CAPTAIN AMERICA

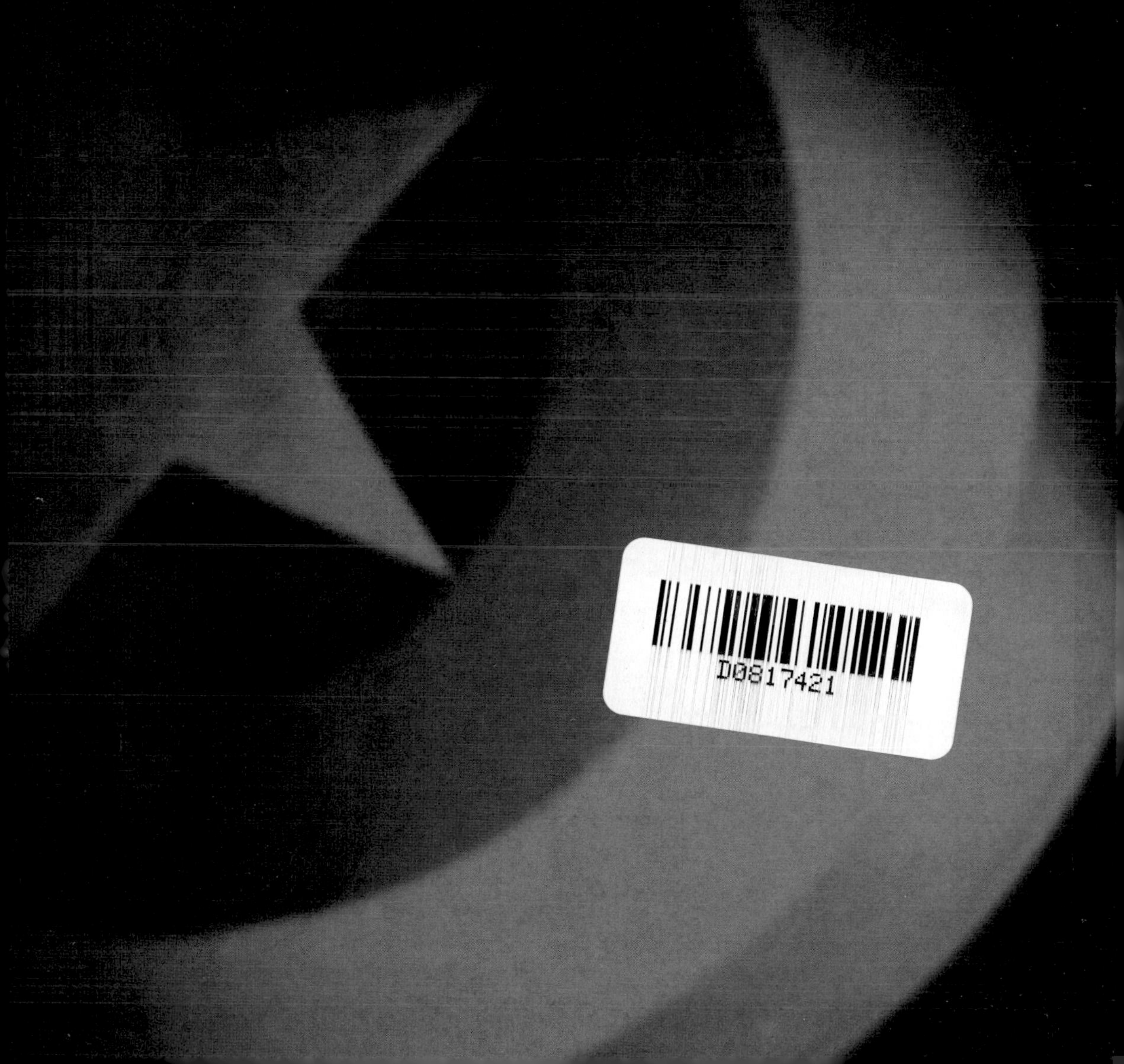

THE DEATH OF
CAPTAIN AMERICA
THE DEATH OF THE DREAM

WRITER: Ed Brubaker

ART: Steve Epting & Mike Perkins

COLOR ART: Frank D'Armata

LETTERER: Virtual Calligraphy's Joe Caramagna

COVER ART: Steve Epting

ASSISTANT EDITORS: Molly Lazer & Aubrey Sitterson

EDITOR: Tom Brevoort

Captain America created by Joe Simon & Jack Kirby

COLLECTION EDITOR: Jennifer Grünwald

ASSISTANT EDITORS: Alex Starbuck & Nelson Ribeiro

EDITOR, SPECIAL PROJECTS: Mark D. Beazley

SENIOR EDITOR, SPECIAL PROJECTS: Jeff Youngquist

SENIOR VICE PRESIDENT OF SALES: David Gabriel

SVP OF BRAND PLANNING & COMMUNICATIONS: Michael Pasciullo

EDITOR IN CHIEF: Axel Alonso

CHIEF CREATIVE OFFICER: Joe Quesada

PUBLISHER: Dan Buckley

EXECUTIVE PRODUCER: Alan Fine

CAPTAIN AMERICA: THE DEATH OF CAPTAIN AMERICA VOL. 1 — THE DEATH OF THE DREAM. Contains material originally published in magazine form as CAPTAIN AMERICA #25-30. Fifth printing 2011. ISBN# 97 7851-2423-8. Published by MARVEL WORLDWIDE, INC., a subsidiary of MARVEL ENTERTAINMENT, LLC. OFFICE OF PUBLICATION: 135 West 50th Street, New York, NY 10020. Copyright © 2007 and 2008 Marvel Charac Inc. All rights reserved. $14.99 per copy in the U.S. and $16.99 in Canada (GST #R127032852); Canadian Agreement #40668537. All characters featured in this issue and the distinctive names and likenesses the and all related indicia are trademarks of Marvel Characters, Inc. No similarity between any of the names, characters, persons, and/or institutions in this magazine with those of any living or dead person or instituti intended, and any such similarity which may exist is purely coincidental. **Printed in the U.S.A.** ALAN FINE, EVP - Office of the President, Marvel Worldwide, Inc. and EVP & CMO Marvel Characters B.V.; DAN BUCH Publisher & President - Print, Animation & Digital Divisions; JOE QUESADA, Chief Creative Officer; DAVID BOGART, SVP of Business Affairs & Talent Management; TOM BREVOORT, SVP of Publishing; C.B. CEBULSKI, S' Creator & Content Development; DAVID GABRIEL, SVP of Publishing Sales & Circulation; MICHAEL PASCIULLO, SVP of Brand Planning & Communications; JIM O'KEEFE, VP of Operations & Logistics; DAN CARR, Exec Director of Publishing Technology; SUSAN CRESPI, Editorial Operations Manager; ALEX MORALES, Publishing Operations Manager; STAN LEE, Chairman Emeritus. For information regarding advertising in Marvel Comi on Marvel.com, please contact John Dokes, SVP Integrated Sales and Marketing, at jdokes@marvel.com. For Marvel subscription inquiries, please call 800-217-9158. **Manufactured between 10/26/11 and 11/1** **by R.R. DONNELLEY, INC., SALEM, VA, USA.**

1 0 9 8 7 6 5

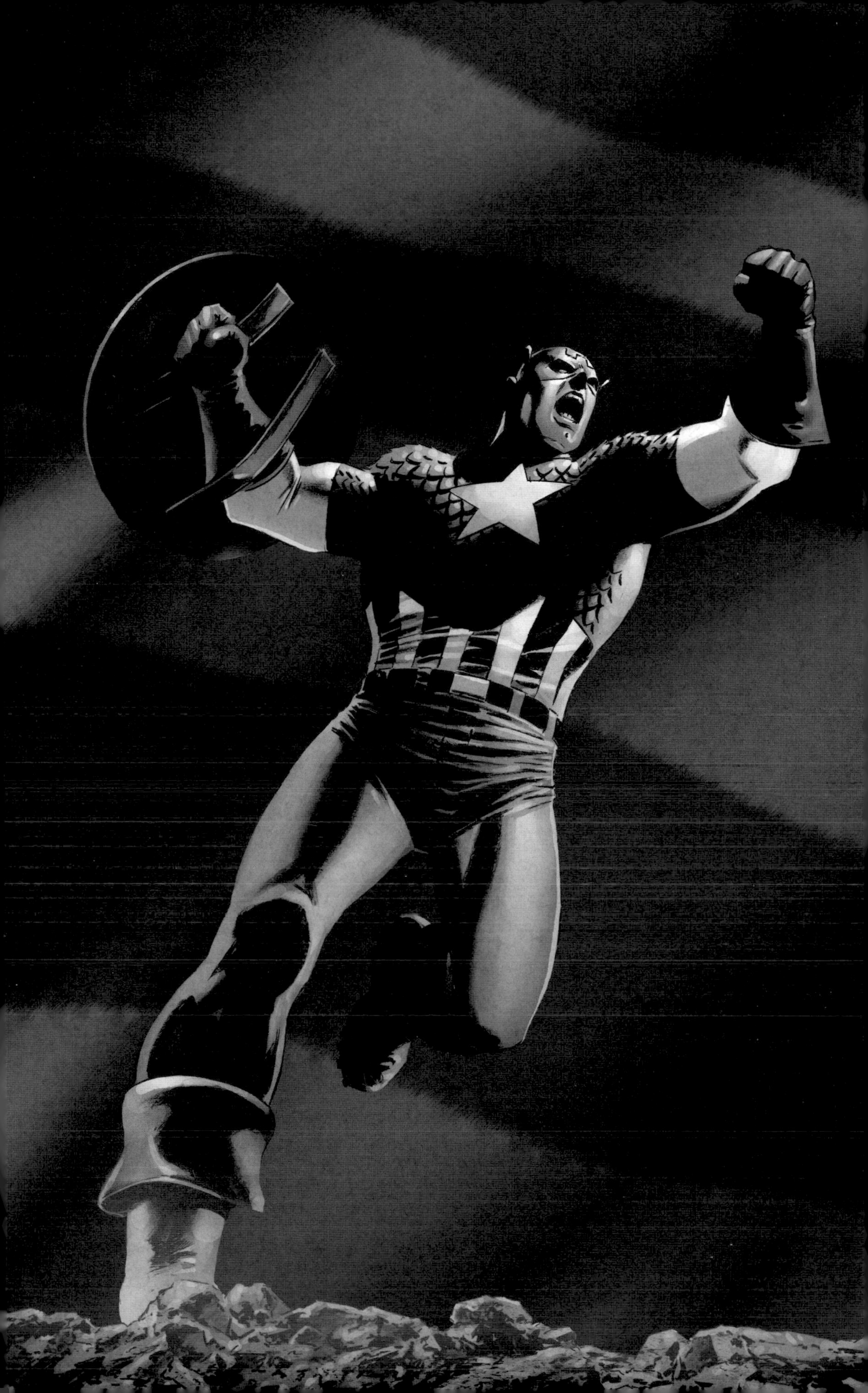

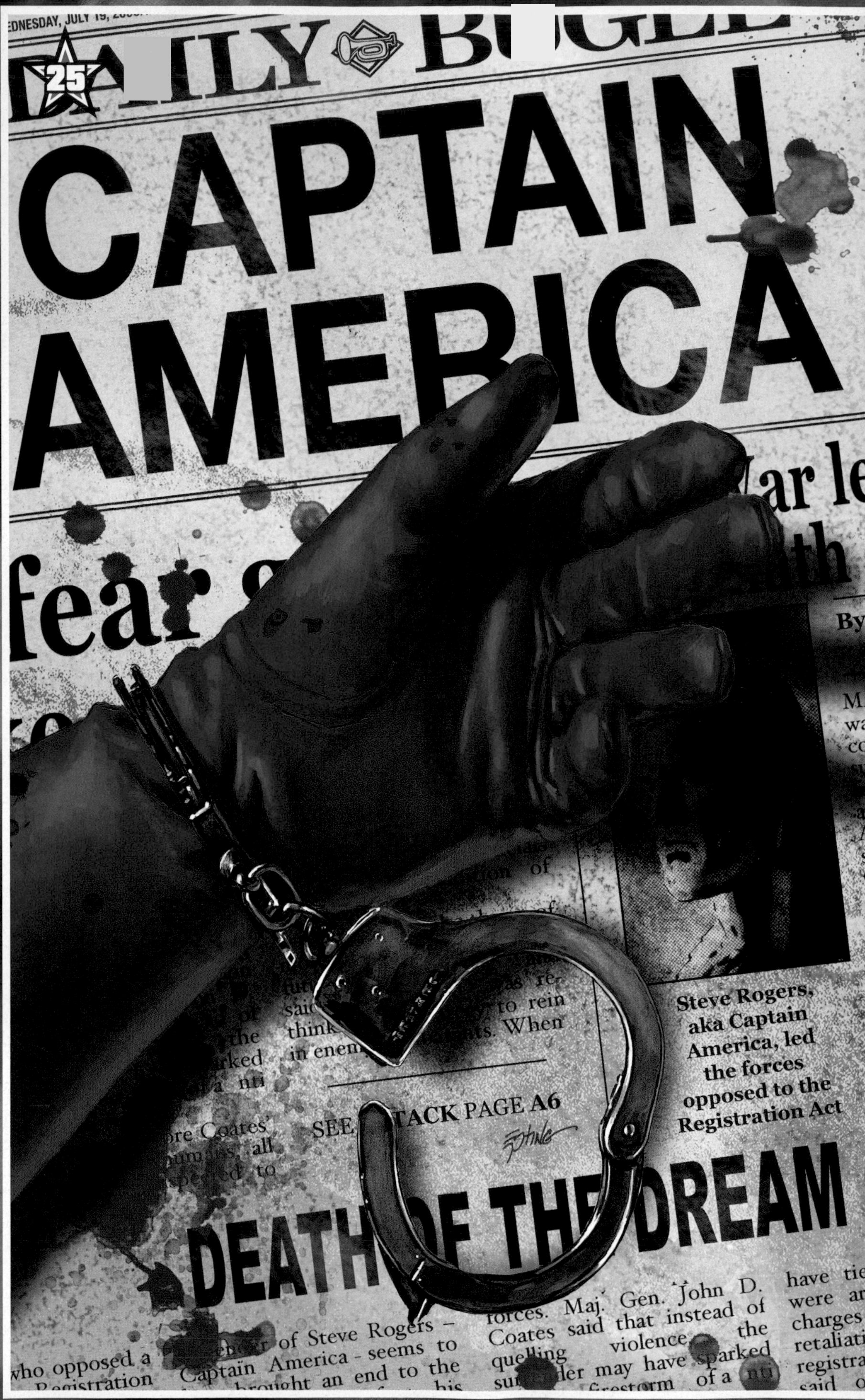

25
CAPTAIN
AMERICA
Steve Rogers, aka Captain America, led the forces opposed to the Registration Act
DEATH
DREAM

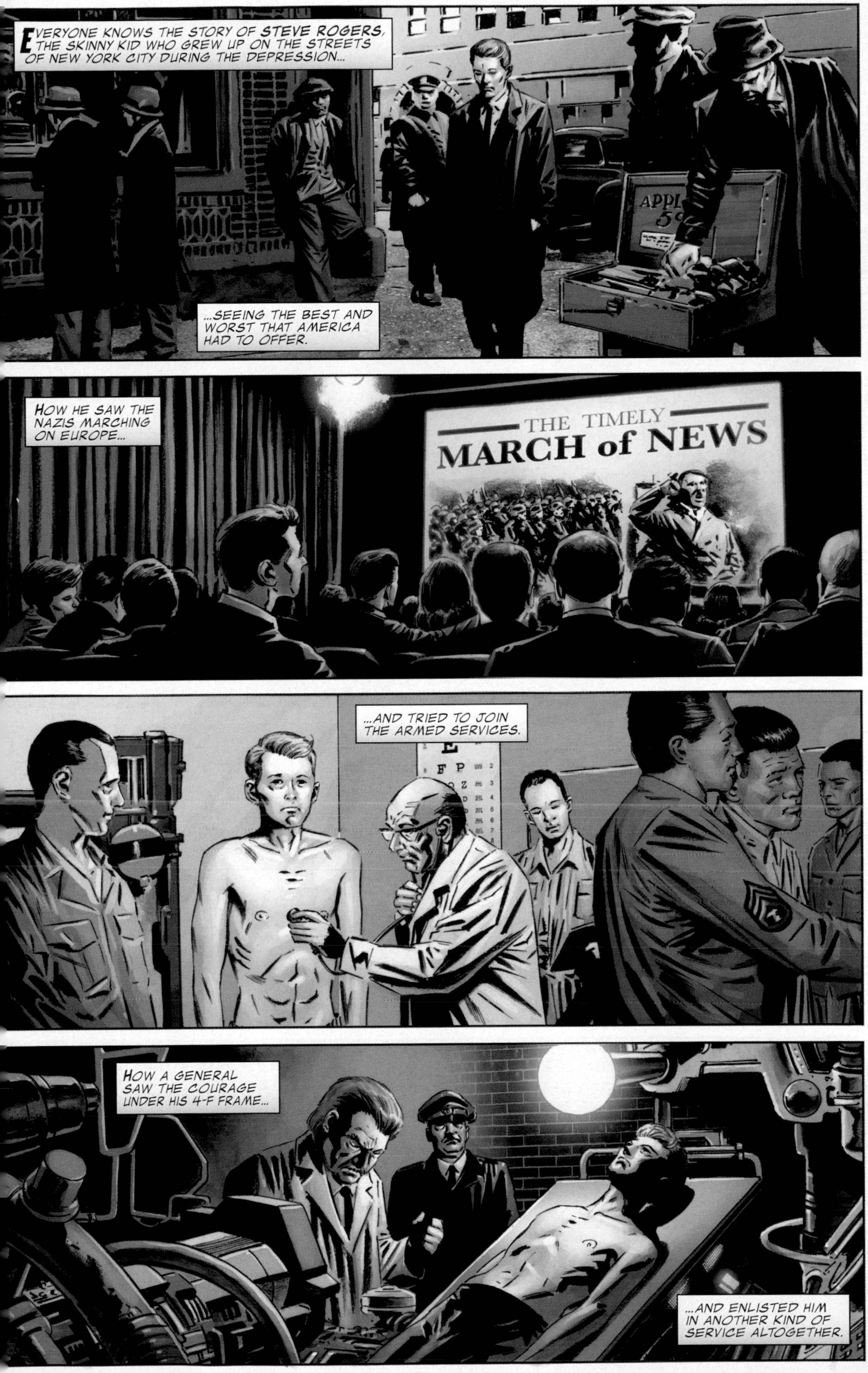
EVERYONE KNOWS THE STORY OF STEVE ROGERS, THE SKINNY KID WHO GREW UP ON THE STREETS OF NEW YORK CITY DURING THE DEPRESSION...
...SEEING THE BEST AND WORST THAT AMERICA HAD TO OFFER.
HOW HE SAW THE NAZIS MARCHING ON EUROPE...
THE TIMELY MARCH of NEWS
...AND TRIED TO JOIN THE ARMED SERVICES.
HOW A GENERAL SAW THE COURAGE UNDER HIS 4-F FRAME...
...AND ENLISTED HIM IN ANOTHER KIND OF SERVICE ALTOGETHER.

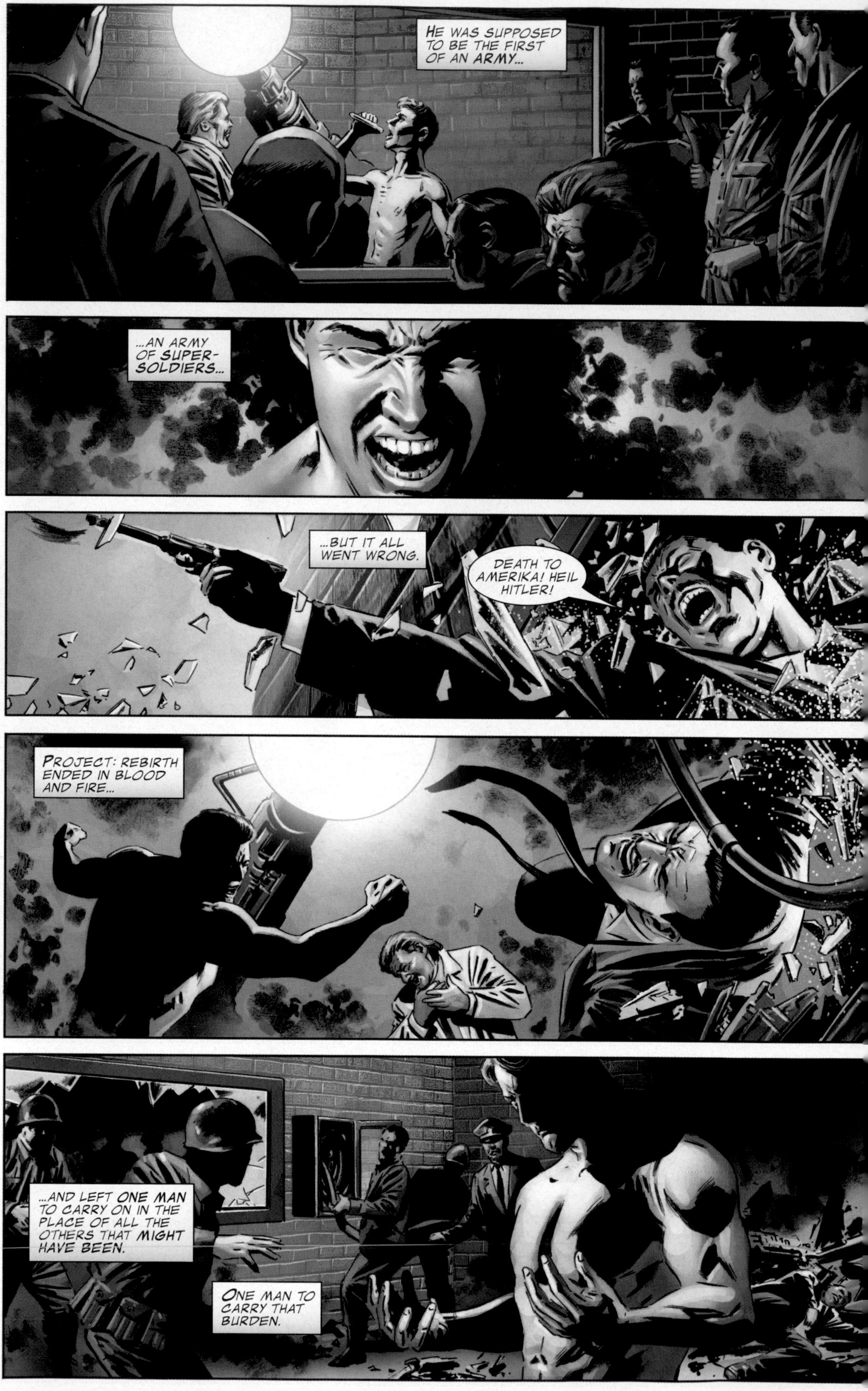
HE WAS SUPPOSED TO BE THE FIRST OF AN ARMY...
...AN ARMY OF SUPER-SOLDIERS...
...BUT IT ALL WENT WRONG.
DEATH TO AMERIKA! HEIL HITLER!
PROJECT: REBIRTH ENDED IN BLOOD AND FIRE...
...AND LEFT ONE MAN TO CARRY ON IN THE PLACE OF ALL THE OTHERS THAT MIGHT HAVE BEEN.
ONE MAN TO CARRY THAT BURDEN.

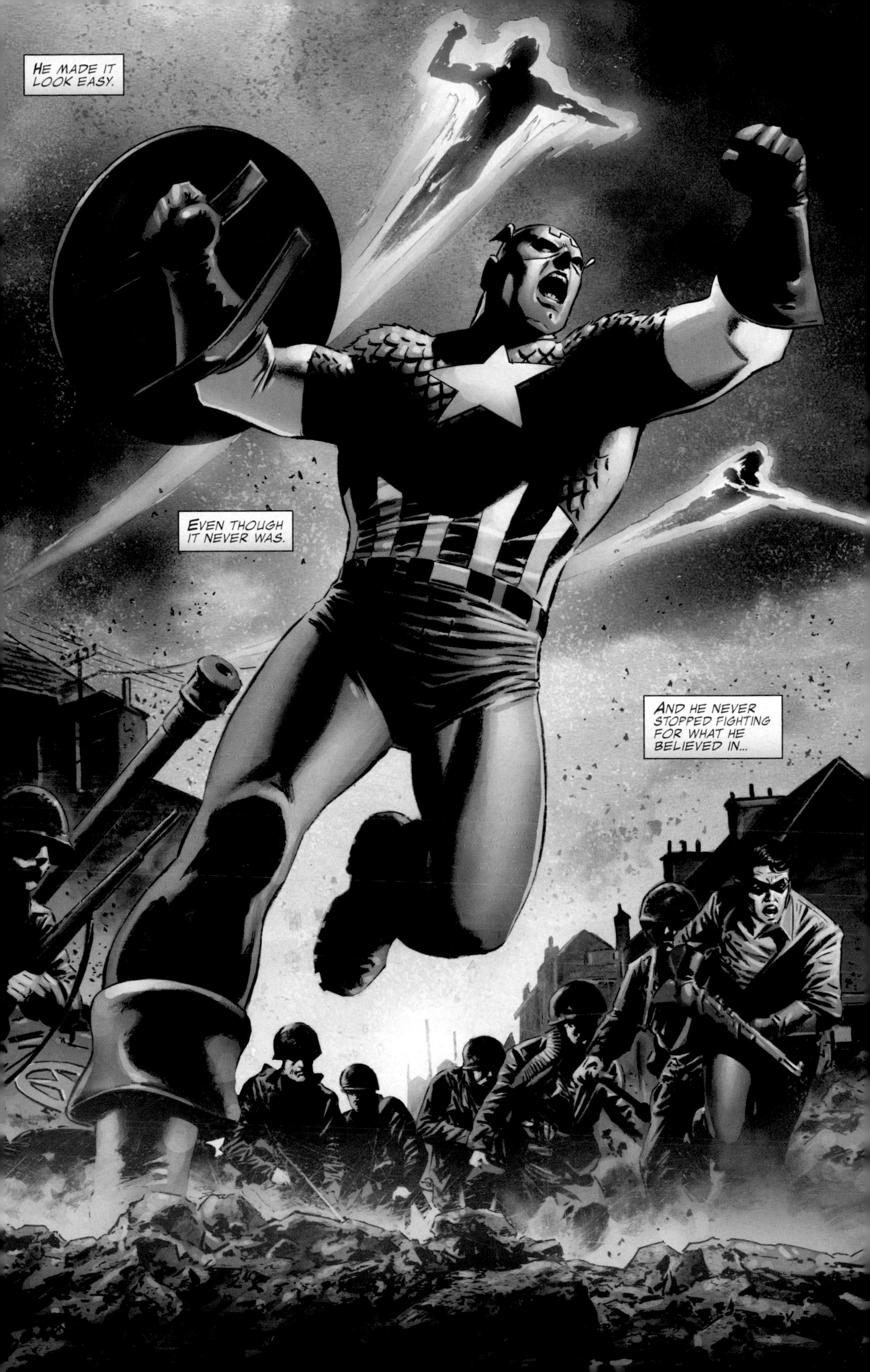
HE MADE IT LOOK EASY.
EVEN THOUGH IT NEVER WAS.
AND HE NEVER STOPPED FIGHTING FOR WHAT HE BELIEVED IN...

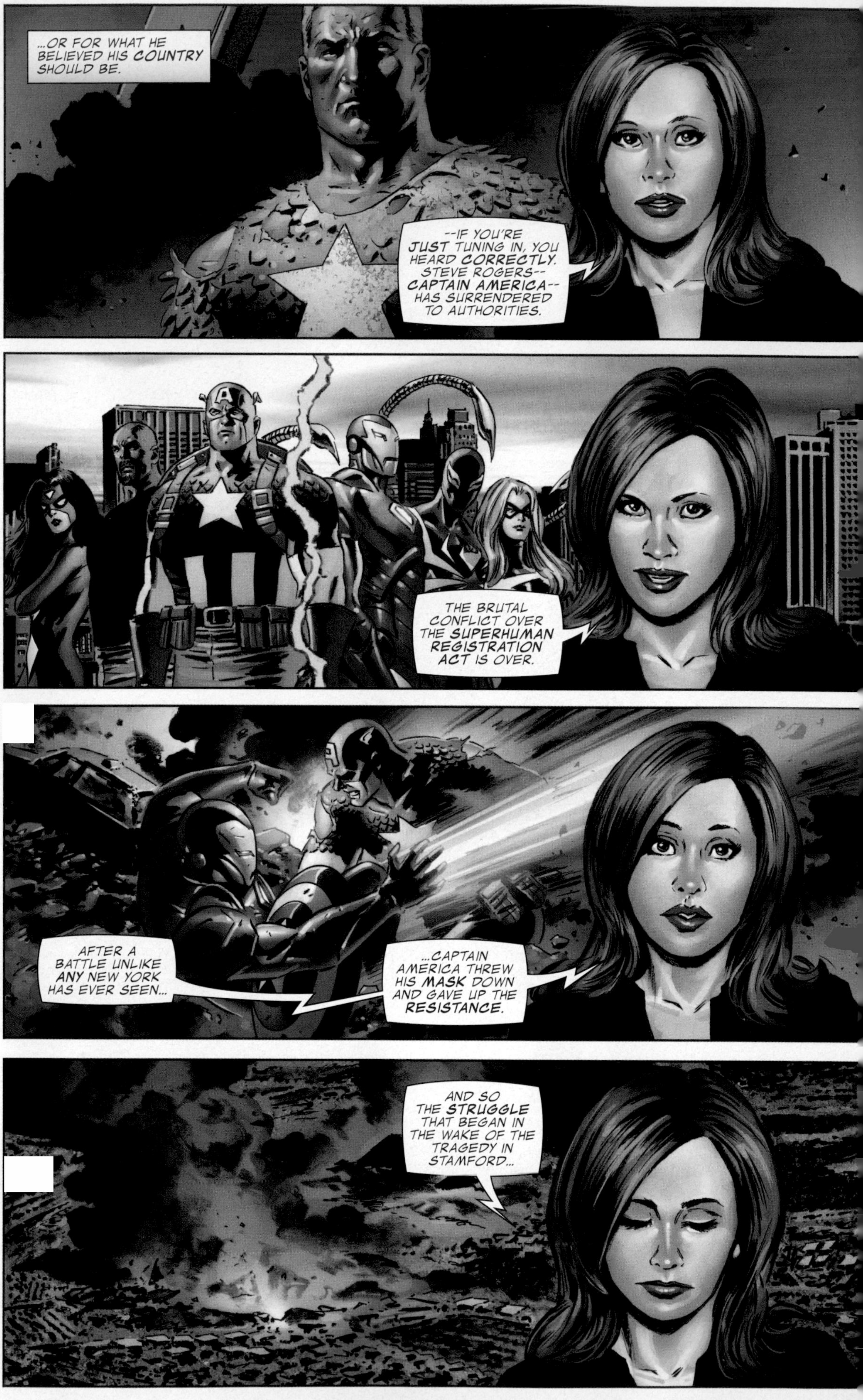
...OR FOR WHAT HE BELIEVED HIS COUNTRY SHOULD BE.
--IF YOU'RE JUST TUNING IN, YOU HEARD CORRECTLY. STEVE ROGERS-- CAPTAIN AMERICA-- HAS SURRENDERED TO AUTHORITIES.
THE BRUTAL CONFLICT OVER THE SUPERHUMAN REGISTRATION ACT IS OVER.
AFTER A BATTLE UNLIKE ANY NEW YORK HAS EVER SEEN...
...CAPTAIN AMERICA THREW HIS MASK DOWN AND GAVE UP THE RESISTANCE.
AND SO THE STRUGGLE THAT BEGAN IN THE WAKE OF THE TRAGEDY IN STAMFORD...

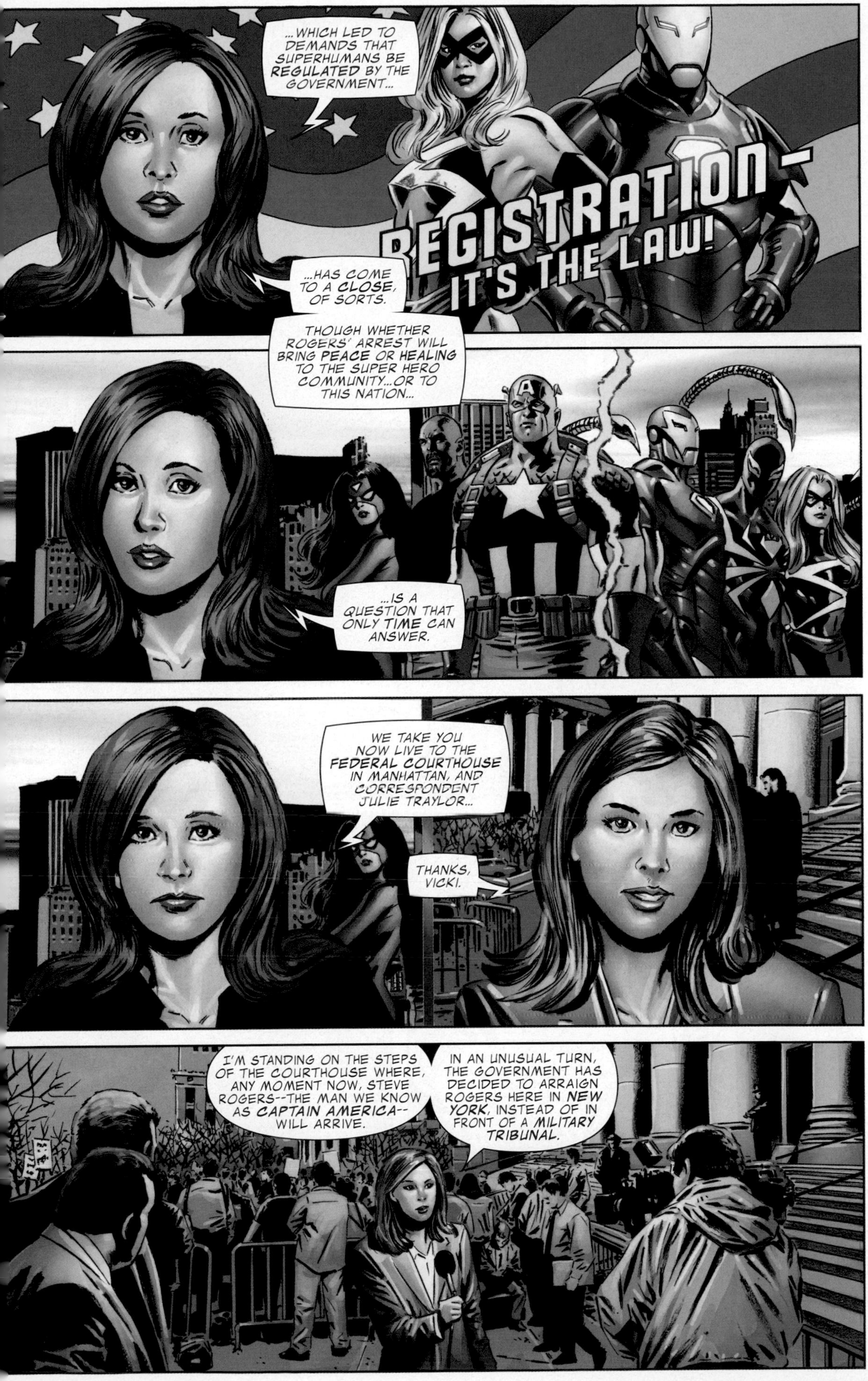
...WHICH LED TO DEMANDS THAT SUPERHUMANS BE REGULATED BY THE GOVERNMENT...
REGISTRATION - IT'S THE LAW!
...HAS COME TO A CLOSE, OF SORTS.
THOUGH WHETHER ROGERS' ARREST WILL BRING PEACE OR HEALING TO THE SUPER HERO COMMUNITY...OR TO THIS NATION...
...IS A QUESTION THAT ONLY TIME CAN ANSWER.
WE TAKE YOU NOW LIVE TO THE FEDERAL COURTHOUSE IN MANHATTAN, AND CORRESPONDENT JULIE TRAYLOR...
THANKS, VICKI.
I'M STANDING ON THE STEPS OF THE COURTHOUSE WHERE, ANY MOMENT NOW, STEVE ROGERS--THE MAN WE KNOW AS CAPTAIN AMERICA--WILL ARRIVE.
IN AN UNUSUAL TURN, THE GOVERNMENT HAS DECIDED TO ARRAIGN ROGERS HERE IN NEW YORK, INSTEAD OF IN FRONT OF A MILITARY TRIBUNAL.

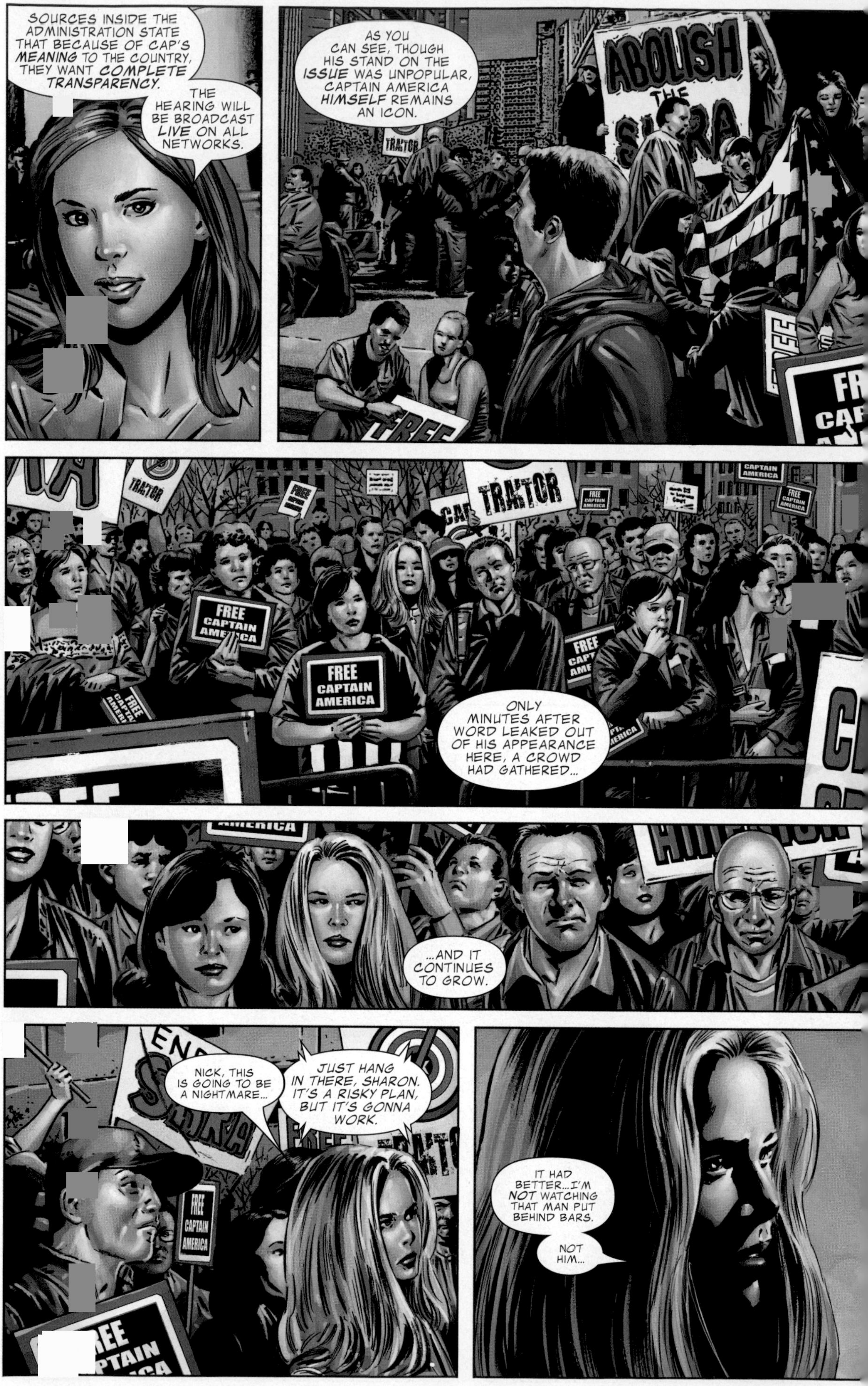
SOURCES INSIDE THE ADMINISTRATION STATE THAT BECAUSE OF CAP'S MEANING TO THE COUNTRY, THEY WANT COMPLETE TRANSPARENCY.
THE HEARING WILL BE BROADCAST LIVE ON ALL NETWORKS.
AS YOU CAN SEE, THOUGH HIS STAND ON THE ISSUE WAS UNPOPULAR, CAPTAIN AMERICA HIMSELF REMAINS AN ICON.
ABOLISH THE
TRAITOR
FREE CAPTAIN AMERICA
FREE CAPTAIN AMERICA
ONLY MINUTES AFTER WORD LEAKED OUT OF HIS APPEARANCE HERE, A CROWD HAD GATHERED...
...AND IT CONTINUES TO GROW.
NICK, THIS IS GOING TO BE A NIGHTMARE...
JUST HANG IN THERE, SHARON. IT'S A RISKY PLAN, BUT IT'S GONNA WORK.
FREE CAPTAIN AMERICA
IT HAD BETTER...I'M NOT WATCHING THAT MAN PUT BEHIND BARS.
NOT HIM...

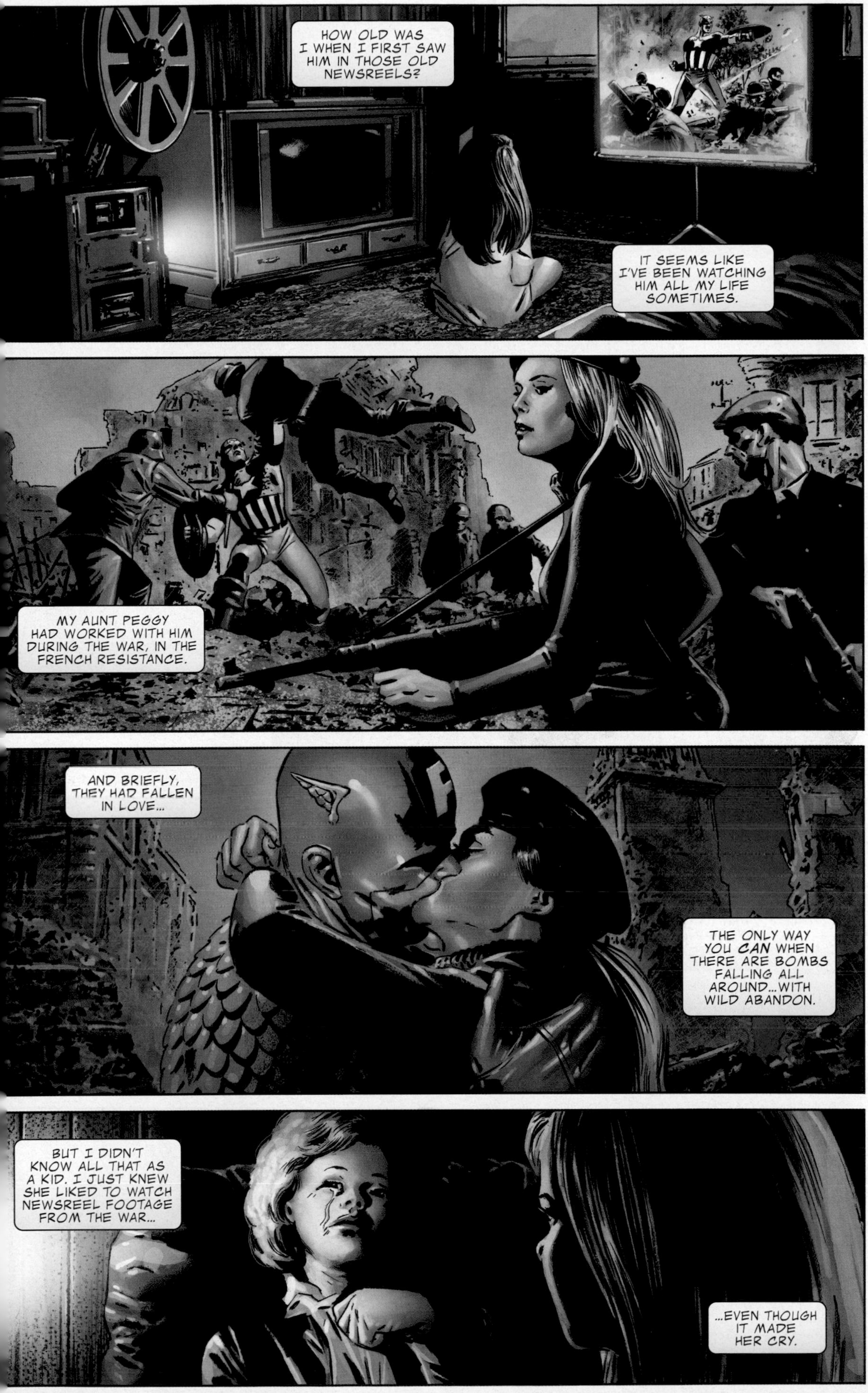
HOW OLD WAS I WHEN I FIRST SAW HIM IN THOSE OLD NEWSREELS?
IT SEEMS LIKE I'VE BEEN WATCHING HIM ALL MY LIFE SOMETIMES.
MY AUNT PEGGY HAD WORKED WITH HIM DURING THE WAR, IN THE FRENCH RESISTANCE.
AND BRIEFLY, THEY HAD FALLEN IN LOVE...
THE ONLY WAY YOU CAN WHEN THERE ARE BOMBS FALLING ALL AROUND...WITH WILD ABANDON.
BUT I DIDN'T KNOW ALL THAT AS A KID. I JUST KNEW SHE LIKED TO WATCH NEWSREEL FOOTAGE FROM THE WAR...
...EVEN THOUGH IT MADE HER CRY.

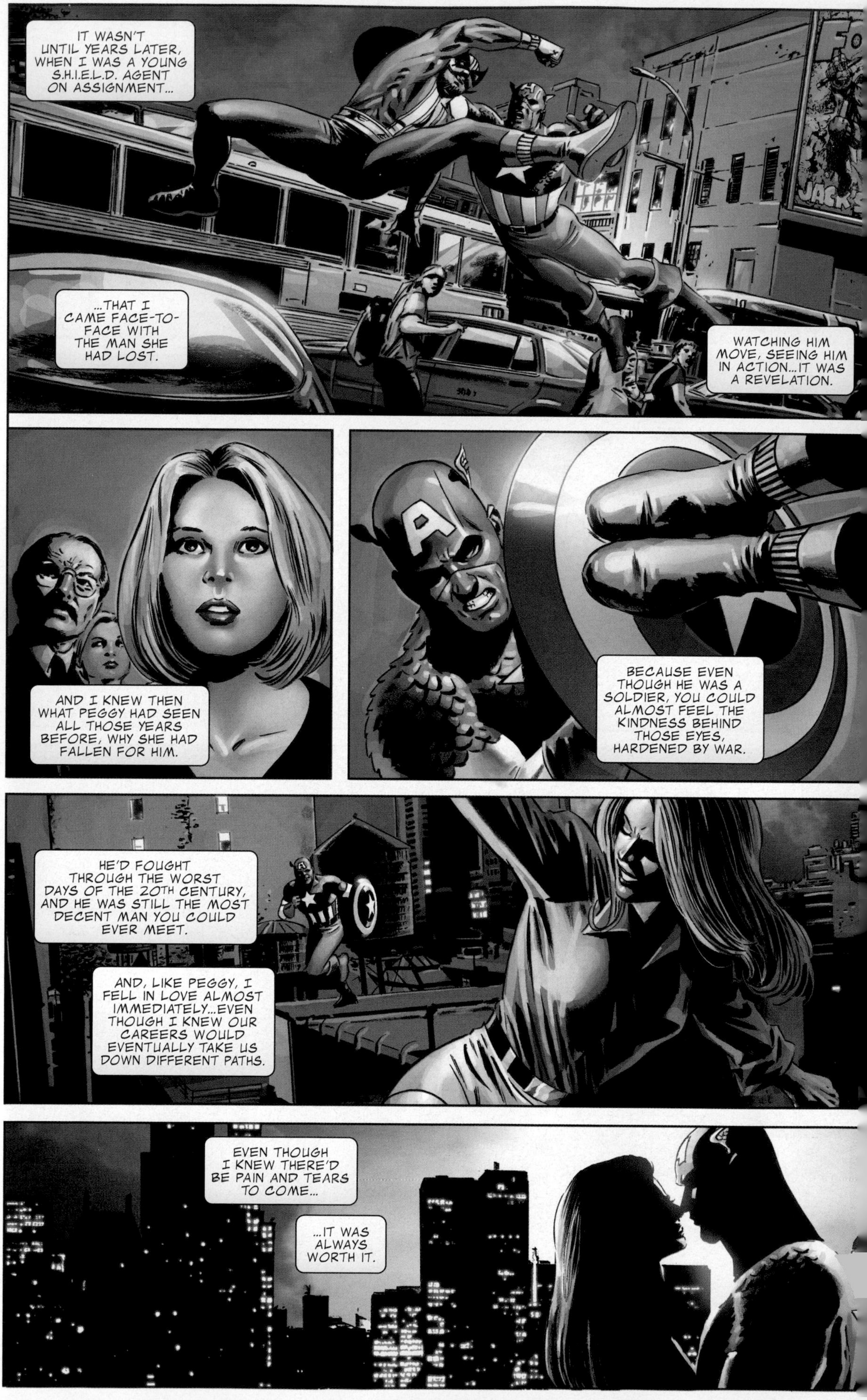
IT WASN'T UNTIL YEARS LATER, WHEN I WAS A YOUNG S.H.I.E.L.D. AGENT ON ASSIGNMENT...
...THAT I CAME FACE-TO-FACE WITH THE MAN SHE HAD LOST.
WATCHING HIM MOVE, SEEING HIM IN ACTION...IT WAS A REVELATION.
AND I KNEW THEN WHAT PEGGY HAD SEEN ALL THOSE YEARS BEFORE, WHY SHE HAD FALLEN FOR HIM.
BECAUSE EVEN THOUGH HE WAS A SOLDIER, YOU COULD ALMOST FEEL THE KINDNESS BEHIND THOSE EYES, HARDENED BY WAR.
HE'D FOUGHT THROUGH THE WORST DAYS OF THE 20TH CENTURY, AND HE WAS STILL THE MOST DECENT MAN YOU COULD EVER MEET.
AND, LIKE PEGGY, I FELL IN LOVE ALMOST IMMEDIATELY...EVEN THOUGH I KNEW OUR CAREERS WOULD EVENTUALLY TAKE US DOWN DIFFERENT PATHS.
EVEN THOUGH I KNEW THERE'D BE PAIN AND TEARS TO COME...
...IT WAS ALWAYS WORTH IT.

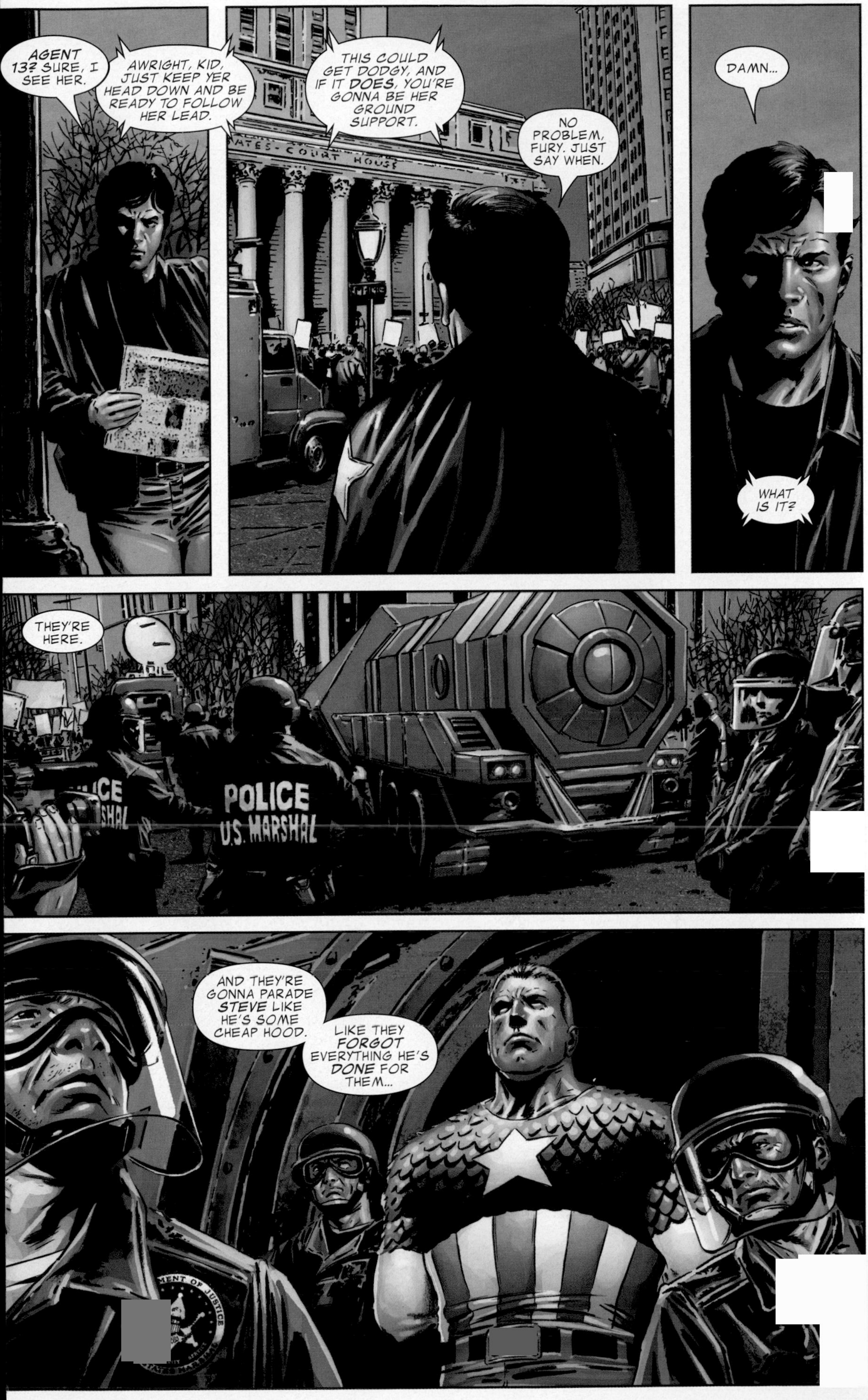
AGENT 13? SURE, I SEE HER.
AWRIGHT, KID, JUST KEEP YER HEAD DOWN AND BE READY TO FOLLOW HER LEAD.
THIS COULD GET DODGY, AND IF IT DOES, YOU'RE GONNA BE HER GROUND SUPPORT.
NO PROBLEM, FURY. JUST SAY WHEN.
DAMN...
WHAT IS IT?
THEY'RE HERE.
POLICE U.S. MARSHAL
AND THEY'RE GONNA PARADE STEVE LIKE HE'S SOME CHEAP HOOD.
LIKE THEY FORGOT EVERYTHING HE'S DONE FOR THEM...

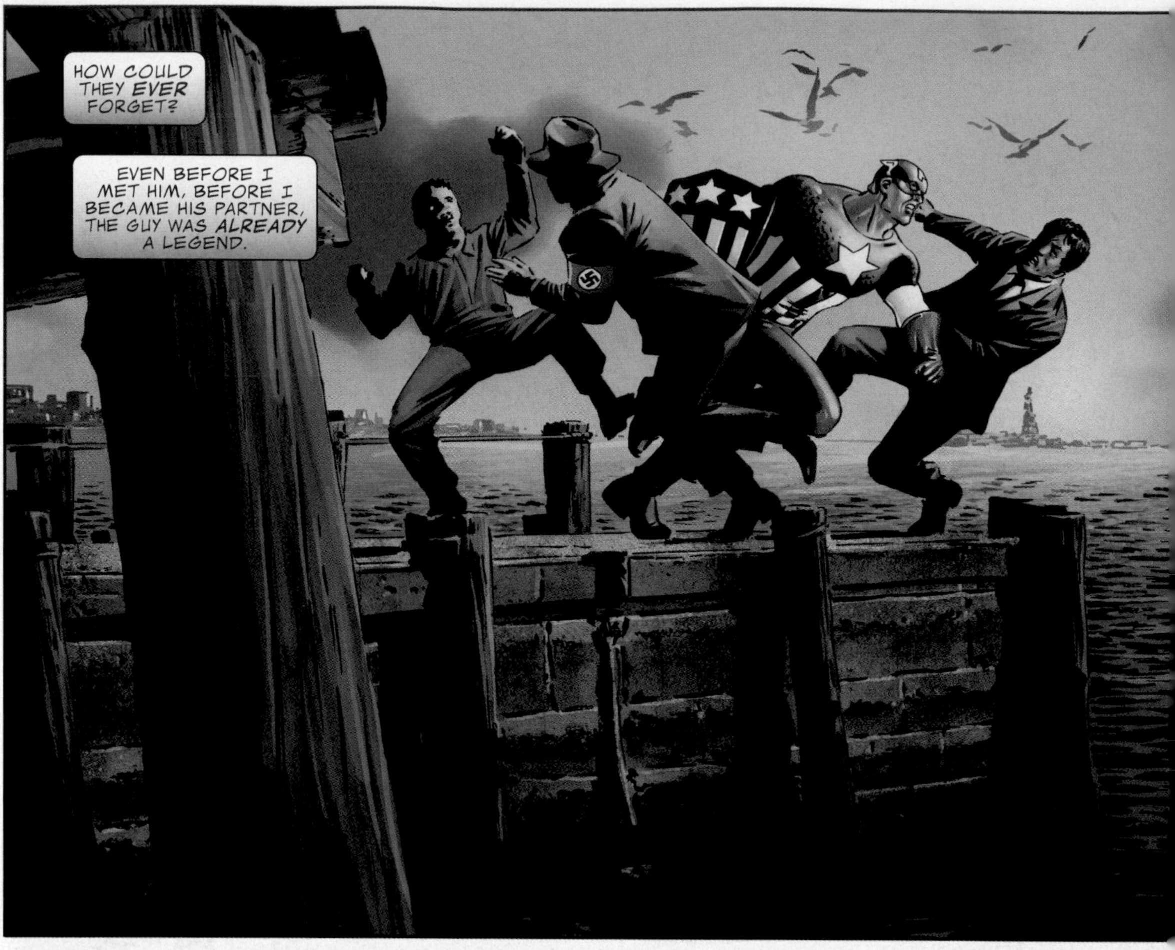
HOW COULD THEY EVER FORGET?
EVEN BEFORE I MET HIM, BEFORE I BECAME HIS PARTNER, THE GUY WAS ALREADY A LEGEND.

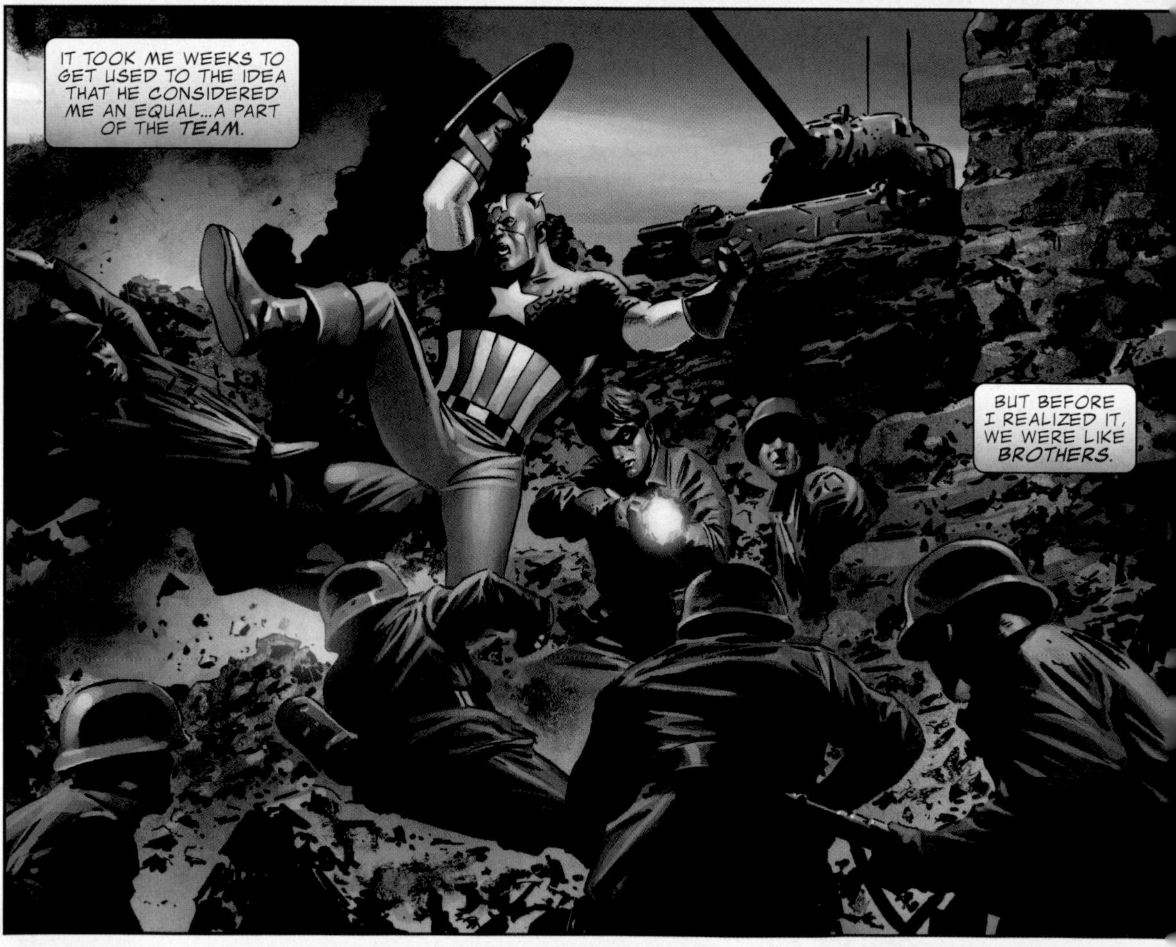
IT TOOK ME WEEKS TO GET USED TO THE IDEA THAT HE CONSIDERED ME AN EQUAL...A PART OF THE TEAM.
BUT BEFORE I REALIZED IT, WE WERE LIKE BROTHERS.

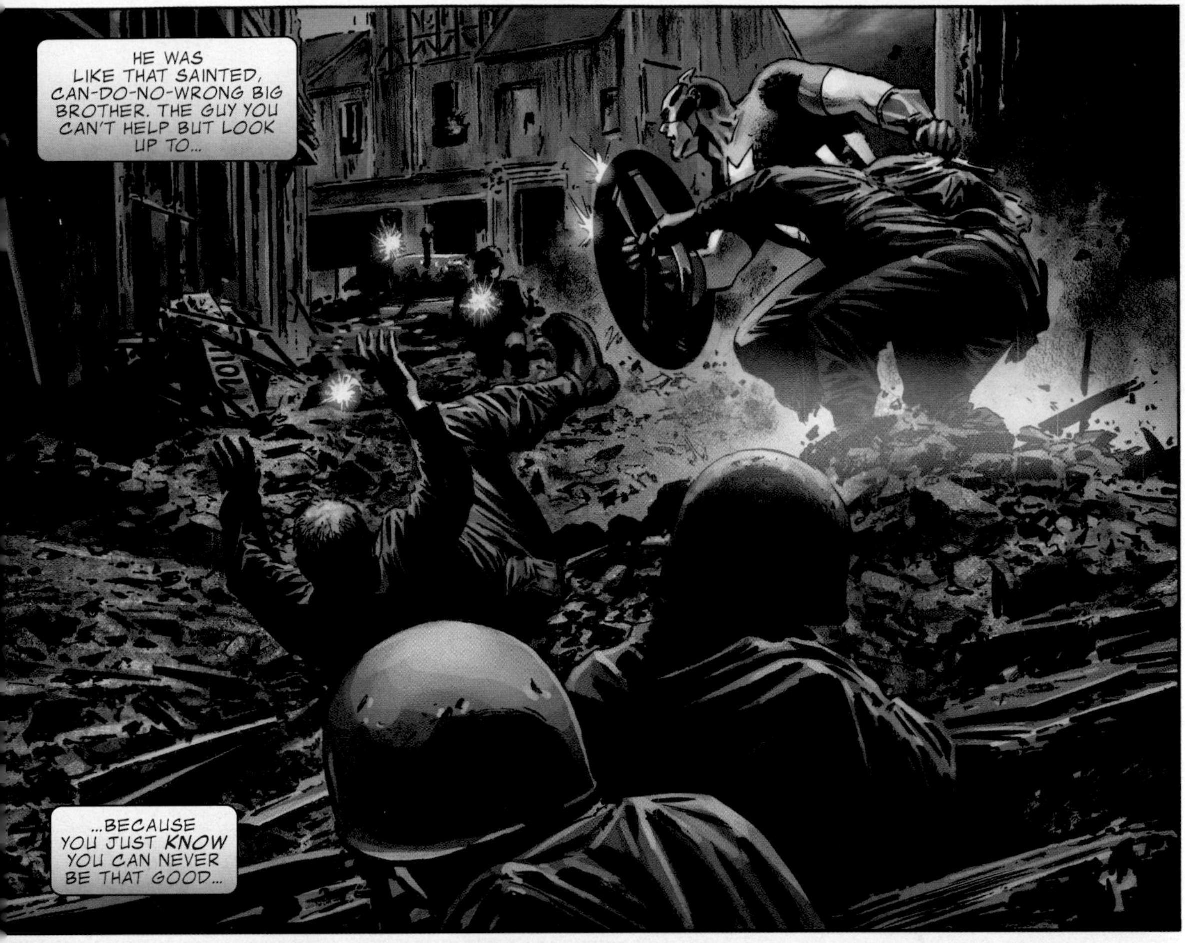
HE WAS LIKE THAT SAINTED, CAN-DO-NO-WRONG BIG BROTHER. THE GUY YOU CAN'T HELP BUT LOOK UP TO...
...BECAUSE YOU JUST KNOW YOU CAN NEVER BE THAT GOOD...
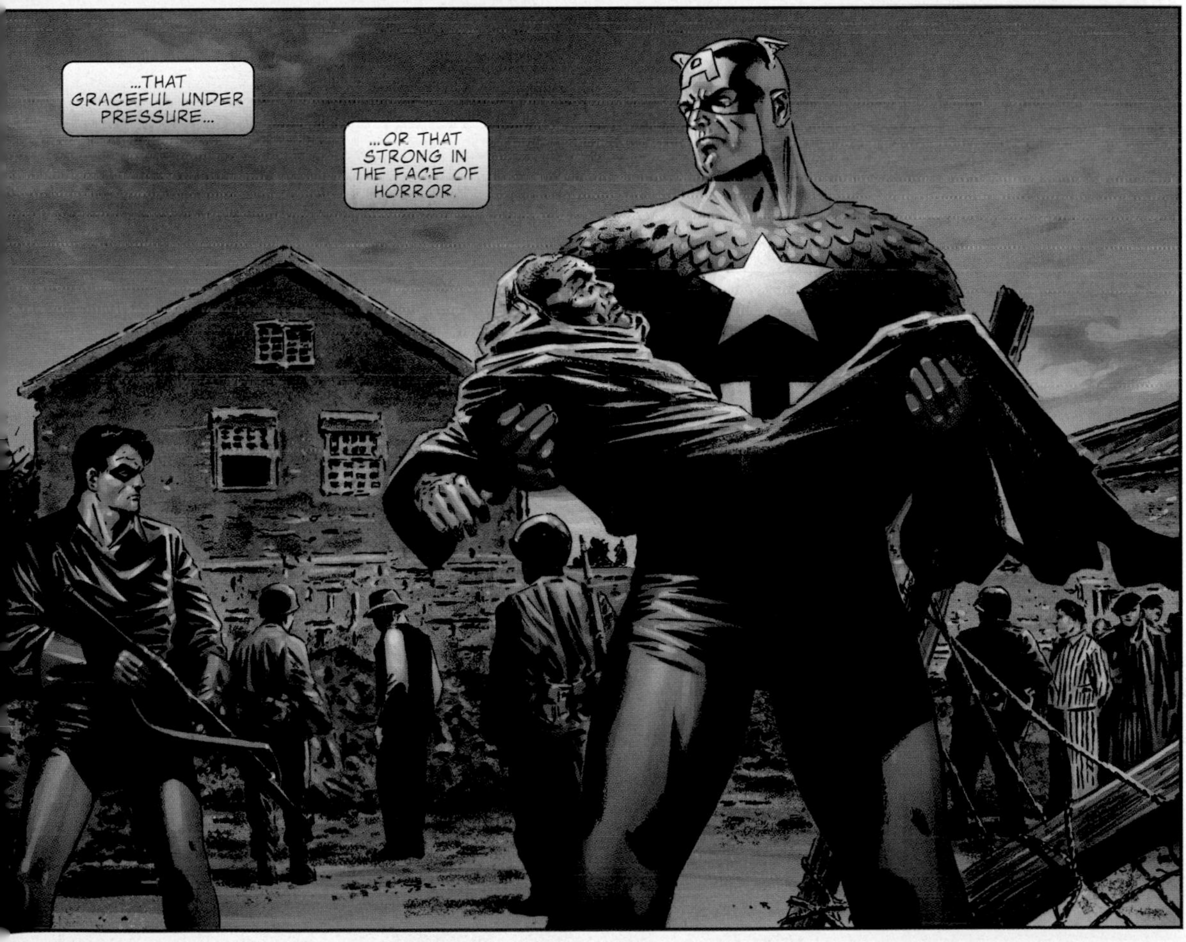
...THAT GRACEFUL UNDER PRESSURE...
...OR THAT STRONG IN THE FACE OF HORROR.

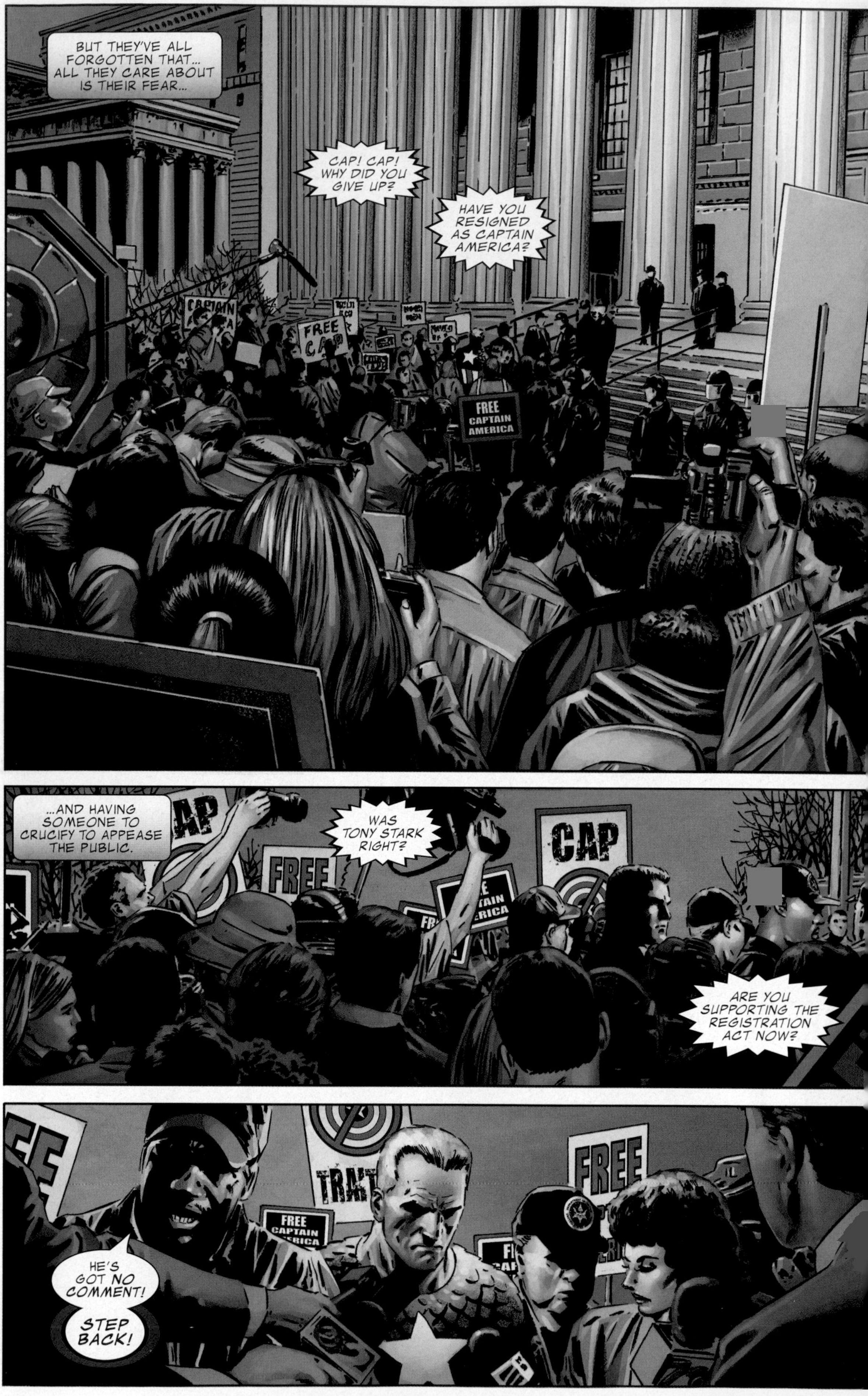
BUT THEY'VE ALL FORGOTTEN THAT... ALL THEY CARE ABOUT IS THEIR FEAR...
CAP! CAP! WHY DID YOU GIVE UP?
HAVE YOU RESIGNED AS CAPTAIN AMERICA?
FREE CAP
FREE CAPTAIN AMERICA
...AND HAVING SOMEONE TO CRUCIFY TO APPEASE THE PUBLIC.
WAS TONY STARK RIGHT?
CAP
ARE YOU SUPPORTING THE REGISTRATION ACT NOW?
FREE CAPTAIN AMERICA
FREE
HE'S GOT NO COMMENT!
STEP BACK!

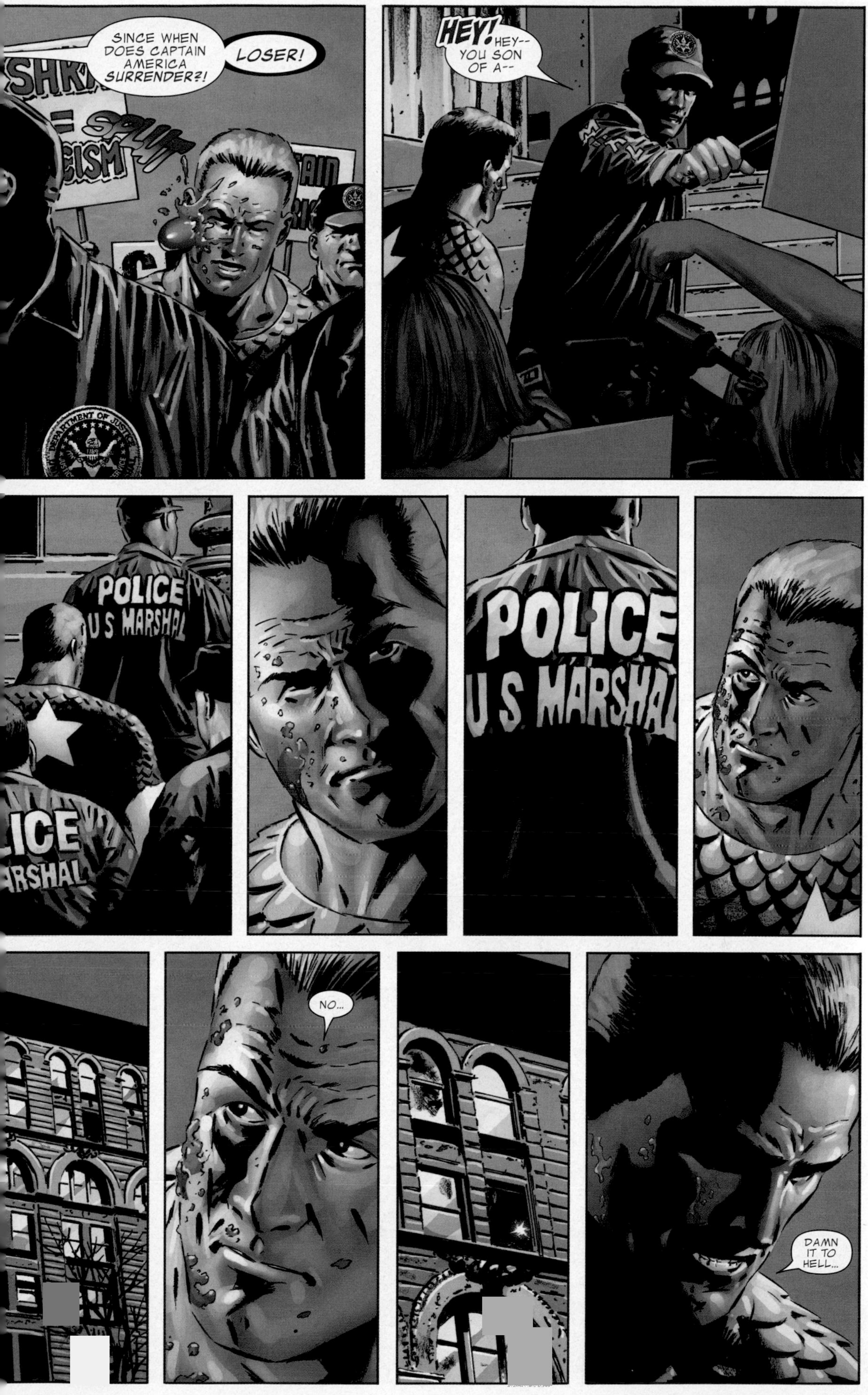
SINCE WHEN DOES CAPTAIN AMERICA SURRENDER?!
LOSER!
SPLUT
HEY!
HEY-- YOU SON OF A--
POLICE U.S. MARSHAL
POLICE U.S. MARSHAL
NO...
DAMN IT TO HELL...

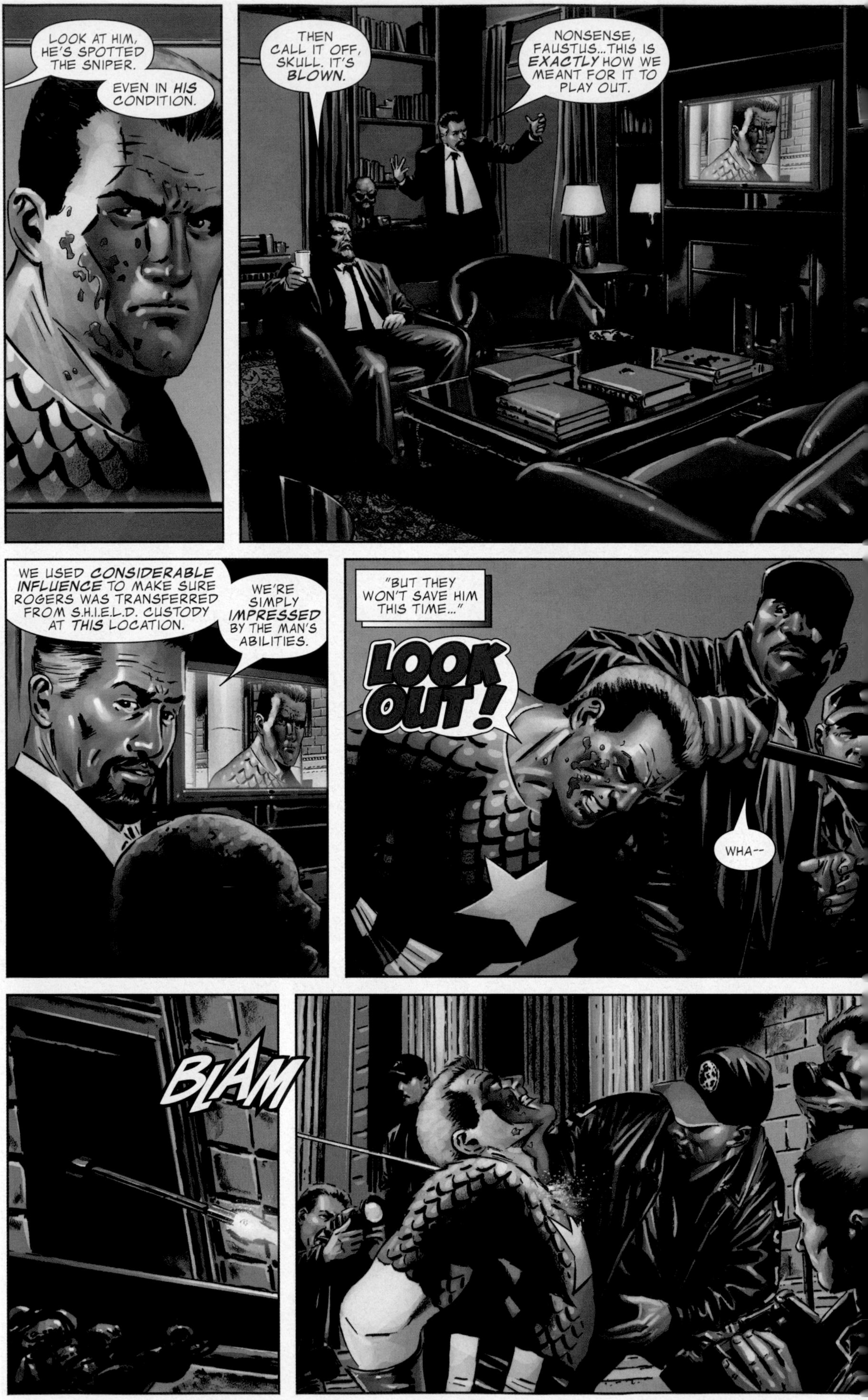
LOOK AT HIM, HE'S SPOTTED THE SNIPER.
EVEN IN HIS CONDITION.
THEN CALL IT OFF, SKULL. IT'S BLOWN.
NONSENSE, FAUSTUS...THIS IS EXACTLY HOW WE MEANT FOR IT TO PLAY OUT.
WE USED CONSIDERABLE INFLUENCE TO MAKE SURE ROGERS WAS TRANSFERRED FROM S.H.I.E.L.D. CUSTODY AT THIS LOCATION.
WE'RE SIMPLY IMPRESSED BY THE MAN'S ABILITIES.
"BUT THEY WON'T SAVE HIM THIS TIME..."
LOOK OUT!
WHA--
BLAM

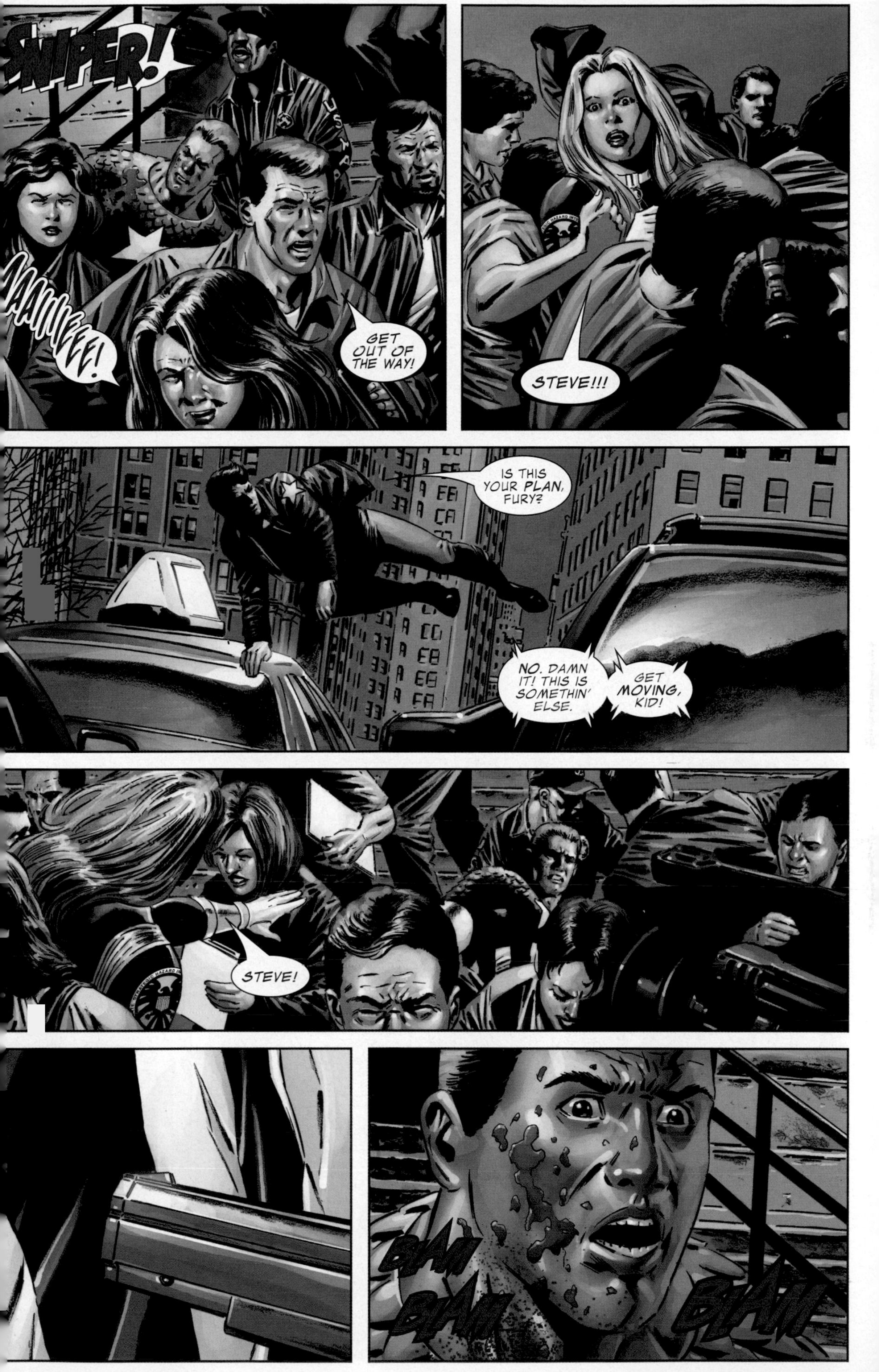
SNIPER!
AAAIIIEEE!
GET OUT OF THE WAY!
STEVE!!!
IS THIS YOUR PLAN, FURY?
NO. DAMN IT! THIS IS SOMETHIN' ELSE.
GET MOVING, KID!
STEVE!
BLAM
BLAM
BLAM

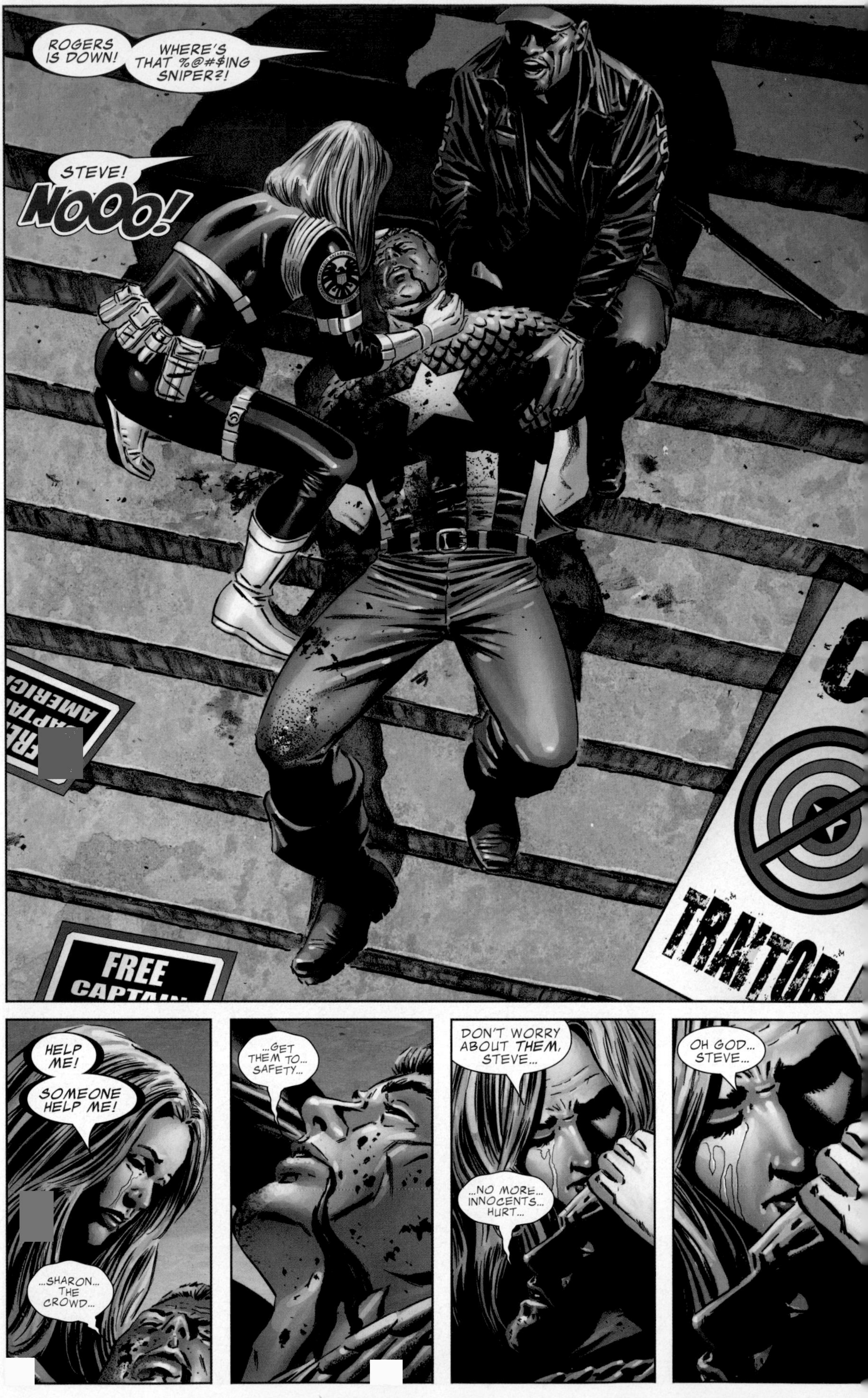
ROGERS IS DOWN!
WHERE'S THAT %@#$ING SNIPER?!
STEVE!
NOOO!
FREE
TRAITOR
HELP ME!
SOMEONE HELP ME!
...SHARON... THE CROWD...
...GET THEM TO... SAFETY...
DON'T WORRY ABOUT THEM, STEVE...
...NO MORE... INNOCENTS... HURT...
OH GOD... STEVE...

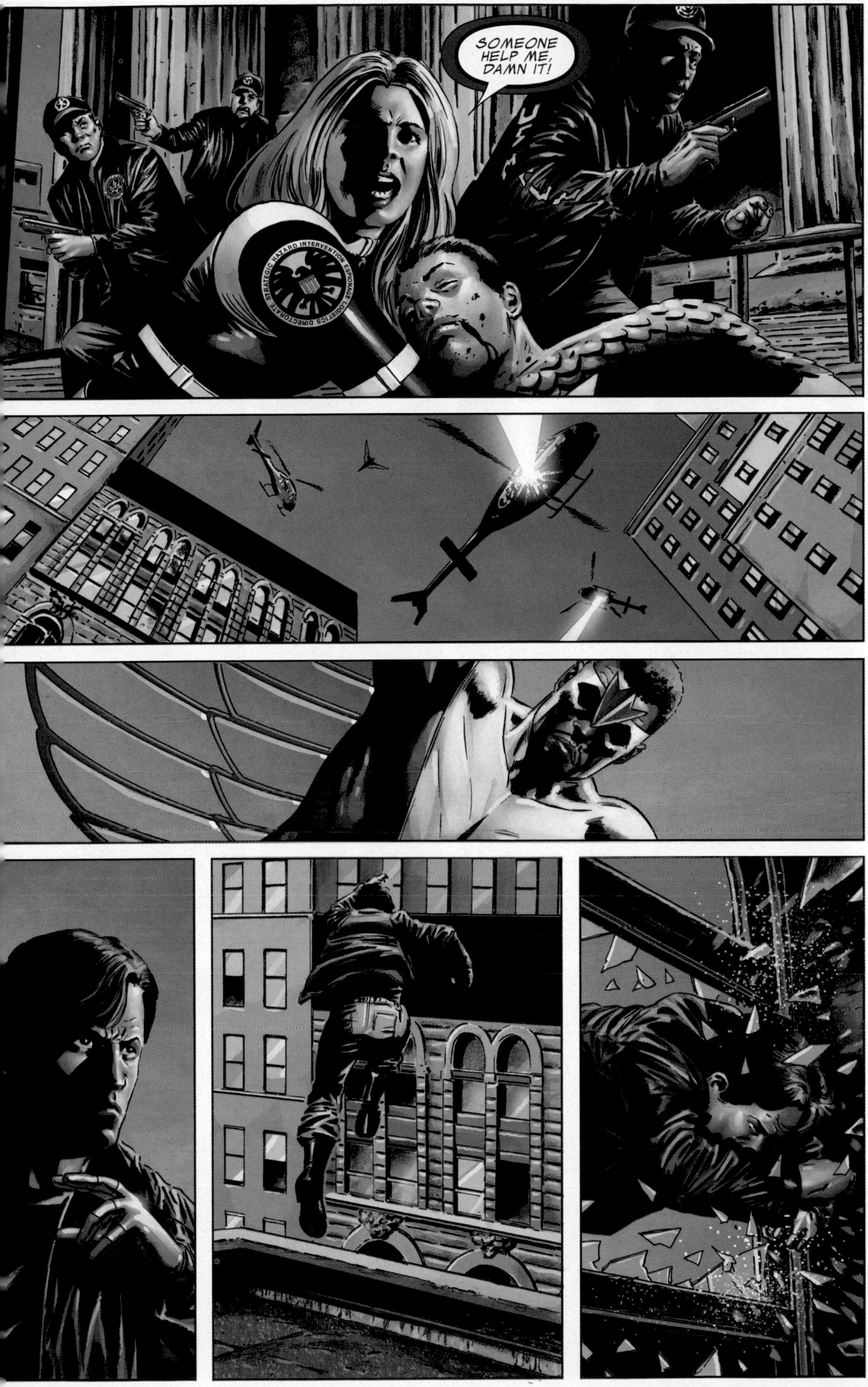
SOMEONE HELP ME, DAMN IT!
STRATEGIC HAZARD INTERVENTION ESPIONAGE LOGISTICS DIRECTORATE

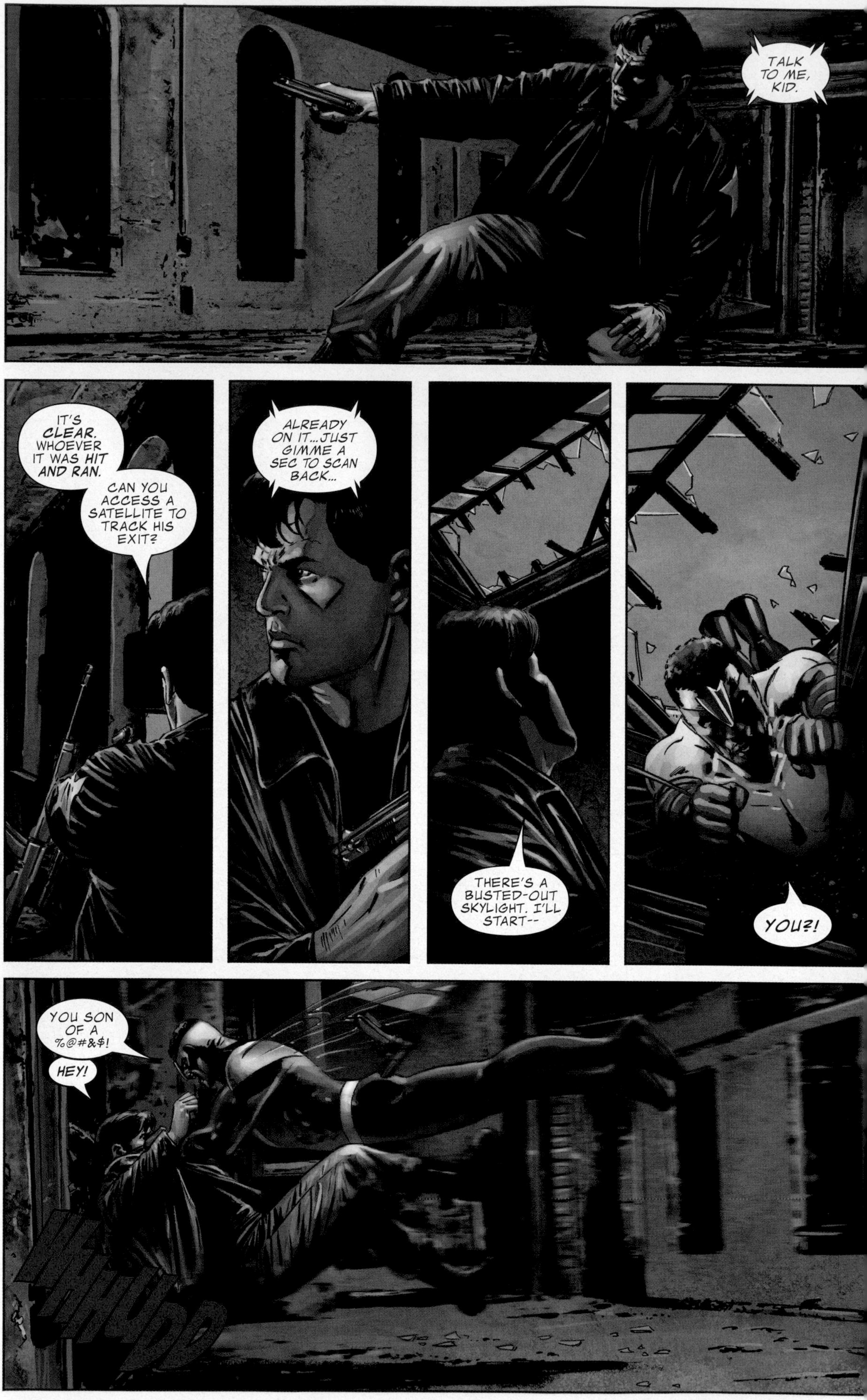
TALK TO ME, KID.
IT'S CLEAR. WHOEVER IT WAS HIT AND RAN.
CAN YOU ACCESS A SATELLITE TO TRACK HIS EXIT?
ALREADY ON IT...JUST GIMME A SEC TO SCAN BACK...
THERE'S A BUSTED-OUT SKYLIGHT. I'LL START--
YOU?!
YOU SON OF A %@#&$!
HEY!

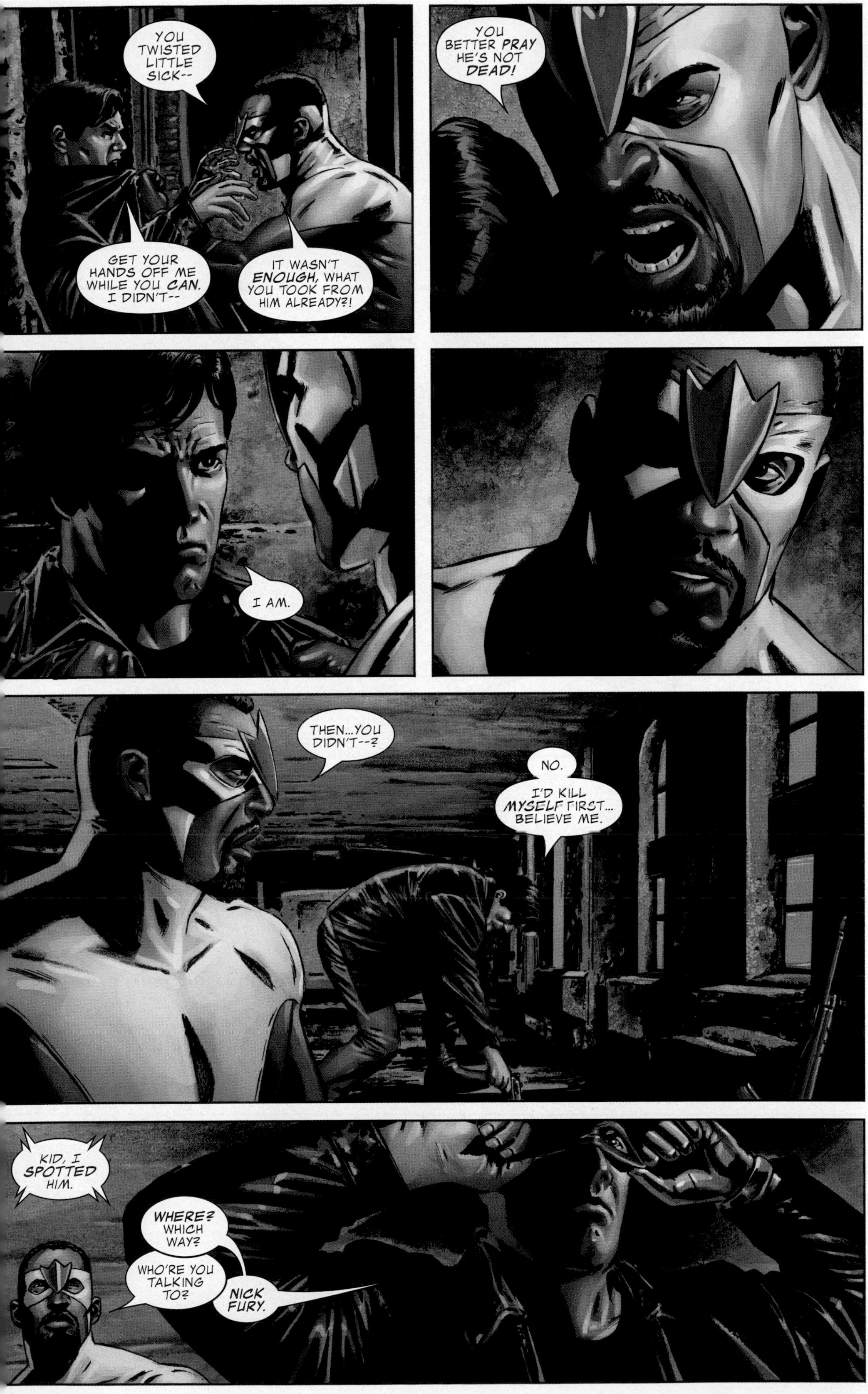
YOU TWISTED LITTLE SICK--
GET YOUR HANDS OFF ME WHILE YOU CAN. I DIDN'T--
IT WASN'T ENOUGH, WHAT YOU TOOK FROM HIM ALREADY?!
YOU BETTER PRAY HE'S NOT DEAD!
I AM.
THEN...YOU DIDN'T--?
NO.
I'D KILL MYSELF FIRST... BELIEVE ME.
KID, I SPOTTED HIM.
WHERE? WHICH WAY?
WHO'RE YOU TALKING TO?
NICK FURY.

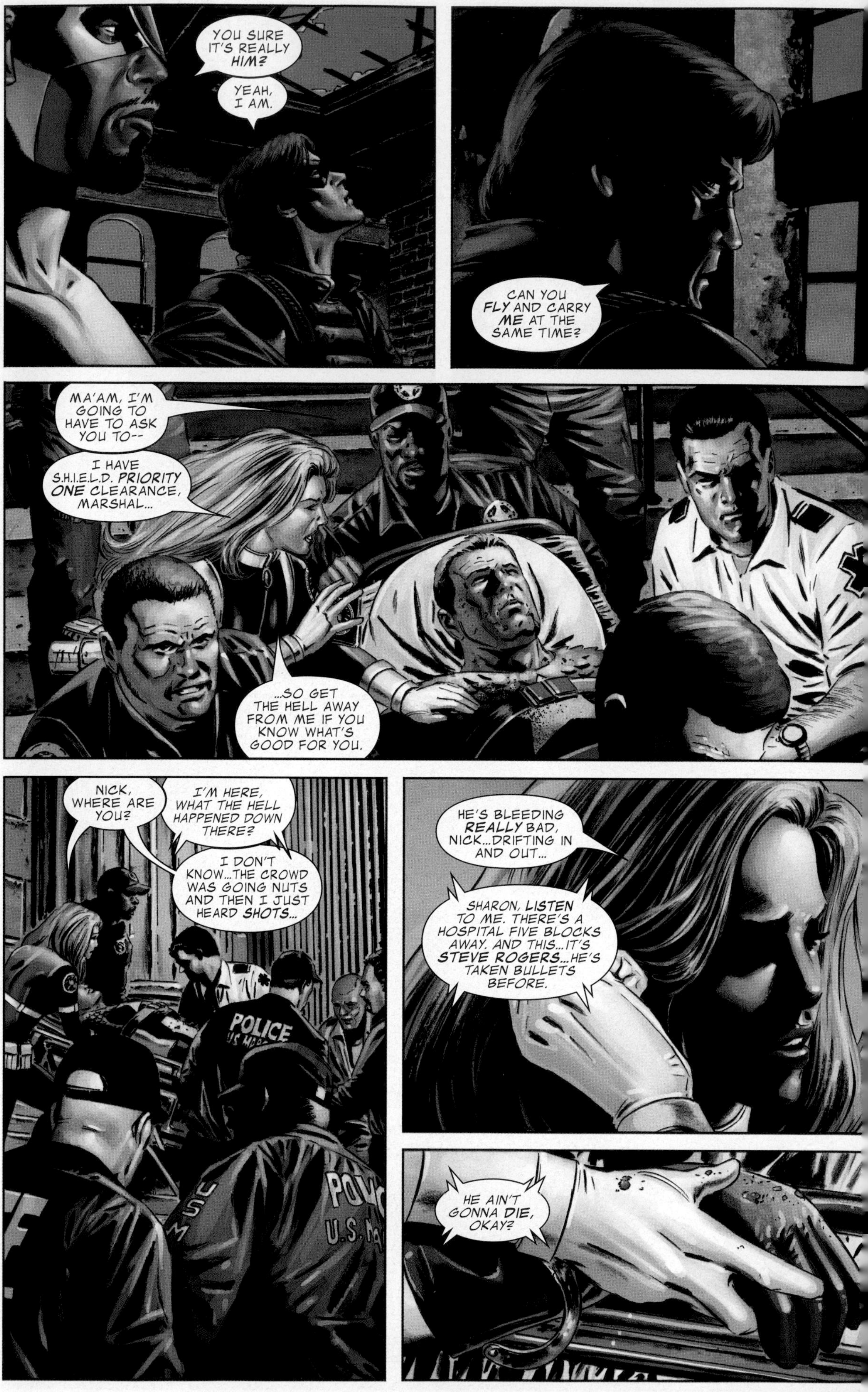

YOU SURE IT'S REALLY HIM?
YEAH, I AM.
CAN YOU FLY AND CARRY ME AT THE SAME TIME?
MA'AM, I'M GOING TO HAVE TO ASK YOU TO--
I HAVE S.H.I.E.L.D. PRIORITY ONE CLEARANCE, MARSHAL...
...SO GET THE HELL AWAY FROM ME IF YOU KNOW WHAT'S GOOD FOR YOU.
NICK, WHERE ARE YOU?
I'M HERE, WHAT THE HELL HAPPENED DOWN THERE?
I DON'T KNOW...THE CROWD WAS GOING NUTS AND THEN I JUST HEARD SHOTS...
POLICE
POLICE U.S.
HE'S BLEEDING REALLY BAD, NICK...DRIFTING IN AND OUT...
SHARON, LISTEN TO ME. THERE'S A HOSPITAL FIVE BLOCKS AWAY. AND THIS...IT'S STEVE ROGERS...HE'S TAKEN BULLETS BEFORE.
HE AIN'T GONNA DIE, OKAY?

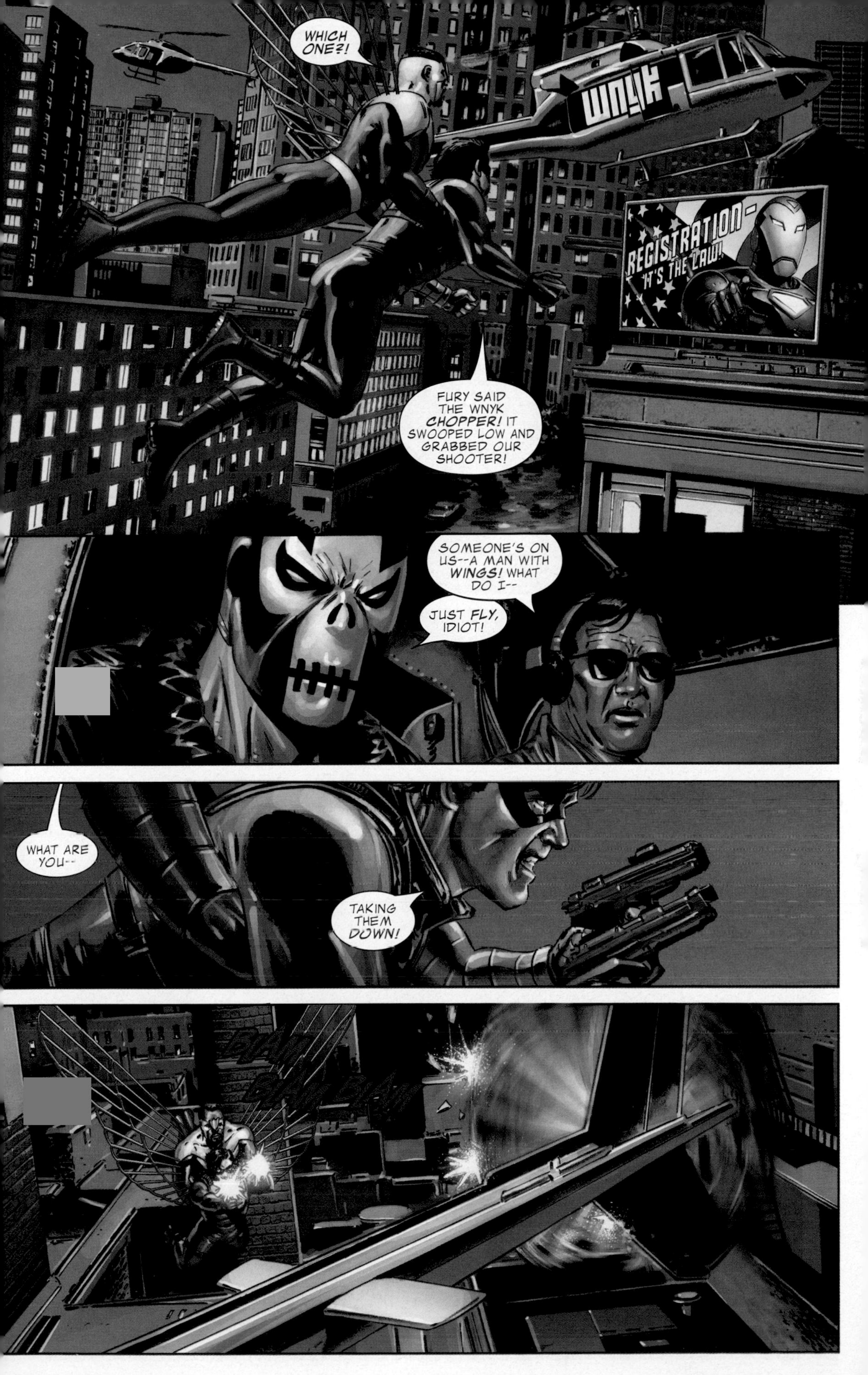
WHICH ONE?!
WNYK
REGISTRATION— IT'S THE LAW!
FURY SAID THE WNYK CHOPPER! IT SWOOPED LOW AND GRABBED OUR SHOOTER!
SOMEONE'S ON US--A MAN WITH WINGS! WHAT DO I--
JUST FLY, IDIOT!
WHAT ARE YOU--
TAKING THEM DOWN!

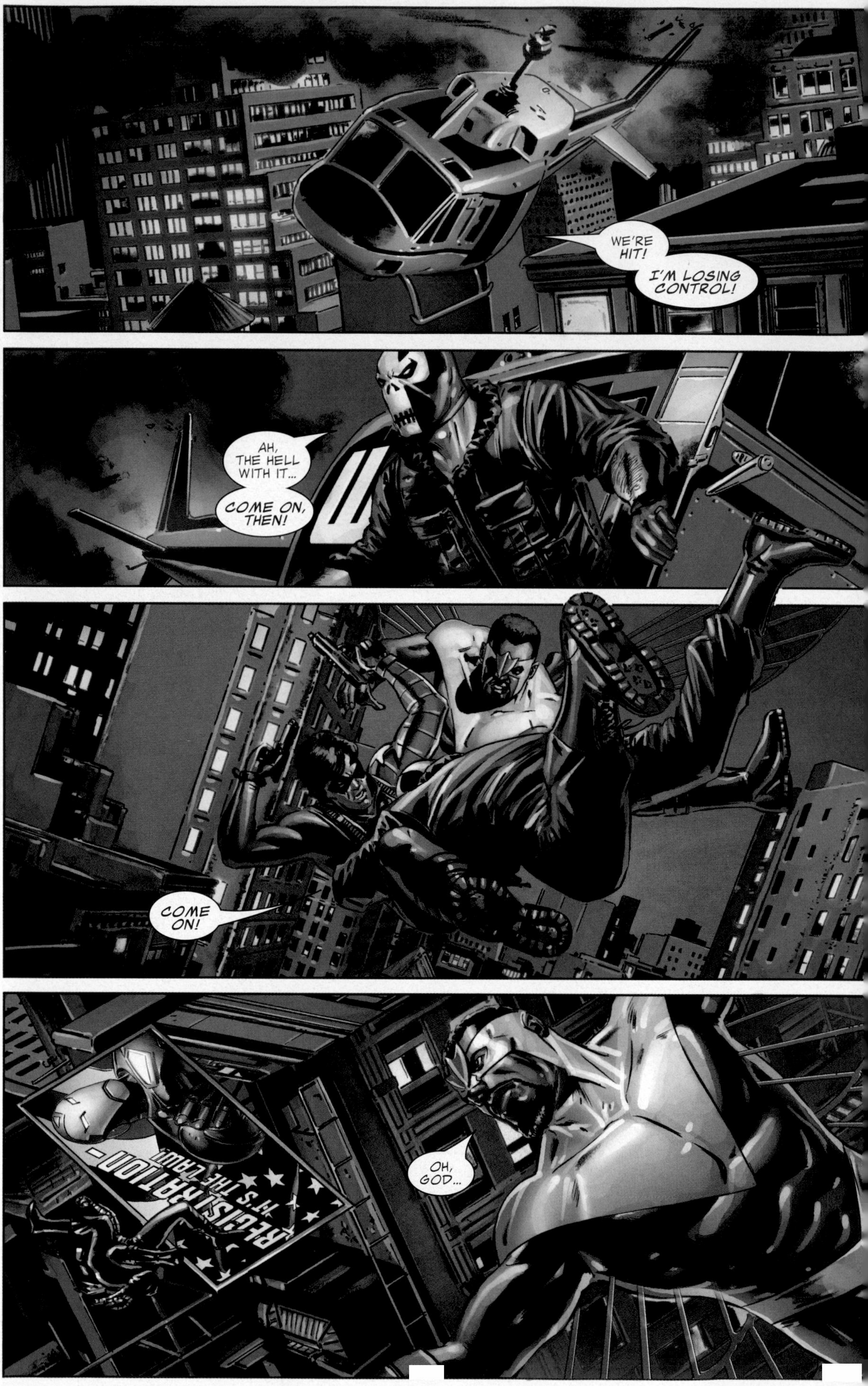
WE'RE HIT!
I'M LOSING CONTROL!
AH, THE HELL WITH IT...
COME ON, THEN!
COME ON!
REGISTRATION - IT'S THE LAW!
OH, GOD...

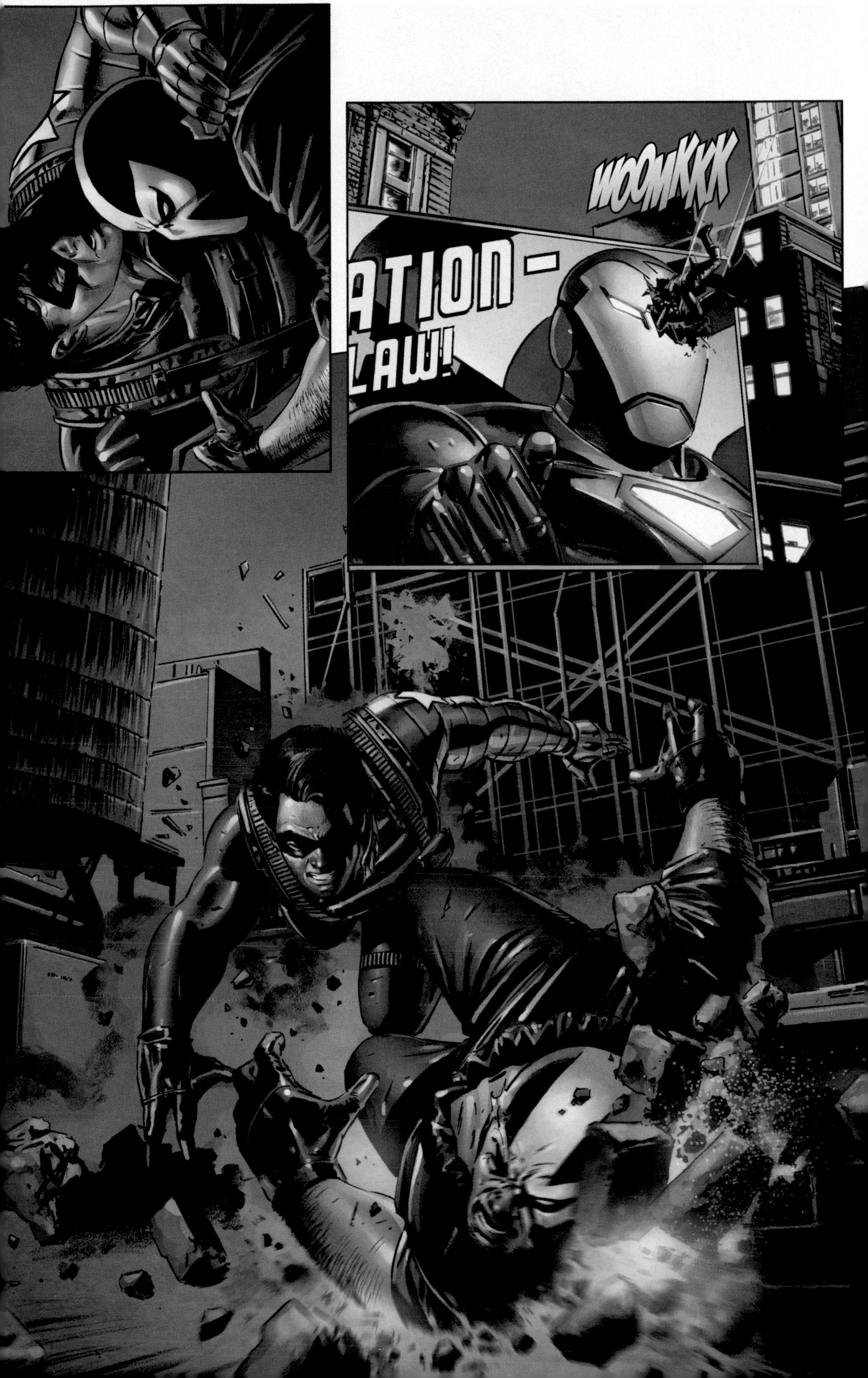
WOOMKKK
ATION-
LAW!

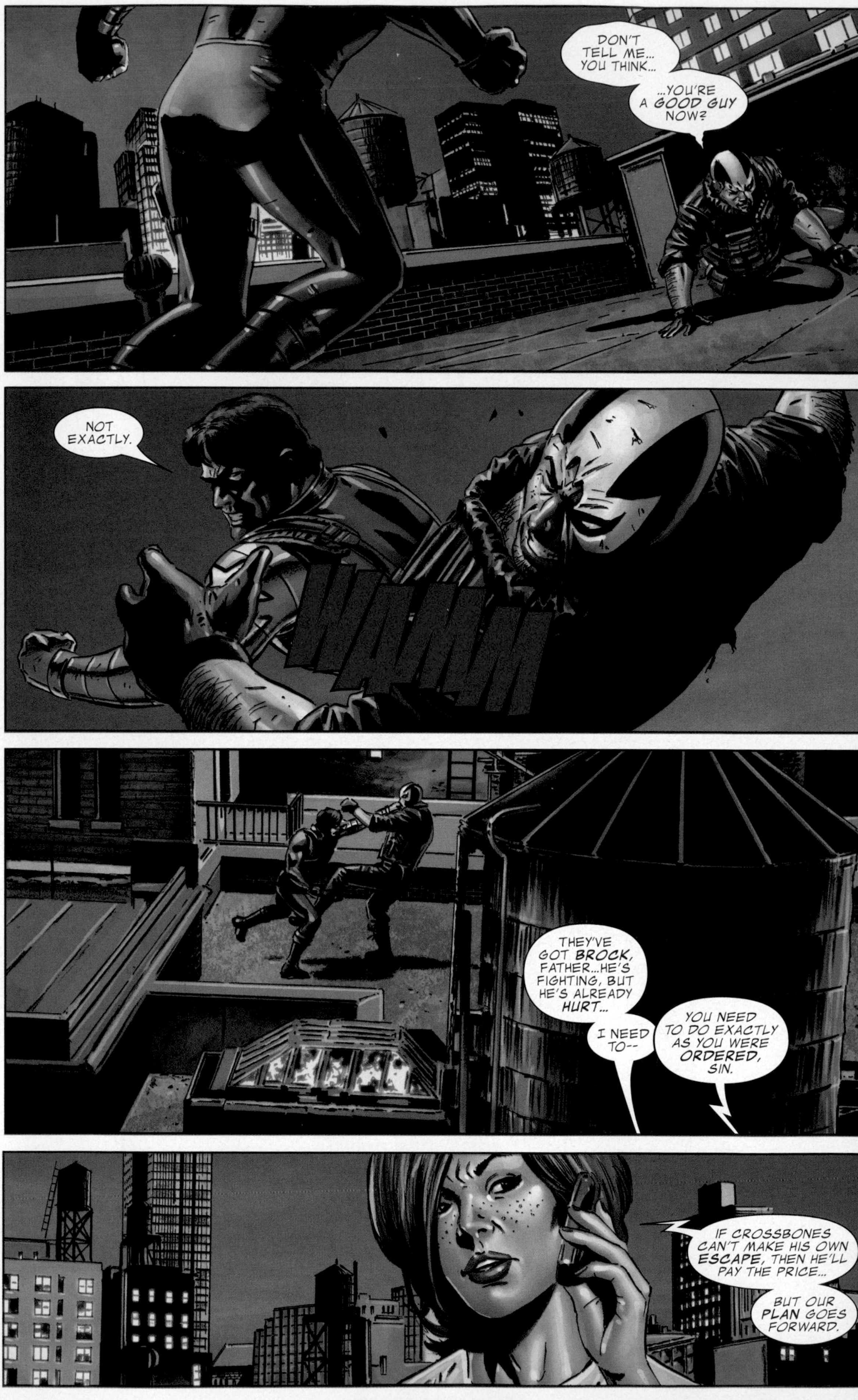
DON'T TELL ME... YOU THINK...
...YOU'RE A GOOD GUY NOW?
NOT EXACTLY.
WAMM
THEY'VE GOT BROCK, FATHER...HE'S FIGHTING, BUT HE'S ALREADY HURT...
I NEED TO--
YOU NEED TO DO EXACTLY AS YOU WERE ORDERED, SIN.
IF CROSSBONES CAN'T MAKE HIS OWN ESCAPE, THEN HE'LL PAY THE PRICE...
BUT OUR PLAN GOES FORWARD.

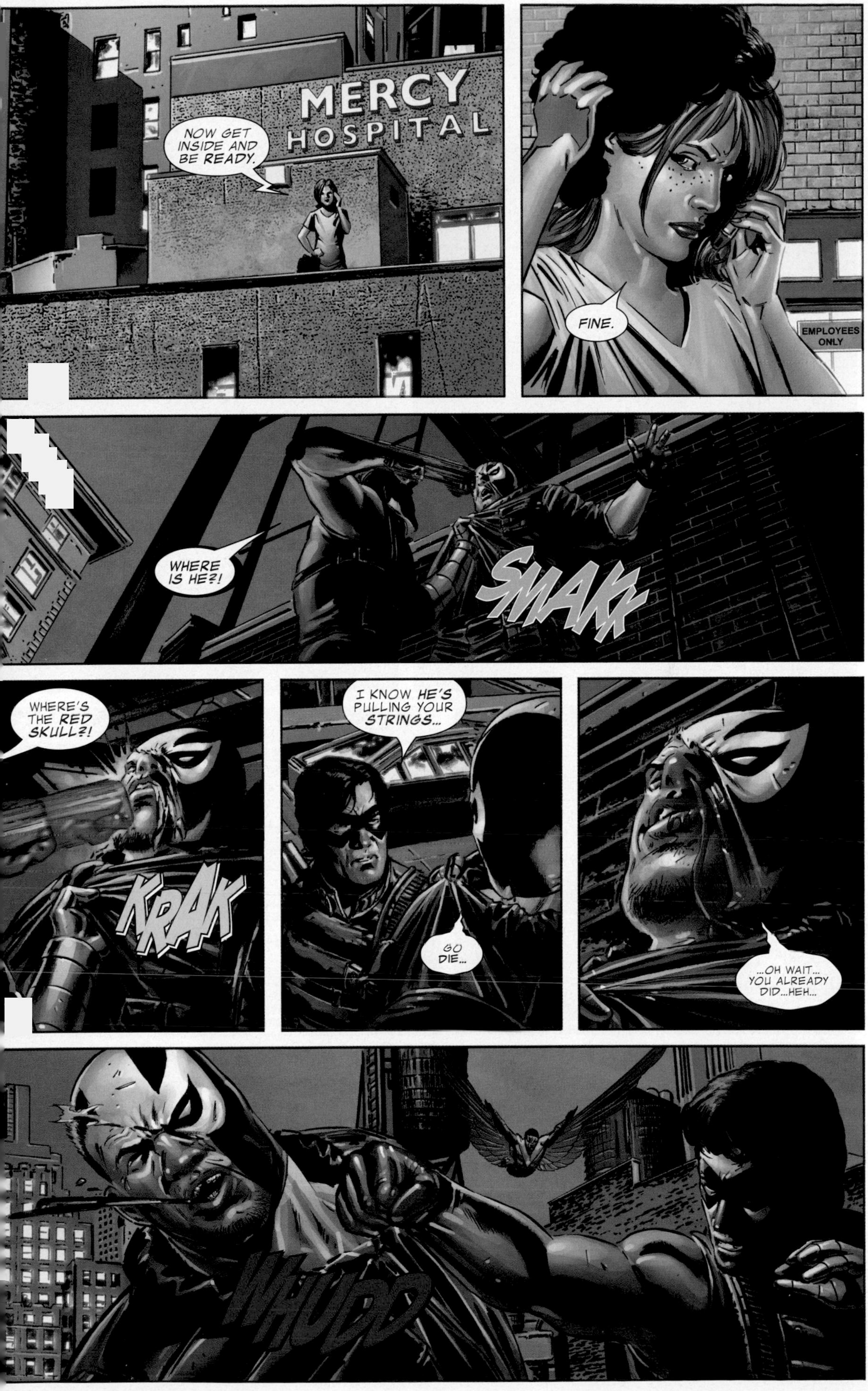
MERCY HOSPITAL
NOW GET INSIDE AND BE READY.
FINE.
EMPLOYEES ONLY
WHERE IS HE?!
SMAKK
WHERE'S THE RED SKULL?!
KRAK
I KNOW HE'S PULLING YOUR STRINGS...
GO DIE...
...OH WAIT... YOU ALREADY DID...HEH...
WHUDD

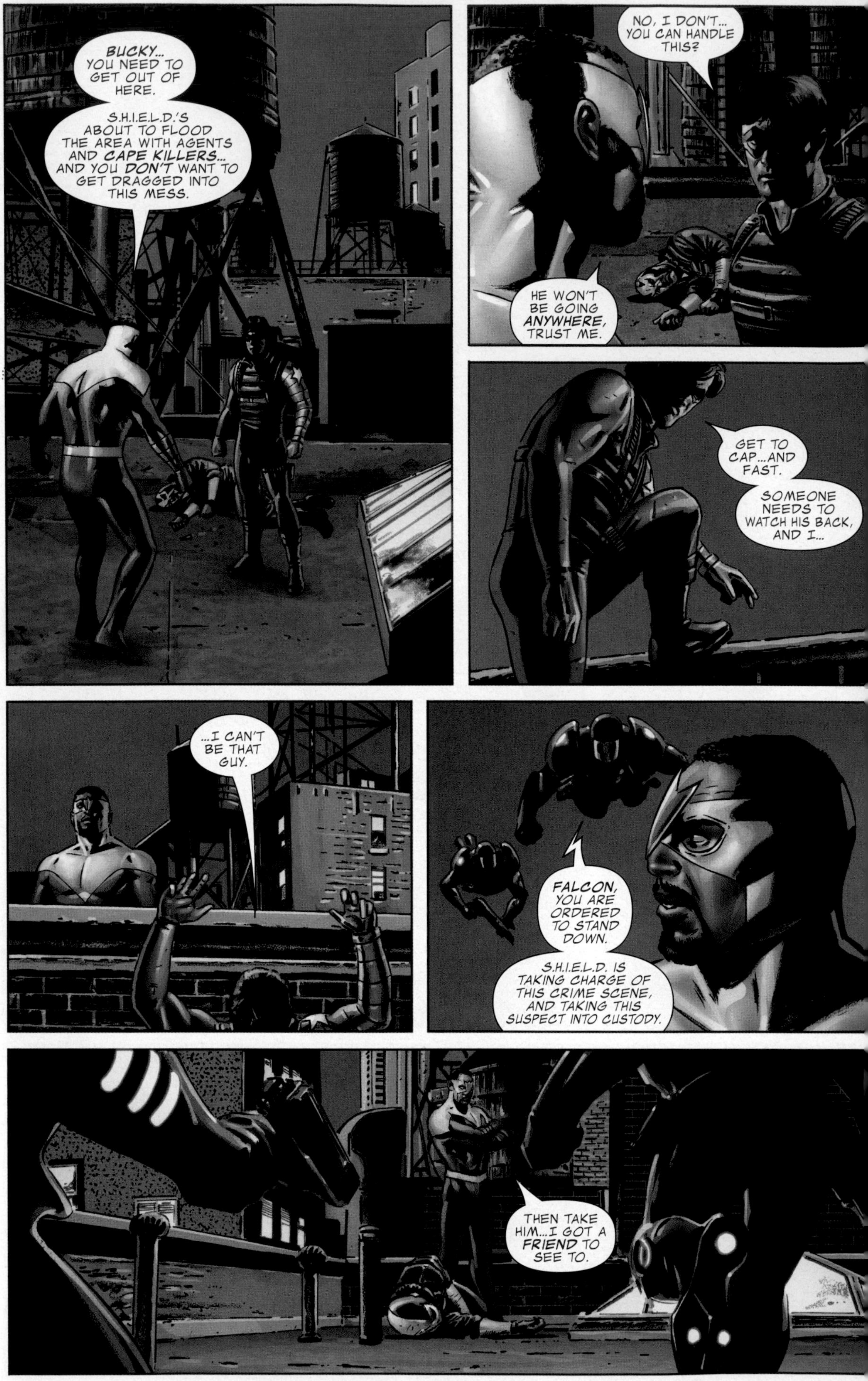
BUCKY... YOU NEED TO GET OUT OF HERE.
S.H.I.E.L.D.'S ABOUT TO FLOOD THE AREA WITH AGENTS AND CAPE KILLERS... AND YOU DON'T WANT TO GET DRAGGED INTO THIS MESS.
NO, I DON'T... YOU CAN HANDLE THIS?
HE WON'T BE GOING ANYWHERE, TRUST ME.
GET TO CAP...AND FAST.
SOMEONE NEEDS TO WATCH HIS BACK, AND I...
...I CAN'T BE THAT GUY.
FALCON, YOU ARE ORDERED TO STAND DOWN.
S.H.I.E.L.D. IS TAKING CHARGE OF THIS CRIME SCENE, AND TAKING THIS SUSPECT INTO CUSTODY.
THEN TAKE HIM...I GOT A FRIEND TO SEE TO.

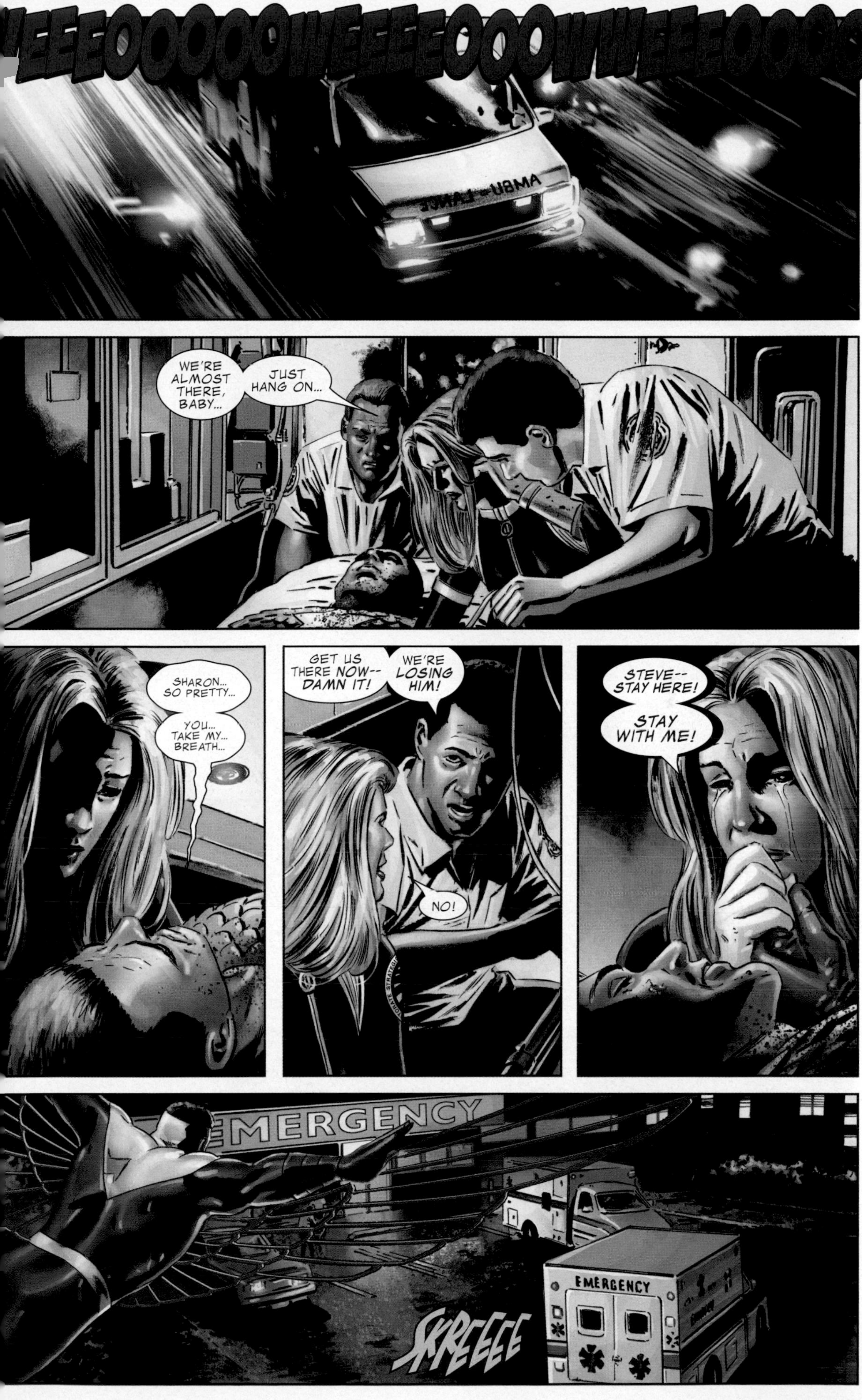

WEEEOOOOOOWEEEEOOOOWWEEEOOOO
AMBU-LANCE
WE'RE ALMOST THERE, BABY...
JUST HANG ON...
SHARON... SO PRETTY...
YOU... TAKE MY... BREATH...
GET US THERE NOW-- DAMN IT!
WE'RE LOSING HIM!
NO!
STEVE-- STAY HERE!
STAY WITH ME!
EMERGENCY
EMERGENCY
SKREEEEE

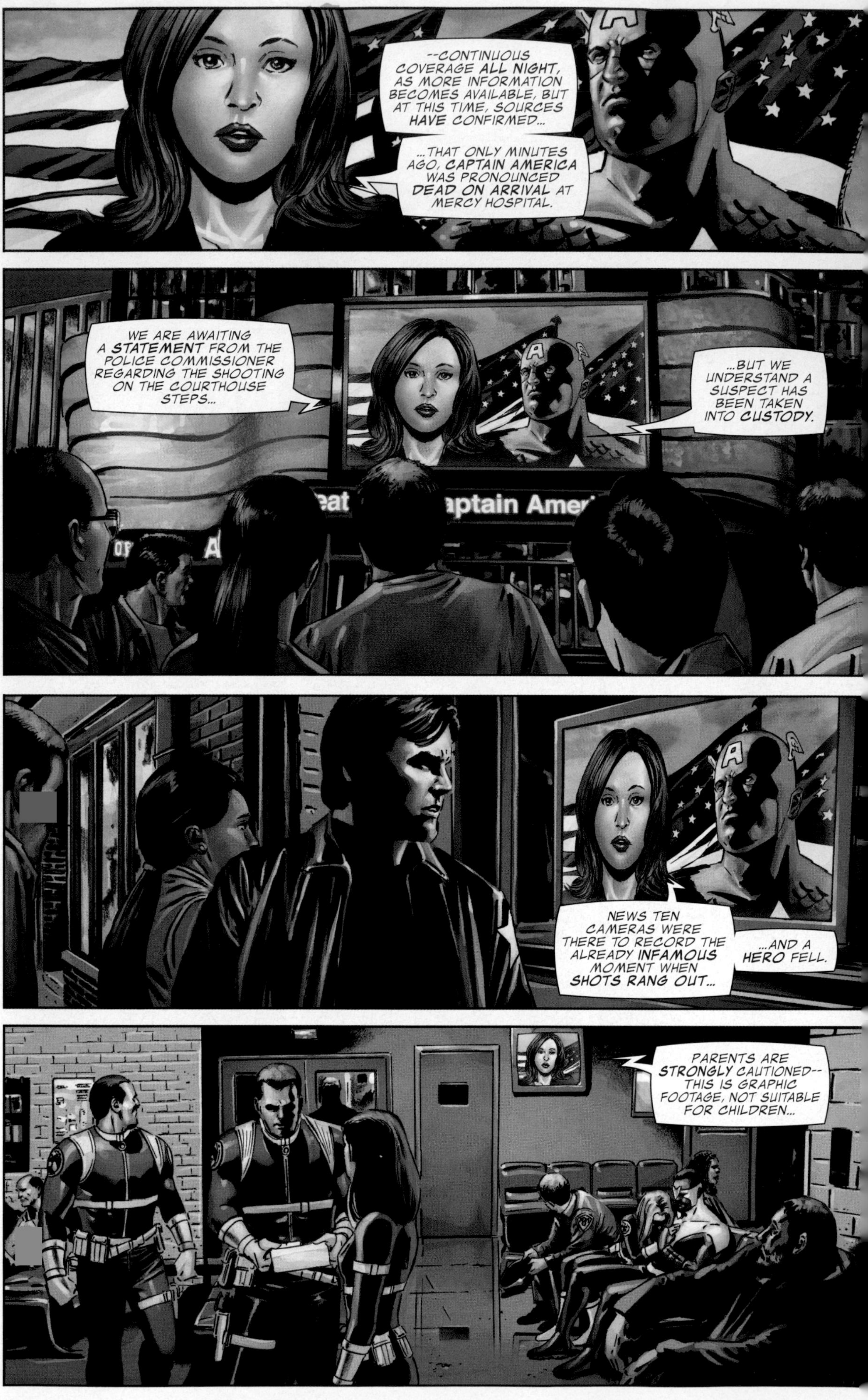
--CONTINUOUS COVERAGE ALL NIGHT, AS MORE INFORMATION BECOMES AVAILABLE, BUT AT THIS TIME, SOURCES HAVE CONFIRMED...
...THAT ONLY MINUTES AGO, CAPTAIN AMERICA WAS PRONOUNCED DEAD ON ARRIVAL AT MERCY HOSPITAL.
WE ARE AWAITING A STATEMENT FROM THE POLICE COMMISSIONER REGARDING THE SHOOTING ON THE COURTHOUSE STEPS...
...BUT WE UNDERSTAND A SUSPECT HAS BEEN TAKEN INTO CUSTODY.
NEWS TEN CAMERAS WERE THERE TO RECORD THE ALREADY INFAMOUS MOMENT WHEN SHOTS RANG OUT...
...AND A HERO FELL.
PARENTS ARE STRONGLY CAUTIONED-- THIS IS GRAPHIC FOOTAGE, NOT SUITABLE FOR CHILDREN...

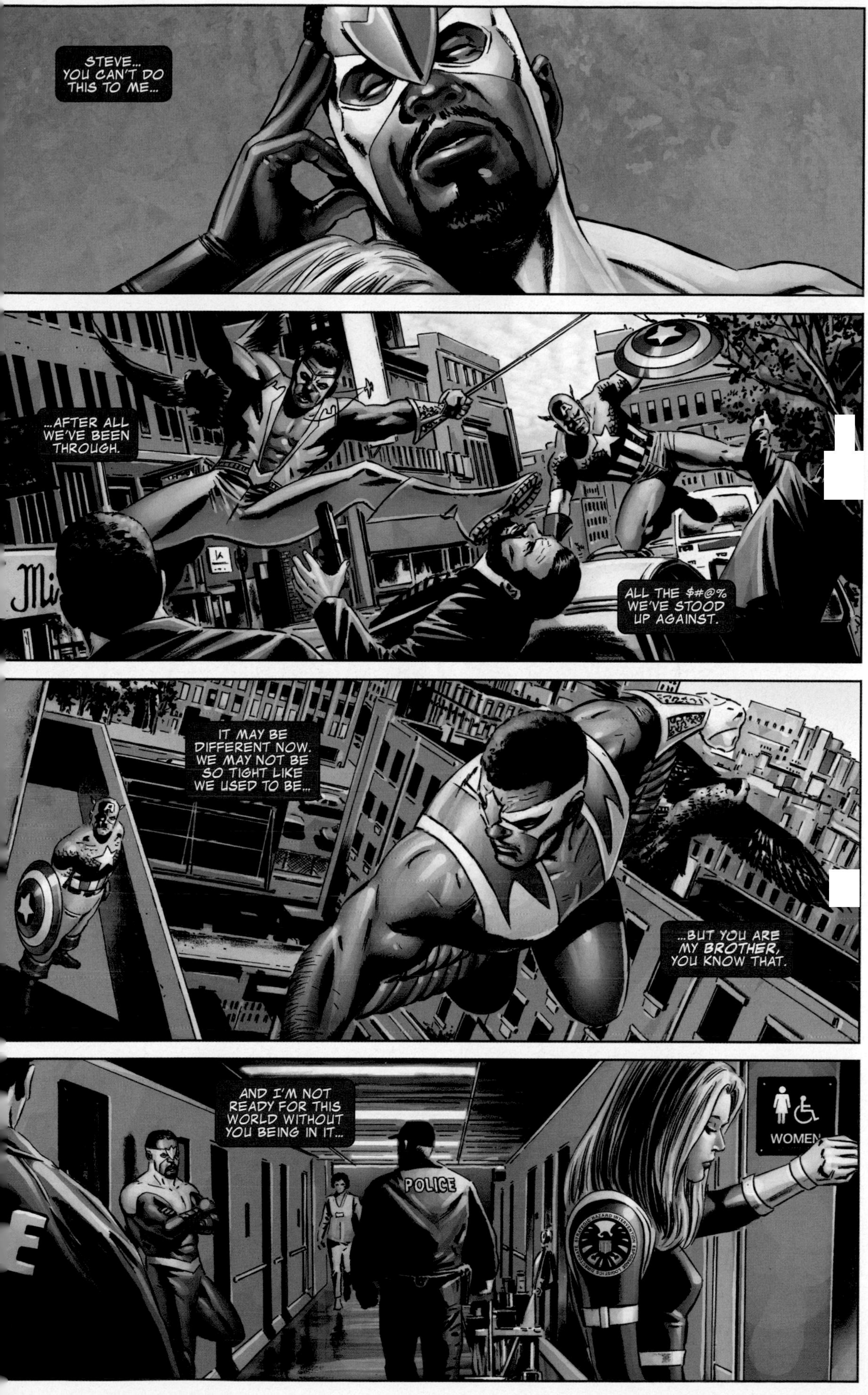
STEVE... YOU CAN'T DO THIS TO ME...
...AFTER ALL WE'VE BEEN THROUGH.
ALL THE $#@% WE'VE STOOD UP AGAINST.
IT MAY BE DIFFERENT NOW. WE MAY NOT BE SO TIGHT LIKE WE USED TO BE...
...BUT YOU ARE MY BROTHER, YOU KNOW THAT.
AND I'M NOT READY FOR THIS WORLD WITHOUT YOU BEING IN IT...
POLICE
WOMEN

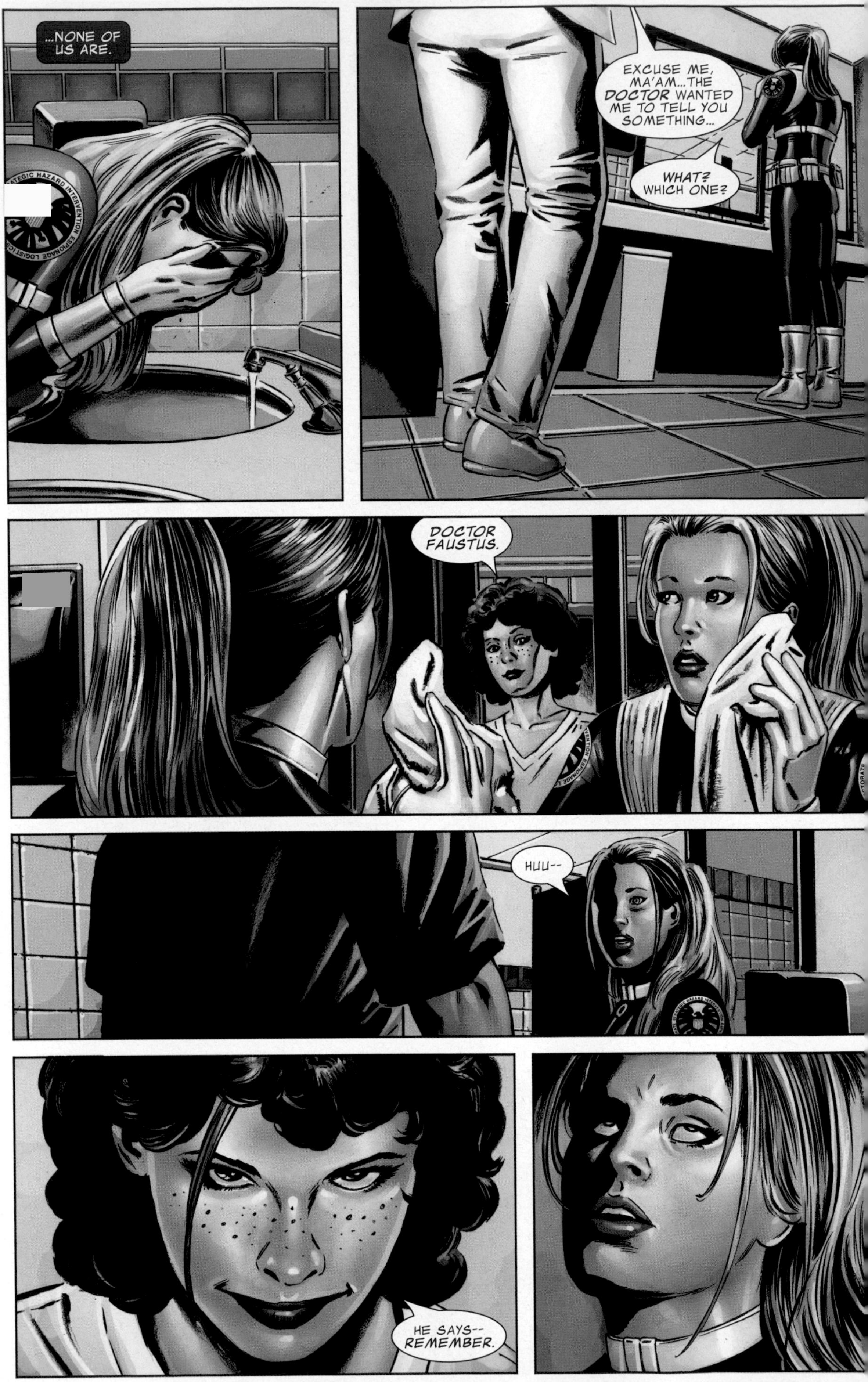
...NONE OF US ARE.
EXCUSE ME, MA'AM...THE DOCTOR WANTED ME TO TELL YOU SOMETHING...
WHAT? WHICH ONE?
DOCTOR FAUSTUS.
HUU--
HE SAYS-- REMEMBER.

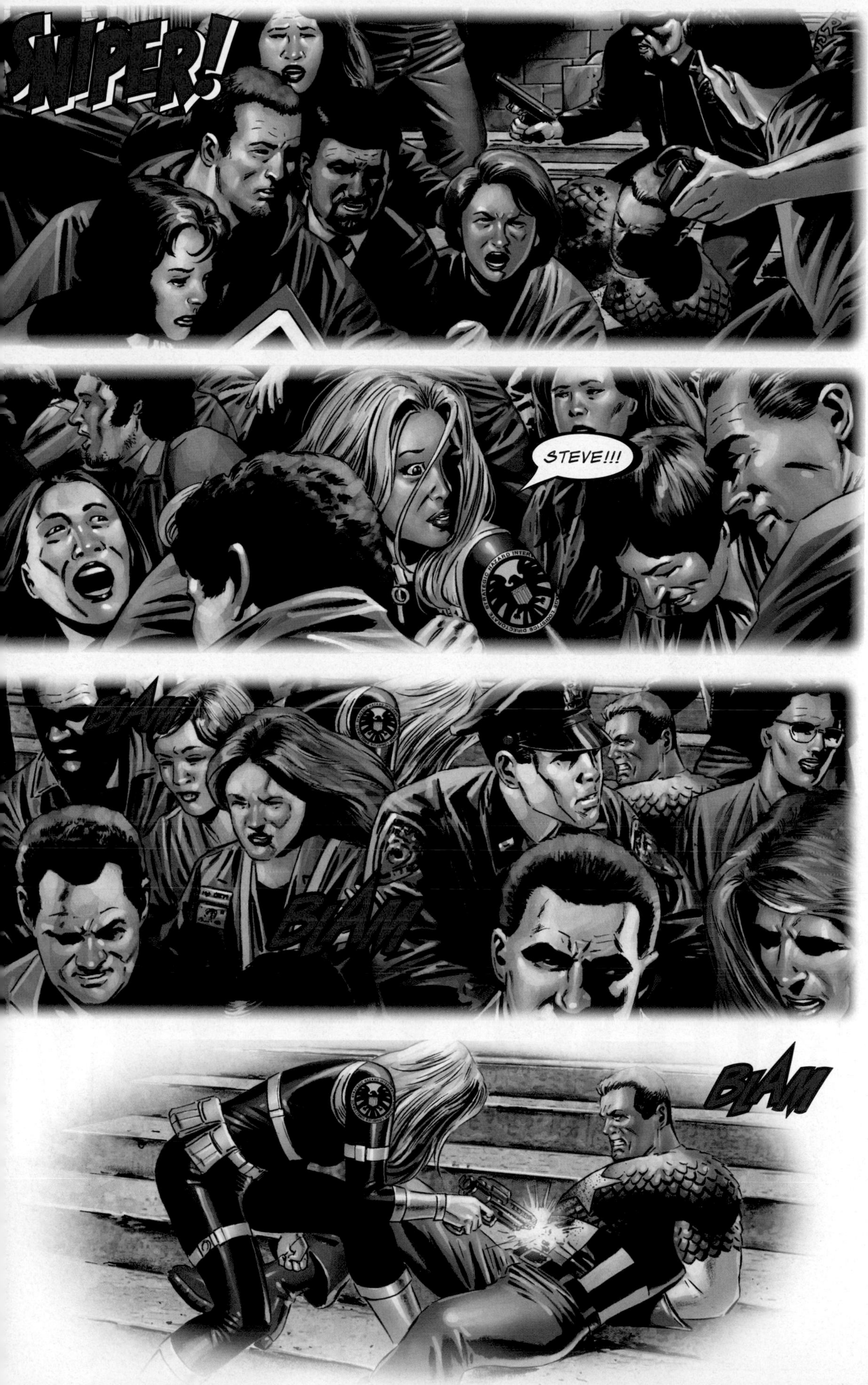
SNIPER!
STEVE!!!
BLAM
BLAM
BLAM

...NO... NO...
...WHAT DID I DO...?
"...WHAT DID I DO?"

The Death Of THE DREAM

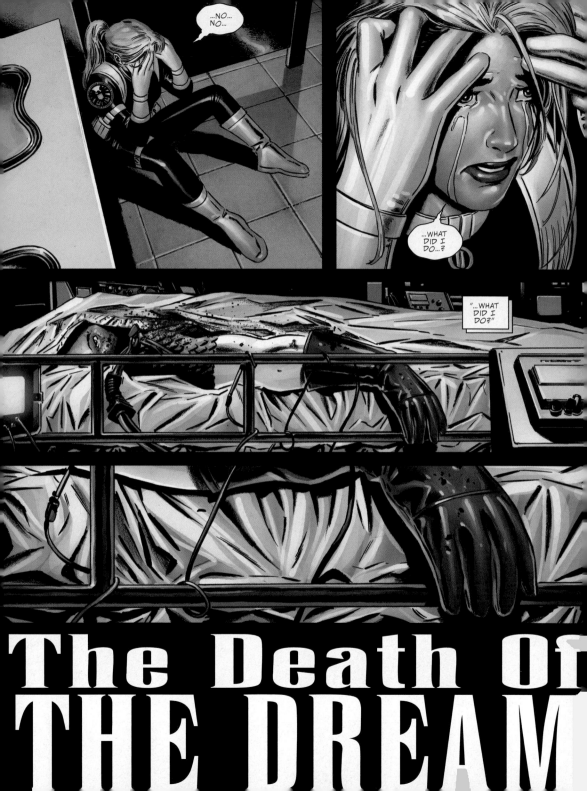

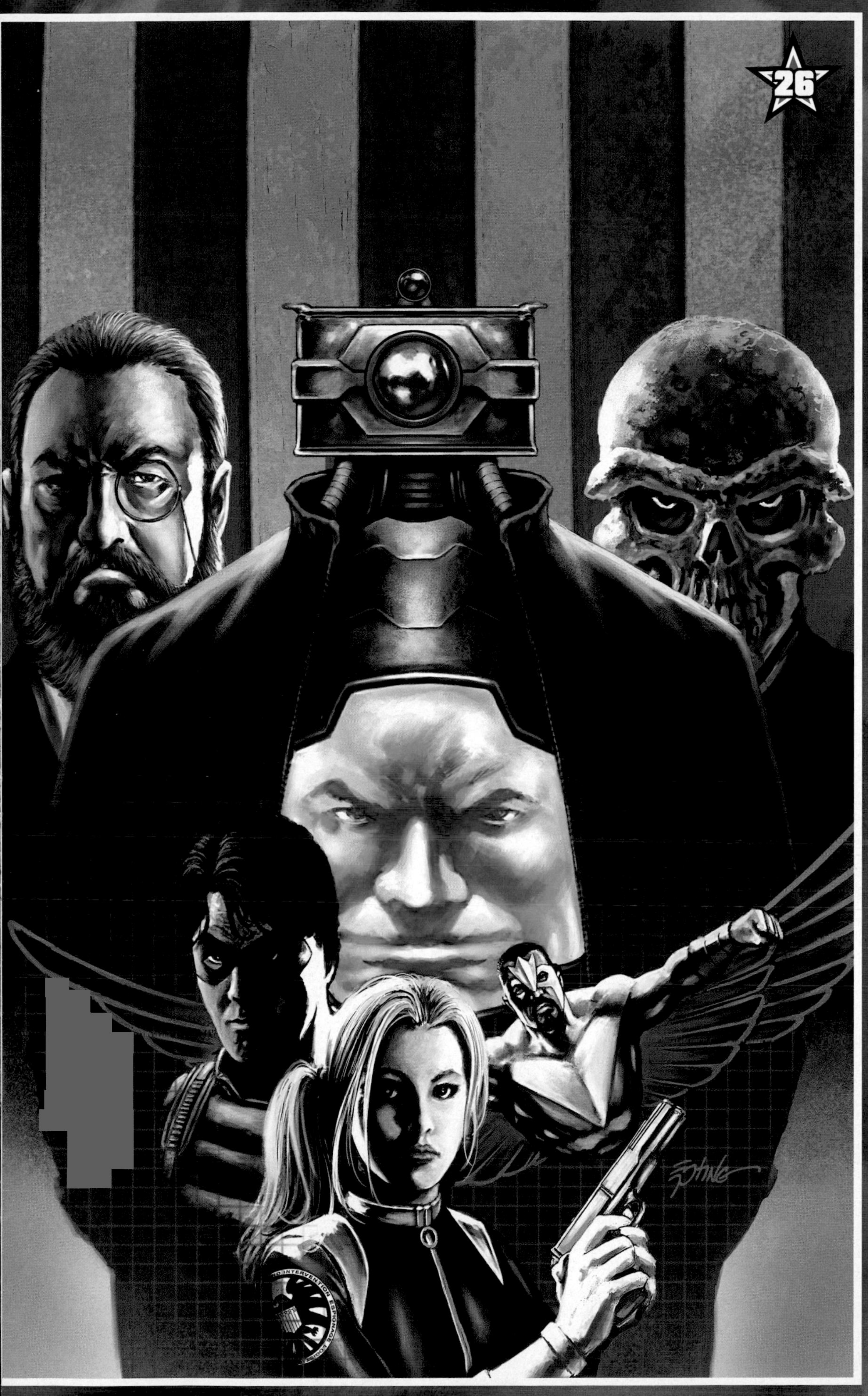

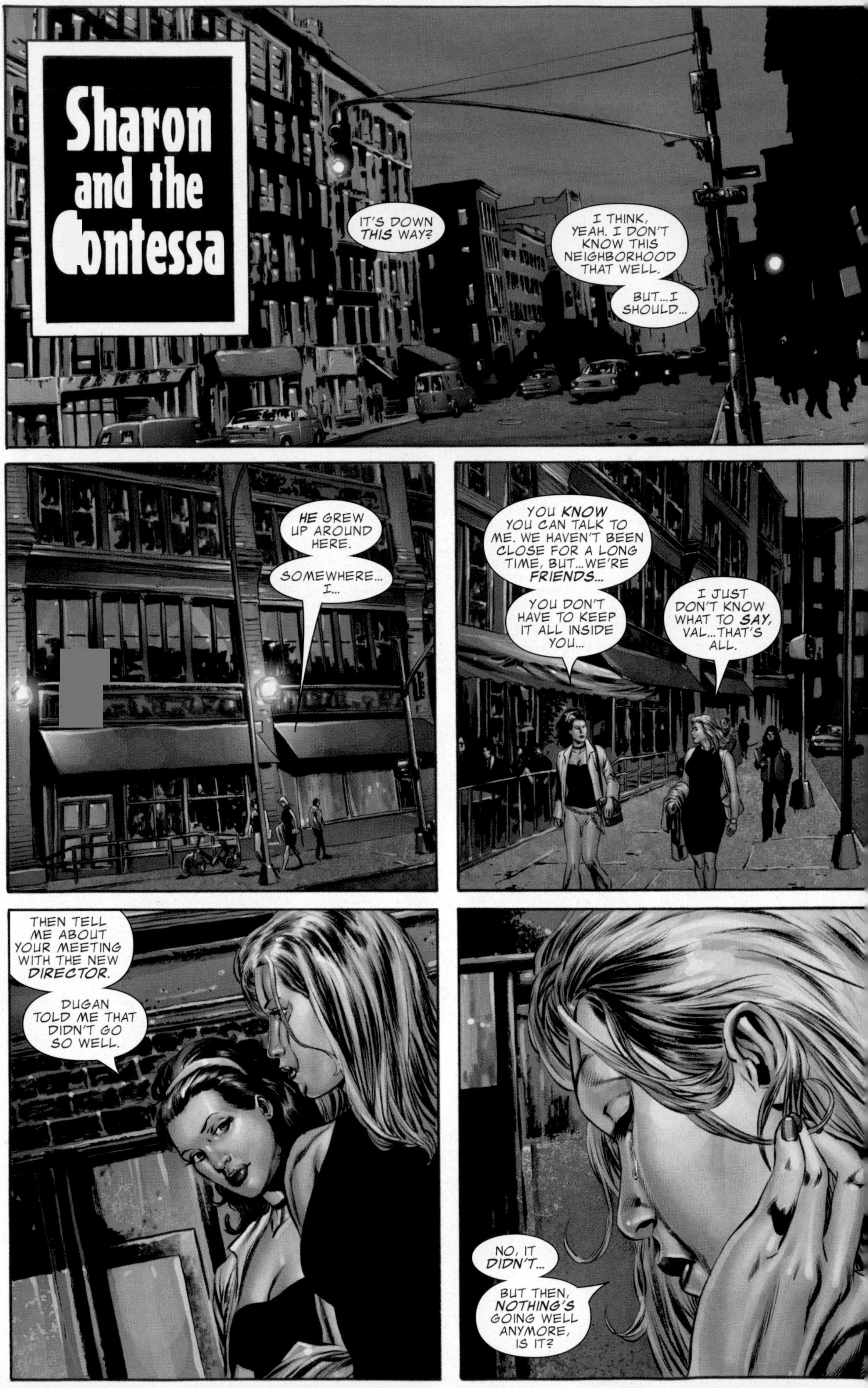
Sharon and the Contessa
IT'S DOWN THIS WAY?
I THINK, YEAH. I DON'T KNOW THIS NEIGHBORHOOD THAT WELL.
BUT...I SHOULD...
HE GREW UP AROUND HERE.
SOMEWHERE... I...
YOU KNOW YOU CAN TALK TO ME. WE HAVEN'T BEEN CLOSE FOR A LONG TIME, BUT...WE'RE FRIENDS...
YOU DON'T HAVE TO KEEP IT ALL INSIDE YOU...
I JUST DON'T KNOW WHAT TO SAY, VAL...THAT'S ALL.
THEN TELL ME ABOUT YOUR MEETING WITH THE NEW DIRECTOR.
DUGAN TOLD ME THAT DIDN'T GO SO WELL.
NO, IT DIDN'T...
BUT THEN, NOTHING'S GOING WELL ANYMORE, IS IT?

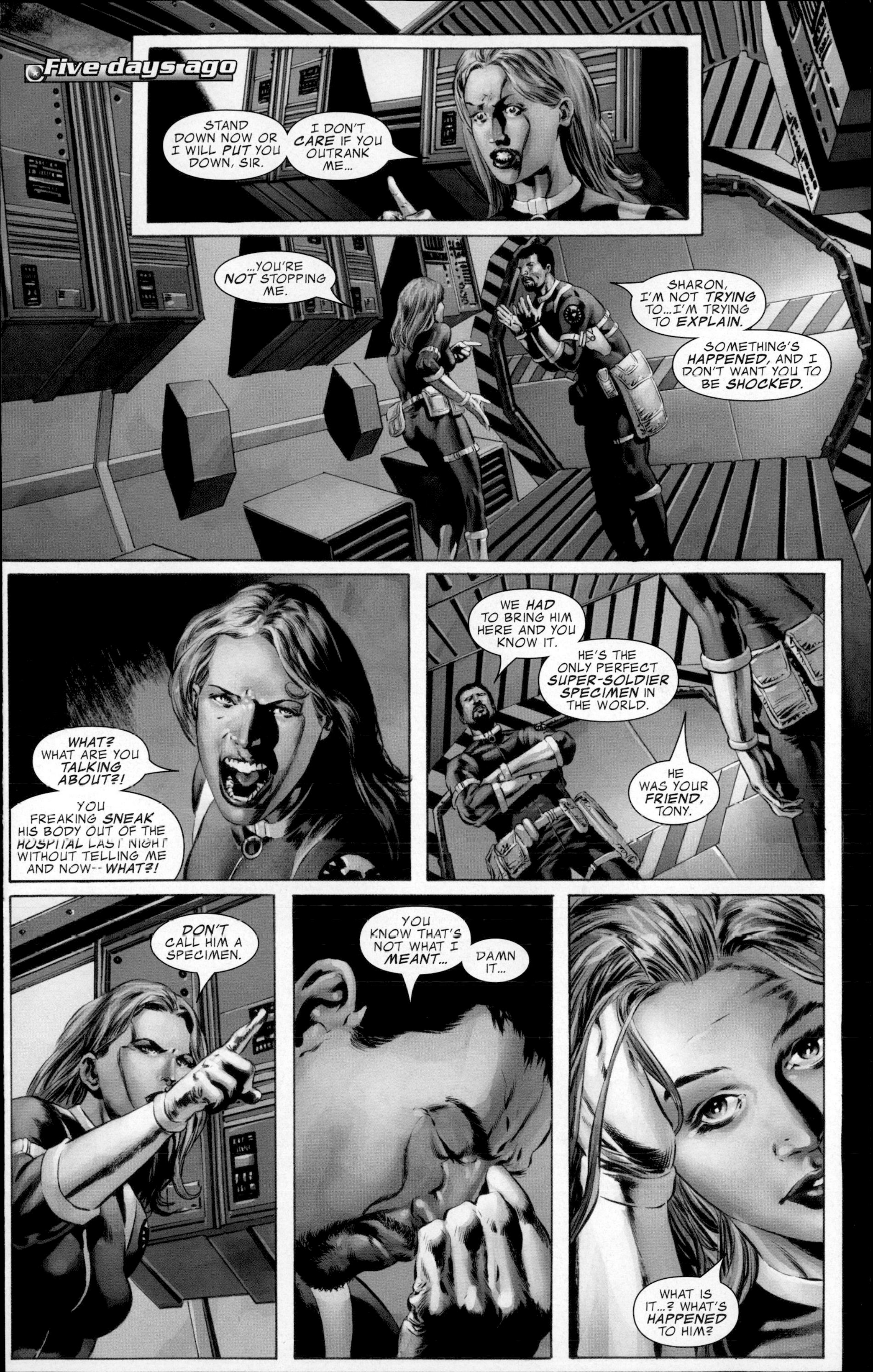
Five days ago
STAND DOWN NOW OR I WILL PUT YOU DOWN, SIR.
I DON'T CARE IF YOU OUTRANK ME...
...YOU'RE NOT STOPPING ME.
SHARON, I'M NOT TRYING TO...I'M TRYING TO EXPLAIN.
SOMETHING'S HAPPENED, AND I DON'T WANT YOU TO BE SHOCKED.
WHAT? WHAT ARE YOU TALKING ABOUT?!
YOU FREAKING SNEAK HIS BODY OUT OF THE HOSPITAL LAST NIGHT WITHOUT TELLING ME AND NOW--WHAT?!
WE HAD TO BRING HIM HERE AND YOU KNOW IT.
HE'S THE ONLY PERFECT SUPER-SOLDIER SPECIMEN IN THE WORLD.
HE WAS YOUR FRIEND, TONY.
DON'T CALL HIM A SPECIMEN.
YOU KNOW THAT'S NOT WHAT I MEANT...
DAMN IT...
WHAT IS IT...? WHAT'S HAPPENED TO HIM?

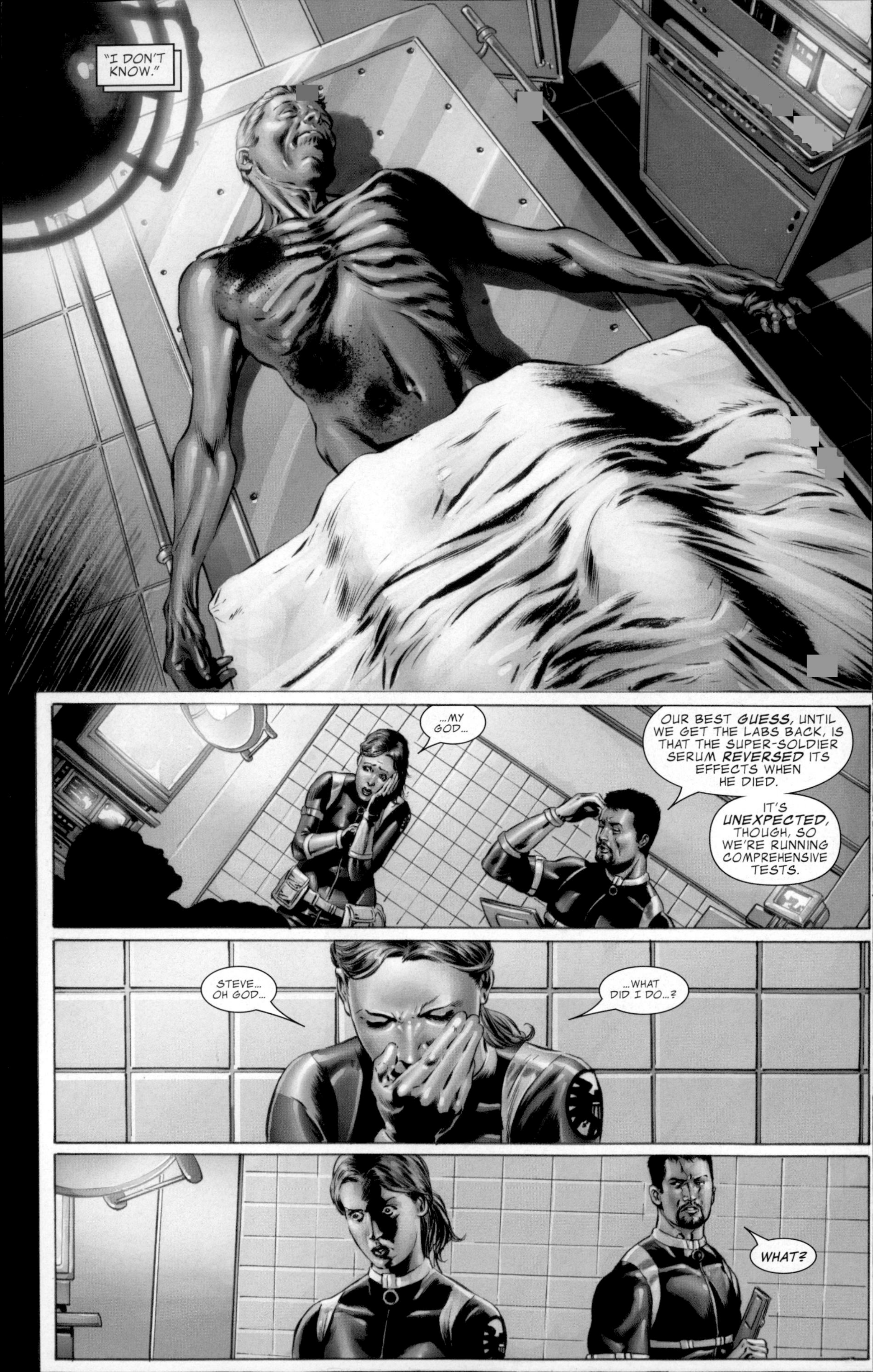
"I DON'T KNOW."
...MY GOD...
OUR BEST GUESS, UNTIL WE GET THE LABS BACK, IS THAT THE SUPER-SOLDIER SERUM REVERSED ITS EFFECTS WHEN HE DIED.
IT'S UNEXPECTED, THOUGH, SO WE'RE RUNNING COMPREHENSIVE TESTS.
STEVE... OH GOD...
...WHAT DID I DO...?
WHAT?

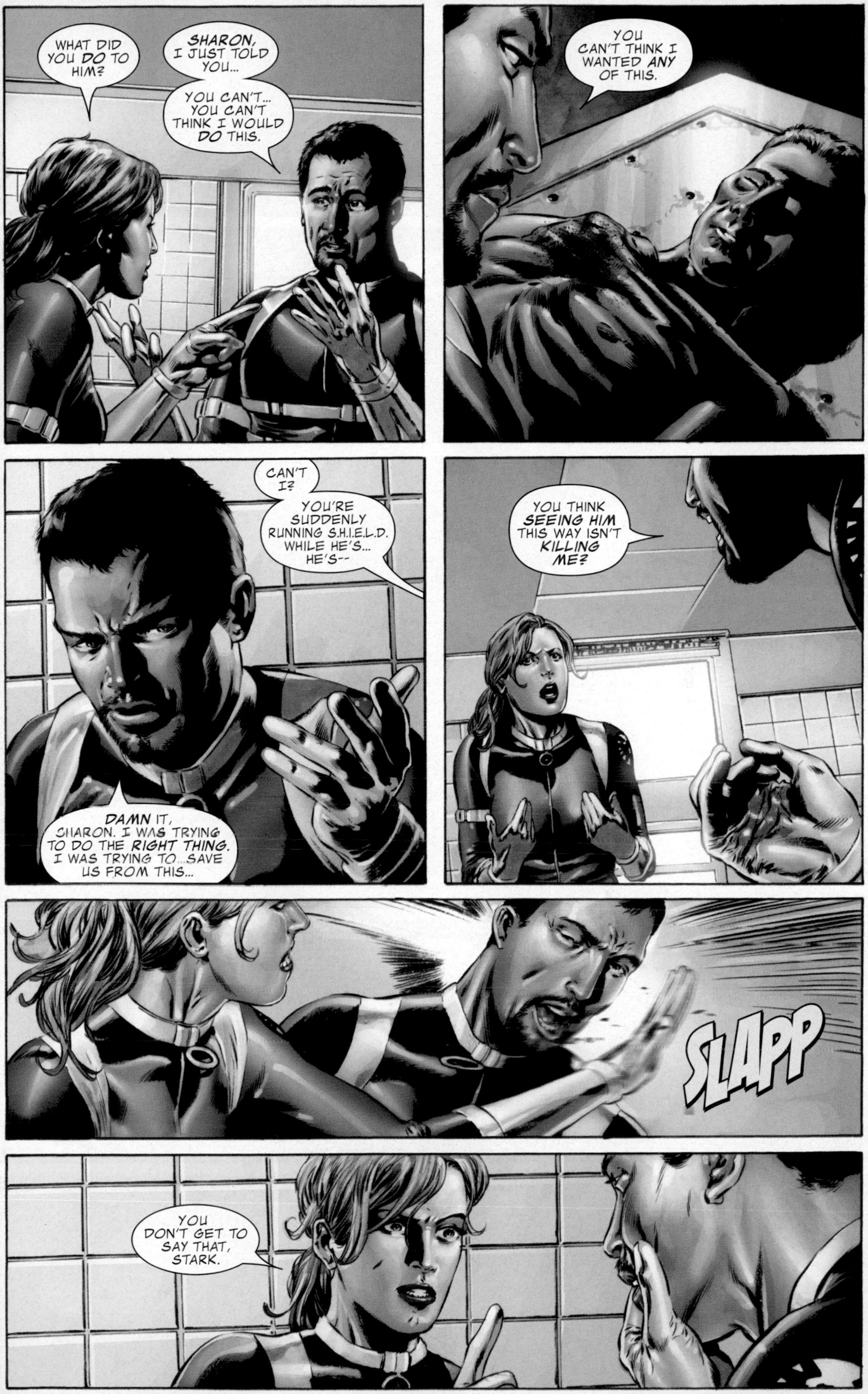
WHAT DID YOU DO TO HIM?
SHARON, I JUST TOLD YOU...
YOU CAN'T... YOU CAN'T THINK I WOULD DO THIS.
YOU CAN'T THINK I WANTED ANY OF THIS.
CAN'T I?
YOU'RE SUDDENLY RUNNING S.H.I.E.L.D. WHILE HE'S... HE'S--
DAMN IT, SHARON. I WAS TRYING TO DO THE RIGHT THING. I WAS TRYING TO...SAVE US FROM THIS...
YOU THINK SEEING HIM THIS WAY ISN'T KILLING ME?
SLAPP
YOU DON'T GET TO SAY THAT, STARK.

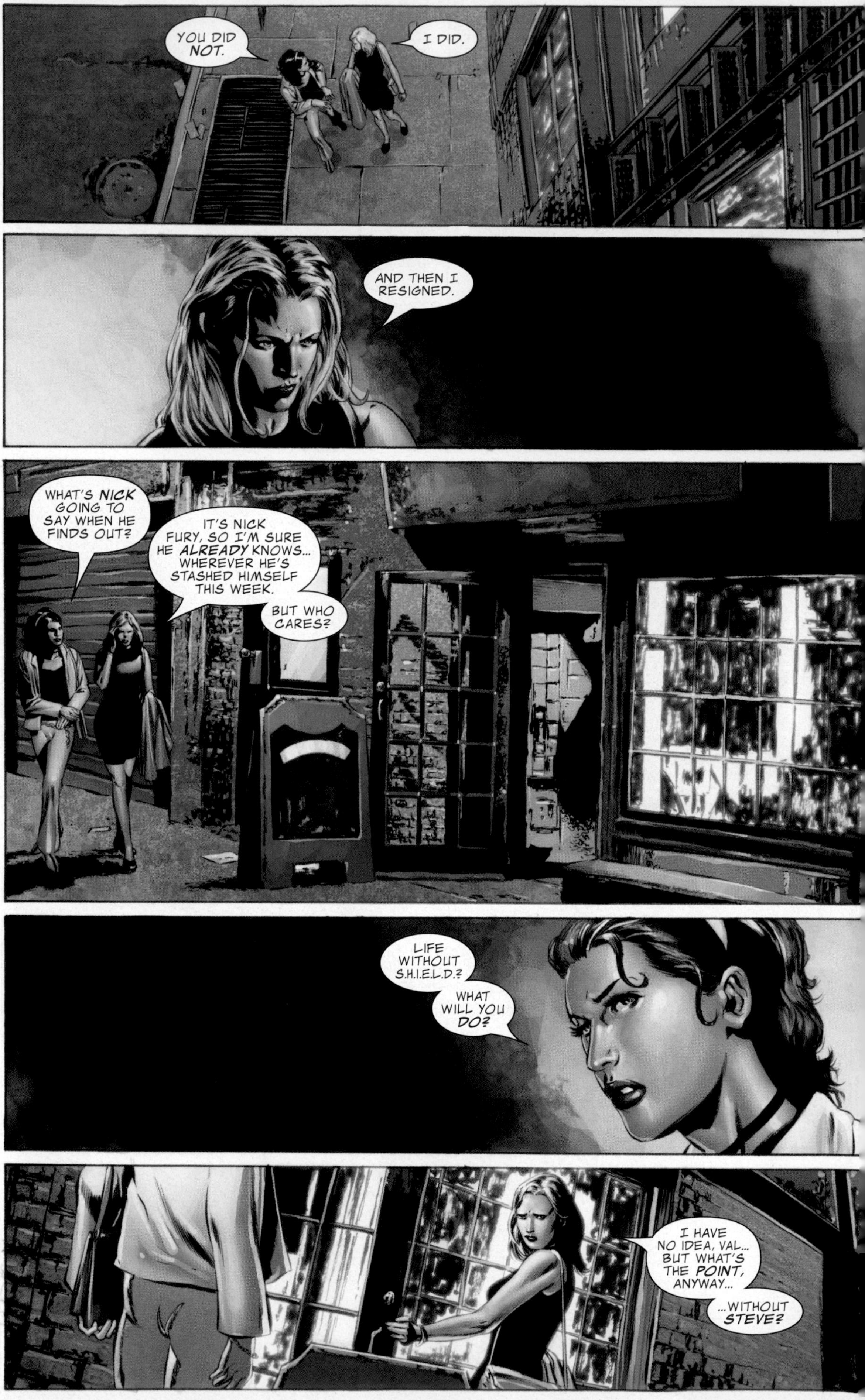
YOU DID NOT.
I DID.
AND THEN I RESIGNED.
WHAT'S NICK GOING TO SAY WHEN HE FINDS OUT?
IT'S NICK FURY, SO I'M SURE HE ALREADY KNOWS... WHEREVER HE'S STASHED HIMSELF THIS WEEK.
BUT WHO CARES?
LIFE WITHOUT S.H.I.E.L.D.?
WHAT WILL YOU DO?
I HAVE NO IDEA, VAL... BUT WHAT'S THE POINT, ANYWAY...
...WITHOUT STEVE?

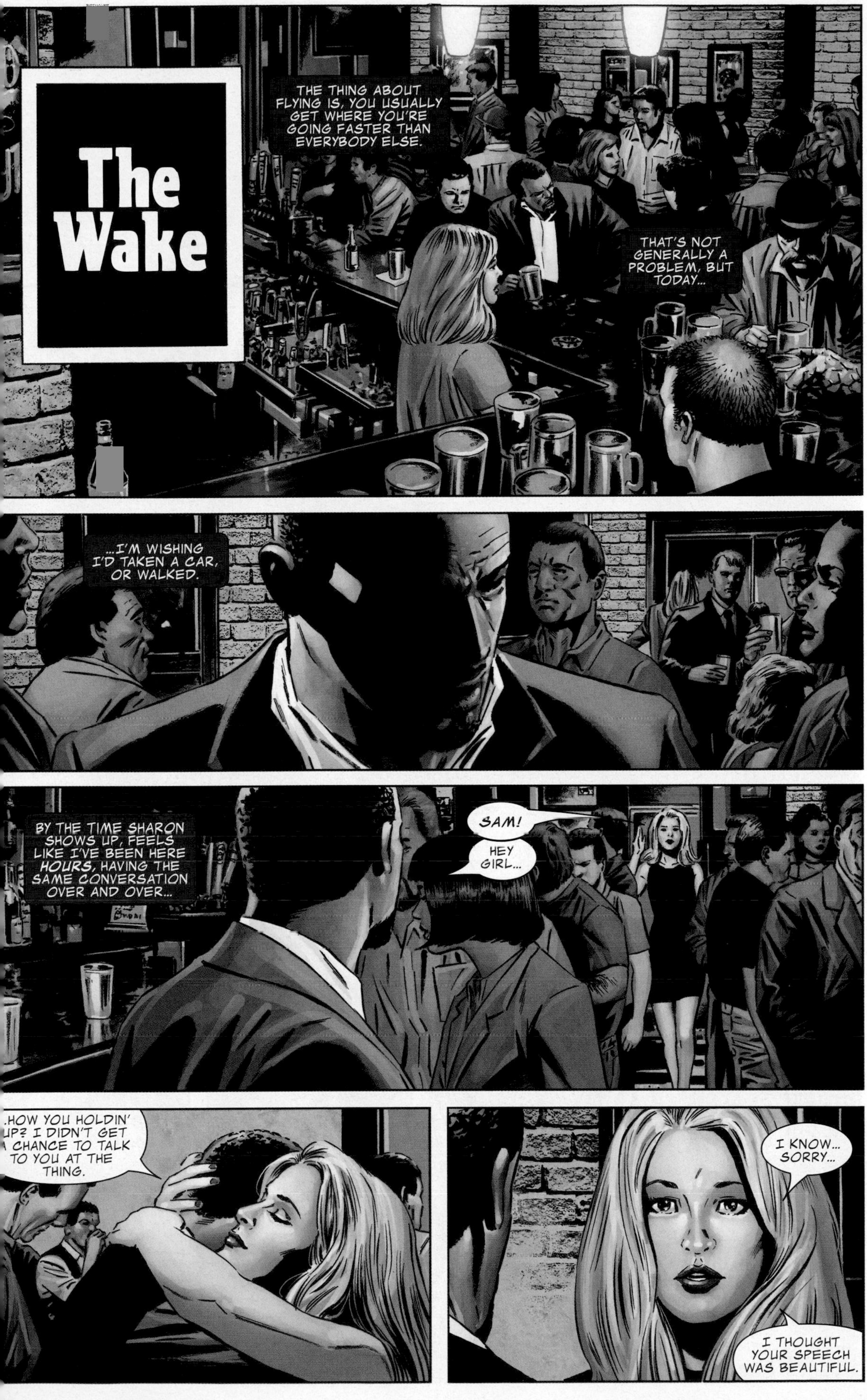
The Wake
THE THING ABOUT FLYING IS, YOU USUALLY GET WHERE YOU'RE GOING FASTER THAN EVERYBODY ELSE.
THAT'S NOT GENERALLY A PROBLEM, BUT TODAY...
...I'M WISHING I'D TAKEN A CAR, OR WALKED.
BY THE TIME SHARON SHOWS UP, FEELS LIKE I'VE BEEN HERE HOURS, HAVING THE SAME CONVERSATION OVER AND OVER...
SAM!
HEY GIRL...
HOW YOU HOLDIN' UP? I DIDN'T GET A CHANCE TO TALK TO YOU AT THE THING.
I KNOW... SORRY...
I THOUGHT YOUR SPEECH WAS BEAUTIFUL.

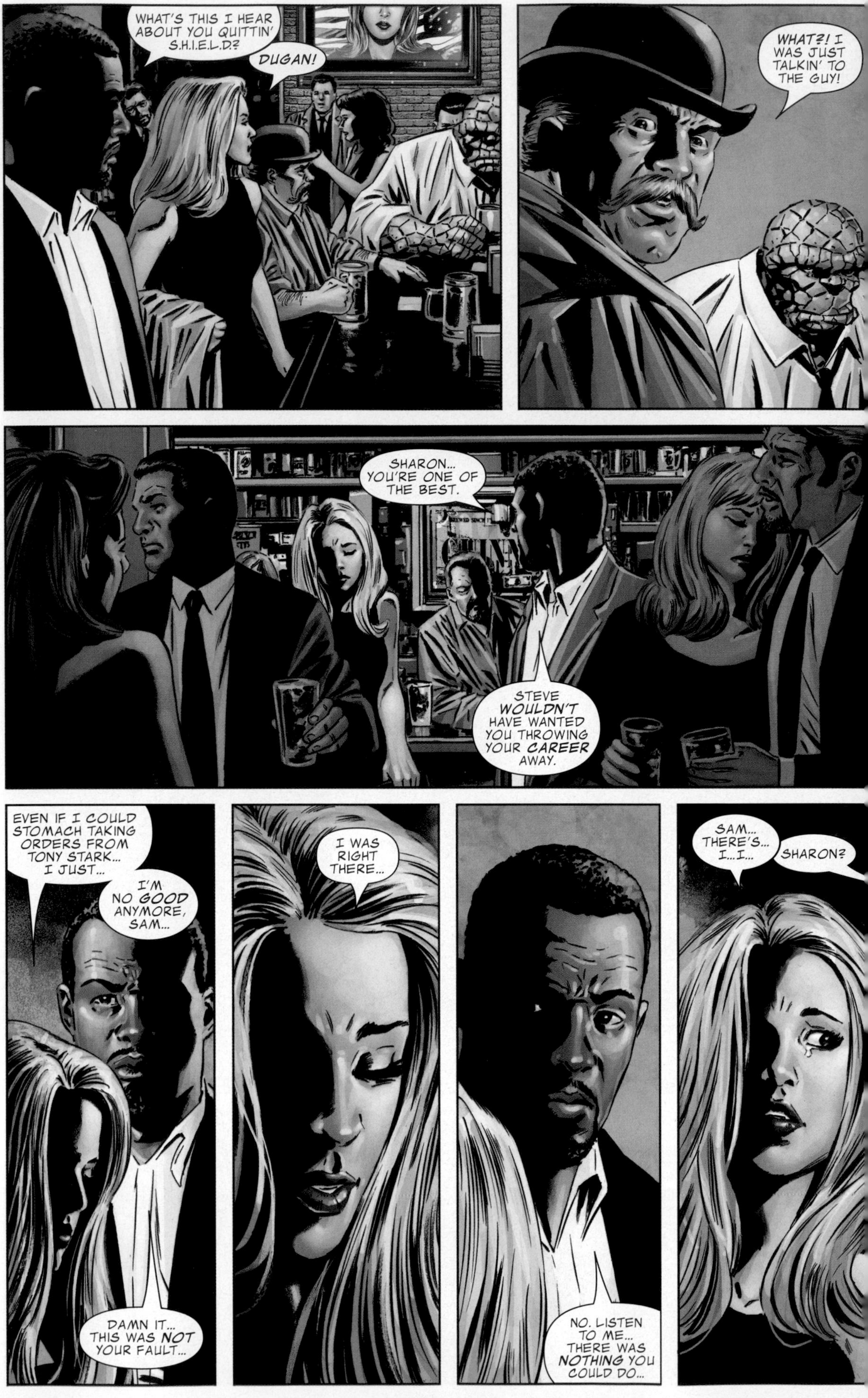
WHAT'S THIS I HEAR ABOUT YOU QUITTIN' S.H.I.E.L.D.?
DUGAN!
WHAT?! I WAS JUST TALKIN' TO THE GUY!
SHARON... YOU'RE ONE OF THE BEST.
STEVE WOULDN'T HAVE WANTED YOU THROWING YOUR CAREER AWAY.
EVEN IF I COULD STOMACH TAKING ORDERS FROM TONY STARK... I JUST...
I'M NO GOOD ANYMORE, SAM...
DAMN IT... THIS WAS NOT YOUR FAULT...
I WAS RIGHT THERE...
NO. LISTEN TO ME... THERE WAS NOTHING YOU COULD DO...
SAM... THERE'S... I... I...
SHARON?

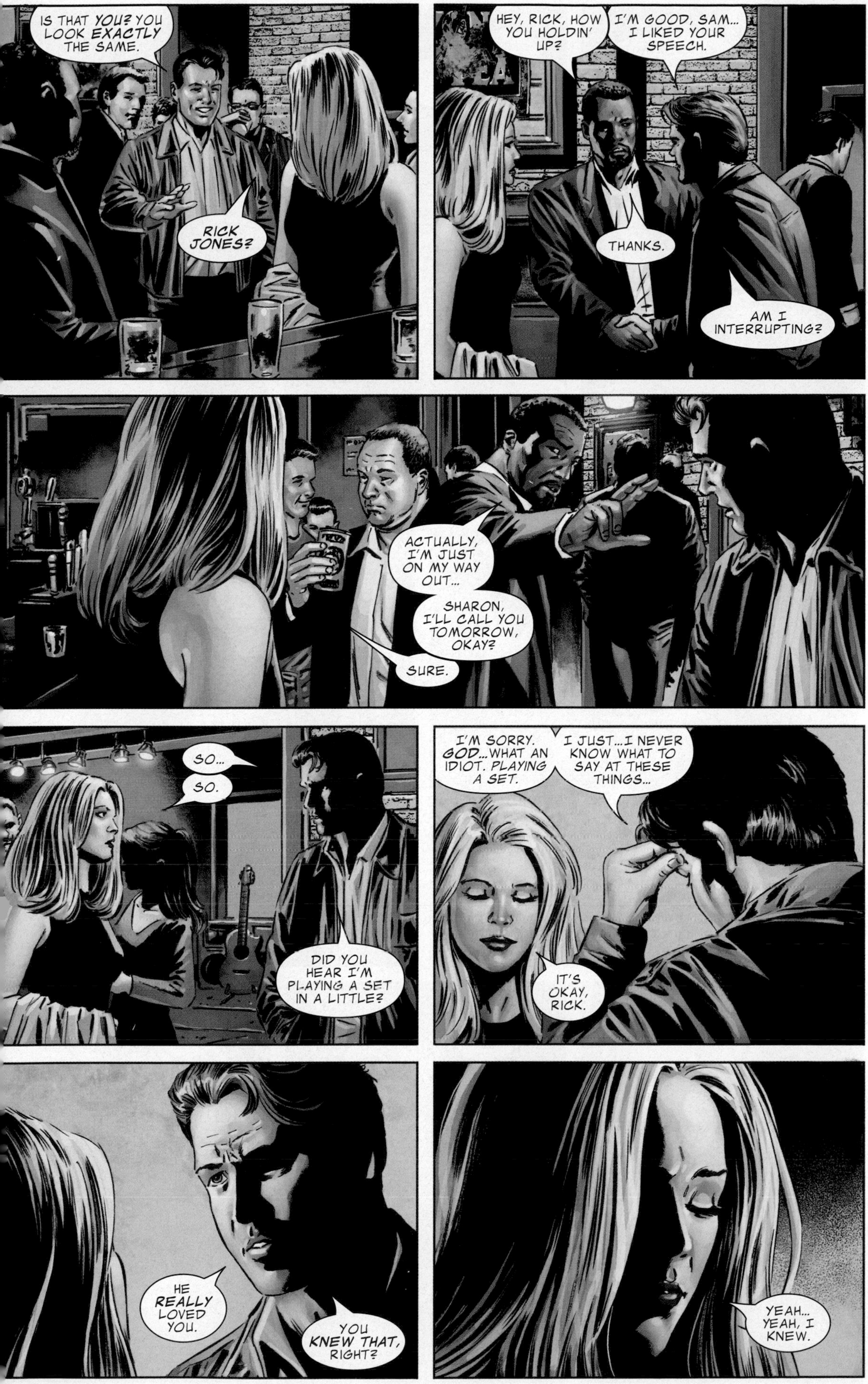
IS THAT YOU? YOU LOOK EXACTLY THE SAME.
RICK JONES?
HEY, RICK, HOW YOU HOLDIN' UP?
I'M GOOD, SAM... I LIKED YOUR SPEECH.
THANKS.
AM I INTERRUPTING?
ACTUALLY, I'M JUST ON MY WAY OUT...
SHARON, I'LL CALL YOU TOMORROW, OKAY?
SURE.
SO...
SO.
DID YOU HEAR I'M PLAYING A SET IN A LITTLE?
I'M SORRY. GOD... WHAT AN IDIOT. PLAYING A SET.
I JUST...I NEVER KNOW WHAT TO SAY AT THESE THINGS...
IT'S OKAY, RICK.
HE REALLY LOVED YOU.
YOU KNEW THAT, RIGHT?
YEAH... YEAH, I KNEW.

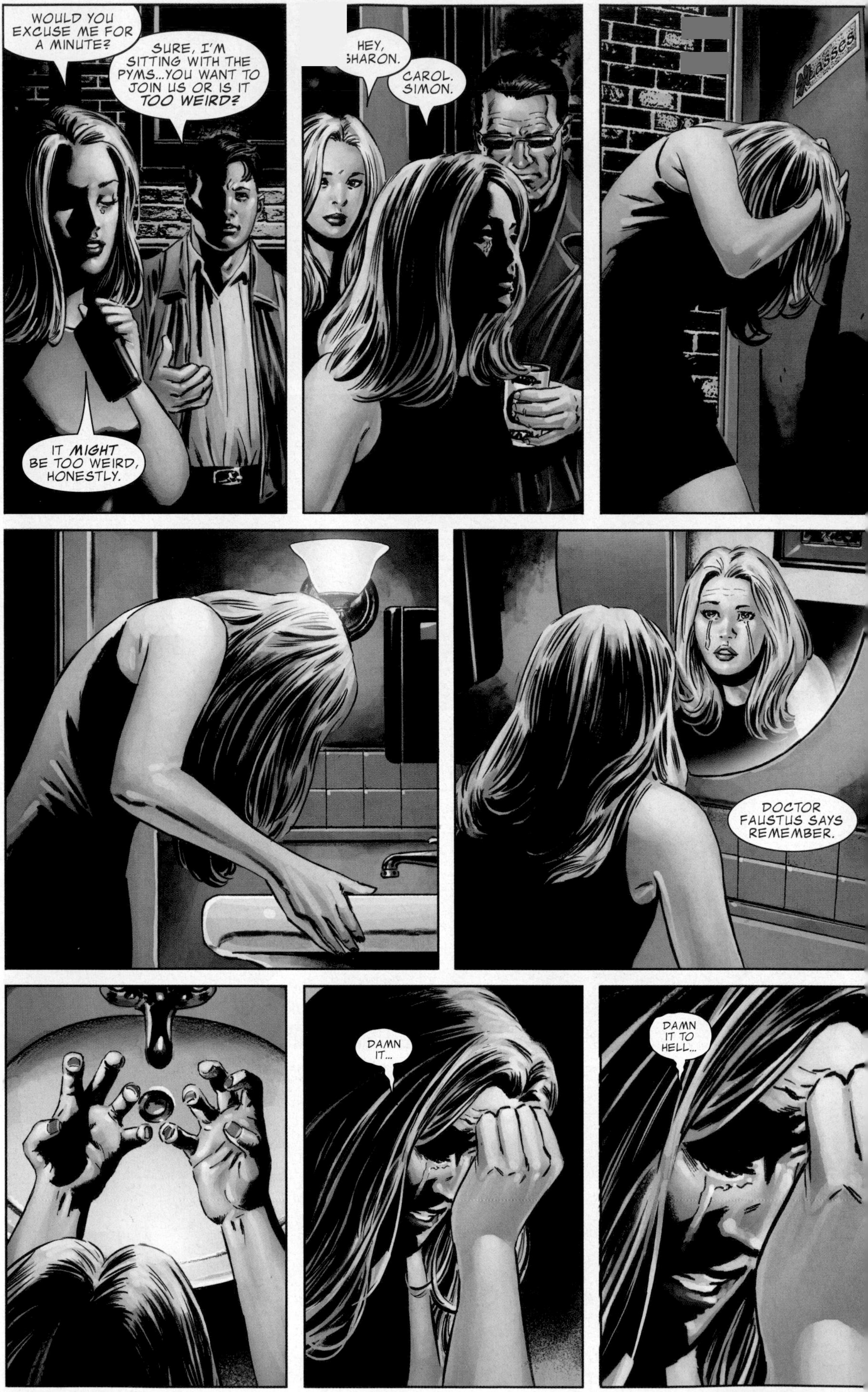
WOULD YOU EXCUSE ME FOR A MINUTE?
SURE, I'M SITTING WITH THE PYMS...YOU WANT TO JOIN US OR IS IT *TOO WEIRD?*
IT *MIGHT* BE TOO WEIRD, HONESTLY.
HEY, SHARON.
CAROL. SIMON.
DOCTOR FAUSTUS SAYS REMEMBER.
DAMN IT...
DAMN IT TO HELL...

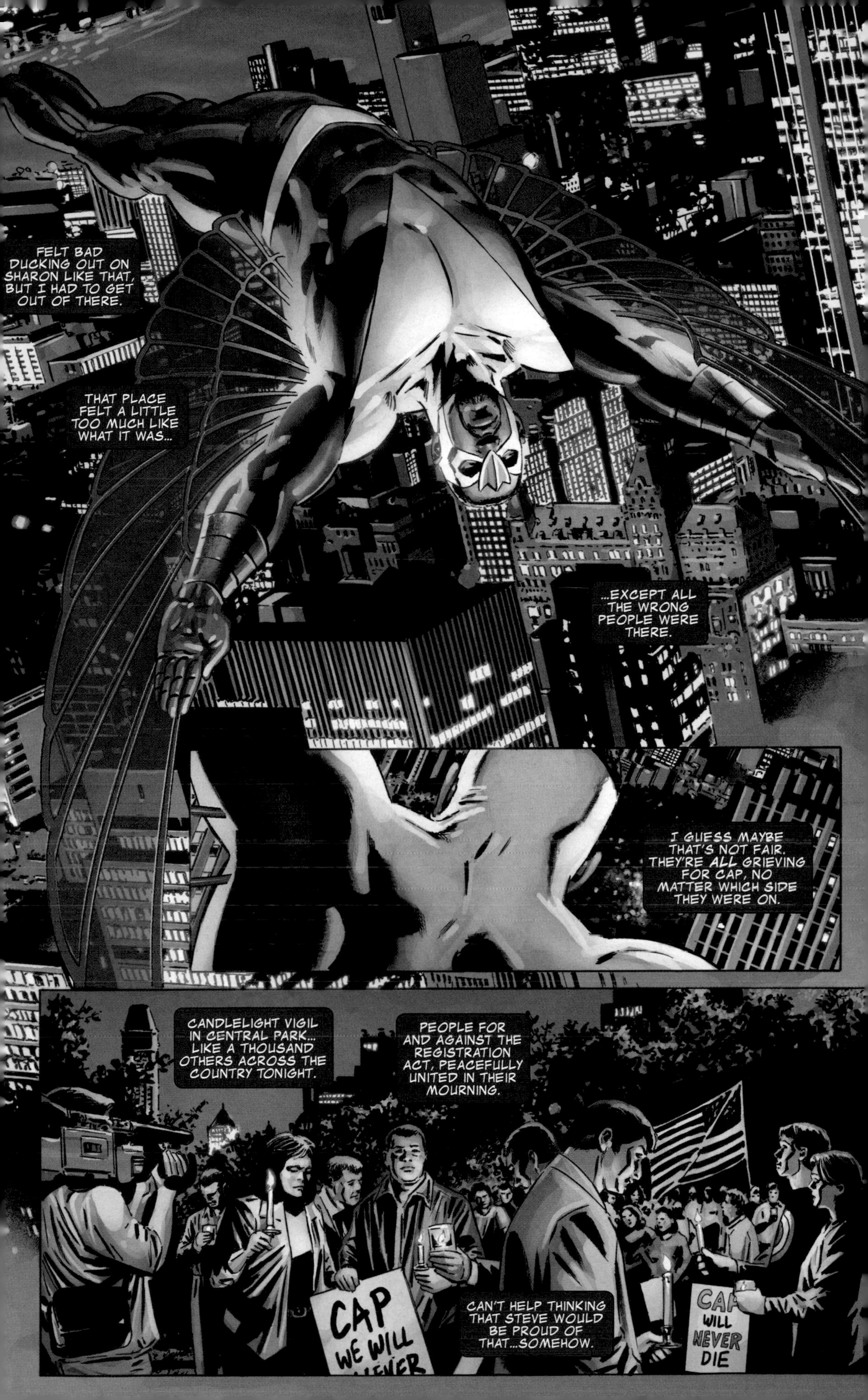
FELT BAD DUCKING OUT ON SHARON LIKE THAT, BUT I HAD TO GET OUT OF THERE.
THAT PLACE FELT A LITTLE TOO MUCH LIKE WHAT IT WAS...
...EXCEPT ALL THE WRONG PEOPLE WERE THERE.
I GUESS MAYBE THAT'S NOT FAIR. THEY'RE ALL GRIEVING FOR CAP, NO MATTER WHICH SIDE THEY WERE ON.
CANDLELIGHT VIGIL IN CENTRAL PARK... LIKE A THOUSAND OTHERS ACROSS THE COUNTRY TONIGHT.
PEOPLE FOR AND AGAINST THE REGISTRATION ACT, PEACEFULLY UNITED IN THEIR MOURNING.
CAP WE WILL
CAN'T HELP THINKING THAT STEVE WOULD BE PROUD OF THAT...SOMEHOW.
WILL NEVER DIE

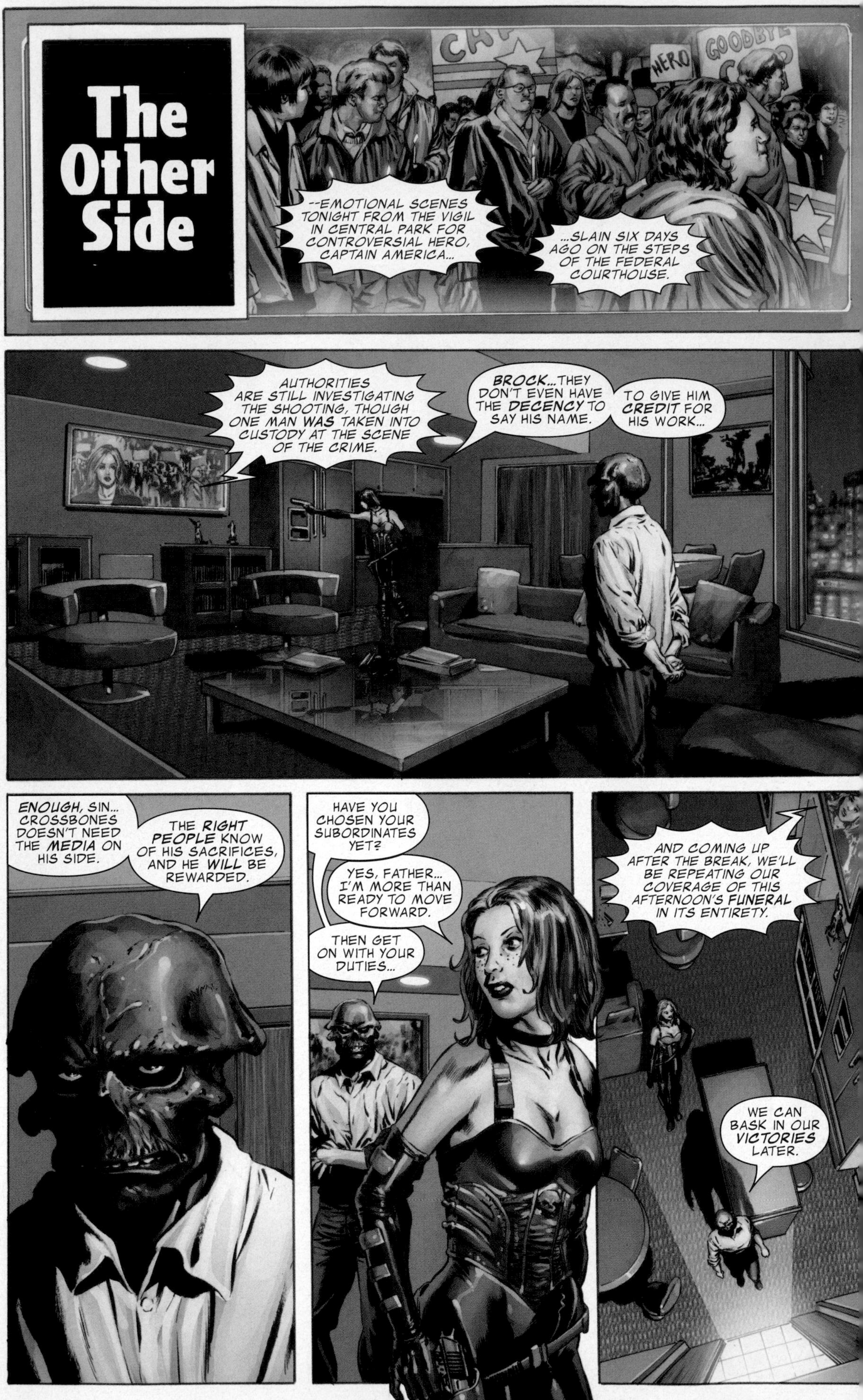
The Other Side
CAP
HERO
GOODBYE
--EMOTIONAL SCENES TONIGHT FROM THE VIGIL IN CENTRAL PARK FOR CONTROVERSIAL HERO, CAPTAIN AMERICA...
...SLAIN SIX DAYS AGO ON THE STEPS OF THE FEDERAL COURTHOUSE.
AUTHORITIES ARE STILL INVESTIGATING THE SHOOTING, THOUGH ONE MAN WAS TAKEN INTO CUSTODY AT THE SCENE OF THE CRIME.
BROCK...THEY DON'T EVEN HAVE THE DECENCY TO SAY HIS NAME.
TO GIVE HIM CREDIT FOR HIS WORK...
ENOUGH, SIN... CROSSBONES DOESN'T NEED THE MEDIA ON HIS SIDE.
THE RIGHT PEOPLE KNOW OF HIS SACRIFICES, AND HE WILL BE REWARDED.
HAVE YOU CHOSEN YOUR SUBORDINATES YET?
YES, FATHER... I'M MORE THAN READY TO MOVE FORWARD.
THEN GET ON WITH YOUR DUTIES...
AND COMING UP AFTER THE BREAK, WE'LL BE REPEATING OUR COVERAGE OF THIS AFTERNOON'S FUNERAL IN ITS ENTIRETY.
WE CAN BASK IN OUR VICTORIES LATER.

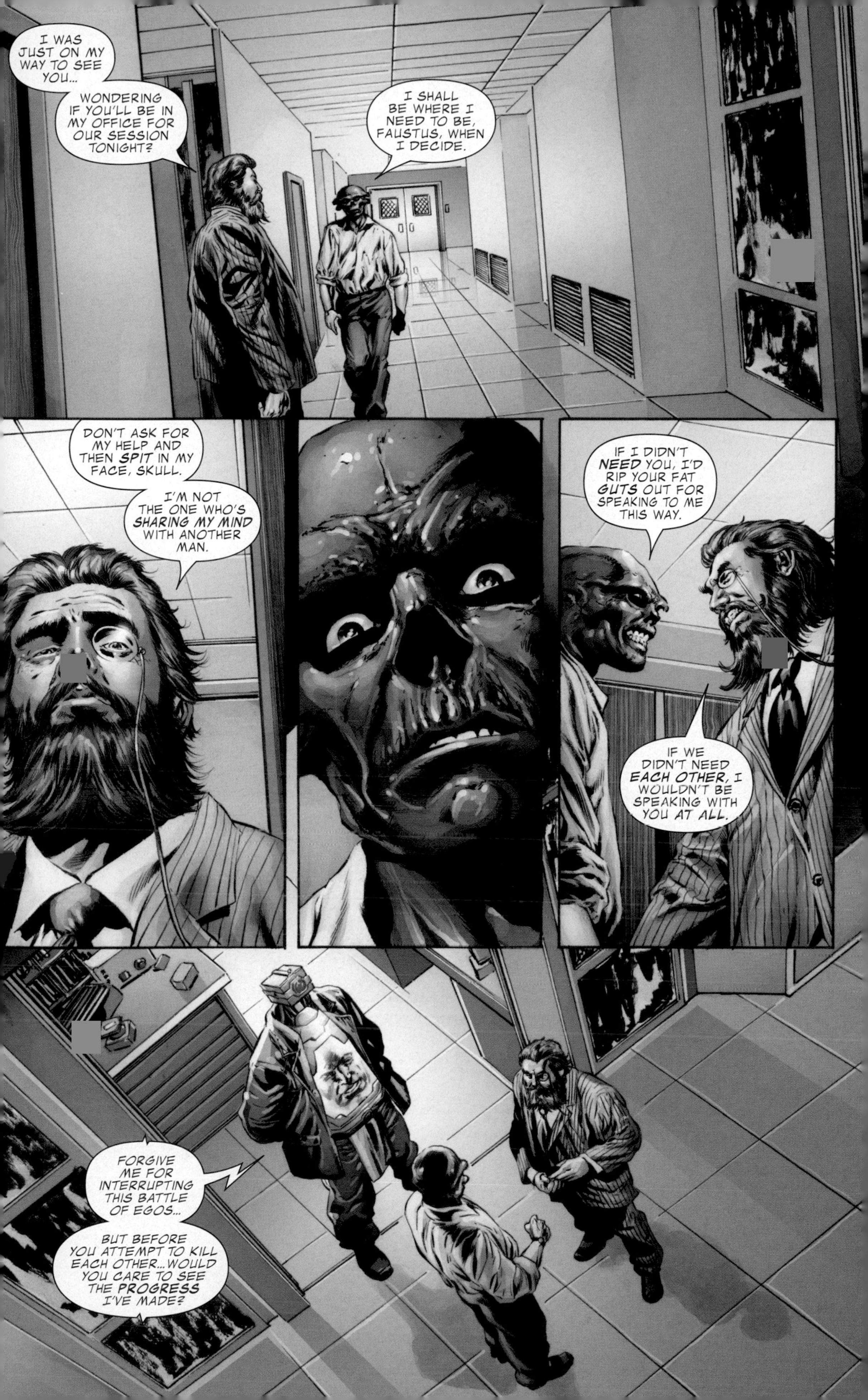
I WAS JUST ON MY WAY TO SEE YOU...
WONDERING IF YOU'LL BE IN MY OFFICE FOR OUR SESSION TONIGHT?
I SHALL BE WHERE I NEED TO BE, FAUSTUS, WHEN I DECIDE.
DON'T ASK FOR MY HELP AND THEN SPIT IN MY FACE, SKULL.
I'M NOT THE ONE WHO'S SHARING MY MIND WITH ANOTHER MAN.
IF I DIDN'T NEED YOU, I'D RIP YOUR FAT GUTS OUT FOR SPEAKING TO ME THIS WAY.
IF WE DIDN'T NEED EACH OTHER, I WOULDN'T BE SPEAKING WITH YOU AT ALL.
FORGIVE ME FOR INTERRUPTING THIS BATTLE OF EGOS...
BUT BEFORE YOU ATTEMPT TO KILL EACH OTHER...WOULD YOU CARE TO SEE THE PROGRESS I'VE MADE?

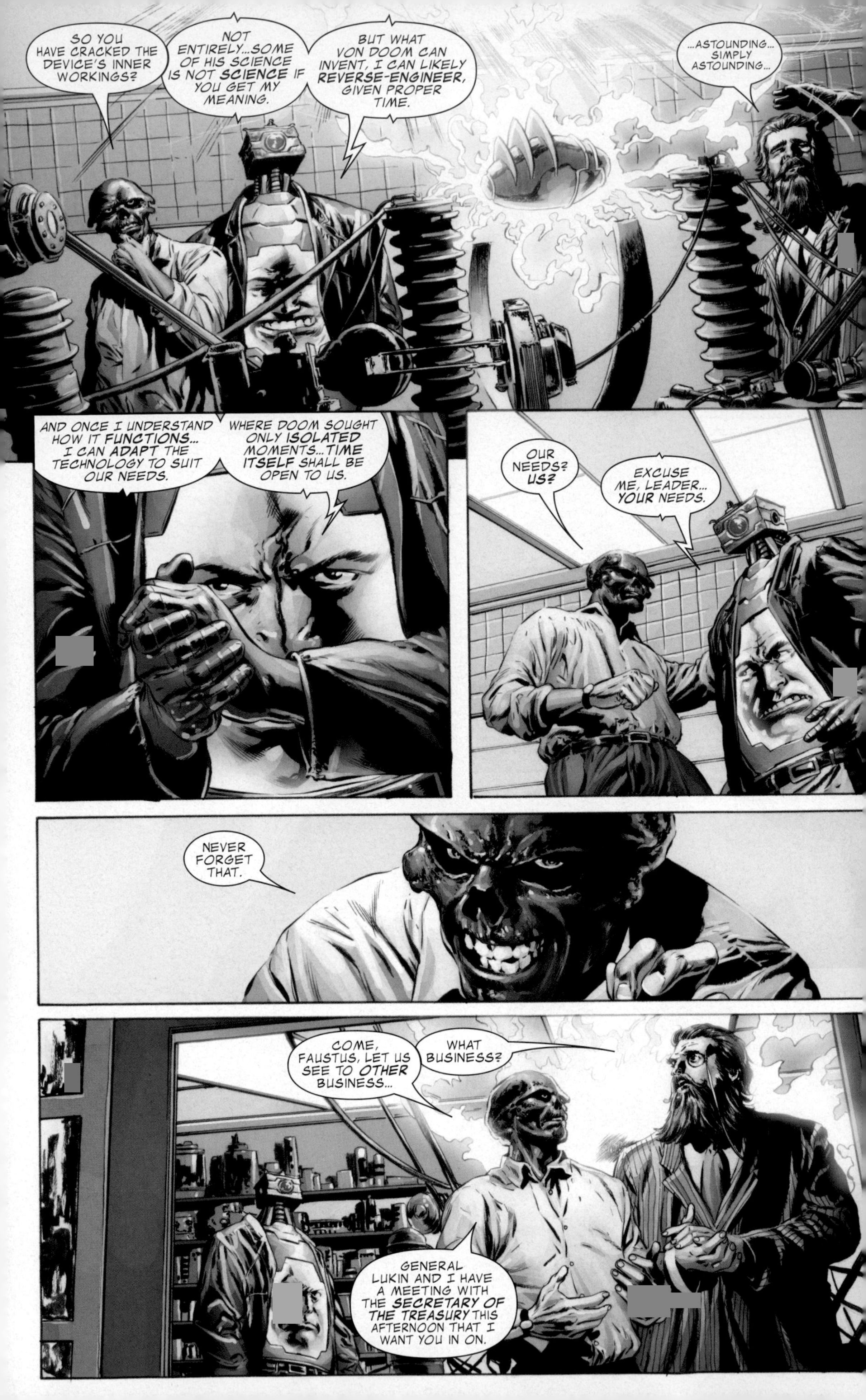
SO YOU HAVE CRACKED THE DEVICE'S INNER WORKINGS?
NOT ENTIRELY...SOME OF HIS SCIENCE IS NOT **SCIENCE** IF YOU GET MY MEANING.
BUT WHAT VON DOOM CAN INVENT, I CAN LIKELY **REVERSE-ENGINEER,** GIVEN PROPER TIME.
...ASTOUNDING... SIMPLY ASTOUNDING...
AND ONCE I UNDERSTAND HOW IT **FUNCTIONS...** I CAN **ADAPT** THE TECHNOLOGY TO SUIT OUR NEEDS.
WHERE DOOM SOUGHT ONLY **ISOLATED** MOMENTS...**TIME ITSELF** SHALL BE OPEN TO US.
OUR NEEDS? ***US?***
EXCUSE ME, LEADER... ***YOUR*** NEEDS.
NEVER FORGET THAT.
COME, FAUSTUS, LET US SEE TO ***OTHER*** BUSINESS...
WHAT BUSINESS?
GENERAL LUKIN AND I HAVE A MEETING WITH THE ***SECRETARY OF THE TREASURY*** THIS AFTERNOON THAT I WANT YOU IN ON.

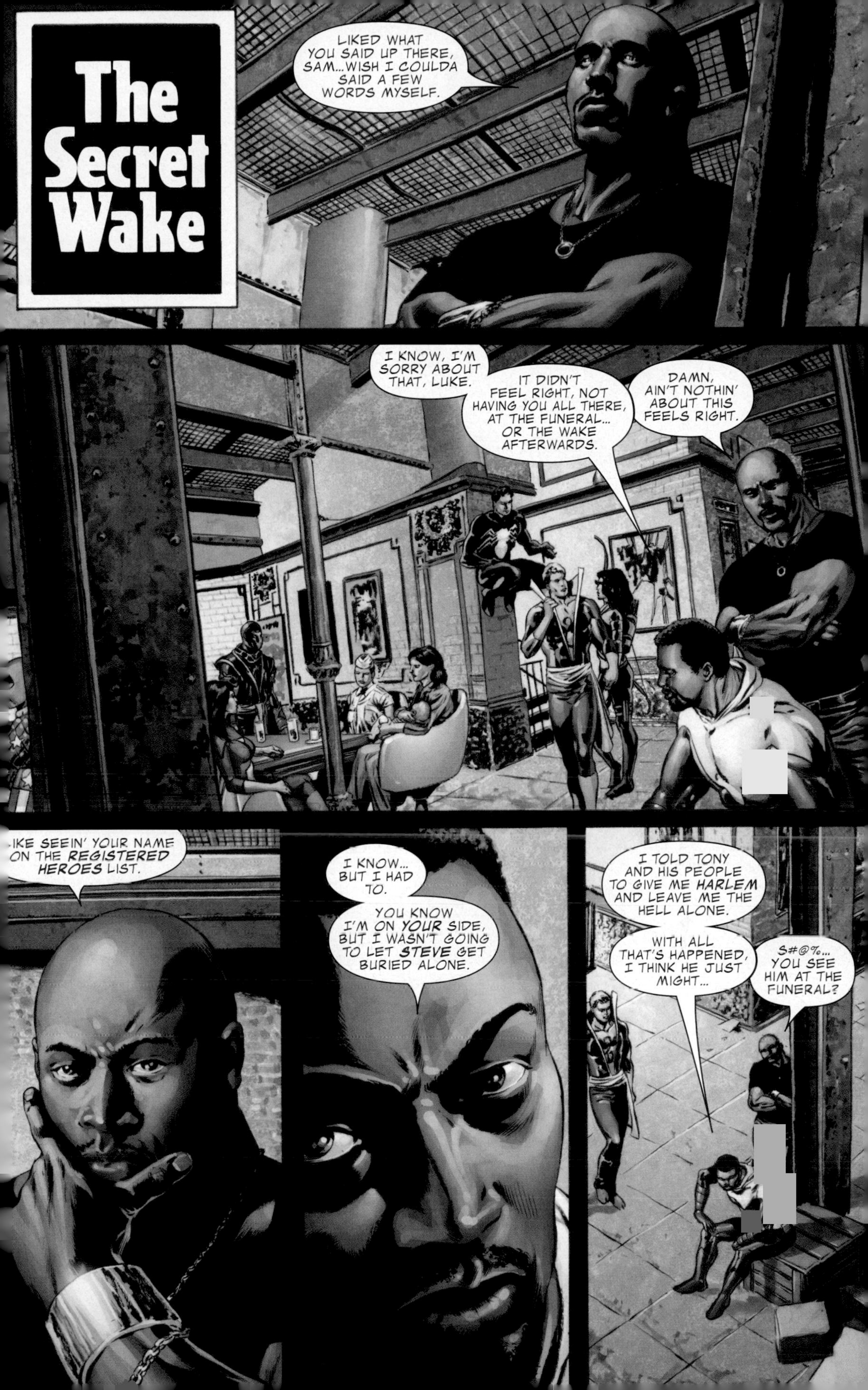

The Secret Wake
LIKED WHAT YOU SAID UP THERE, SAM...WISH I COULDA SAID A FEW WORDS MYSELF.
I KNOW, I'M SORRY ABOUT THAT, LUKE.
IT DIDN'T FEEL RIGHT, NOT HAVING YOU ALL THERE, AT THE FUNERAL... OR THE WAKE AFTERWARDS.
DAMN, AIN'T NOTHIN' ABOUT THIS FEELS RIGHT.
-IKE SEEIN' YOUR NAME ON THE REGISTERED HEROES LIST.
I KNOW... BUT I HAD TO.
YOU KNOW I'M ON YOUR SIDE, BUT I WASN'T GOING TO LET STEVE GET BURIED ALONE.
I TOLD TONY AND HIS PEOPLE TO GIVE ME HARLEM AND LEAVE ME THE HELL ALONE.
WITH ALL THAT'S HAPPENED, I THINK HE JUST MIGHT...
S#@%... YOU SEE HIM AT THE FUNERAL?

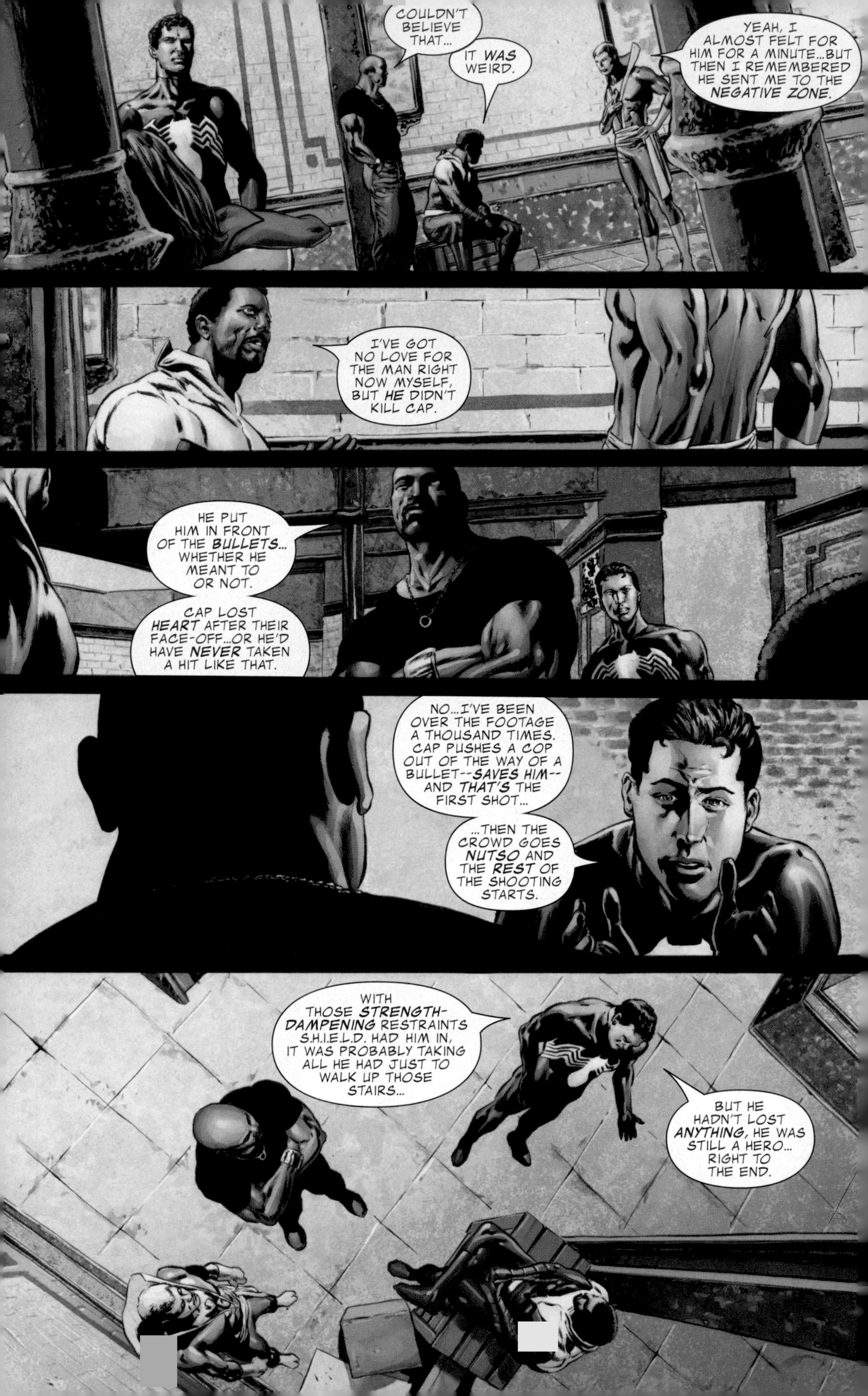
COULDN'T BELIEVE THAT...
IT WAS WEIRD.
YEAH, I ALMOST FELT FOR HIM FOR A MINUTE...BUT THEN I REMEMBERED HE SENT ME TO THE NEGATIVE ZONE.
I'VE GOT NO LOVE FOR THE MAN RIGHT NOW MYSELF, BUT HE DIDN'T KILL CAP.
HE PUT HIM IN FRONT OF THE BULLETS... WHETHER HE MEANT TO OR NOT.
CAP LOST HEART AFTER THEIR FACE-OFF...OR HE'D HAVE NEVER TAKEN A HIT LIKE THAT.
NO...I'VE BEEN OVER THE FOOTAGE A THOUSAND TIMES. CAP PUSHES A COP OUT OF THE WAY OF A BULLET--SAVES HIM--AND THAT'S THE FIRST SHOT...
...THEN THE CROWD GOES NUTSO AND THE REST OF THE SHOOTING STARTS.
WITH THOSE STRENGTH-DAMPENING RESTRAINTS S.H.I.E.L.D. HAD HIM IN, IT WAS PROBABLY TAKING ALL HE HAD JUST TO WALK UP THOSE STAIRS...
BUT HE HADN'T LOST ANYTHING, HE WAS STILL A HERO... RIGHT TO THE END.

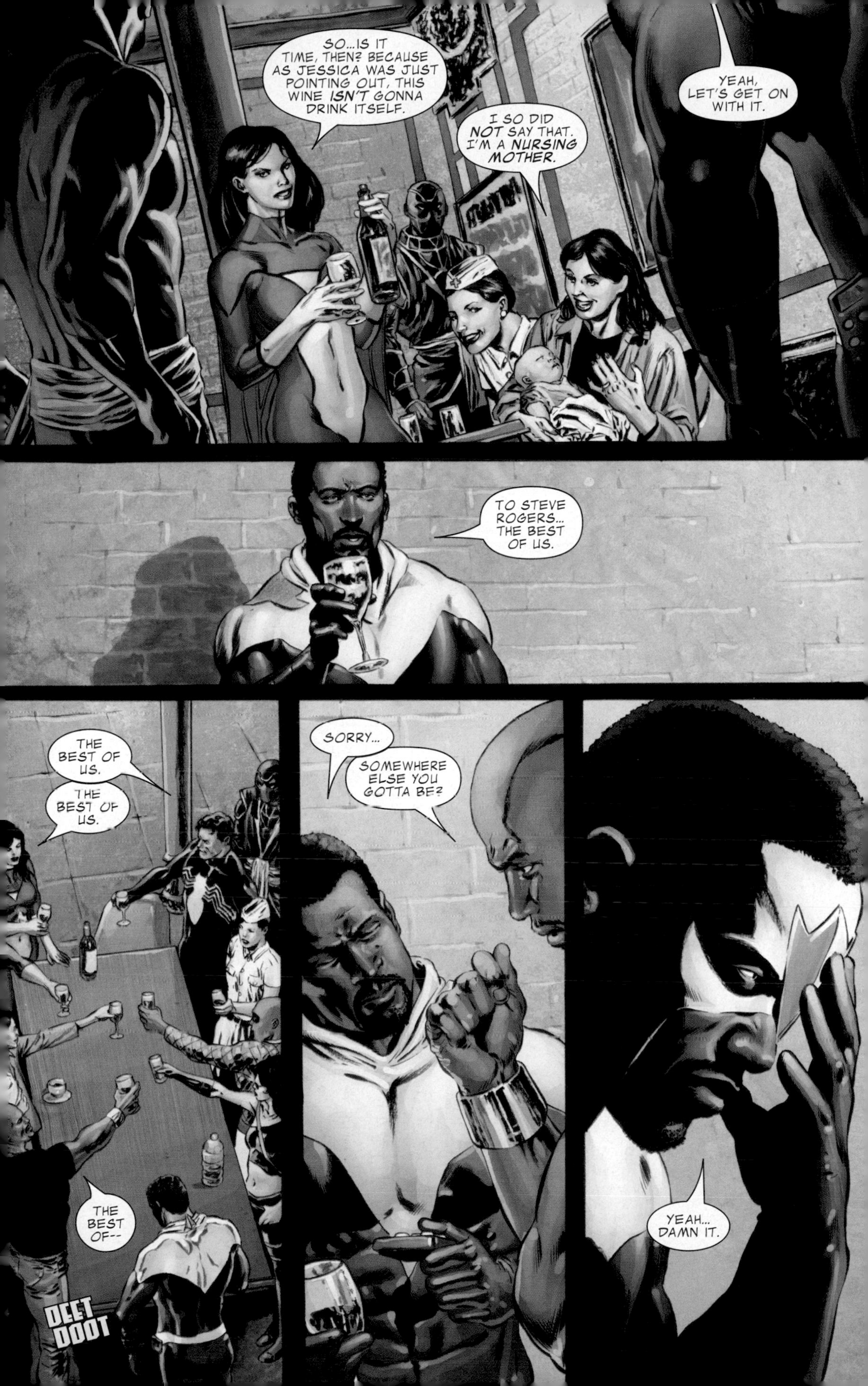
SO...IS IT TIME, THEN? BECAUSE AS JESSICA WAS JUST POINTING OUT, THIS WINE ISN'T GONNA DRINK ITSELF.
I SO DID NOT SAY THAT. I'M A NURSING MOTHER.
YEAH, LET'S GET ON WITH IT.
TO STEVE ROGERS... THE BEST OF US.
THE BEST OF US.
THE BEST OF US.
THE BEST OF--
DEET DOOT
SORRY...
SOMEWHERE ELSE YOU GOTTA BE?
YEAH... DAMN IT.

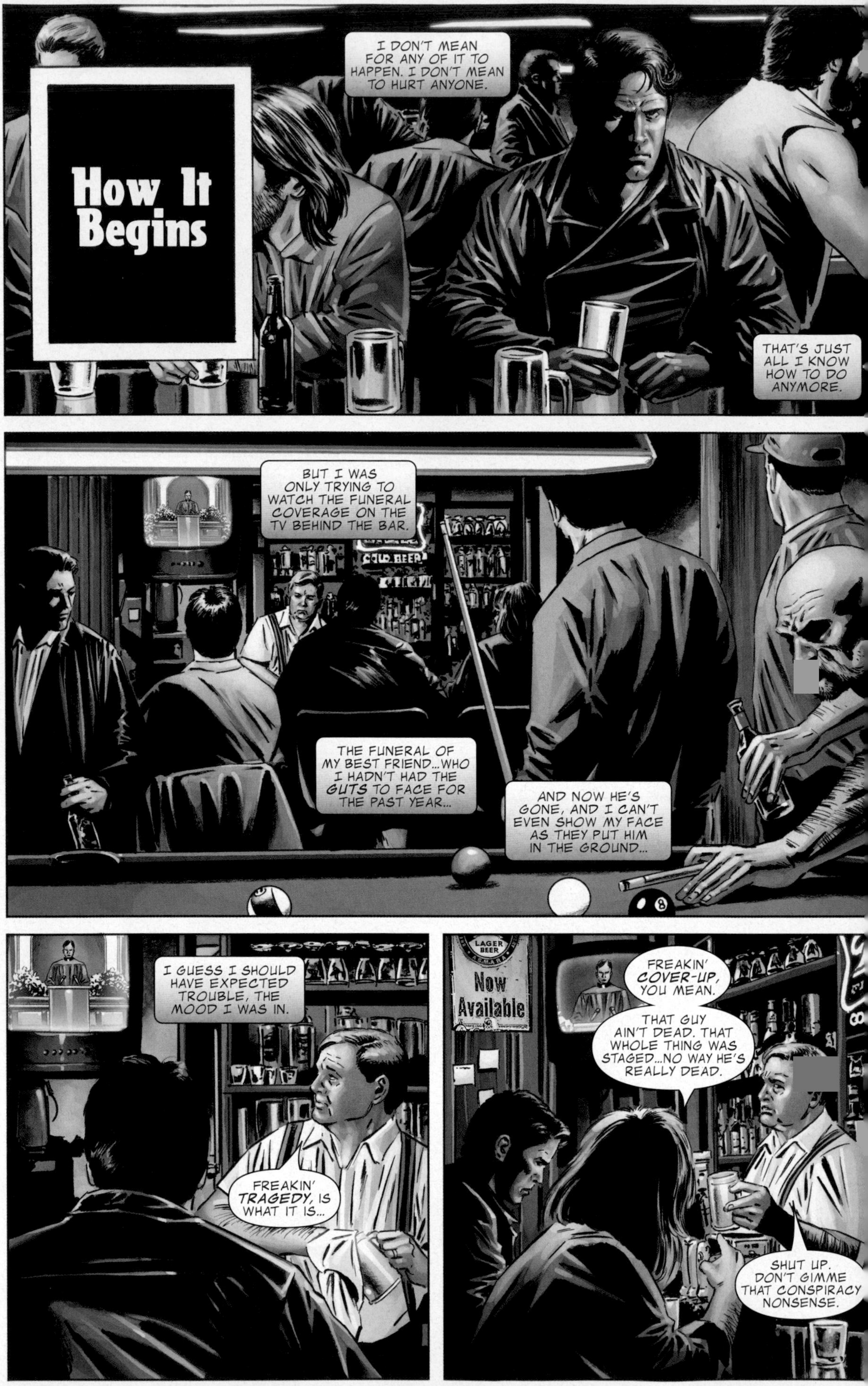
How It Begins
I DON'T MEAN FOR ANY OF IT TO HAPPEN. I DON'T MEAN TO HURT ANYONE.
THAT'S JUST ALL I KNOW HOW TO DO ANYMORE.
BUT I WAS ONLY TRYING TO WATCH THE FUNERAL COVERAGE ON THE TV BEHIND THE BAR.
COLD BEER
THE FUNERAL OF MY BEST FRIEND...WHO I HADN'T HAD THE GUTS TO FACE FOR THE PAST YEAR...
AND NOW HE'S GONE, AND I CAN'T EVEN SHOW MY FACE AS THEY PUT HIM IN THE GROUND...
I GUESS I SHOULD HAVE EXPECTED TROUBLE, THE MOOD I WAS IN.
FREAKIN' TRAGEDY, IS WHAT IT IS...
LAGER BEER
Now Available
FREAKIN' COVER-UP, YOU MEAN.
THAT GUY AIN'T DEAD. THAT WHOLE THING WAS STAGED...NO WAY HE'S REALLY DEAD.
SHUT UP. DON'T GIMME THAT CONSPIRACY NONSENSE.

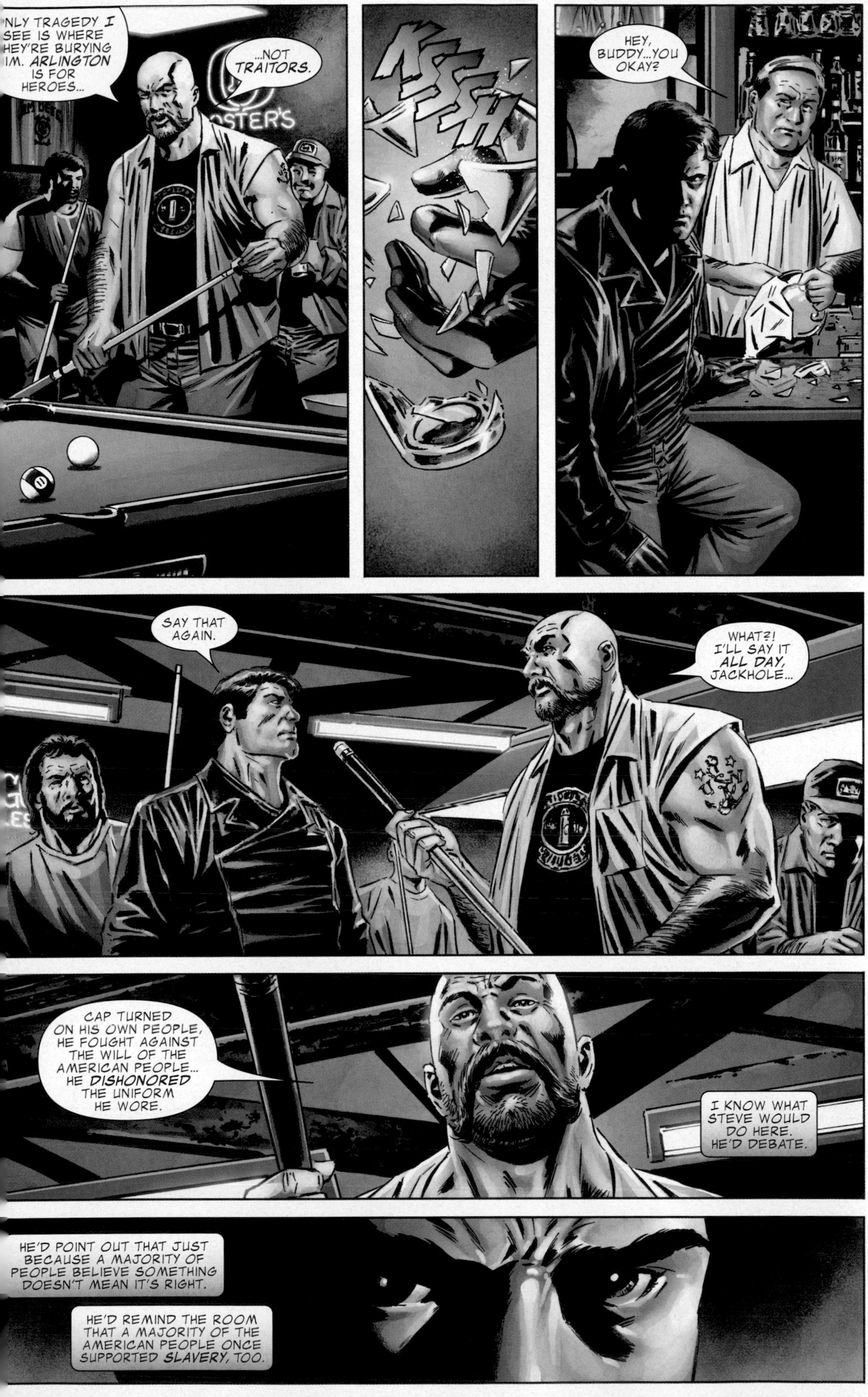

NLY TRAGEDY I SEE IS WHERE HEY'RE BURYING IM. ARLINGTON IS FOR HEROES...
...NOT TRAITORS.
OSTER'S
KSSH
HEY, BUDDY...YOU OKAY?
SAY THAT AGAIN.
WHAT?! I'LL SAY IT ALL DAY, JACKHOLE...
CAP TURNED ON HIS OWN PEOPLE, HE FOUGHT AGAINST THE WILL OF THE AMERICAN PEOPLE... HE DISHONORED THE UNIFORM HE WORE.
I KNOW WHAT STEVE WOULD DO HERE. HE'D DEBATE.
HE'D POINT OUT THAT JUST BECAUSE A MAJORITY OF PEOPLE BELIEVE SOMETHING DOESN'T MEAN IT'S RIGHT.
HE'D REMIND THE ROOM THAT A MAJORITY OF THE AMERICAN PEOPLE ONCE SUPPORTED SLAVERY, TOO.

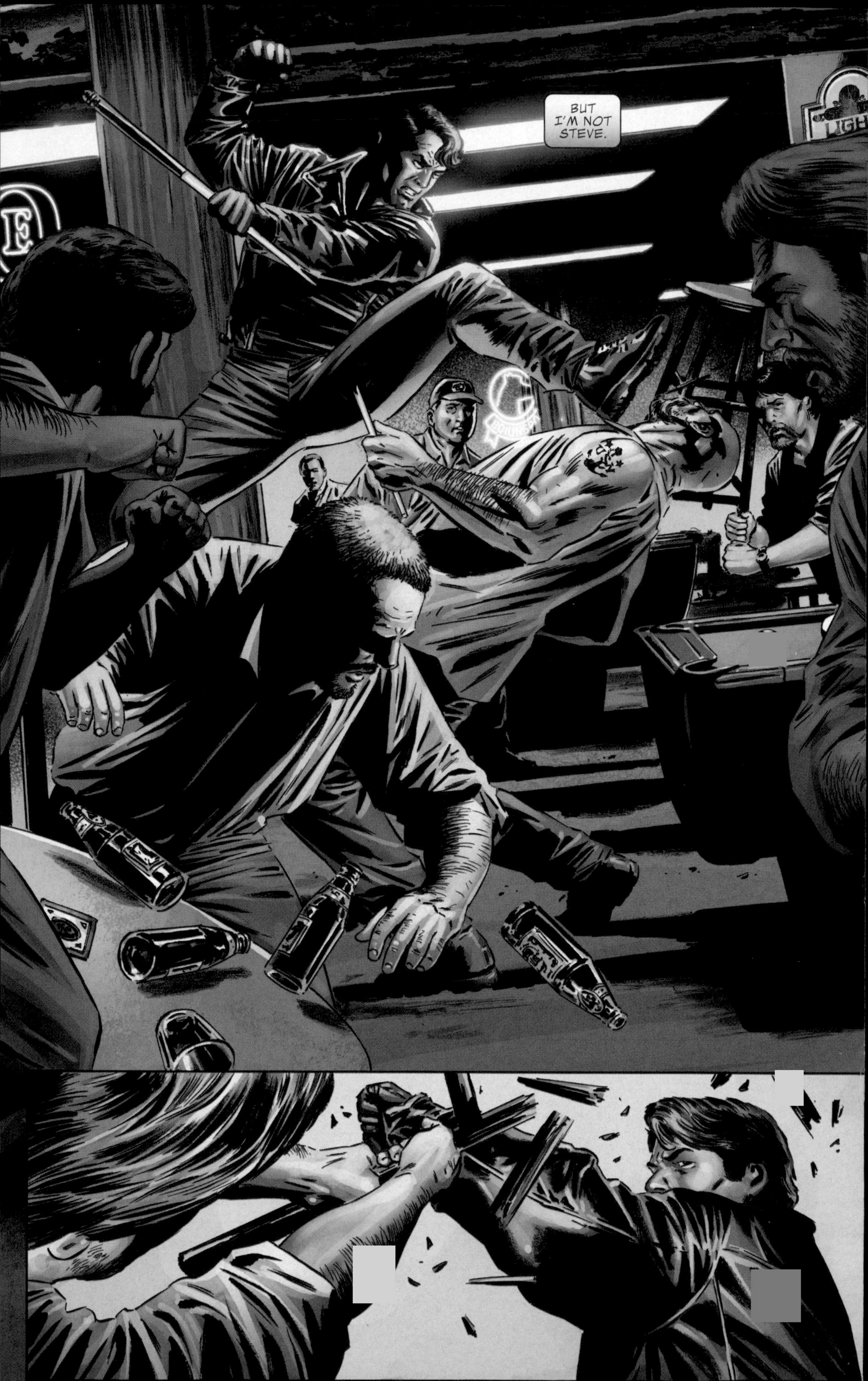
BUT I'M NOT STEVE.

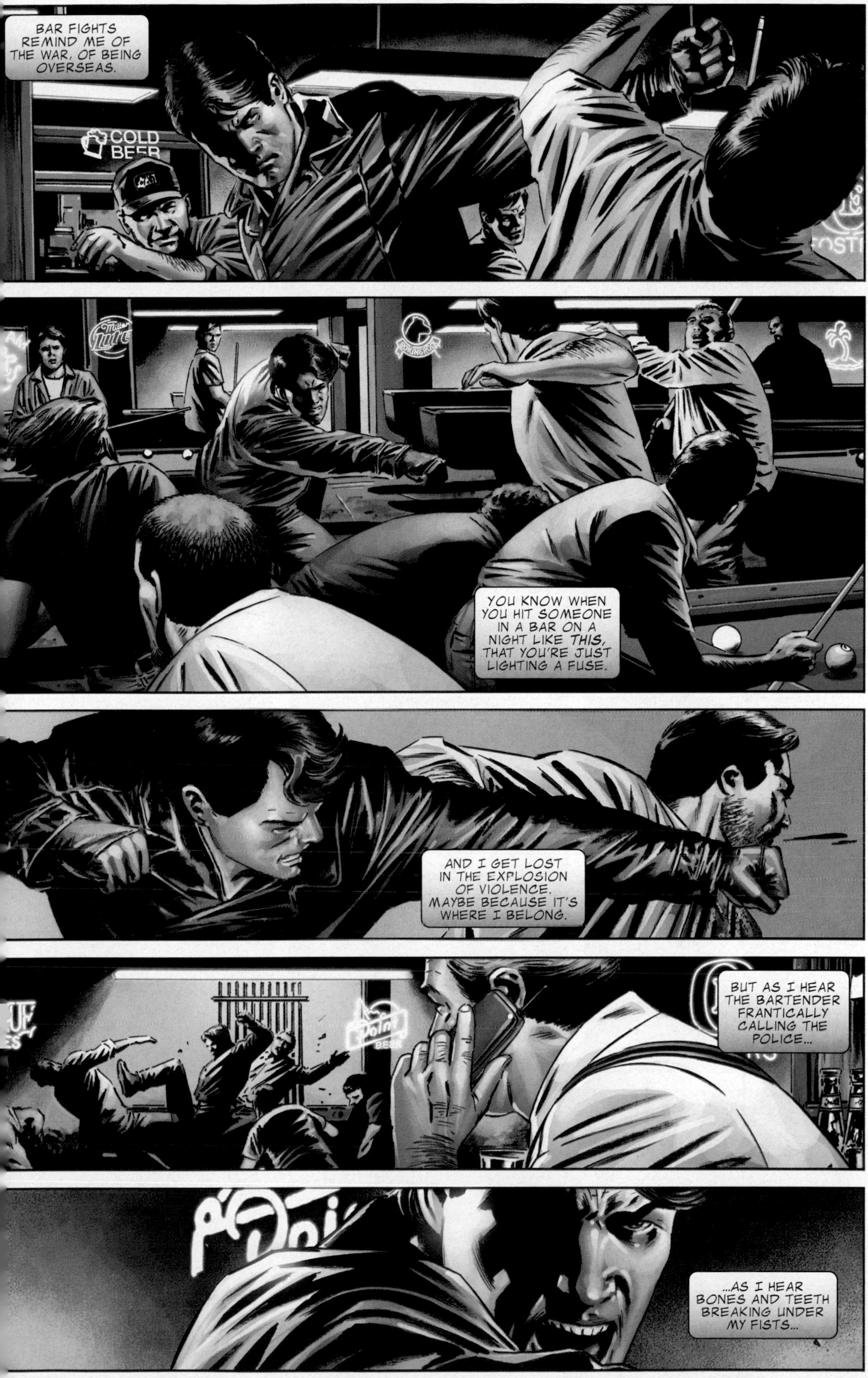
BAR FIGHTS REMIND ME OF THE WAR, OF BEING OVERSEAS.
COLD BEER
YOU KNOW WHEN YOU HIT SOMEONE IN A BAR ON A NIGHT LIKE THIS, THAT YOU'RE JUST LIGHTING A FUSE.
AND I GET LOST IN THE EXPLOSION OF VIOLENCE. MAYBE BECAUSE IT'S WHERE I BELONG.
BUT AS I HEAR THE BARTENDER FRANTICALLY CALLING THE POLICE...
...AS I HEAR BONES AND TEETH BREAKING UNDER MY FISTS...

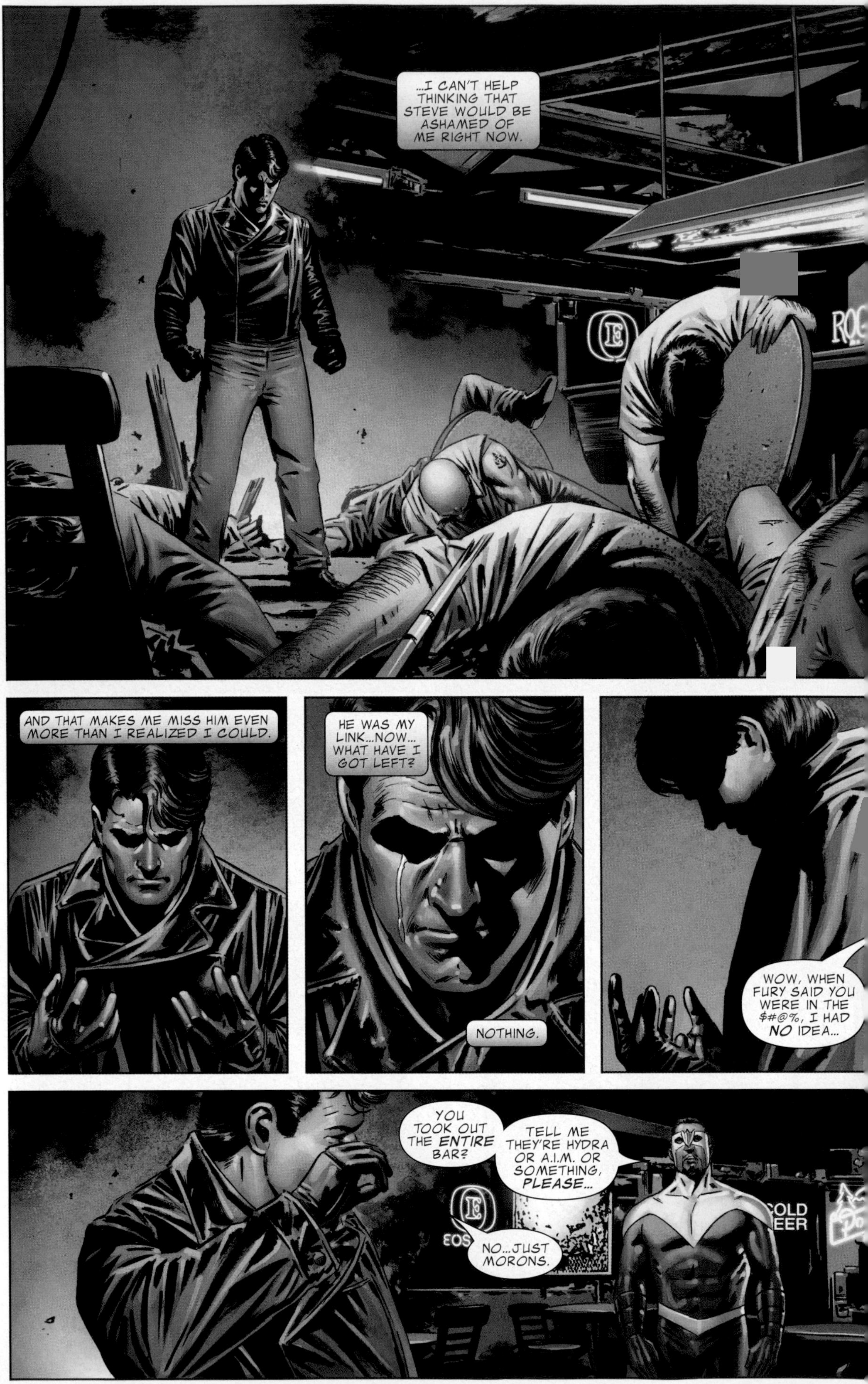

...I CAN'T HELP THINKING THAT STEVE WOULD BE ASHAMED OF ME RIGHT NOW.
AND THAT MAKES ME MISS HIM EVEN MORE THAN I REALIZED I COULD.
HE WAS MY LINK...NOW... WHAT HAVE I GOT LEFT?
NOTHING.
WOW, WHEN FURY SAID YOU WERE IN THE $#@%, I HAD **NO** IDEA...
YOU TOOK OUT THE **ENTIRE** BAR?
TELL ME THEY'RE HYDRA OR A.I.M. OR SOMETHING, ***PLEASE***...
NO...JUST MORONS.

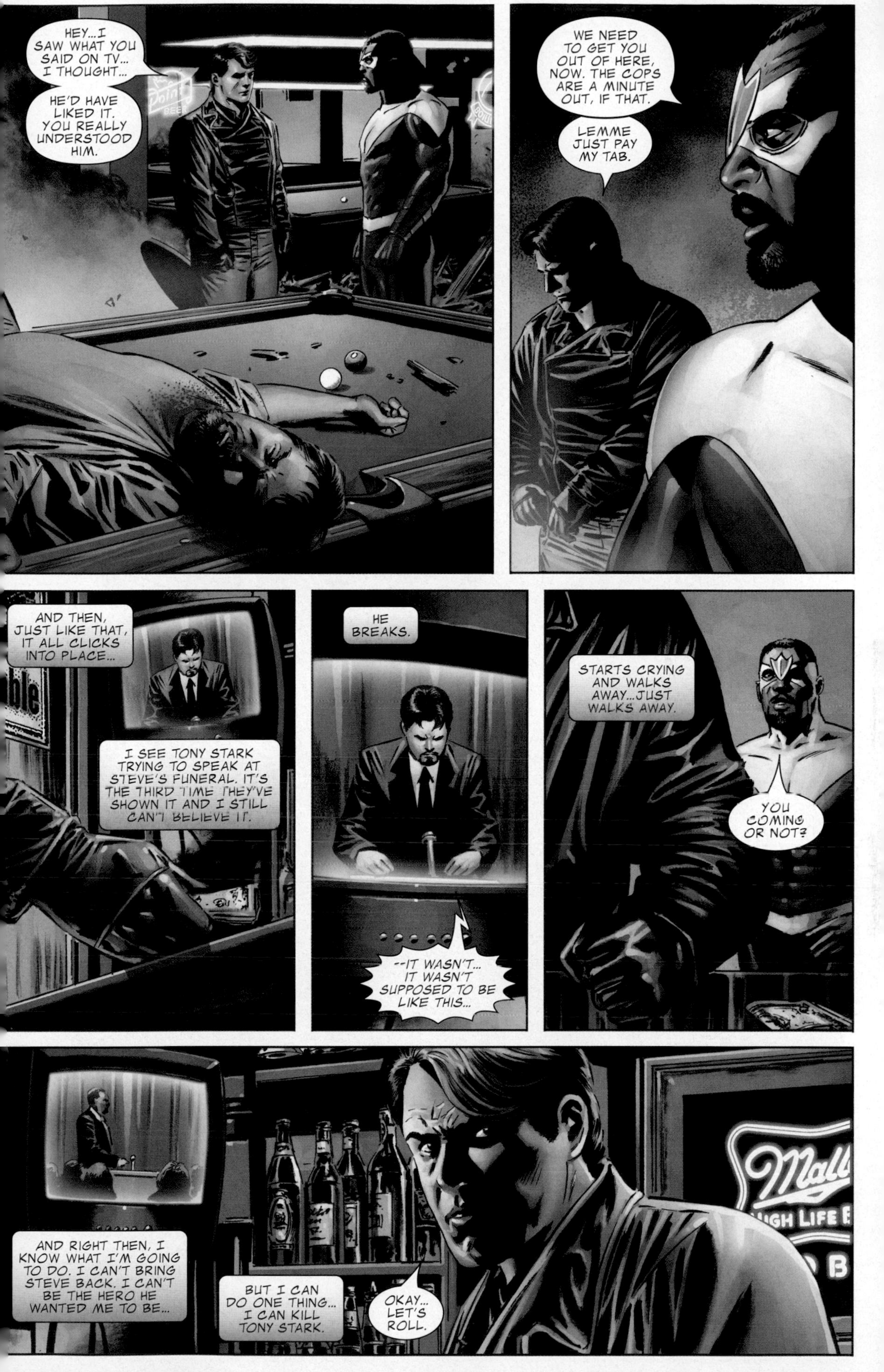
HEY...I SAW WHAT YOU SAID ON TV... I THOUGHT...
HE'D HAVE LIKED IT. YOU REALLY UNDERSTOOD HIM.
WE NEED TO GET YOU OUT OF HERE, NOW. THE COPS ARE A MINUTE OUT, IF THAT.
LEMME JUST PAY MY TAB.
AND THEN, JUST LIKE THAT, IT ALL CLICKS INTO PLACE...
I SEE TONY STARK TRYING TO SPEAK AT STEVE'S FUNERAL. IT'S THE THIRD TIME THEY'VE SHOWN IT AND I STILL CAN'T BELIEVE IT.
HE BREAKS.
--IT WASN'T... IT WASN'T SUPPOSED TO BE LIKE THIS...
STARTS CRYING AND WALKS AWAY...JUST WALKS AWAY.
YOU COMING OR NOT?
AND RIGHT THEN, I KNOW WHAT I'M GOING TO DO. I CAN'T BRING STEVE BACK. I CAN'T BE THE HERO HE WANTED ME TO BE...
BUT I CAN DO ONE THING... I CAN KILL TONY STARK.
OKAY... LET'S ROLL.

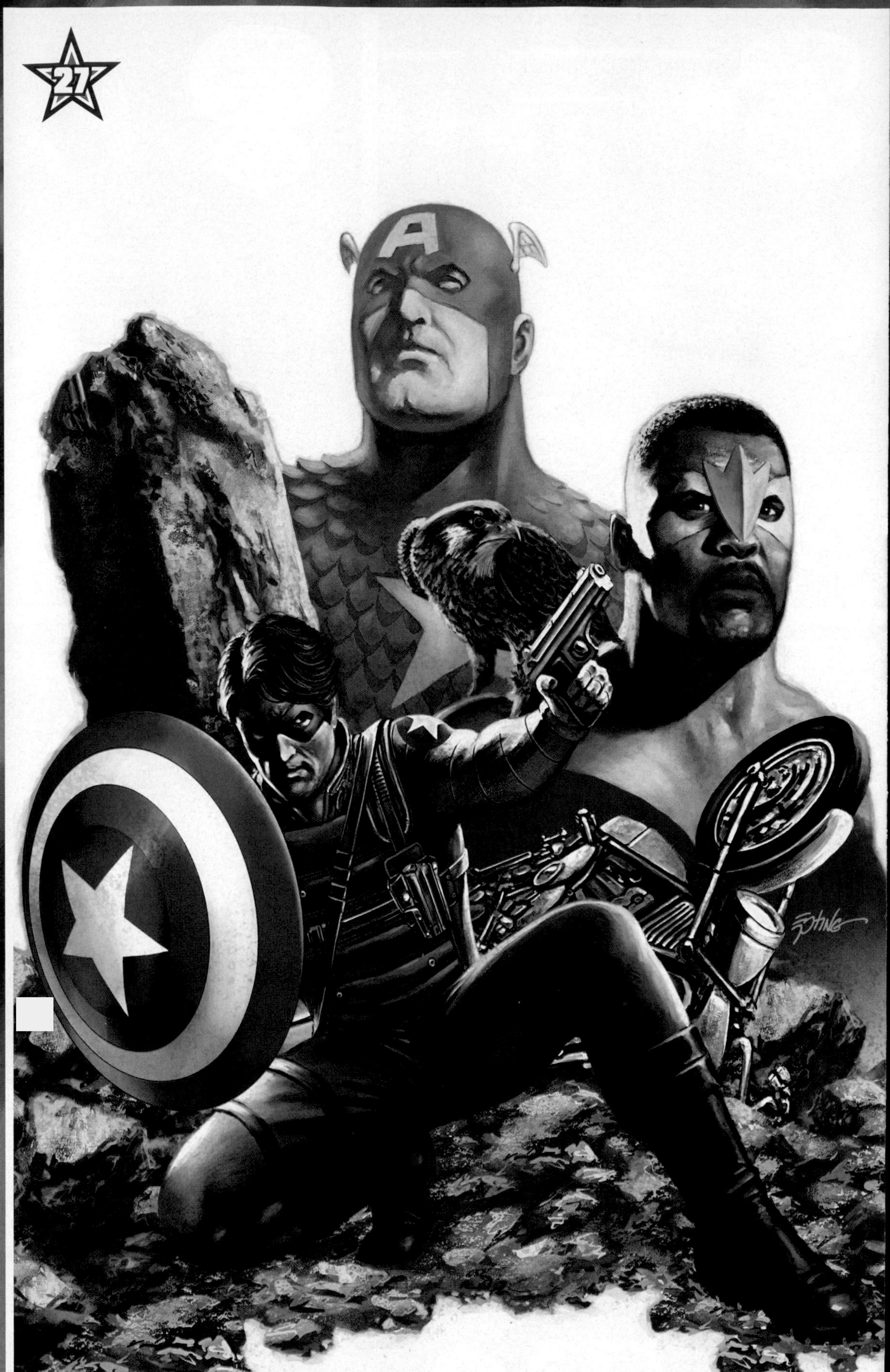
27

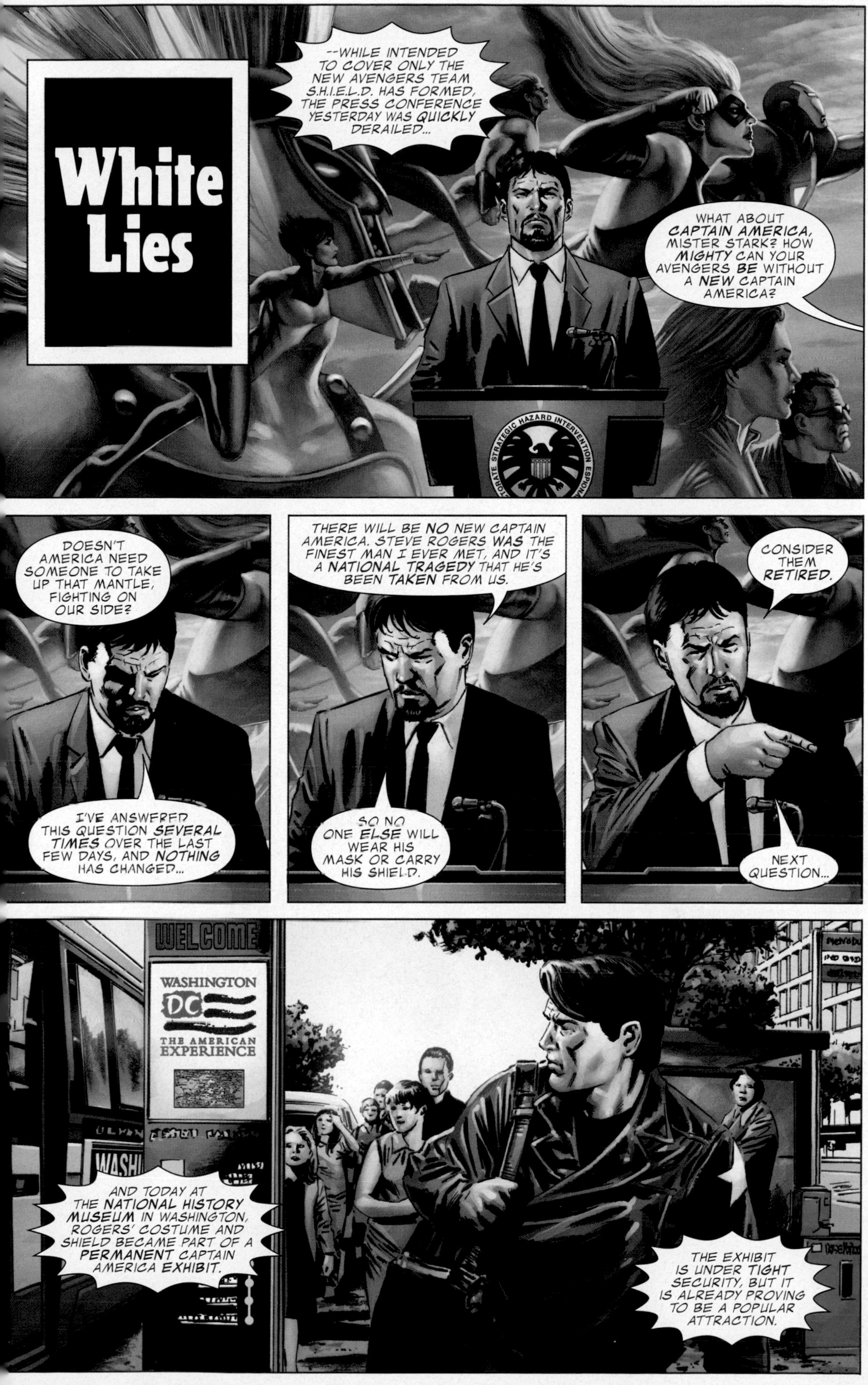
White Lies
--WHILE INTENDED TO COVER ONLY THE NEW AVENGERS TEAM S.H.I.E.L.D. HAS FORMED, THE PRESS CONFERENCE YESTERDAY WAS QUICKLY DERAILED...
WHAT ABOUT CAPTAIN AMERICA, MISTER STARK? HOW MIGHTY CAN YOUR AVENGERS BE WITHOUT A NEW CAPTAIN AMERICA?
DOESN'T AMERICA NEED SOMEONE TO TAKE UP THAT MANTLE, FIGHTING ON OUR SIDE?
I'VE ANSWERED THIS QUESTION SEVERAL TIMES OVER THE LAST FEW DAYS, AND NOTHING HAS CHANGED...
THERE WILL BE NO NEW CAPTAIN AMERICA. STEVE ROGERS WAS THE FINEST MAN I EVER MET, AND IT'S A NATIONAL TRAGEDY THAT HE'S BEEN TAKEN FROM US.
SO NO ONE ELSE WILL WEAR HIS MASK OR CARRY HIS SHIELD.
CONSIDER THEM RETIRED.
NEXT QUESTION...
WELCOME
WASHINGTON DC THE AMERICAN EXPERIENCE
AND TODAY AT THE NATIONAL HISTORY MUSEUM IN WASHINGTON, ROGERS' COSTUME AND SHIELD BECAME PART OF A PERMANENT CAPTAIN AMERICA EXHIBIT.
THE EXHIBIT IS UNDER TIGHT SECURITY, BUT IT IS ALREADY PROVING TO BE A POPULAR ATTRACTION.

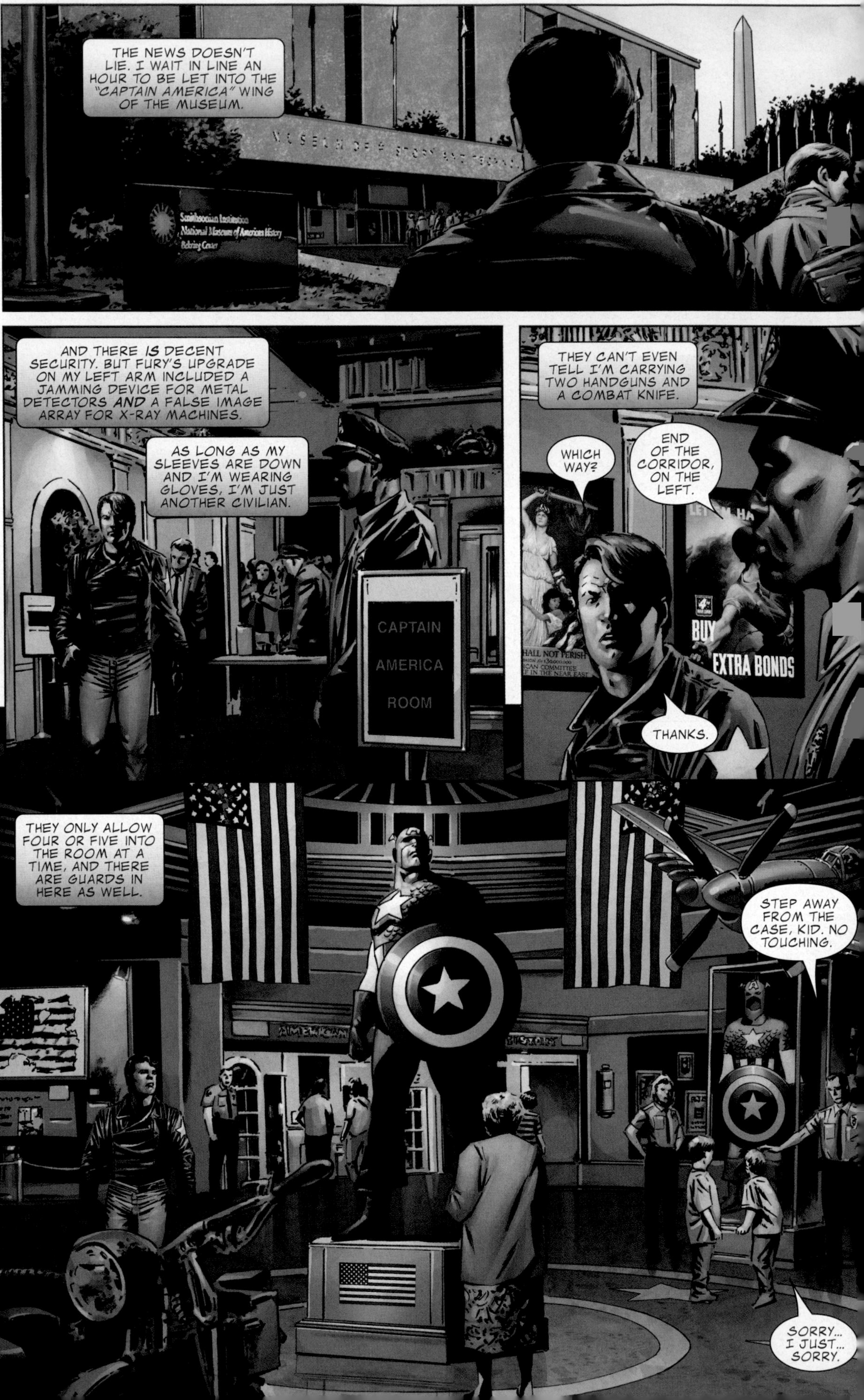
THE NEWS DOESN'T LIE. I WAIT IN LINE AN HOUR TO BE LET INTO THE "CAPTAIN AMERICA" WING OF THE MUSEUM.
Smithsonian Institution
National Museum of American History
Behring Center
AND THERE IS DECENT SECURITY. BUT FURY'S UPGRADE ON MY LEFT ARM INCLUDED A JAMMING DEVICE FOR METAL DETECTORS AND A FALSE IMAGE ARRAY FOR X-RAY MACHINES.
AS LONG AS MY SLEEVES ARE DOWN AND I'M WEARING GLOVES, I'M JUST ANOTHER CIVILIAN.
CAPTAIN AMERICA ROOM
THEY CAN'T EVEN TELL I'M CARRYING TWO HANDGUNS AND A COMBAT KNIFE.
WHICH WAY?
END OF THE CORRIDOR, ON THE LEFT.
BUY
EXTRA BONDS
THANKS.
THEY ONLY ALLOW FOUR OR FIVE INTO THE ROOM AT A TIME, AND THERE ARE GUARDS IN HERE AS WELL.
STEP AWAY FROM THE CASE, KID. NO TOUCHING.
SORRY... I JUST... SORRY.

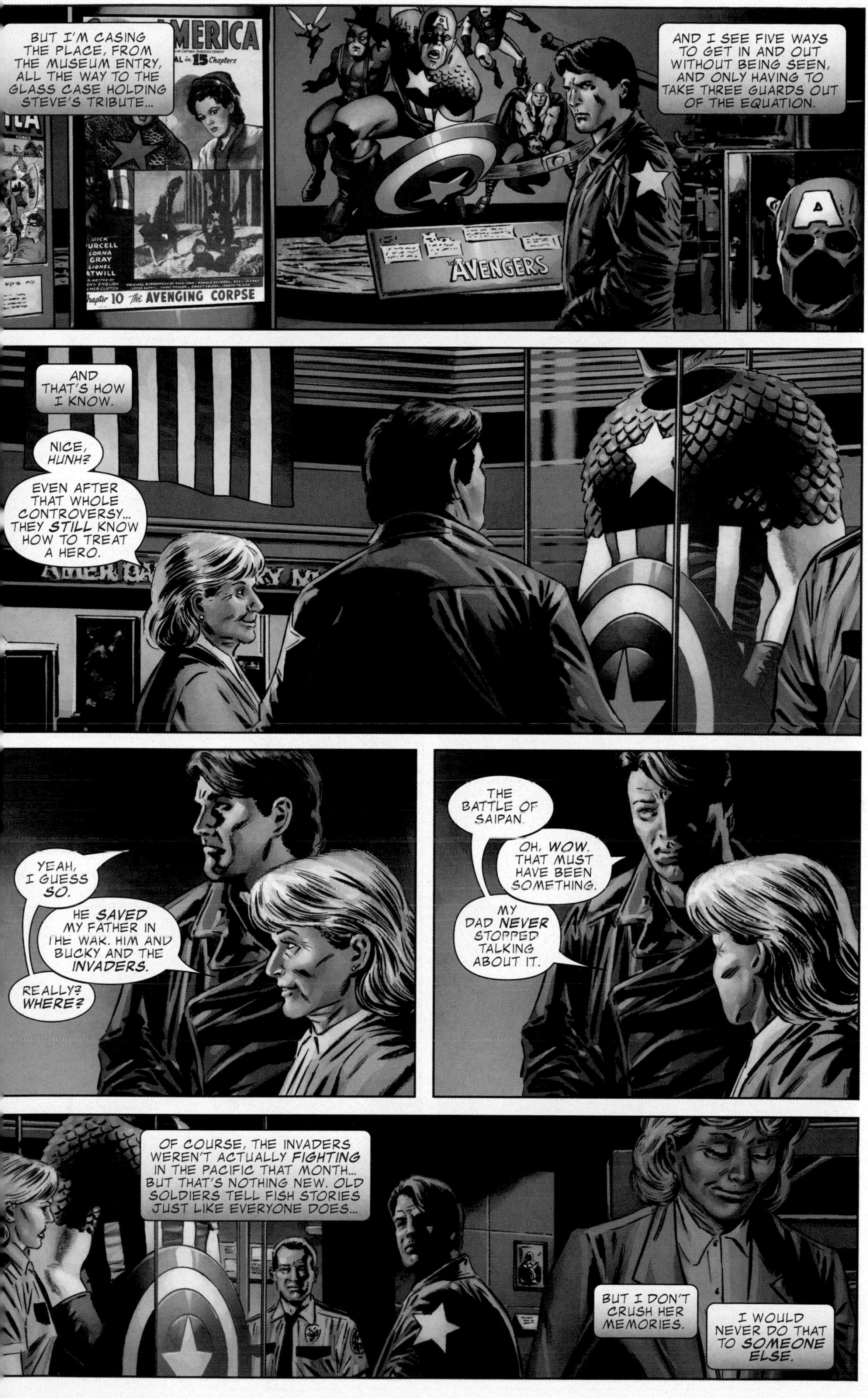
BUT I'M CASING THE PLACE, FROM THE MUSEUM ENTRY, ALL THE WAY TO THE GLASS CASE HOLDING STEVE'S TRIBUTE...
AMERICA
15 Chapters
DICK PURCELL LORNA GRAY LIONEL ATWILL
Chapter 10 The AVENGING CORPSE
THE AVENGERS
AND I SEE FIVE WAYS TO GET IN AND OUT WITHOUT BEING SEEN, AND ONLY HAVING TO TAKE THREE GUARDS OUT OF THE EQUATION.
AND THAT'S HOW I KNOW.
NICE, HUNH?
EVEN AFTER THAT WHOLE CONTROVERSY... THEY STILL KNOW HOW TO TREAT A HERO.
YEAH, I GUESS SO.
HE SAVED MY FATHER IN THE WAR. HIM AND BUCKY AND THE INVADERS.
REALLY? WHERE?
THE BATTLE OF SAIPAN.
OH, WOW. THAT MUST HAVE BEEN SOMETHING.
MY DAD NEVER STOPPED TALKING ABOUT IT.
OF COURSE, THE INVADERS WEREN'T ACTUALLY FIGHTING IN THE PACIFIC THAT MONTH... BUT THAT'S NOTHING NEW. OLD SOLDIERS TELL FISH STORIES JUST LIKE EVERYONE DOES...
BUT I DON'T CRUSH HER MEMORIES.
I WOULD NEVER DO THAT TO SOMEONE ELSE.

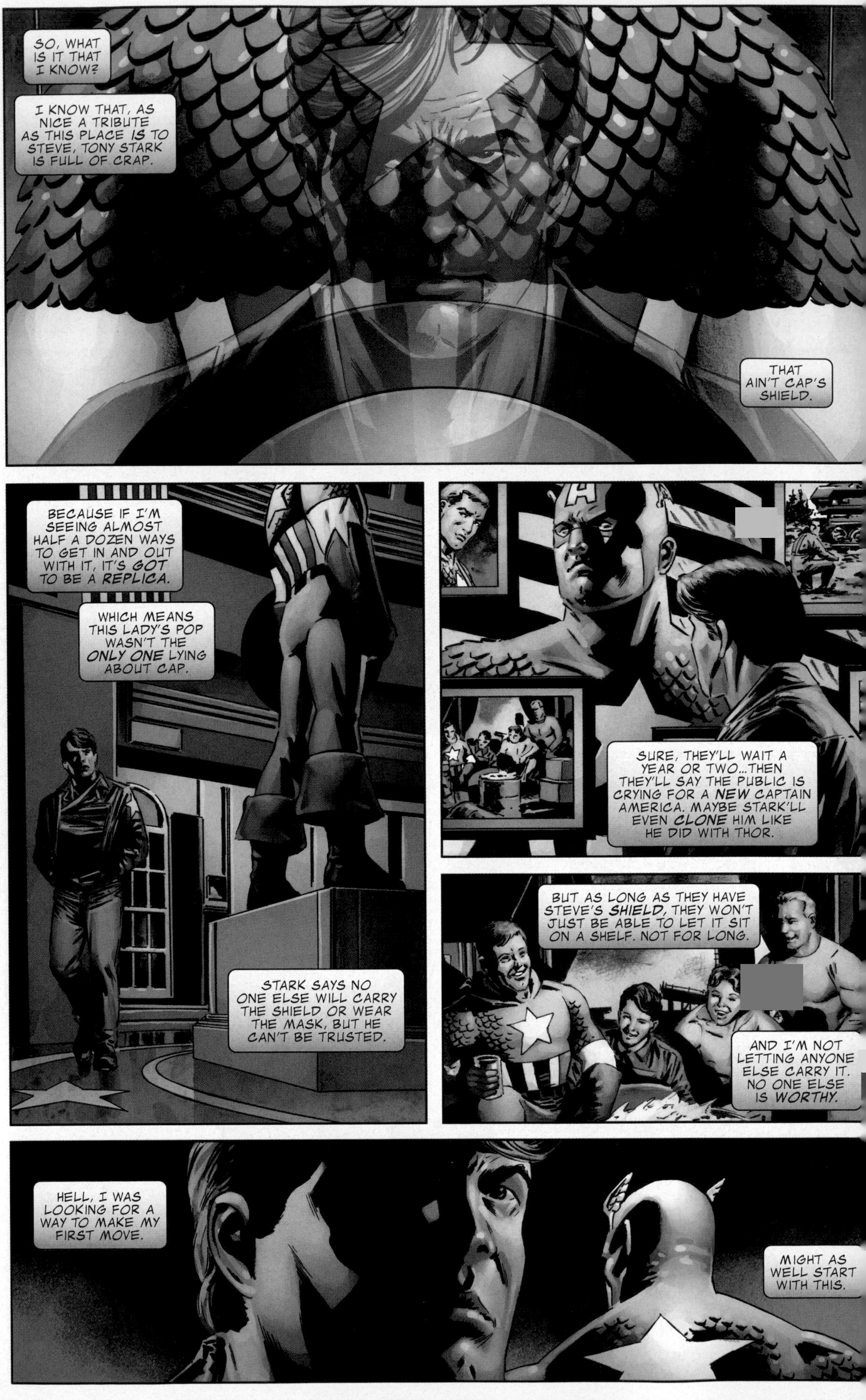
SO, WHAT IS IT THAT I KNOW?
I KNOW THAT, AS NICE A TRIBUTE AS THIS PLACE IS TO STEVE, TONY STARK IS FULL OF CRAP.
THAT AIN'T CAP'S SHIELD.
BECAUSE IF I'M SEEING ALMOST HALF A DOZEN WAYS TO GET IN AND OUT WITH IT, IT'S GOT TO BE A REPLICA.
WHICH MEANS THIS LADY'S POP WASN'T THE ONLY ONE LYING ABOUT CAP.
STARK SAYS NO ONE ELSE WILL CARRY THE SHIELD OR WEAR THE MASK, BUT HE CAN'T BE TRUSTED.
SURE, THEY'LL WAIT A YEAR OR TWO...THEN THEY'LL SAY THE PUBLIC IS CRYING FOR A NEW CAPTAIN AMERICA. MAYBE STARK'LL EVEN CLONE HIM LIKE HE DID WITH THOR.
BUT AS LONG AS THEY HAVE STEVE'S SHIELD, THEY WON'T JUST BE ABLE TO LET IT SIT ON A SHELF. NOT FOR LONG.
AND I'M NOT LETTING ANYONE ELSE CARRY IT. NO ONE ELSE IS WORTHY.
HELL, I WAS LOOKING FOR A WAY TO MAKE MY FIRST MOVE.
MIGHT AS WELL START WITH THIS.

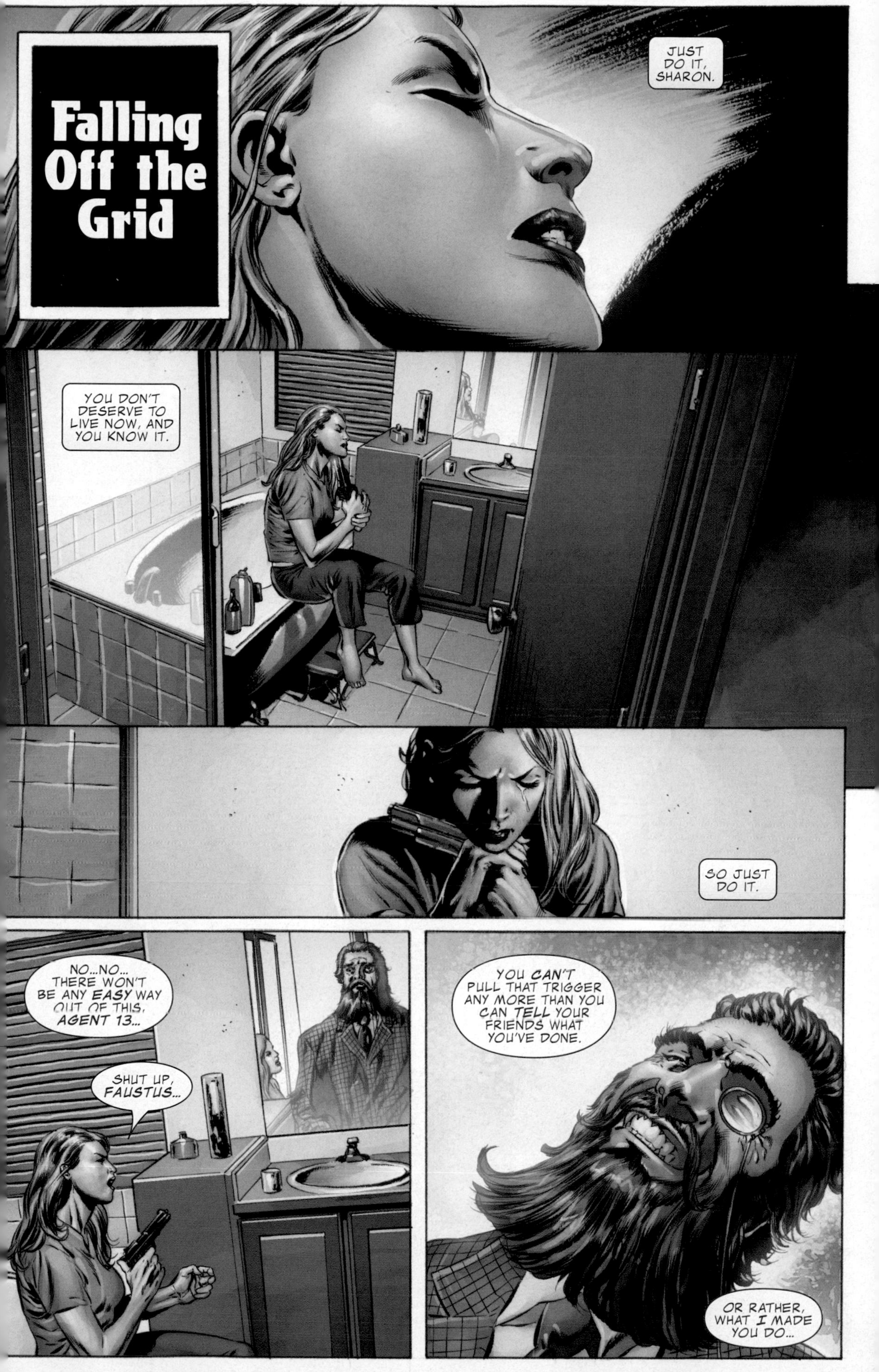
Falling Off the Grid
JUST DO IT, SHARON.
YOU DON'T DESERVE TO LIVE NOW, AND YOU KNOW IT.
SO JUST DO IT.
NO...NO... THERE WON'T BE ANY EASY WAY OUT OF THIS, AGENT 13...
SHUT UP, FAUSTUS...
YOU CAN'T PULL THAT TRIGGER ANY MORE THAN YOU CAN TELL YOUR FRIENDS WHAT YOU'VE DONE.
OR RATHER, WHAT I MADE YOU DO...

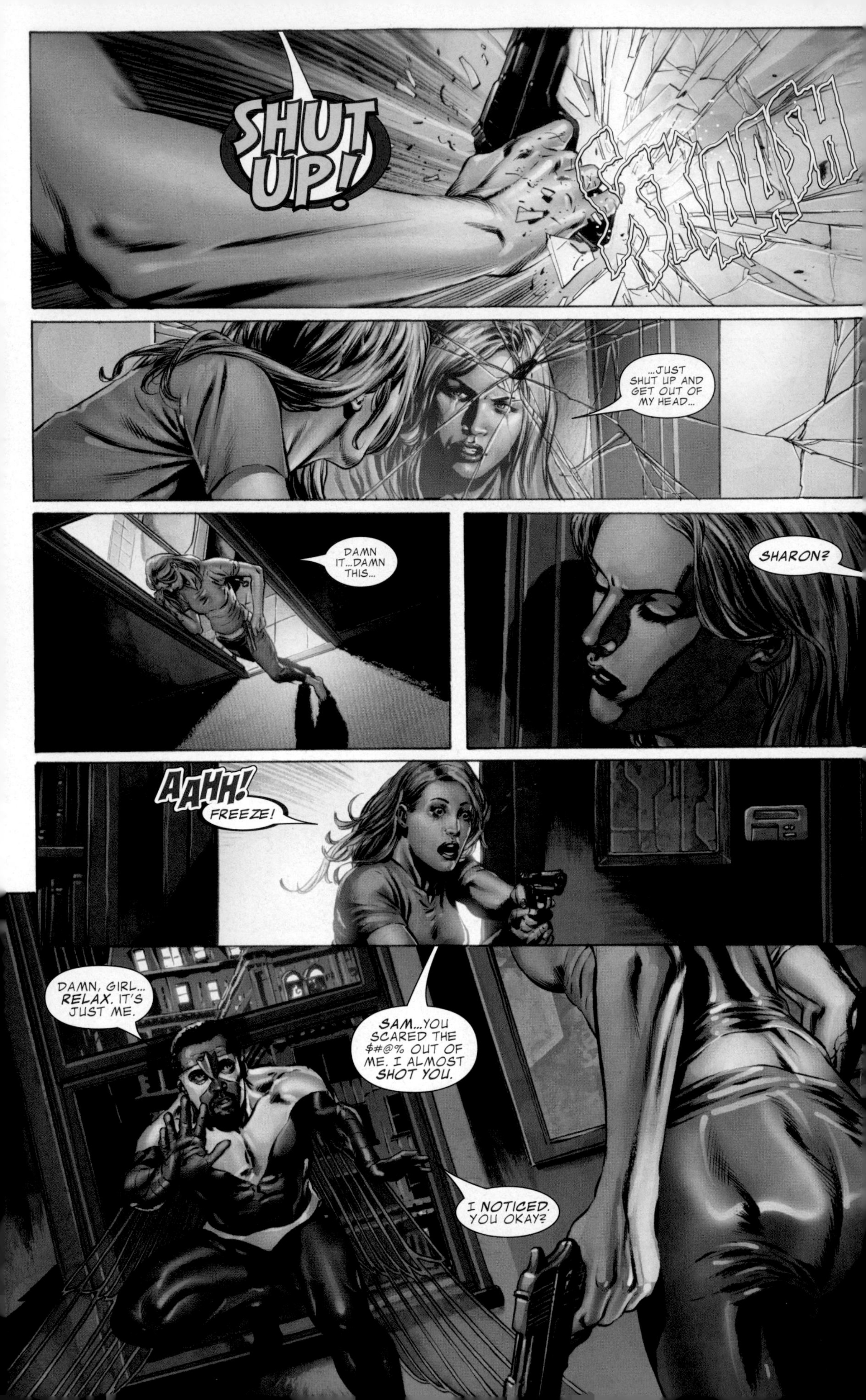

SHUT UP!
SKNOSH
...JUST SHUT UP AND GET OUT OF MY HEAD...
DAMN IT...DAMN THIS...
SHARON?
AAHH!
FREEZE!
DAMN, GIRL... RELAX. IT'S JUST ME.
SAM...YOU SCARED THE $#@% OUT OF ME. I ALMOST SHOT YOU.
I NOTICED. YOU OKAY?

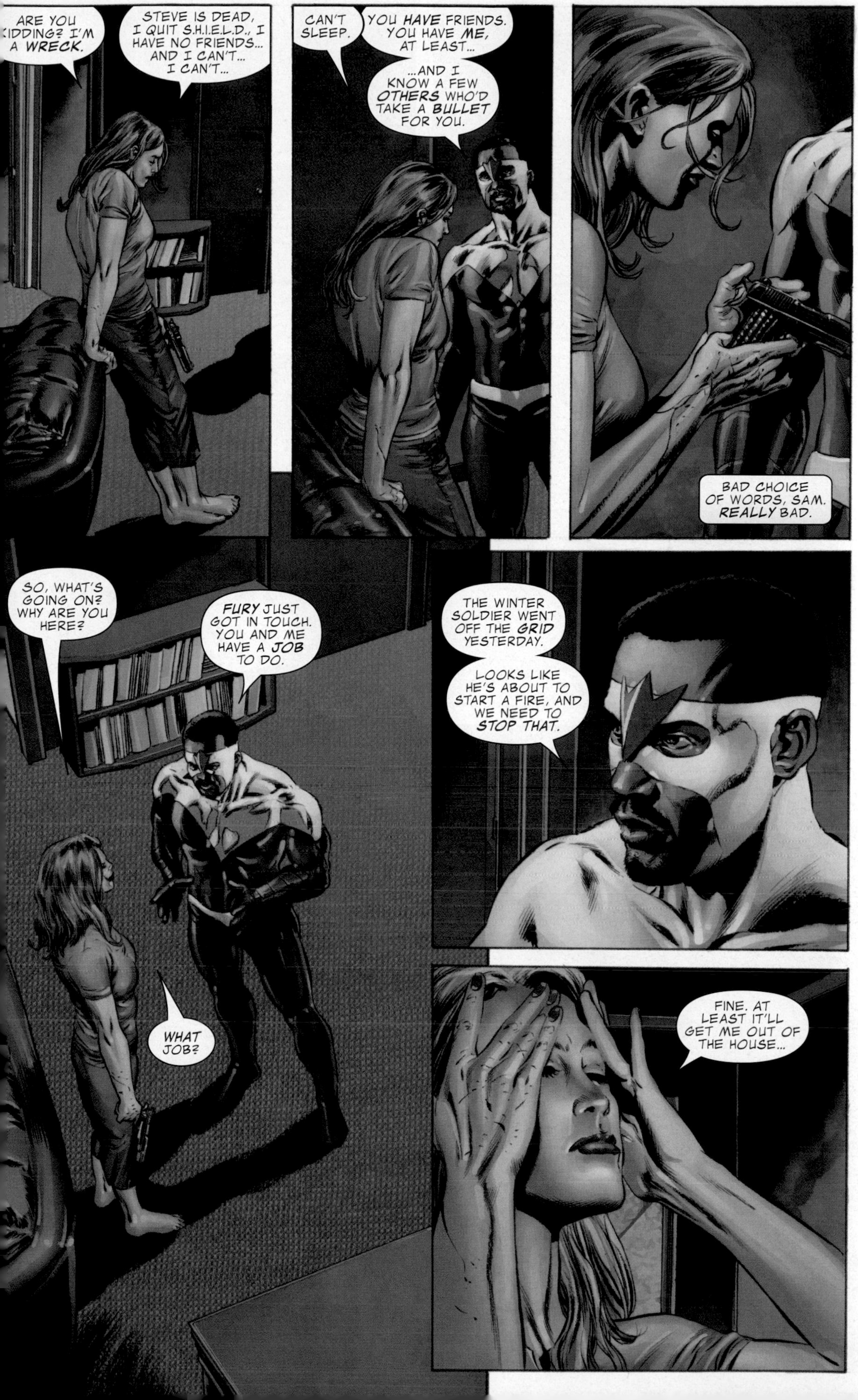
ARE YOU KIDDING? I'M A WRECK.
STEVE IS DEAD, I QUIT S.H.I.E.L.D., I HAVE NO FRIENDS... AND I CAN'T... I CAN'T...
CAN'T SLEEP.
YOU HAVE FRIENDS. YOU HAVE ME, AT LEAST...
...AND I KNOW A FEW OTHERS WHO'D TAKE A BULLET FOR YOU.
BAD CHOICE OF WORDS, SAM. REALLY BAD.
SO, WHAT'S GOING ON? WHY ARE YOU HERE?
FURY JUST GOT IN TOUCH. YOU AND ME HAVE A JOB TO DO.
WHAT JOB?
THE WINTER SOLDIER WENT OFF THE GRID YESTERDAY.
LOOKS LIKE HE'S ABOUT TO START A FIRE, AND WE NEED TO STOP THAT.
FINE. AT LEAST IT'LL GET ME OUT OF THE HOUSE...

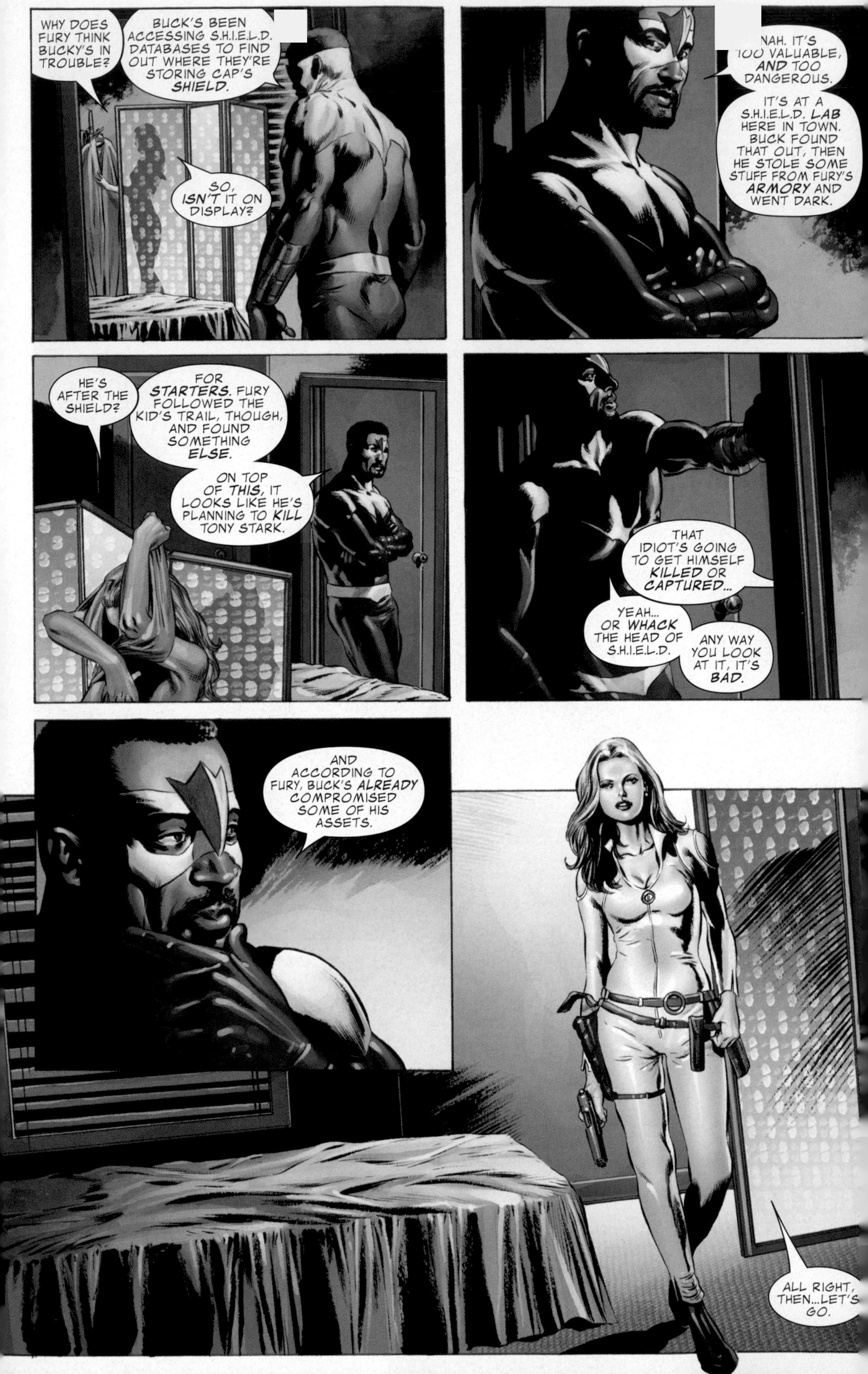
WHY DOES FURY THINK BUCKY'S IN TROUBLE?
BUCK'S BEEN ACCESSING S.H.I.E.L.D. DATABASES TO FIND OUT WHERE THEY'RE STORING CAP'S SHIELD.
SO, ISN'T IT ON DISPLAY?
NAH. IT'S TOO VALUABLE, AND TOO DANGEROUS.
IT'S AT A S.H.I.E.L.D. LAB HERE IN TOWN. BUCK FOUND THAT OUT, THEN HE STOLE SOME STUFF FROM FURY'S ARMORY AND WENT DARK.
HE'S AFTER THE SHIELD?
FOR STARTERS. FURY FOLLOWED THE KID'S TRAIL, THOUGH, AND FOUND SOMETHING ELSE.
ON TOP OF THIS, IT LOOKS LIKE HE'S PLANNING TO KILL TONY STARK.
THAT IDIOT'S GOING TO GET HIMSELF KILLED OR CAPTURED...
YEAH... OR WHACK THE HEAD OF S.H.I.E.L.D.
ANY WAY YOU LOOK AT IT, IT'S BAD.
AND ACCORDING TO FURY, BUCK'S ALREADY COMPROMISED SOME OF HIS ASSETS.
ALL RIGHT, THEN...LET'S GO.

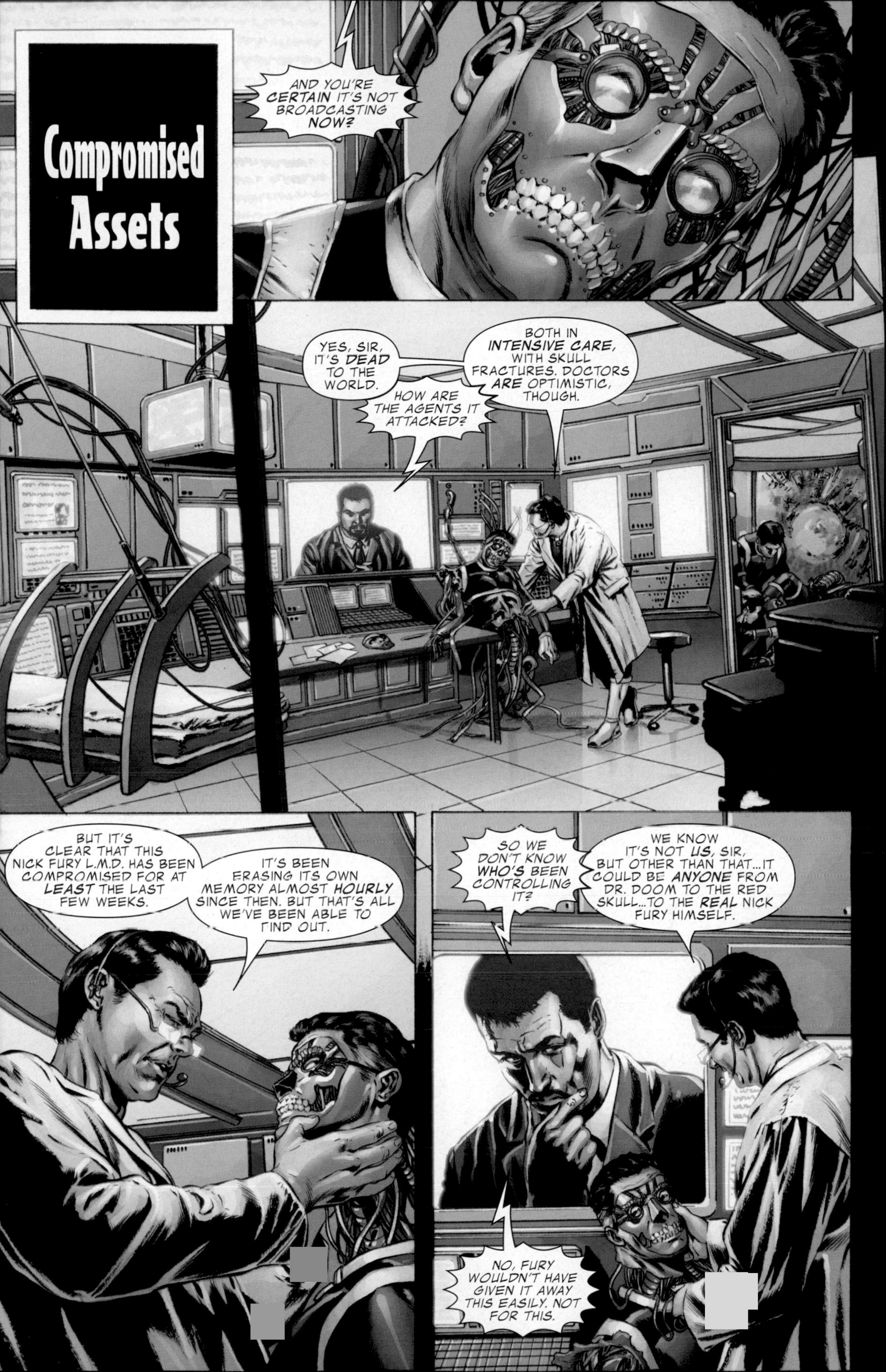
Compromised Assets
AND YOU'RE CERTAIN IT'S NOT BROADCASTING NOW?
YES, SIR, IT'S DEAD TO THE WORLD.
HOW ARE THE AGENTS IT ATTACKED?
BOTH IN INTENSIVE CARE, WITH SKULL FRACTURES. DOCTORS ARE OPTIMISTIC, THOUGH.
BUT IT'S CLEAR THAT THIS NICK FURY L.M.D. HAS BEEN COMPROMISED FOR AT LEAST THE LAST FEW WEEKS.
IT'S BEEN ERASING ITS OWN MEMORY ALMOST HOURLY SINCE THEN. BUT THAT'S ALL WE'VE BEEN ABLE TO FIND OUT.
SO WE DON'T KNOW WHO'S BEEN CONTROLLING IT?
WE KNOW IT'S NOT US, SIR, BUT OTHER THAN THAT...IT COULD BE ANYONE FROM DR. DOOM TO THE RED SKULL...TO THE REAL NICK FURY HIMSELF.
NO, FURY WOULDN'T HAVE GIVEN IT AWAY THIS EASILY. NOT FOR THIS.

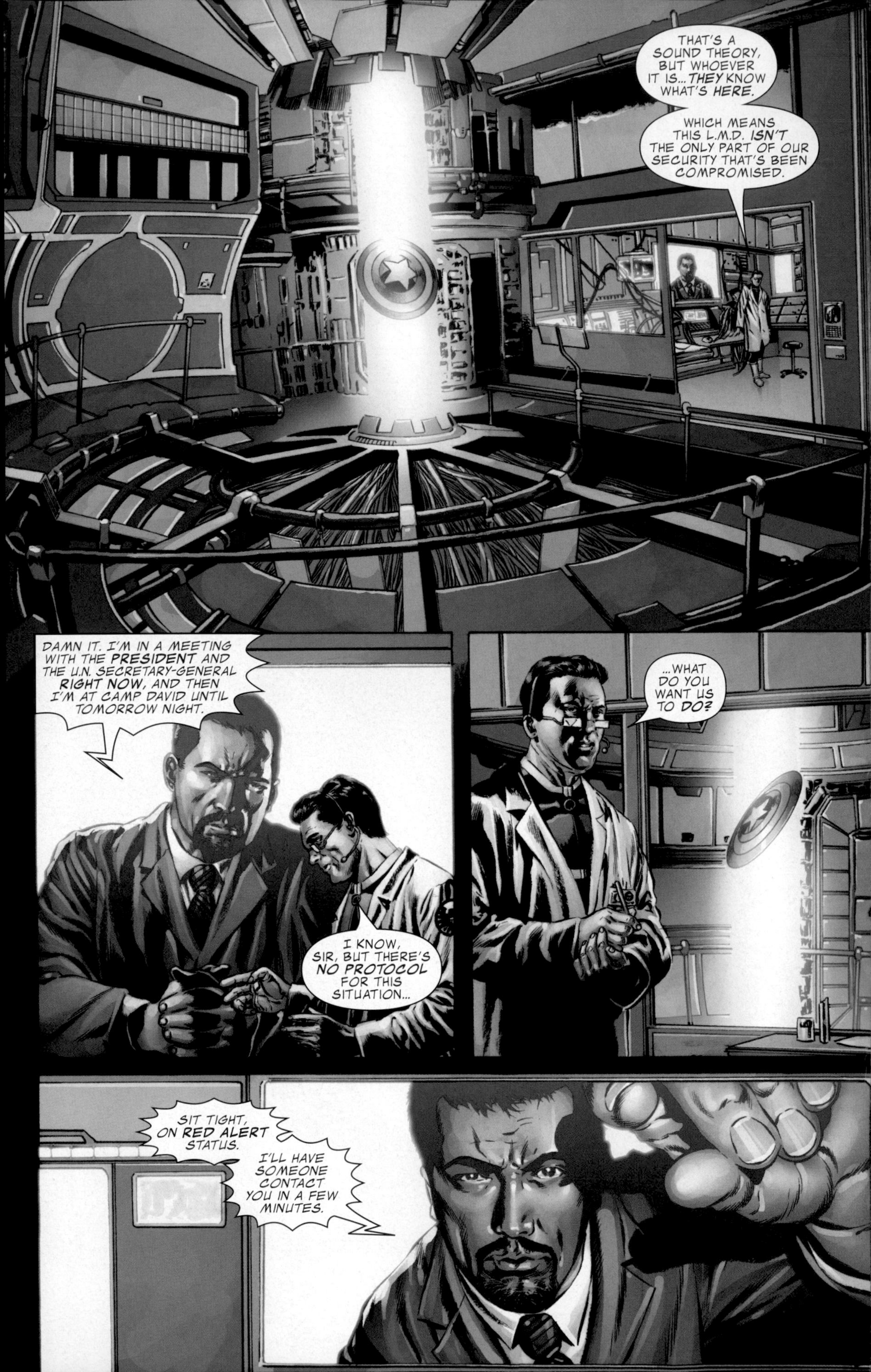
THAT'S A SOUND THEORY, BUT WHOEVER IT IS... THEY KNOW WHAT'S HERE.
WHICH MEANS THIS L.M.D. ISN'T THE ONLY PART OF OUR SECURITY THAT'S BEEN COMPROMISED.
DAMN IT. I'M IN A MEETING WITH THE PRESIDENT AND THE U.N. SECRETARY-GENERAL RIGHT NOW, AND THEN I'M AT CAMP DAVID UNTIL TOMORROW NIGHT.
I KNOW, SIR, BUT THERE'S NO PROTOCOL FOR THIS SITUATION...
...WHAT DO YOU WANT US TO DO?
SIT TIGHT, ON RED ALERT STATUS.
I'LL HAVE SOMEONE CONTACT YOU IN A FEW MINUTES.

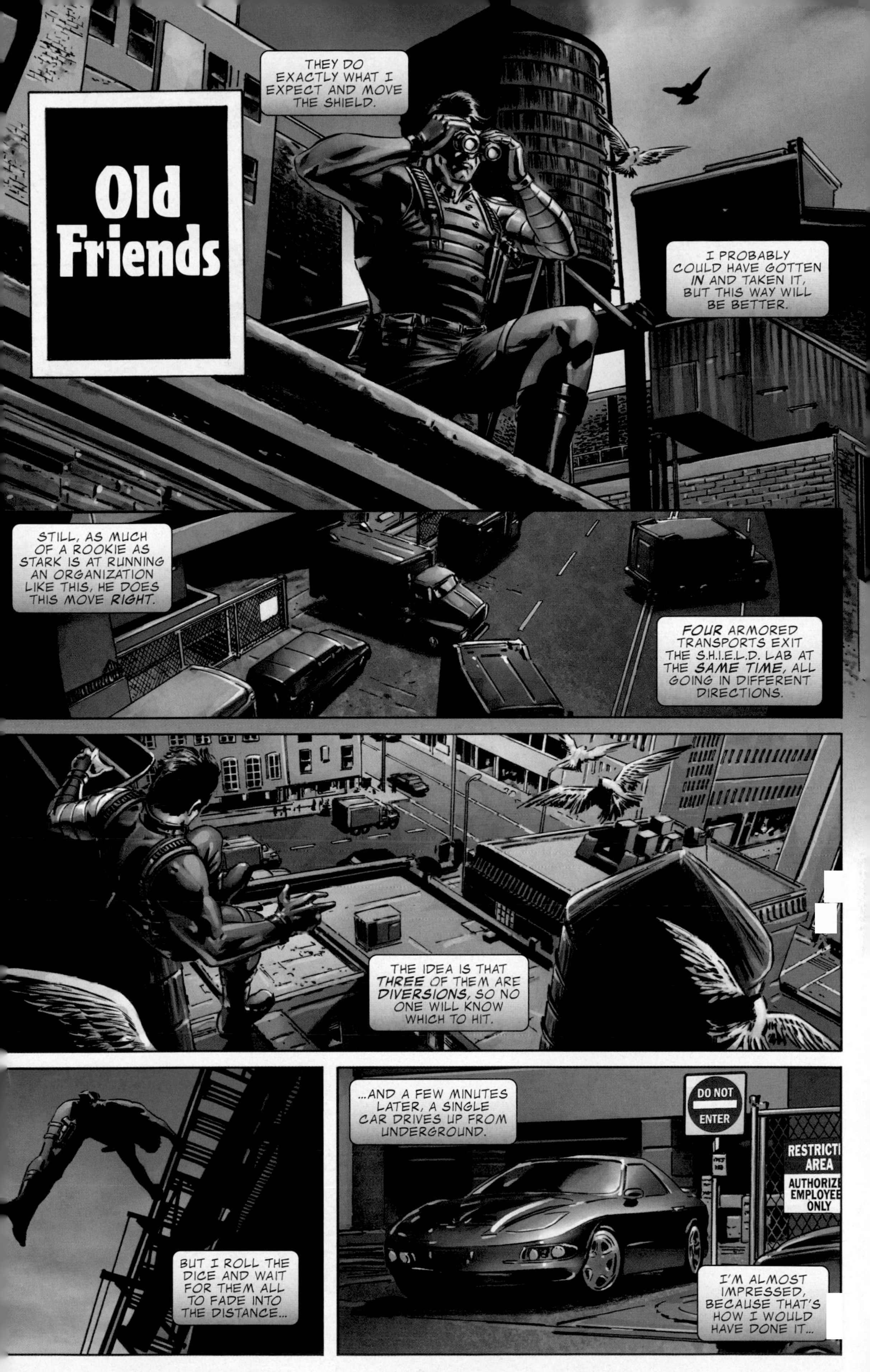
THEY DO EXACTLY WHAT I EXPECT AND MOVE THE SHIELD.
Old Friends
I PROBABLY COULD HAVE GOTTEN IN AND TAKEN IT, BUT THIS WAY WILL BE BETTER.
STILL, AS MUCH OF A ROOKIE AS STARK IS AT RUNNING AN ORGANIZATION LIKE THIS, HE DOES THIS MOVE RIGHT.
FOUR ARMORED TRANSPORTS EXIT THE S.H.I.E.L.D. LAB AT THE SAME TIME, ALL GOING IN DIFFERENT DIRECTIONS.
THE IDEA IS THAT THREE OF THEM ARE DIVERSIONS, SO NO ONE WILL KNOW WHICH TO HIT.
BUT I ROLL THE DICE AND WAIT FOR THEM ALL TO FADE INTO THE DISTANCE...
...AND A FEW MINUTES LATER, A SINGLE CAR DRIVES UP FROM UNDERGROUND.
DO NOT ENTER
I'M ALMOST IMPRESSED, BECAUSE THAT'S HOW I WOULD HAVE DONE IT...

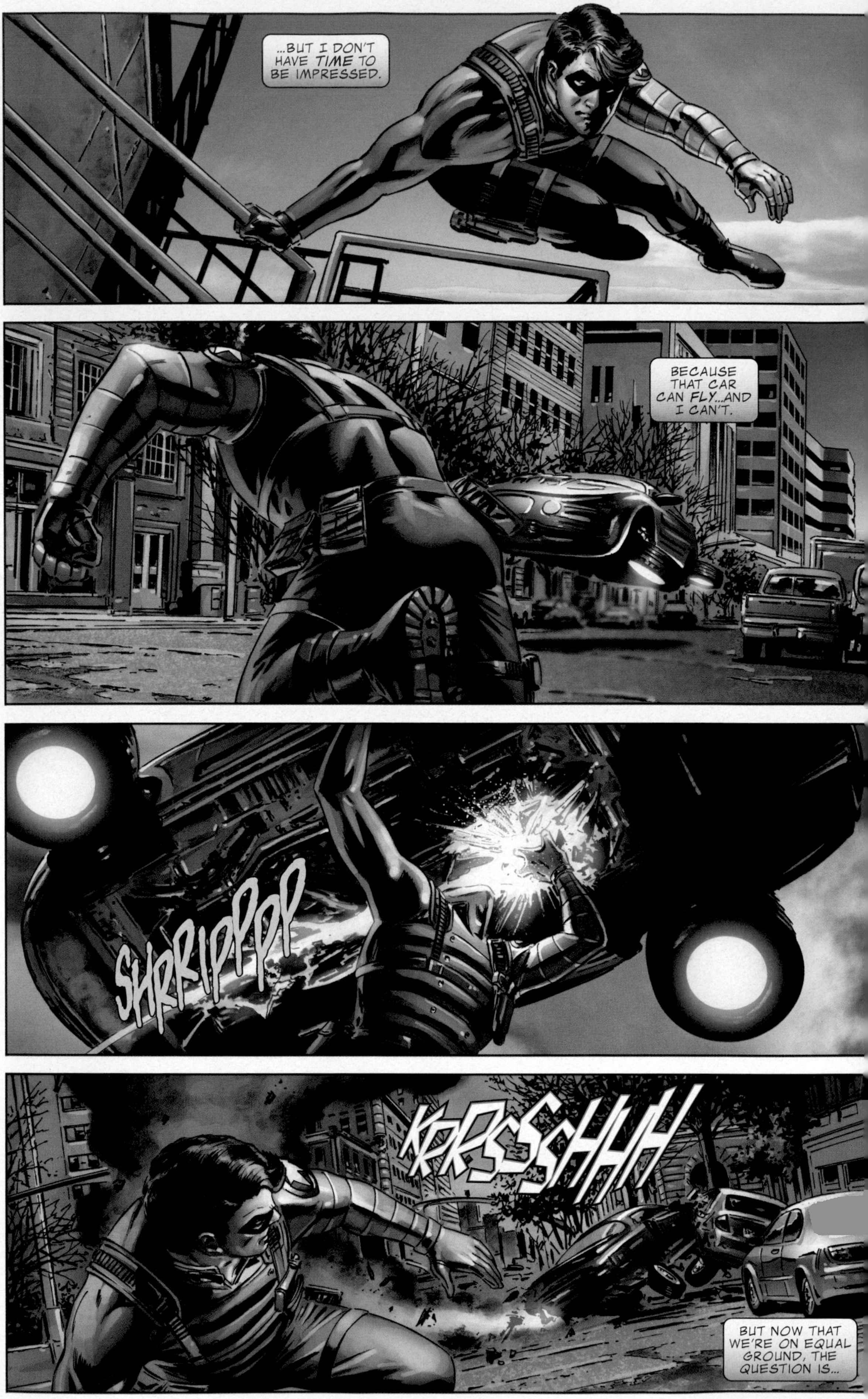
...BUT I DON'T HAVE TIME TO BE IMPRESSED.
BECAUSE THAT CAR CAN FLY...AND I CAN'T.
SHRIPPPP
KRRSSSHHH
BUT NOW THAT WE'RE ON EQUAL GROUND, THE QUESTION IS...

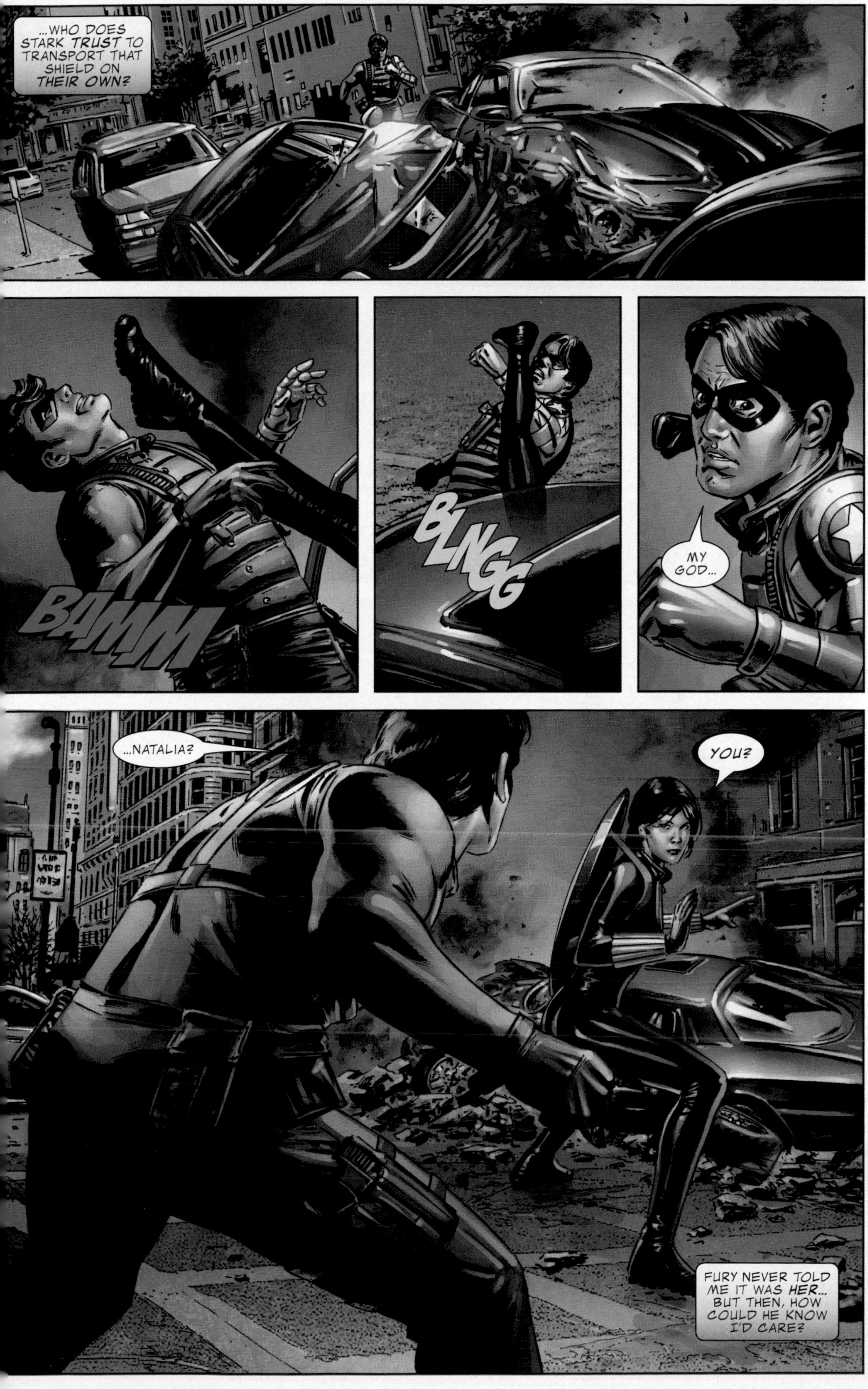
...WHO DOES STARK TRUST TO TRANSPORT THAT SHIELD ON THEIR OWN?
BAMM
BLNGG
MY GOD...
...NATALIA?
YOU?
FURY NEVER TOLD ME IT WAS HER... BUT THEN, HOW COULD HE KNOW I'D CARE?

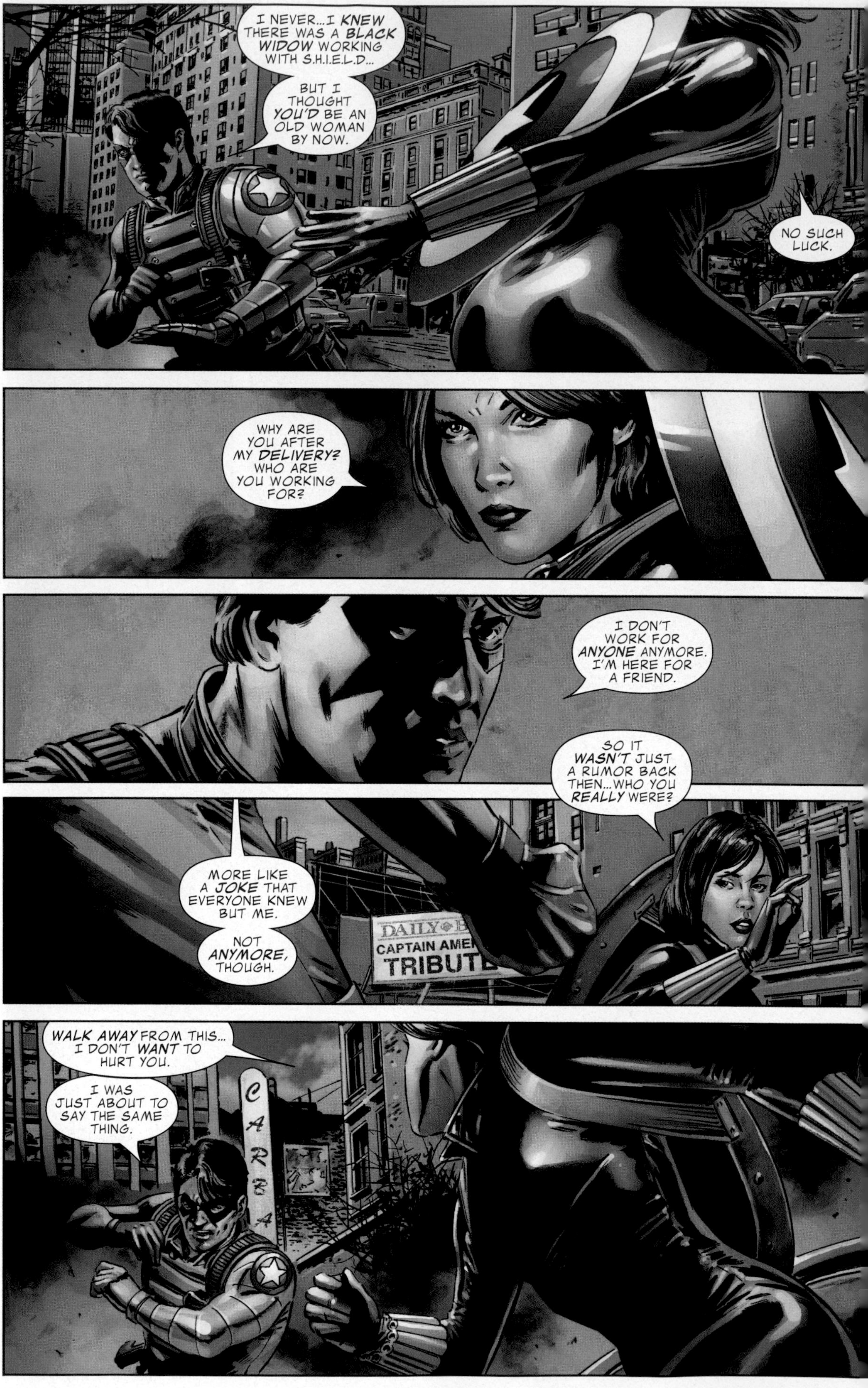
I NEVER...I KNEW THERE WAS A BLACK WIDOW WORKING WITH S.H.I.E.L.D...
BUT I THOUGHT YOU'D BE AN OLD WOMAN BY NOW.
NO SUCH LUCK.
WHY ARE YOU AFTER MY DELIVERY? WHO ARE YOU WORKING FOR?
I DON'T WORK FOR ANYONE ANYMORE. I'M HERE FOR A FRIEND.
SO IT WASN'T JUST A RUMOR BACK THEN...WHO YOU REALLY WERE?
MORE LIKE A JOKE THAT EVERYONE KNEW BUT ME.
NOT ANYMORE, THOUGH.
DAILY B
CAPTAIN AMER
TRIBUTE
WALK AWAY FROM THIS... I DON'T WANT TO HURT YOU.
I WAS JUST ABOUT TO SAY THE SAME THING.
CARBA

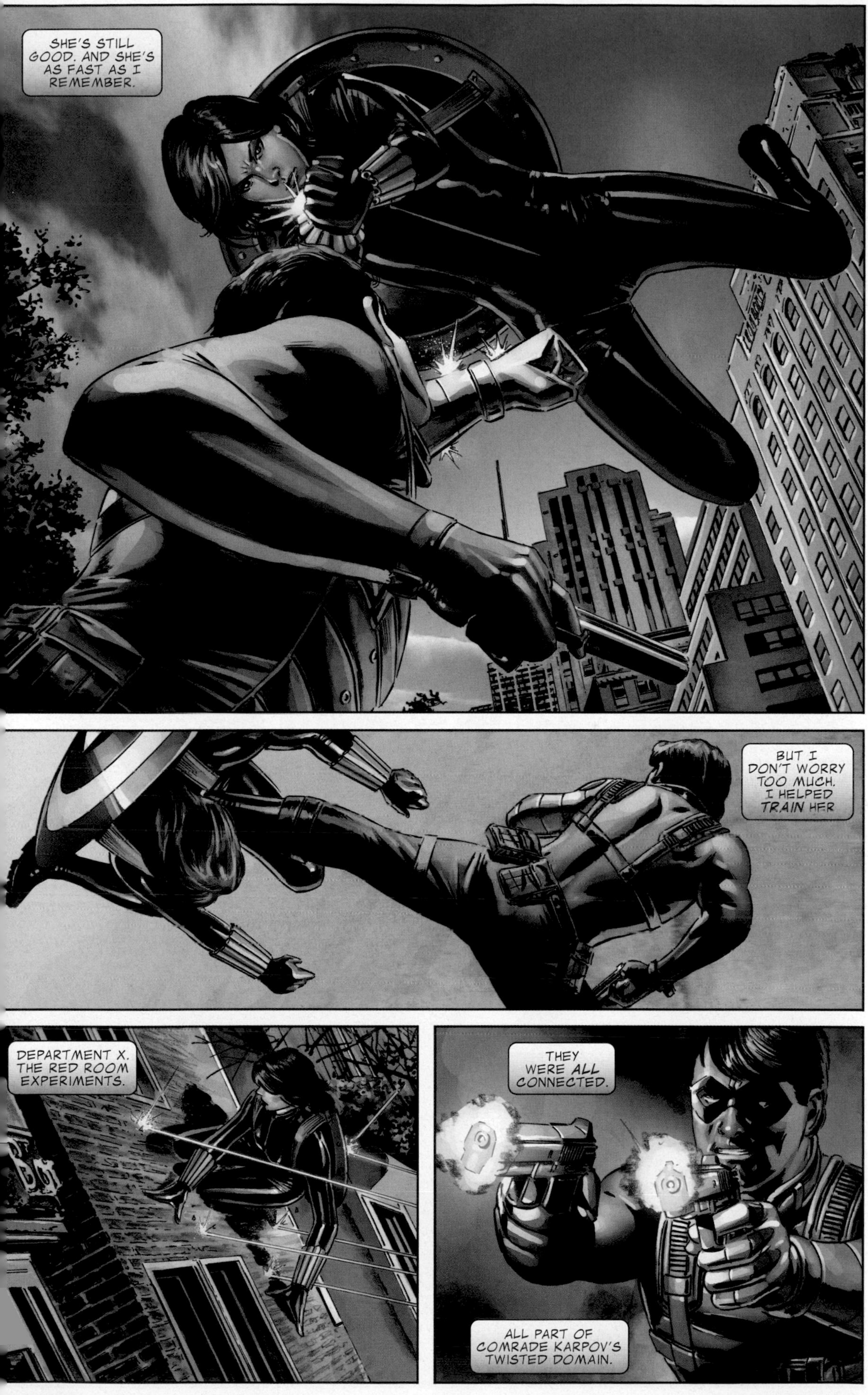
SHE'S STILL GOOD. AND SHE'S AS FAST AS I REMEMBER.
BUT I DON'T WORRY TOO MUCH. I HELPED TRAIN HER
DEPARTMENT X. THE RED ROOM EXPERIMENTS.
THEY WERE ALL CONNECTED.
ALL PART OF COMRADE KARPOV'S TWISTED DOMAIN.

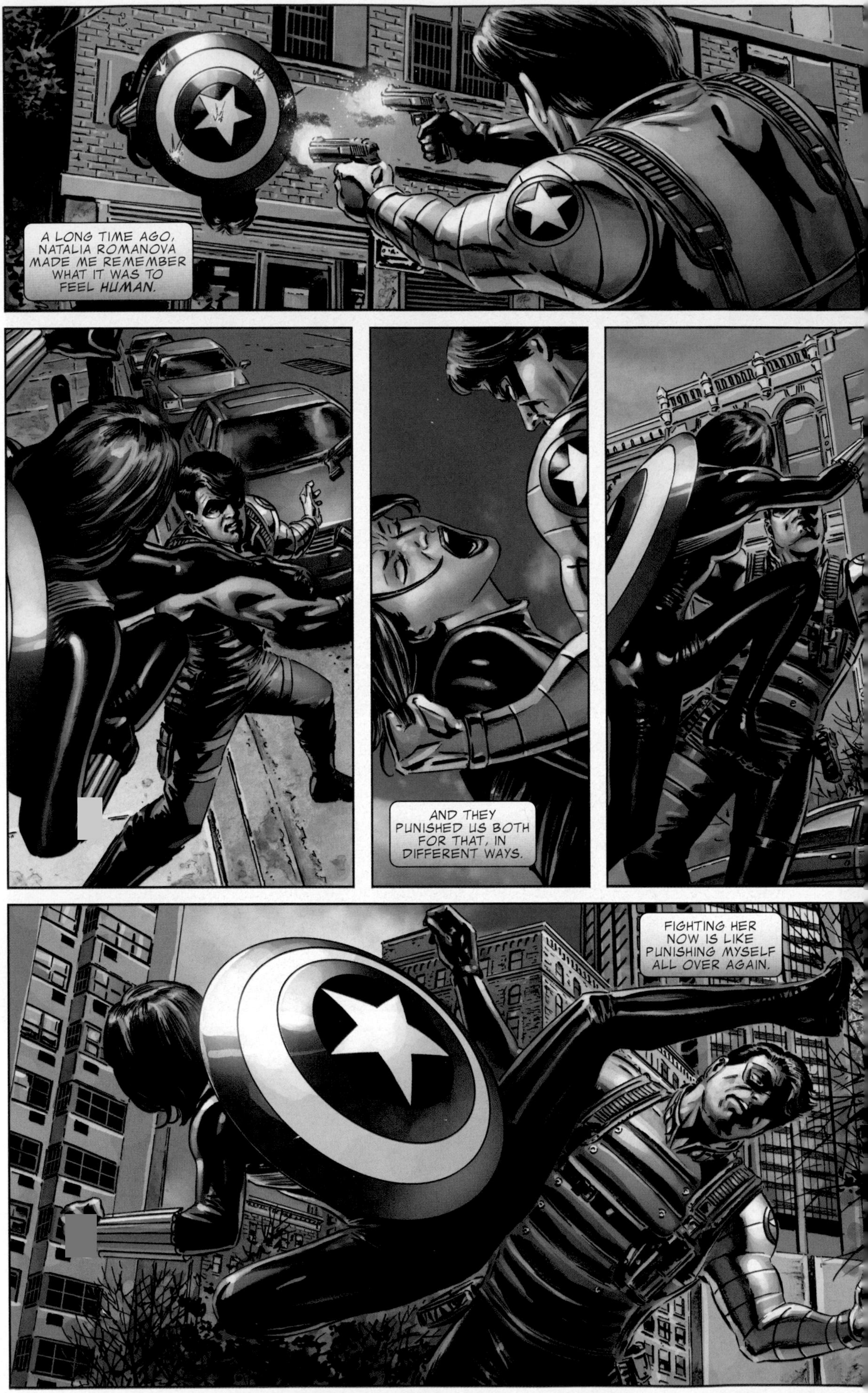
A LONG TIME AGO, NATALIA ROMANOVA MADE ME REMEMBER WHAT IT WAS TO FEEL HUMAN.
AND THEY PUNISHED US BOTH FOR THAT, IN DIFFERENT WAYS.
FIGHTING HER NOW IS LIKE PUNISHING MYSELF ALL OVER AGAIN.

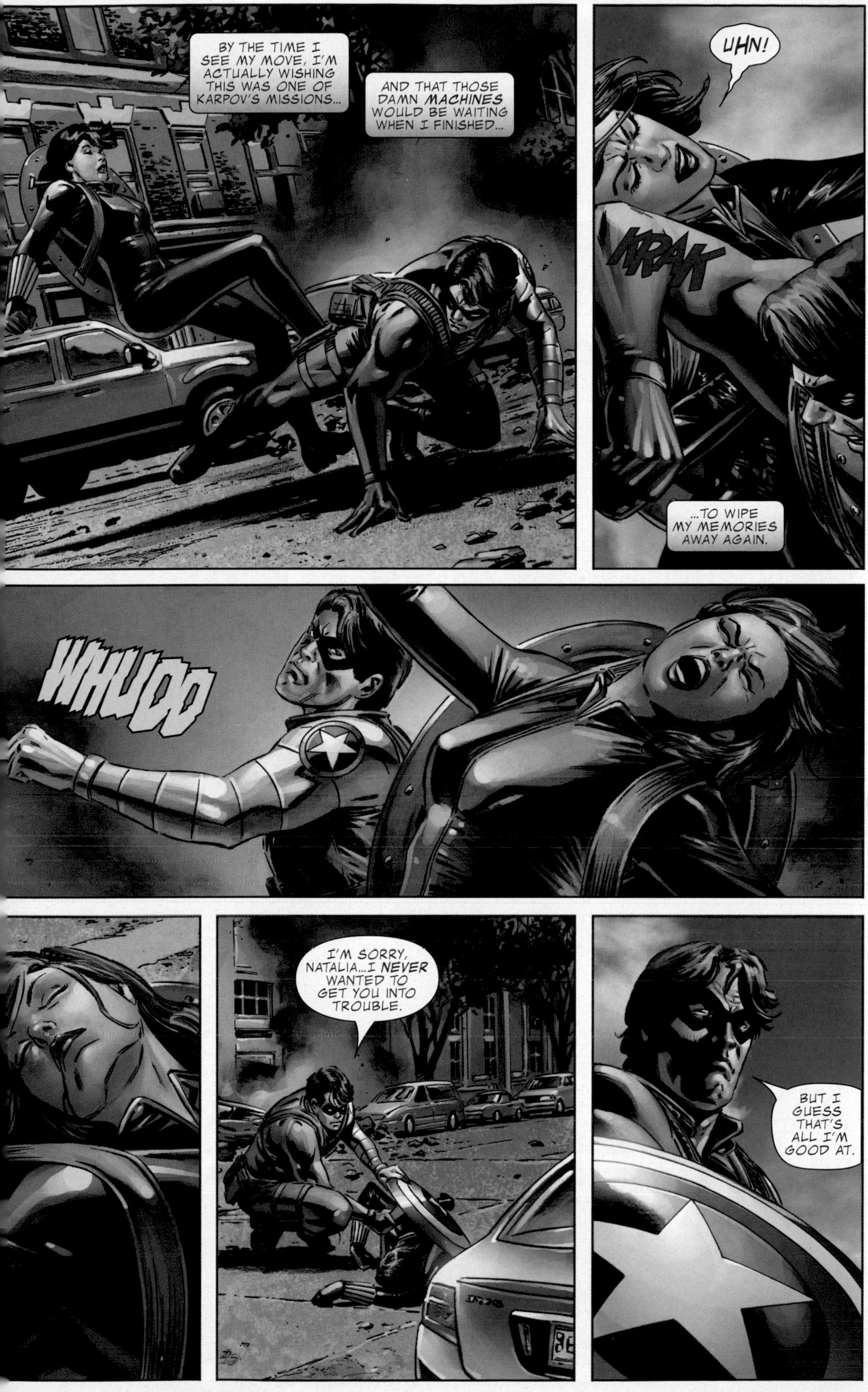
BY THE TIME I SEE MY MOVE, I'M ACTUALLY WISHING THIS WAS ONE OF KARPOV'S MISSIONS...
AND THAT THOSE DAMN MACHINES WOULD BE WAITING WHEN I FINISHED...
UHN!
KRAK
...TO WIPE MY MEMORIES AWAY AGAIN.
WHUDD
I'M SORRY, NATALIA...I NEVER WANTED TO GET YOU INTO TROUBLE.
BUT I GUESS THAT'S ALL I'M GOOD AT.

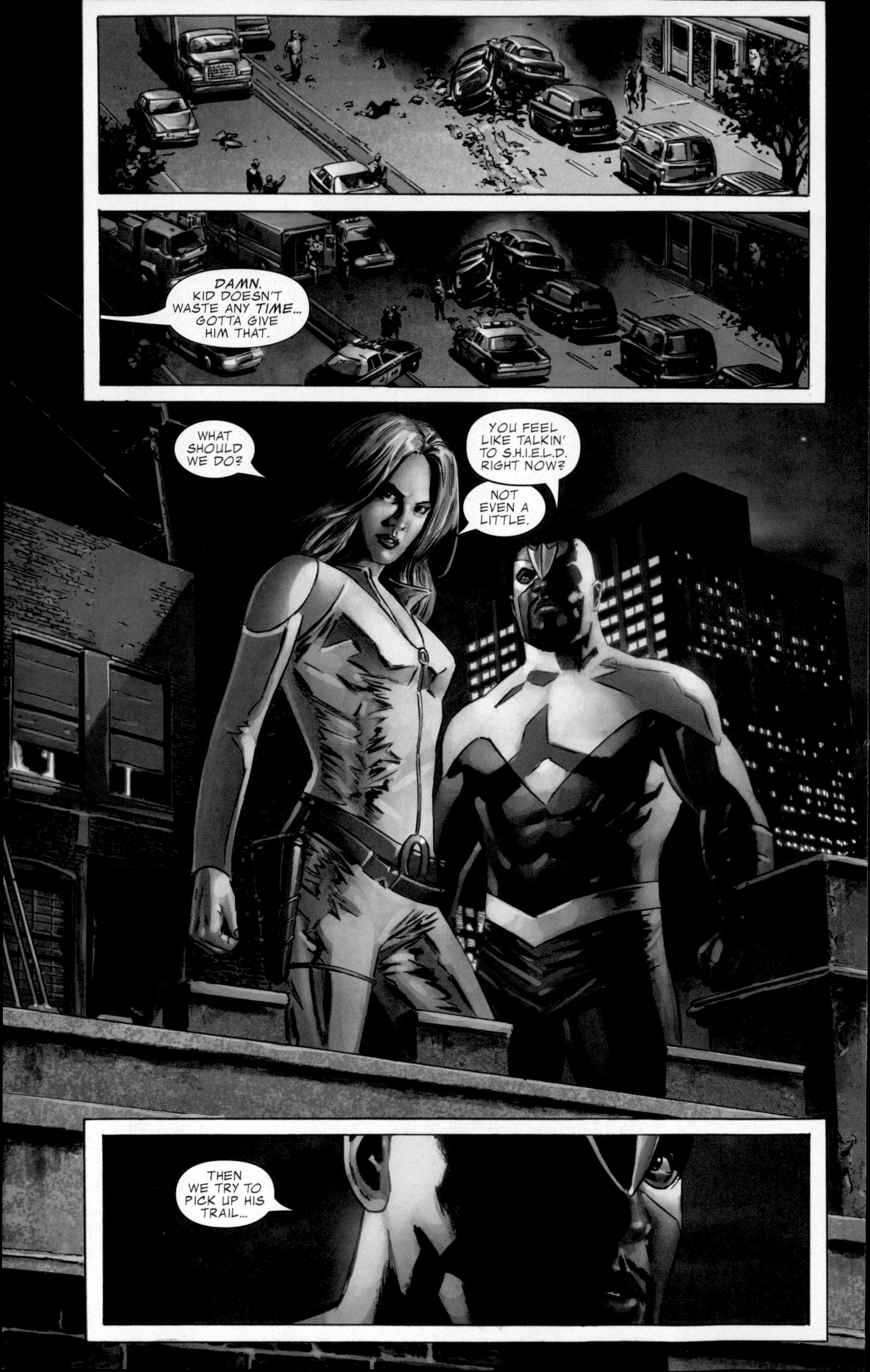
DAMN. KID DOESN'T WASTE ANY TIME... GOTTA GIVE HIM THAT.
WHAT SHOULD WE DO?
YOU FEEL LIKE TALKIN' TO S.H.I.E.L.D. RIGHT NOW?
NOT EVEN A LITTLE.
THEN WE TRY TO PICK UP HIS TRAIL...

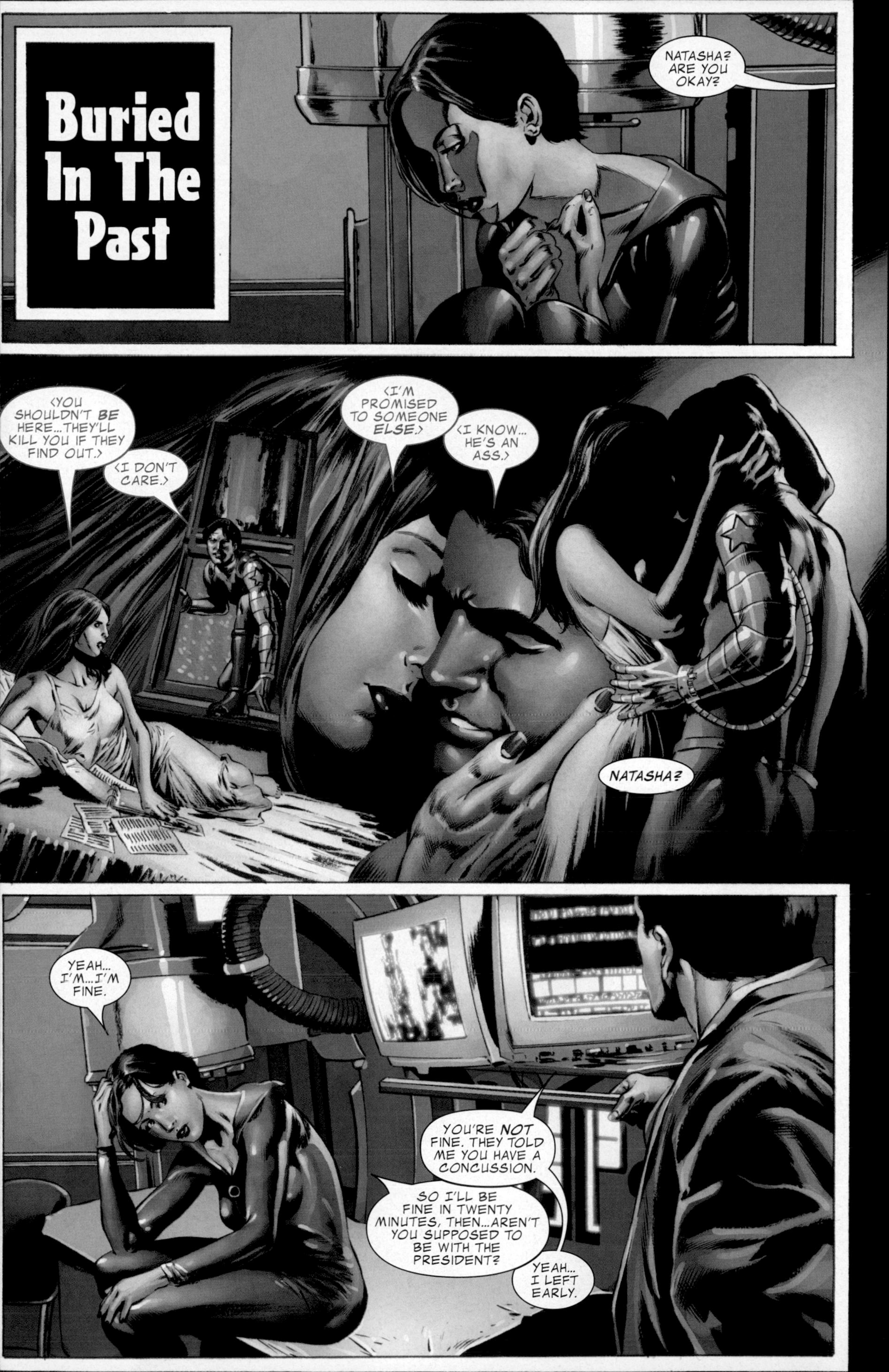
Buried In The Past
NATASHA? ARE YOU OKAY?
<YOU SHOULDN'T BE HERE...THEY'LL KILL YOU IF THEY FIND OUT.>
<I DON'T CARE.>
<I'M PROMISED TO SOMEONE ELSE.>
<I KNOW... HE'S AN ASS.>
NATASHA?
YEAH... I'M...I'M FINE.
YOU'RE NOT FINE. THEY TOLD ME YOU HAVE A CONCUSSION.
SO I'LL BE FINE IN TWENTY MINUTES, THEN...AREN'T YOU SUPPOSED TO BE WITH THE PRESIDENT?
YEAH... I LEFT EARLY.

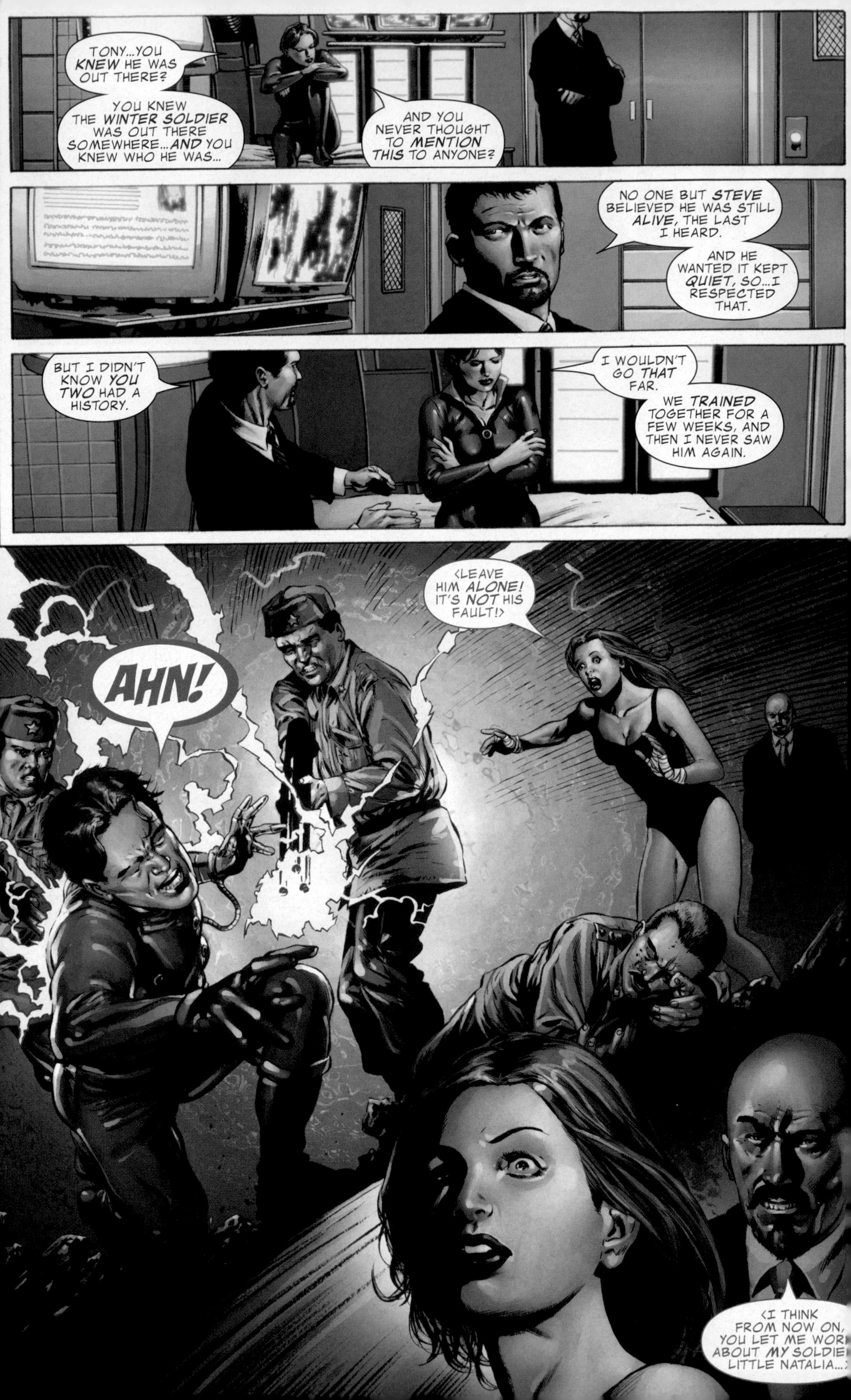
TONY...YOU KNEW HE WAS OUT THERE?
YOU KNEW THE WINTER SOLDIER WAS OUT THERE SOMEWHERE...AND YOU KNEW WHO HE WAS...
AND YOU NEVER THOUGHT TO MENTION THIS TO ANYONE?
NO ONE BUT STEVE BELIEVED HE WAS STILL ALIVE, THE LAST I HEARD.
AND HE WANTED IT KEPT QUIET, SO...I RESPECTED THAT.
BUT I DIDN'T KNOW YOU TWO HAD A HISTORY.
I WOULDN'T GO THAT FAR.
WE TRAINED TOGETHER FOR A FEW WEEKS, AND THEN I NEVER SAW HIM AGAIN.
<LEAVE HIM ALONE! IT'S NOT HIS FAULT!>
AHN!
<I THINK FROM NOW ON, YOU LET ME WOR
ABOUT MY SOLDIE
LITTLE NATALIA...>

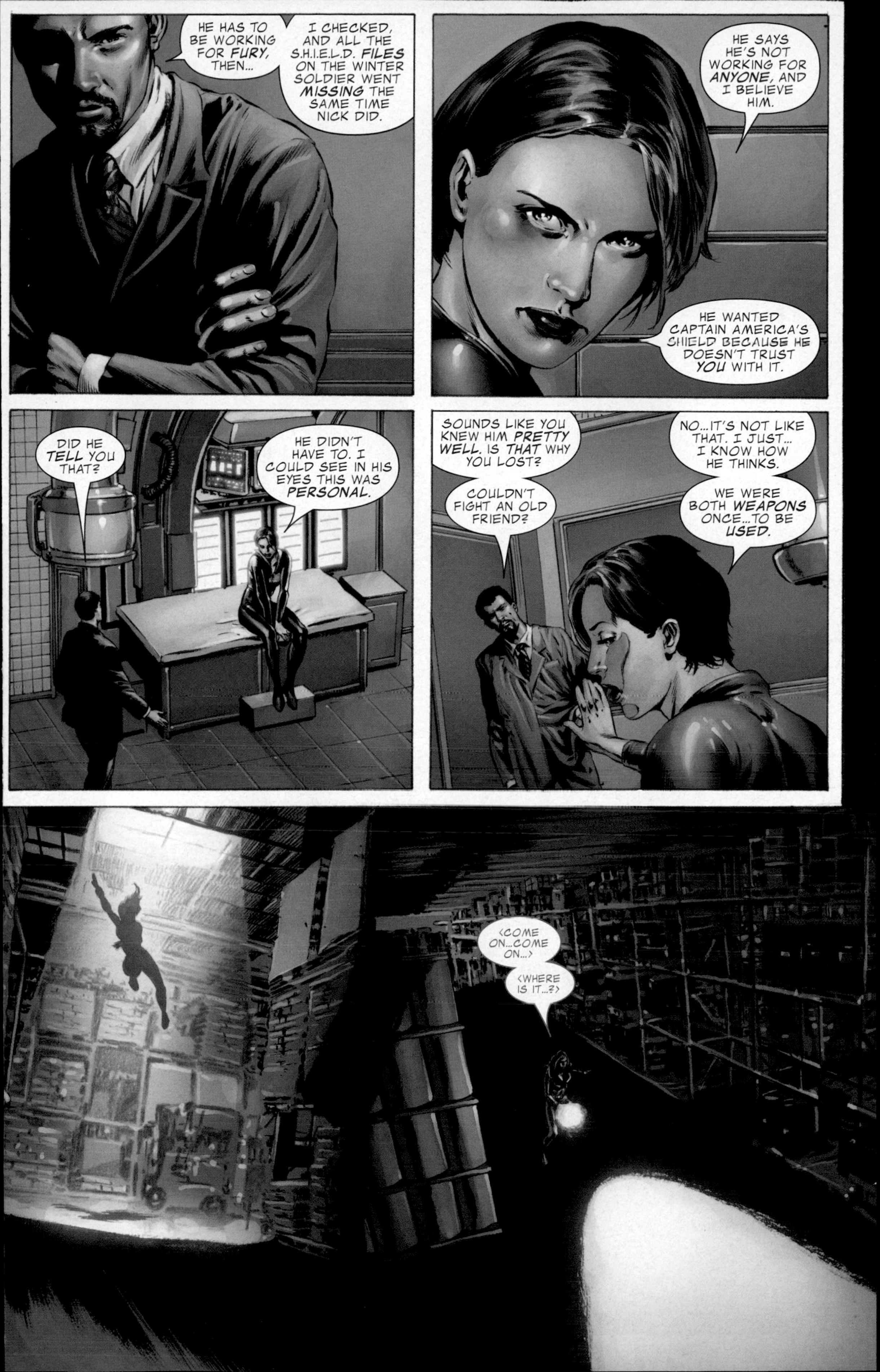
HE HAS TO BE WORKING FOR FURY, THEN...
I CHECKED, AND ALL THE S.H.I.E.L.D. FILES ON THE WINTER SOLDIER WENT MISSING THE SAME TIME NICK DID.
HE SAYS HE'S NOT WORKING FOR ANYONE, AND I BELIEVE HIM.
HE WANTED CAPTAIN AMERICA'S SHIELD BECAUSE HE DOESN'T TRUST YOU WITH IT.
DID HE TELL YOU THAT?
HE DIDN'T HAVE TO. I COULD SEE IN HIS EYES THIS WAS PERSONAL.
SOUNDS LIKE YOU KNEW HIM PRETTY WELL. IS THAT WHY YOU LOST?
COULDN'T FIGHT AN OLD FRIEND?
NO...IT'S NOT LIKE THAT. I JUST... I KNOW HOW HE THINKS.
WE WERE BOTH WEAPONS ONCE...TO BE USED.
<COME ON...COME ON...>
<WHERE IS IT...?>

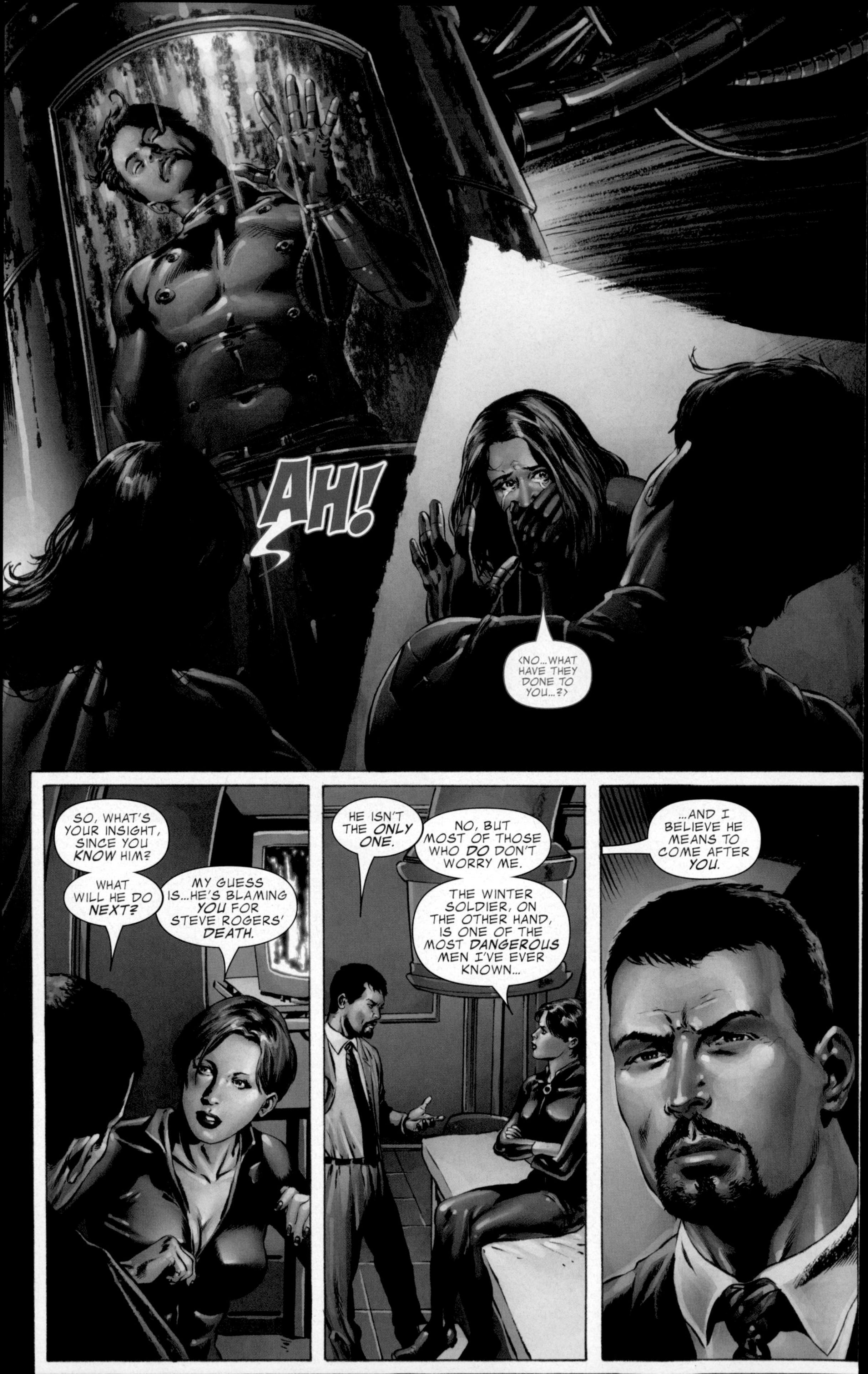
AH!
<NO...WHAT HAVE THEY DONE TO YOU...?>
SO, WHAT'S YOUR INSIGHT, SINCE YOU KNOW HIM?
WHAT WILL HE DO NEXT?
MY GUESS IS...HE'S BLAMING YOU FOR STEVE ROGERS' DEATH.
HE ISN'T THE ONLY ONE.
NO, BUT MOST OF THOSE WHO DO DON'T WORRY ME.
THE WINTER SOLDIER, ON THE OTHER HAND, IS ONE OF THE MOST DANGEROUS MEN I'VE EVER KNOWN...
...AND I BELIEVE HE MEANS TO COME AFTER YOU.

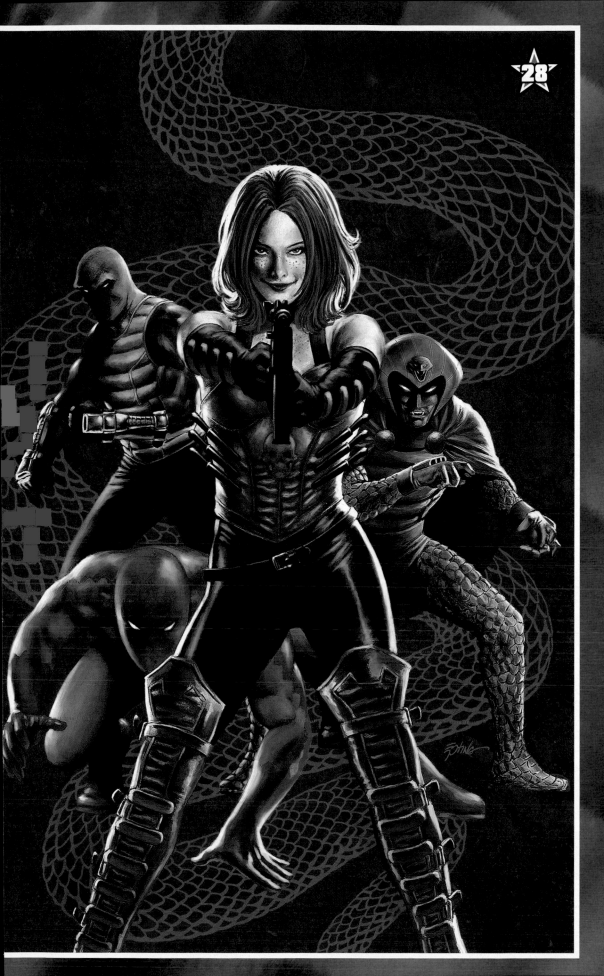

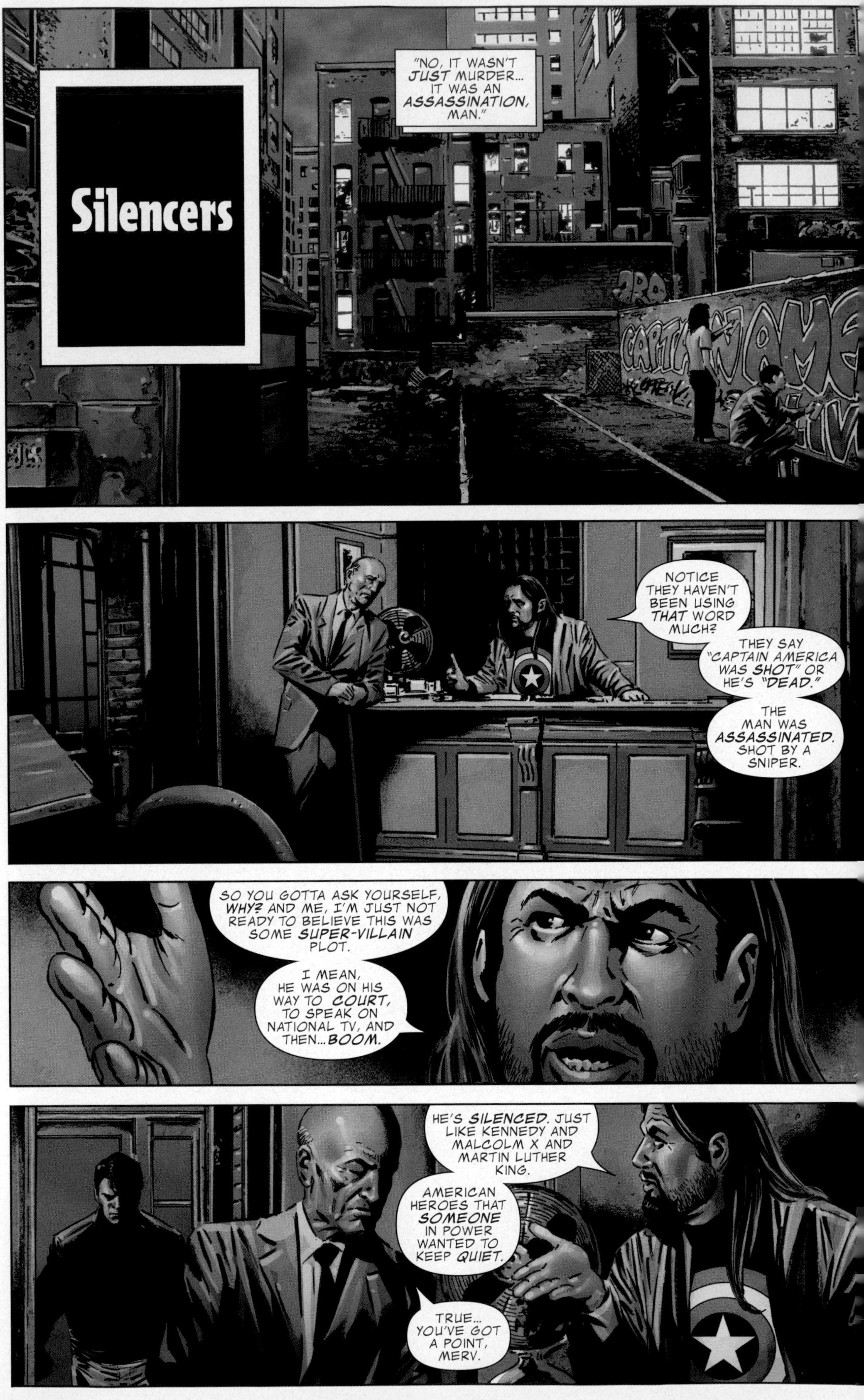

Silencers
"NO, IT WASN'T JUST MURDER... IT WAS AN ASSASSINATION, MAN."
NOTICE THEY HAVEN'T BEEN USING THAT WORD MUCH?
THEY SAY "CAPTAIN AMERICA WAS SHOT" OR HE'S "DEAD."
THE MAN WAS ASSASSINATED. SHOT BY A SNIPER.
SO YOU GOTTA ASK YOURSELF, WHY? AND ME, I'M JUST NOT READY TO BELIEVE THIS WAS SOME SUPER-VILLAIN PLOT.
I MEAN, HE WAS ON HIS WAY TO COURT, TO SPEAK ON NATIONAL TV, AND THEN...BOOM.
HE'S SILENCED. JUST LIKE KENNEDY AND MALCOLM X AND MARTIN LUTHER KING.
AMERICAN HEROES THAT SOMEONE IN POWER WANTED TO KEEP QUIET.
TRUE... YOU'VE GOT A POINT, MERV.

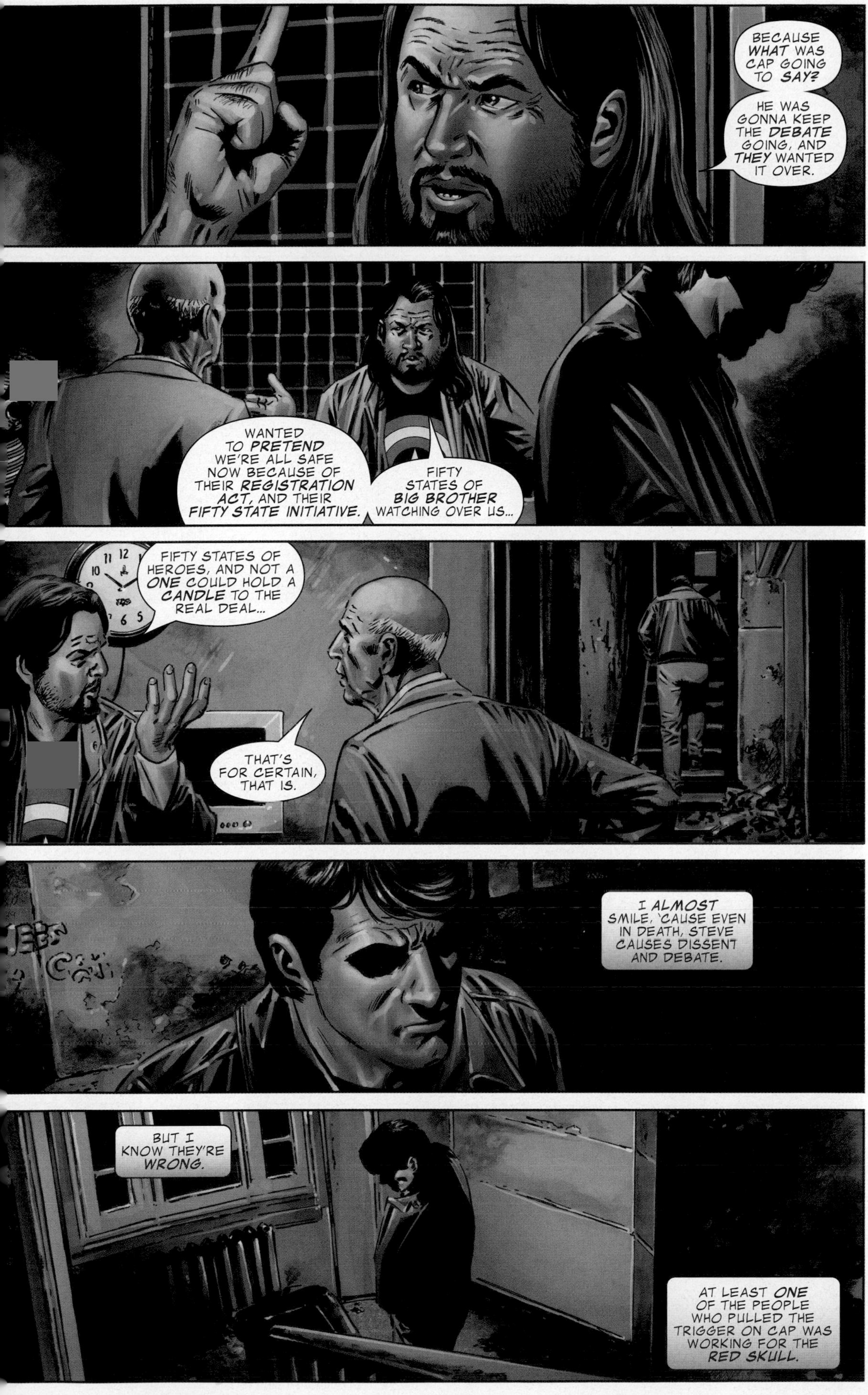

BECAUSE WHAT WAS CAP GOING TO SAY?
HE WAS GONNA KEEP THE DEBATE GOING, AND THEY WANTED IT OVER.
WANTED TO PRETEND WE'RE ALL SAFE NOW BECAUSE OF THEIR REGISTRATION ACT, AND THEIR FIFTY STATE INITIATIVE.
FIFTY STATES OF BIG BROTHER WATCHING OVER US...
FIFTY STATES OF HEROES, AND NOT A ONE COULD HOLD A CANDLE TO THE REAL DEAL...
THAT'S FOR CERTAIN, THAT IS.
I ALMOST SMILE, 'CAUSE EVEN IN DEATH, STEVE CAUSES DISSENT AND DEBATE.
BUT I KNOW THEY'RE WRONG.
AT LEAST ONE OF THE PEOPLE WHO PULLED THE TRIGGER ON CAP WAS WORKING FOR THE RED SKULL.

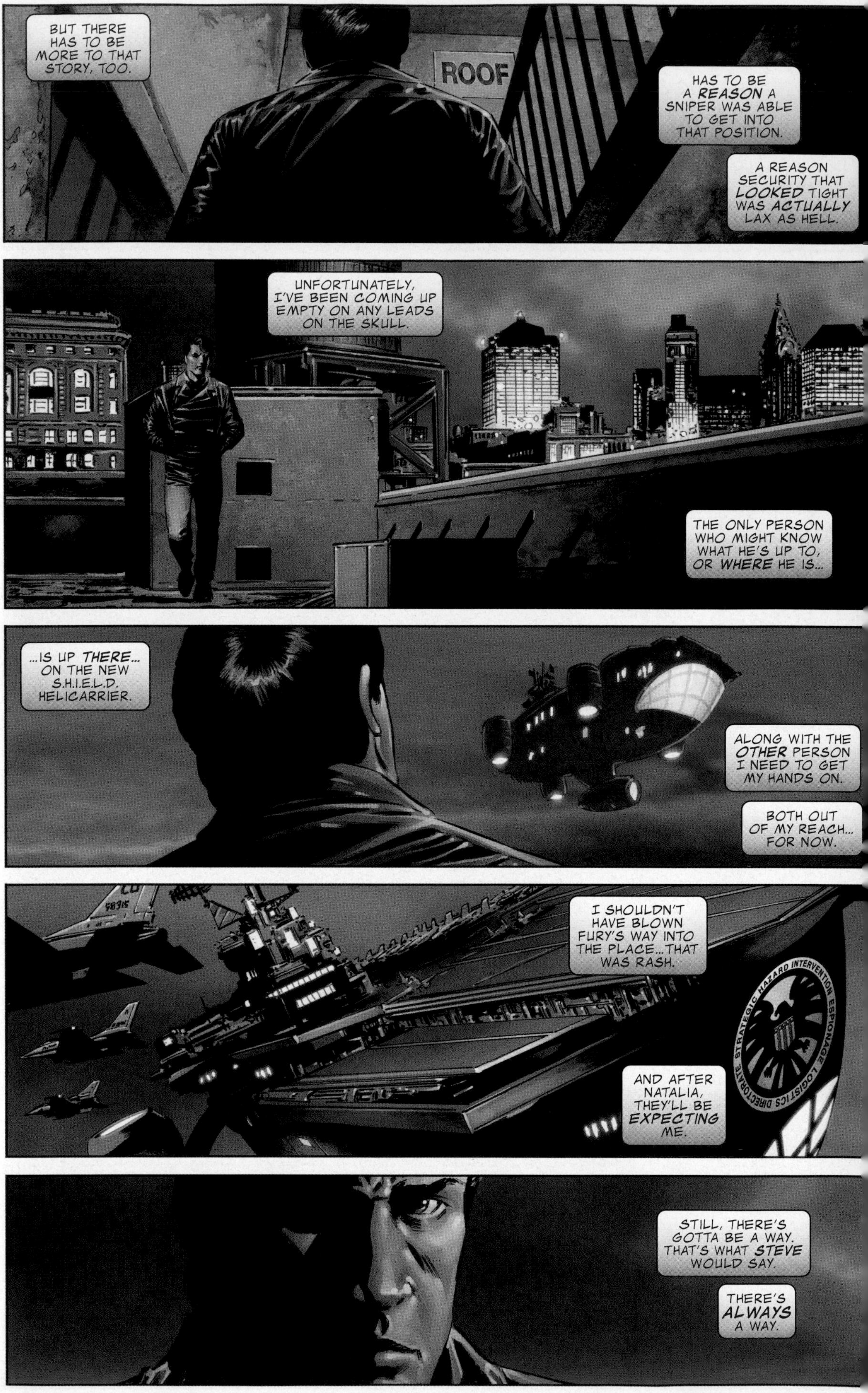
BUT THERE HAS TO BE MORE TO THAT STORY, TOO.
ROOF
HAS TO BE A REASON A SNIPER WAS ABLE TO GET INTO THAT POSITION.
A REASON SECURITY THAT LOOKED TIGHT WAS ACTUALLY LAX AS HELL.
UNFORTUNATELY, I'VE BEEN COMING UP EMPTY ON ANY LEADS ON THE SKULL.
THE ONLY PERSON WHO MIGHT KNOW WHAT HE'S UP TO, OR WHERE HE IS...
...IS UP THERE... ON THE NEW S.H.I.E.L.D. HELICARRIER.
ALONG WITH THE OTHER PERSON I NEED TO GET MY HANDS ON.
BOTH OUT OF MY REACH... FOR NOW.
I SHOULDN'T HAVE BLOWN FURY'S WAY INTO THE PLACE...THAT WAS RASH.
STRATEGIC HAZARD INTERVENTION ESPIONAGE LOGISTICS DIRECTORATE
AND AFTER NATALIA, THEY'LL BE EXPECTING ME.
STILL, THERE'S GOTTA BE A WAY. THAT'S WHAT STEVE WOULD SAY.
THERE'S ALWAYS A WAY.

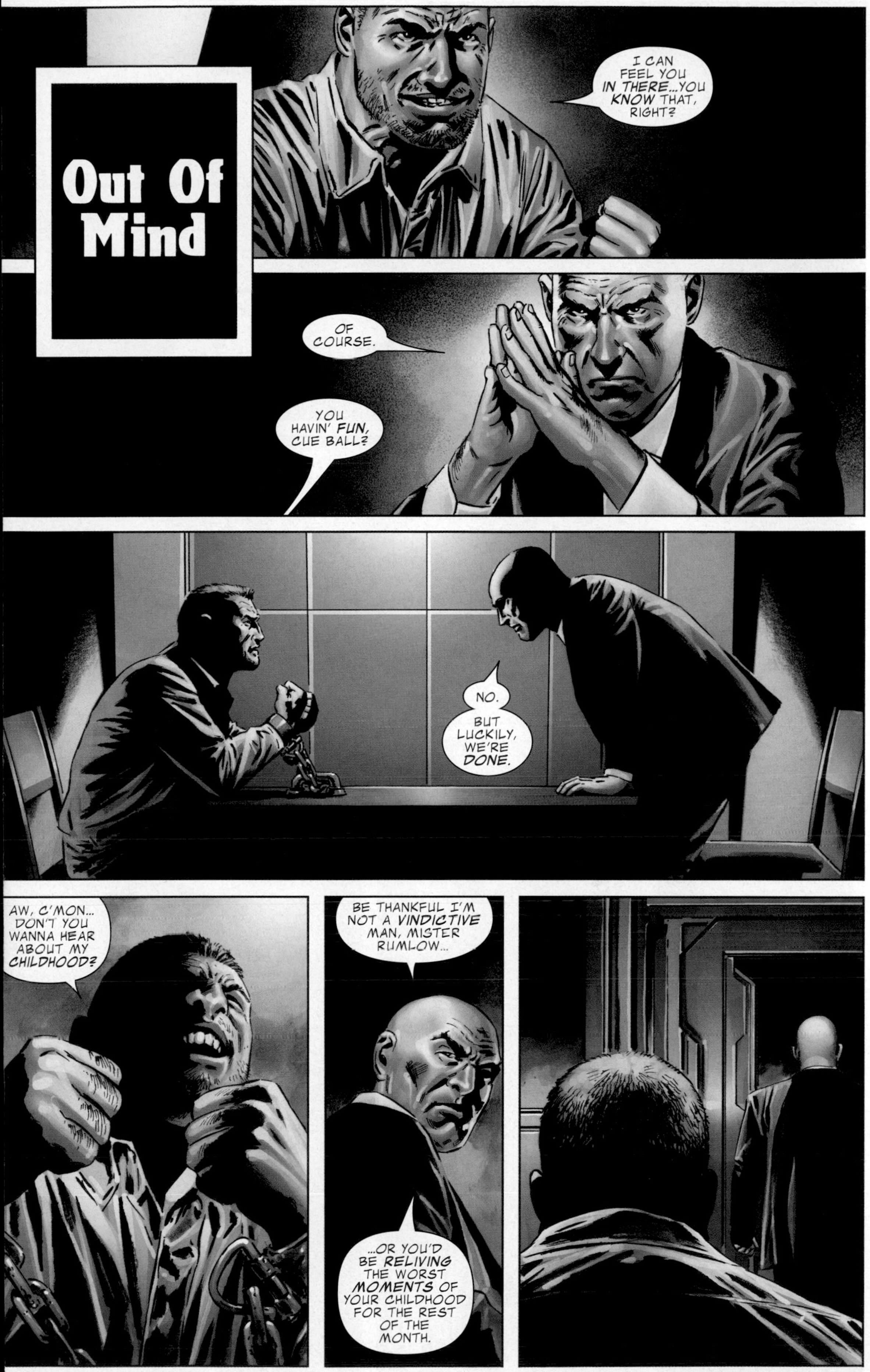
Out Of Mind
I CAN FEEL YOU IN THERE...YOU KNOW THAT, RIGHT?
OF COURSE.
YOU HAVIN' FUN, CUE BALL?
NO.
BUT LUCKILY, WE'RE DONE.
AW, C'MON... DON'T YOU WANNA HEAR ABOUT MY CHILDHOOD?
BE THANKFUL I'M NOT A VINDICTIVE MAN, MISTER RUMLOW...
...OR YOU'D BE RELIVING THE WORST MOMENTS OF YOUR CHILDHOOD FOR THE REST OF THE MONTH.

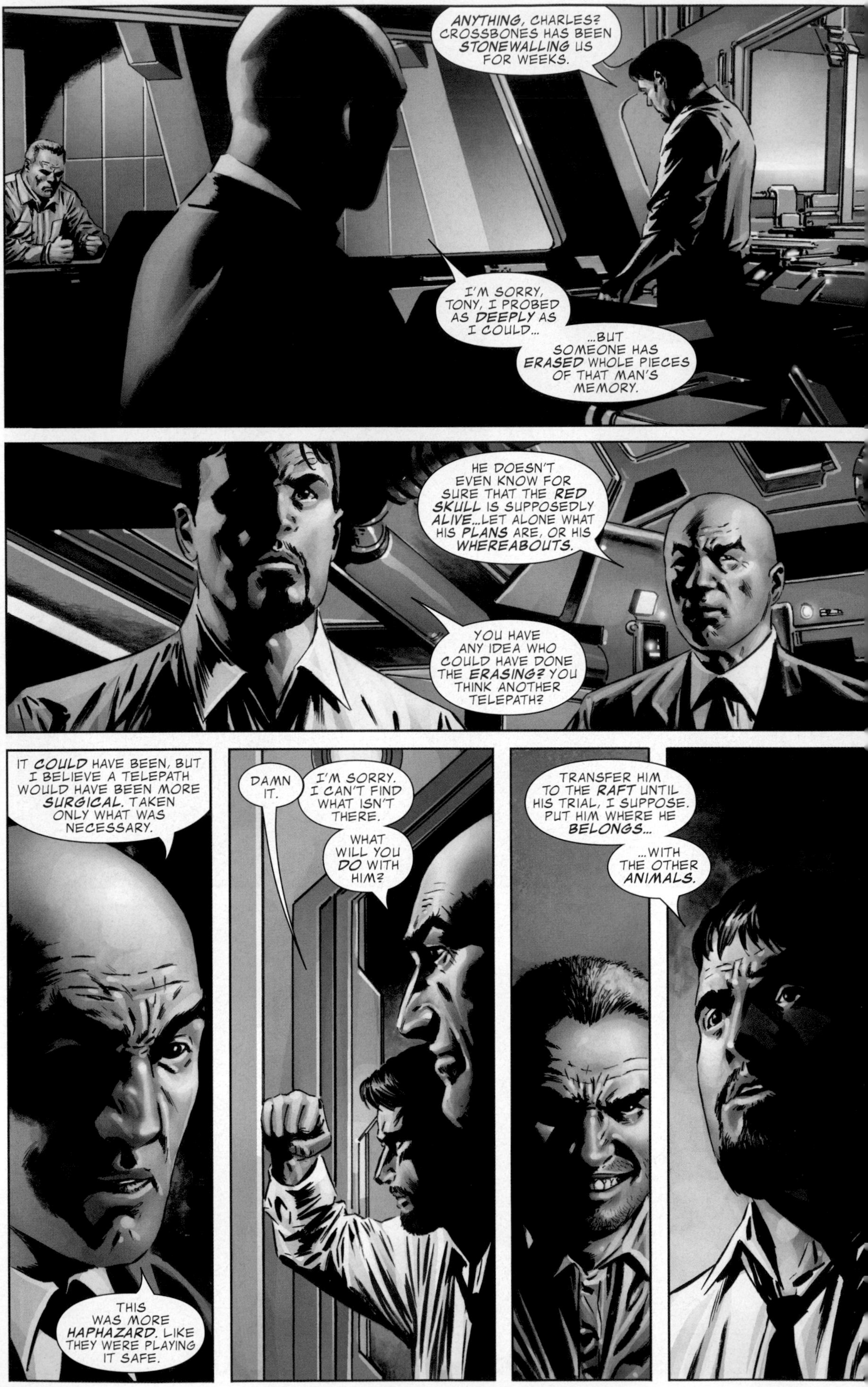

ANYTHING, CHARLES? CROSSBONES HAS BEEN STONEWALLING US FOR WEEKS.
I'M SORRY, TONY, I PROBED AS DEEPLY AS I COULD...
...BUT SOMEONE HAS ERASED WHOLE PIECES OF THAT MAN'S MEMORY.
HE DOESN'T EVEN KNOW FOR SURE THAT THE RED SKULL IS SUPPOSEDLY ALIVE...LET ALONE WHAT HIS PLANS ARE, OR HIS WHEREABOUTS.
YOU HAVE ANY IDEA WHO COULD HAVE DONE THE ERASING? YOU THINK ANOTHER TELEPATH?
IT COULD HAVE BEEN, BUT I BELIEVE A TELEPATH WOULD HAVE BEEN MORE SURGICAL. TAKEN ONLY WHAT WAS NECESSARY.
THIS WAS MORE HAPHAZARD. LIKE THEY WERE PLAYING IT SAFE.
DAMN IT.
I'M SORRY. I CAN'T FIND WHAT ISN'T THERE.
WHAT WILL YOU DO WITH HIM?
TRANSFER HIM TO THE RAFT UNTIL HIS TRIAL, I SUPPOSE. PUT HIM WHERE HE BELONGS...
...WITH THE OTHER ANIMALS.

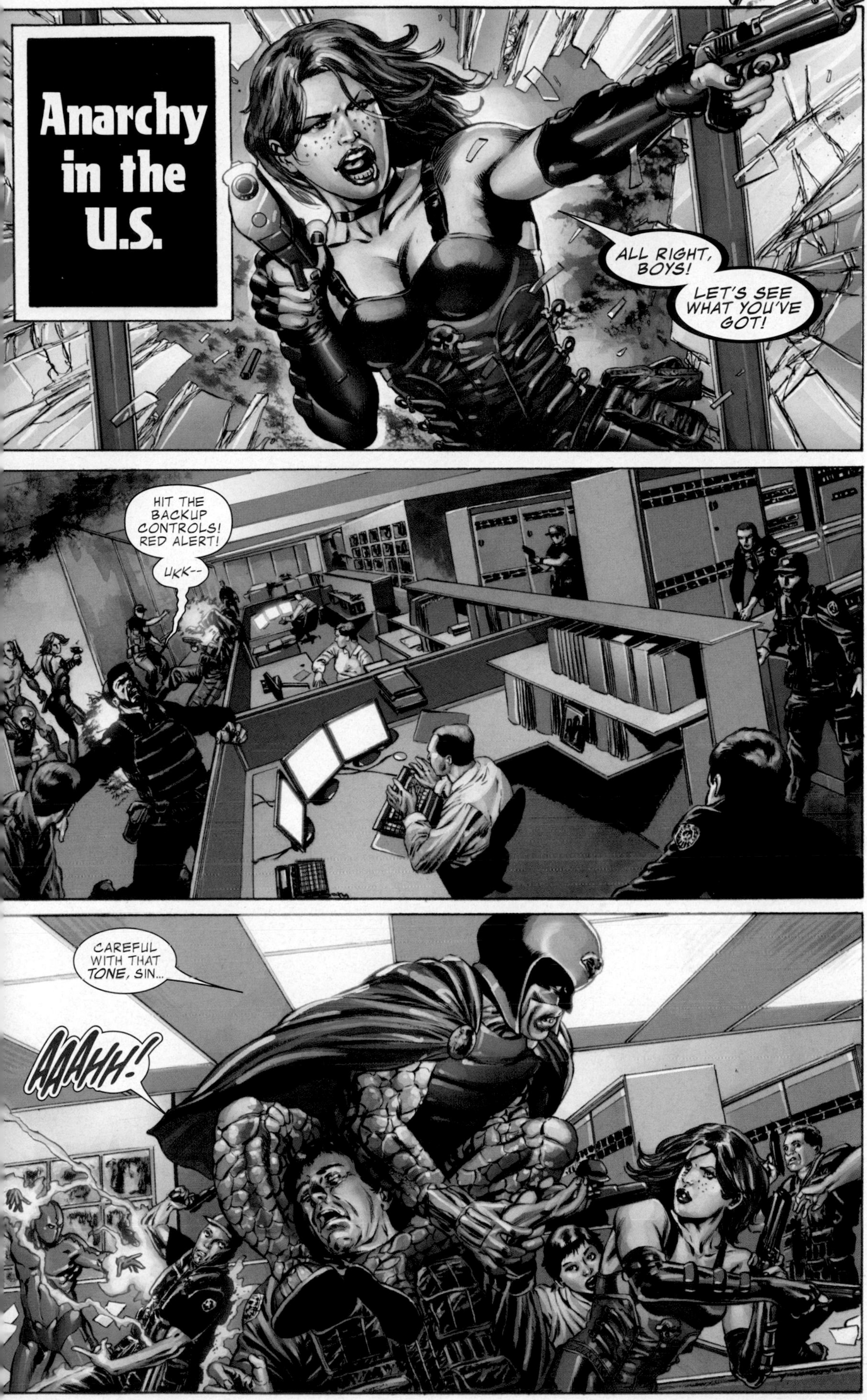
Anarchy in the U.S.
ALL RIGHT, BOYS!
LET'S SEE WHAT YOU'VE GOT!
HIT THE BACKUP CONTROLS! RED ALERT!
UKK--
CAREFUL WITH THAT TONE, SIN...
AAAHH!

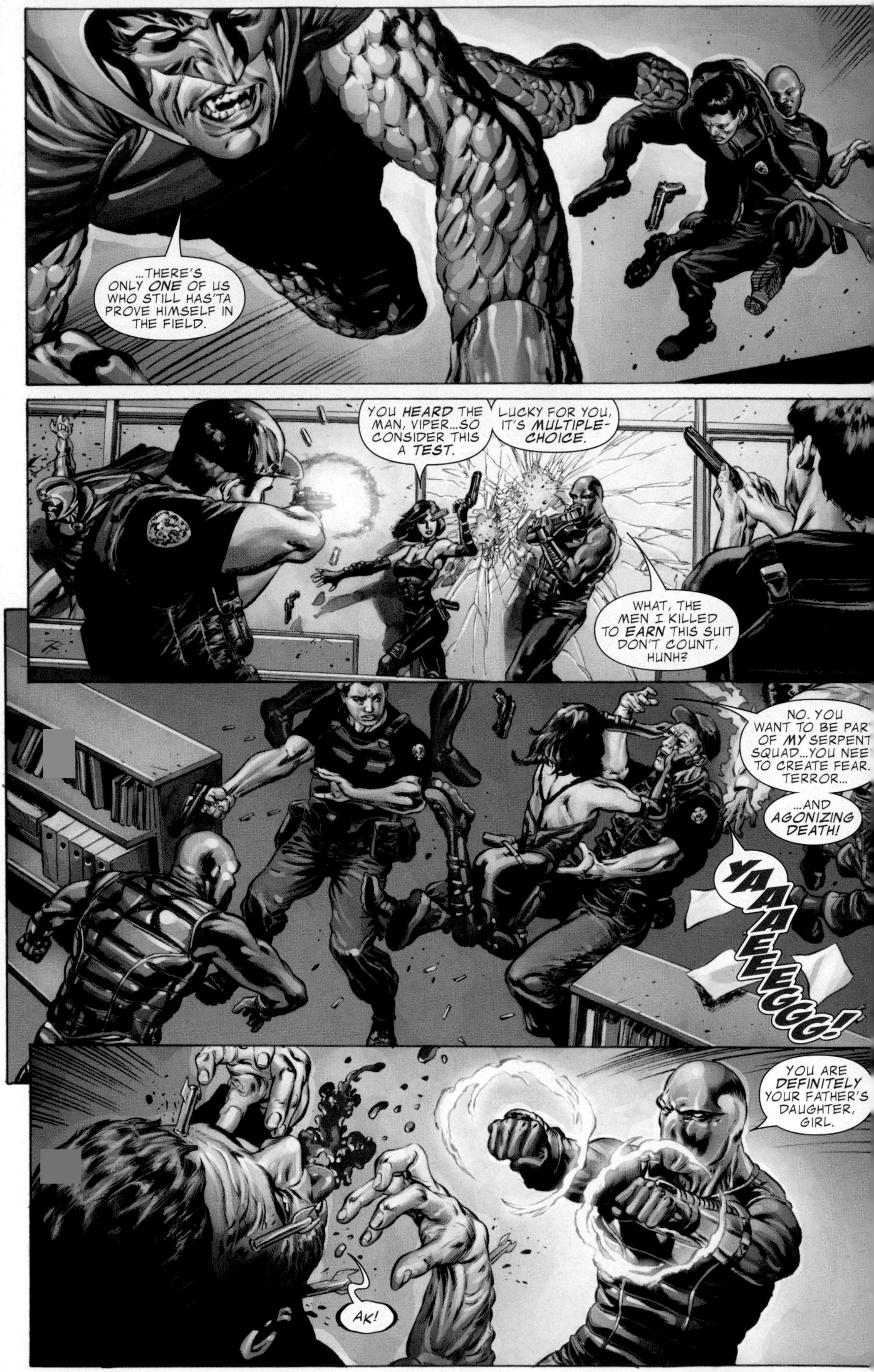
...THERE'S ONLY ONE OF US WHO STILL HAS'TA PROVE HIMSELF IN THE FIELD.
YOU HEARD THE MAN, VIPER...SO CONSIDER THIS A TEST.
LUCKY FOR YOU, IT'S MULTIPLE-CHOICE.
WHAT, THE MEN I KILLED TO EARN THIS SUIT DON'T COUNT, HUNH?
NO. YOU WANT TO BE PAR OF MY SERPENT SQUAD...YOU NEE TO CREATE FEAR. TERROR...
...AND AGONIZING DEATH!
YAAAEEEGGG!
YOU ARE DEFINITELY YOUR FATHER'S DAUGHTER, GIRL.
AK!

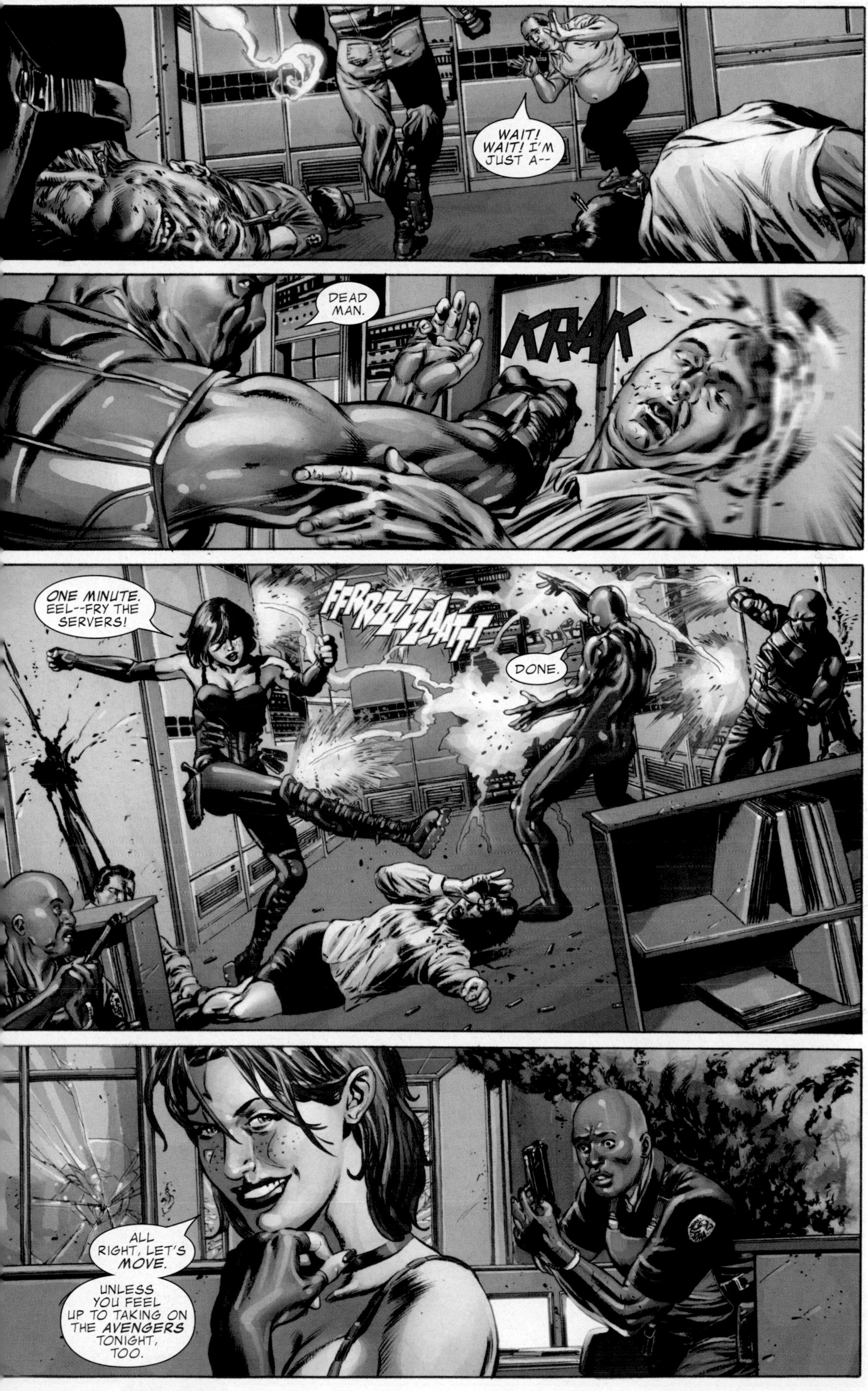
WAIT! WAIT! I'M JUST A--
DEAD MAN.
KRAK
ONE MINUTE. EEL--FRY THE SERVERS!
FFRRZZZZZAATT
DONE.
ALL RIGHT, LET'S *MOVE*.
UNLESS YOU FEEL UP TO TAKING ON THE *AVENGERS* TONIGHT, TOO.

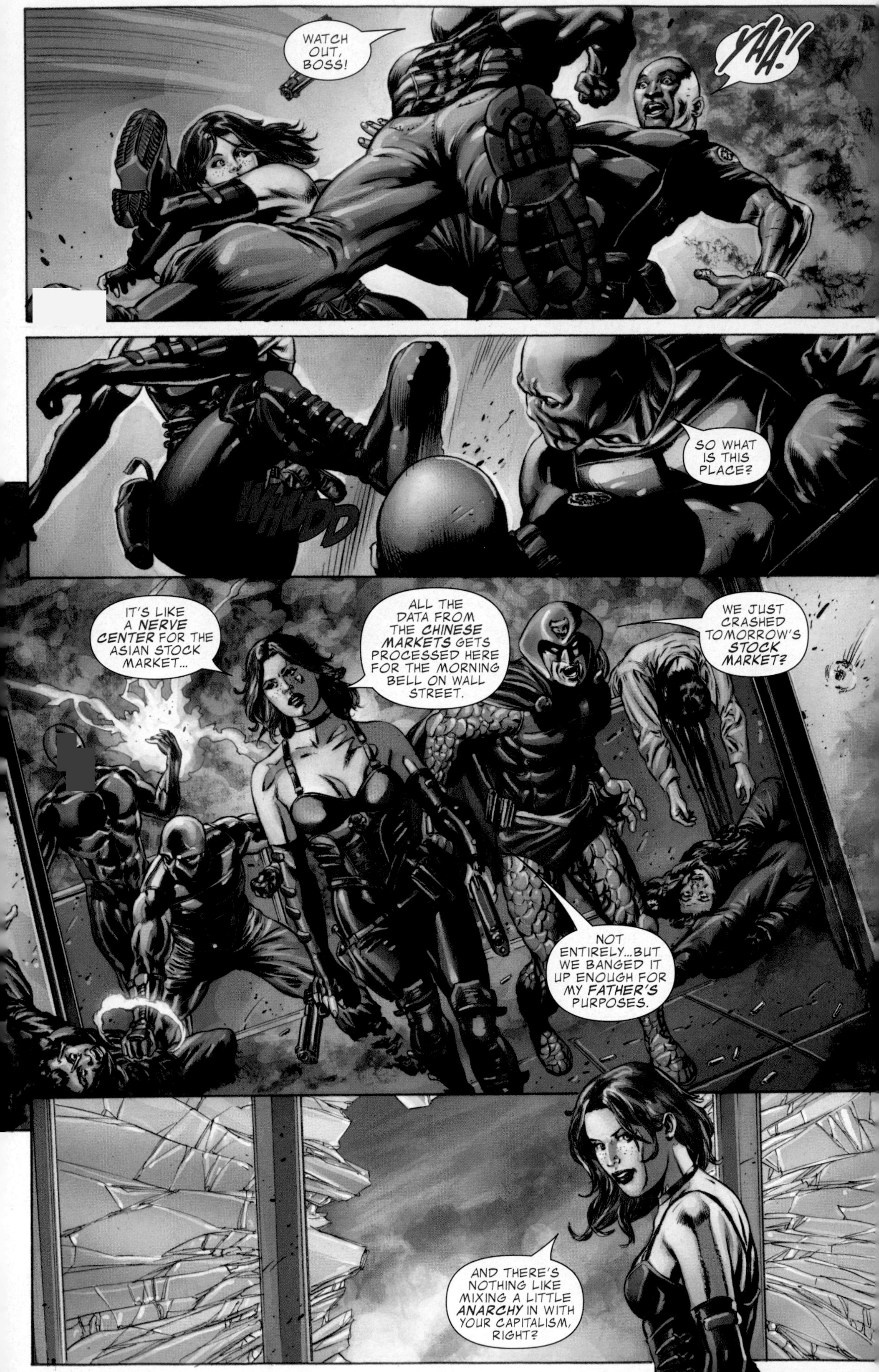
WATCH OUT, BOSS!
YAA!
WHUDD
SO WHAT IS THIS PLACE?
IT'S LIKE A **NERVE CENTER** FOR THE ASIAN STOCK MARKET...
ALL THE DATA FROM THE **CHINESE MARKETS** GETS PROCESSED HERE FOR THE MORNING BELL ON WALL STREET.
WE JUST CRASHED TOMORROW'S **STOCK MARKET**?
NOT ENTIRELY...BUT WE BANGED IT UP ENOUGH FOR MY **FATHER'S** PURPOSES.
AND THERE'S NOTHING LIKE MIXING A LITTLE **ANARCHY** IN WITH YOUR CAPITALISM, RIGHT?

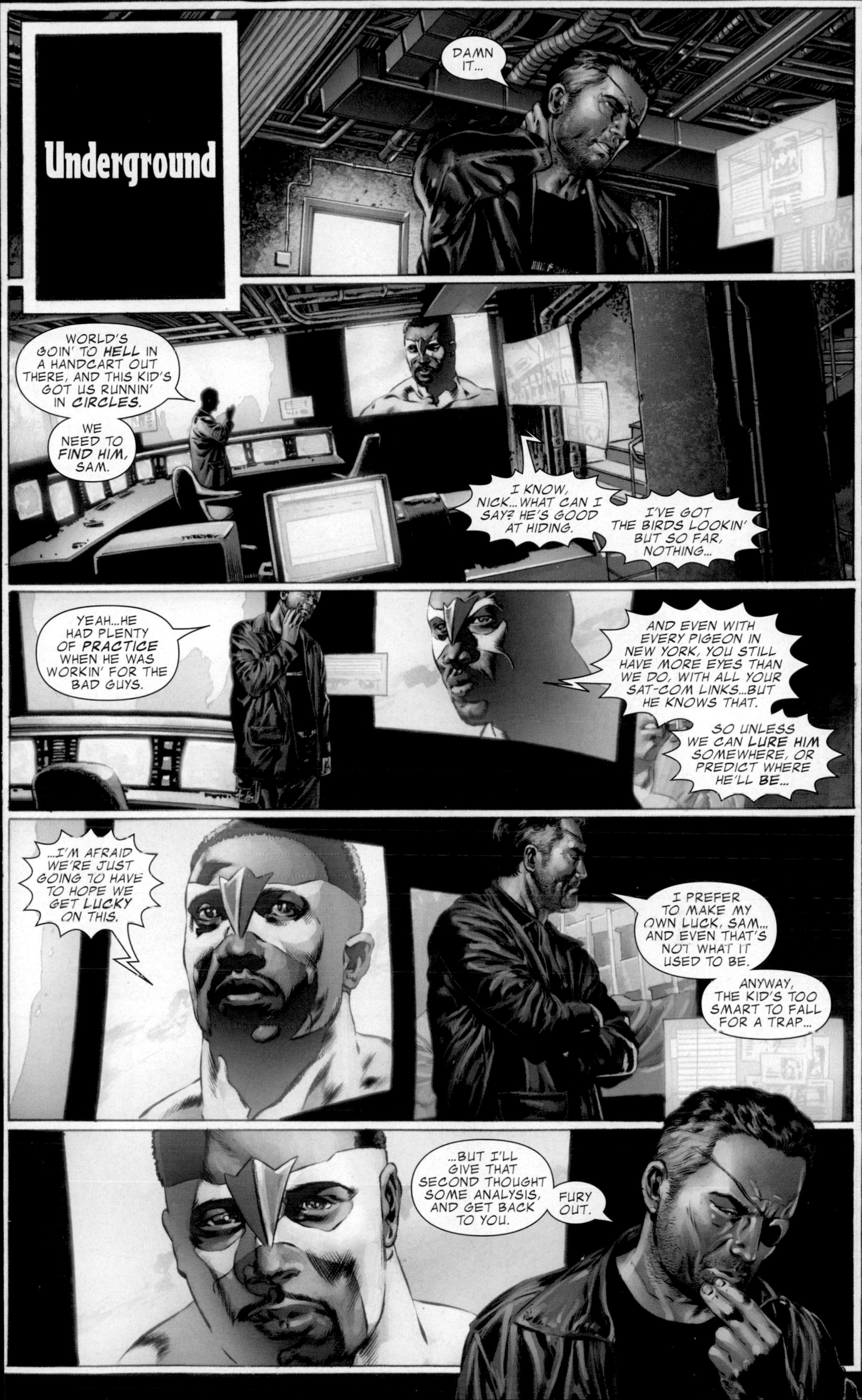

Underground
DAMN IT...
WORLD'S GOIN' TO HELL IN A HANDCART OUT THERE, AND THIS KID'S GOT US RUNNIN' IN CIRCLES.
WE NEED TO FIND HIM, SAM.
I KNOW, NICK...WHAT CAN I SAY? HE'S GOOD AT HIDING.
I'VE GOT THE BIRDS LOOKIN' BUT SO FAR, NOTHING...
YEAH...HE HAD PLENTY OF PRACTICE WHEN HE WAS WORKIN' FOR THE BAD GUYS.
AND EVEN WITH EVERY PIGEON IN NEW YORK, YOU STILL HAVE MORE EYES THAN WE DO, WITH ALL YOUR SAT-COM LINKS...BUT HE KNOWS THAT.
SO UNLESS WE CAN LURE HIM SOMEWHERE, OR PREDICT WHERE HE'LL BE...
...I'M AFRAID WE'RE JUST GOING TO HAVE TO HOPE WE GET LUCKY ON THIS.
I PREFER TO MAKE MY OWN LUCK, SAM... AND EVEN THAT'S NOT WHAT IT USED TO BE.
ANYWAY, THE KID'S TOO SMART TO FALL FOR A TRAP...
...BUT I'LL GIVE THAT SECOND THOUGHT SOME ANALYSIS, AND GET BACK TO YOU.
FURY OUT.

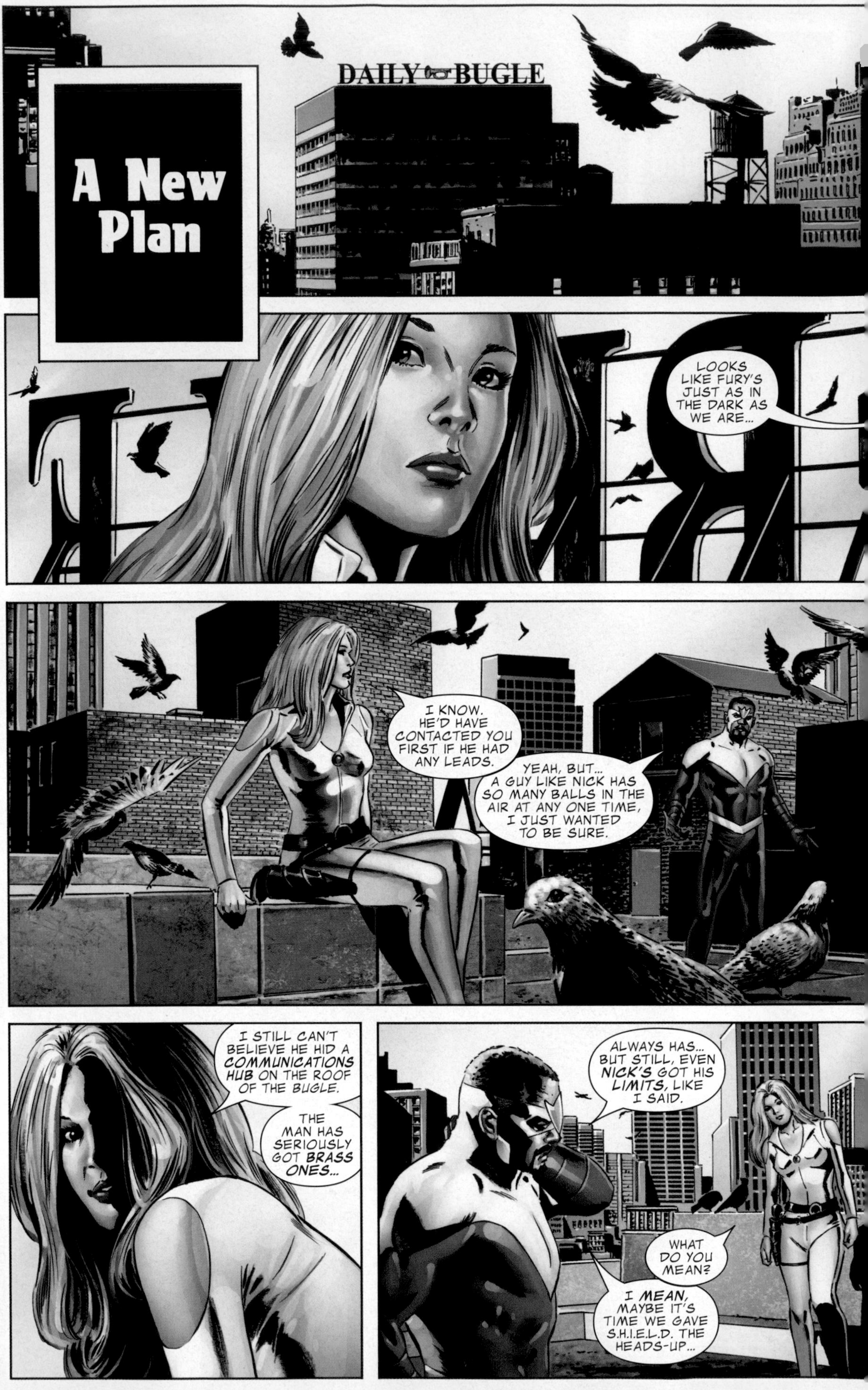
DAILY BUGLE
A New Plan
LOOKS LIKE FURY'S JUST AS IN THE DARK AS WE ARE...
I KNOW. HE'D HAVE CONTACTED YOU FIRST IF HE HAD ANY LEADS.
YEAH, BUT... A GUY LIKE NICK HAS SO MANY BALLS IN THE AIR AT ANY ONE TIME, I JUST WANTED TO BE SURE.
I STILL CAN'T BELIEVE HE HID A COMMUNICATIONS HUB ON THE ROOF OF THE BUGLE.
THE MAN HAS SERIOUSLY GOT BRASS ONES...
ALWAYS HAS... BUT STILL, EVEN NICK'S GOT HIS LIMITS, LIKE I SAID.
WHAT DO YOU MEAN?
I MEAN, MAYBE IT'S TIME WE GAVE S.H.I.E.L.D. THE HEADS-UP...

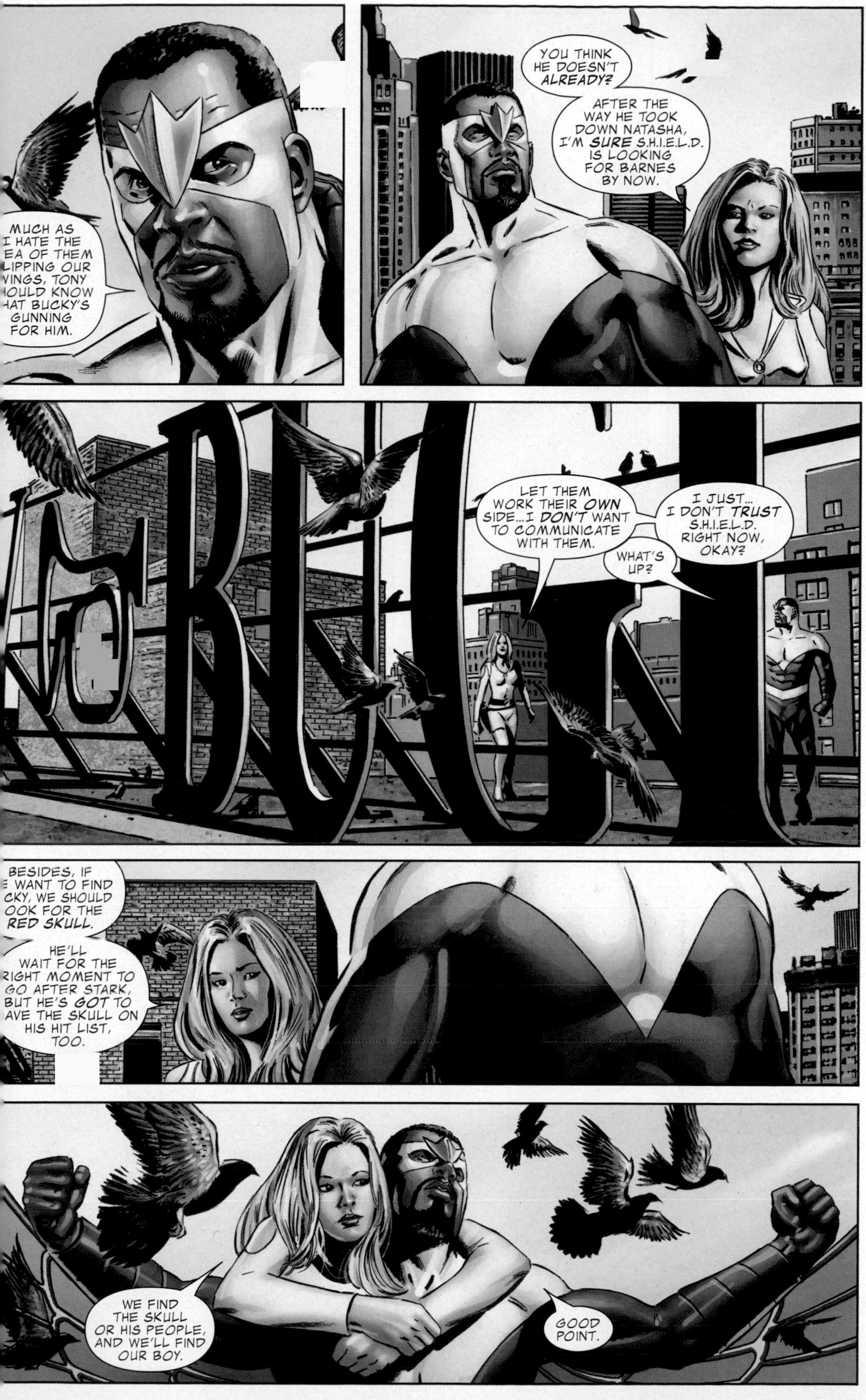
MUCH AS I HATE THE EA OF THEM LIPPING OUR VINGS, TONY HOULD KNOW HAT BUCKY'S GUNNING FOR HIM.
YOU THINK HE DOESN'T ALREADY?
AFTER THE WAY HE TOOK DOWN NATASHA, I'M SURE S.H.I.E.L.D. IS LOOKING FOR BARNES BY NOW.
I JUST... I DON'T TRUST S.H.I.E.L.D. RIGHT NOW, OKAY?
WHAT'S UP?
LET THEM WORK THEIR OWN SIDE...I DON'T WANT TO COMMUNICATE WITH THEM.
BESIDES, IF E WANT TO FIND CKY, WE SHOULD OOK FOR THE RED SKULL.
HE'LL WAIT FOR THE RIGHT MOMENT TO GO AFTER STARK, BUT HE'S GOT TO AVE THE SKULL ON HIS HIT LIST, TOO.
WE FIND THE SKULL OR HIS PEOPLE, AND WE'LL FIND OUR BOY.
GOOD POINT.

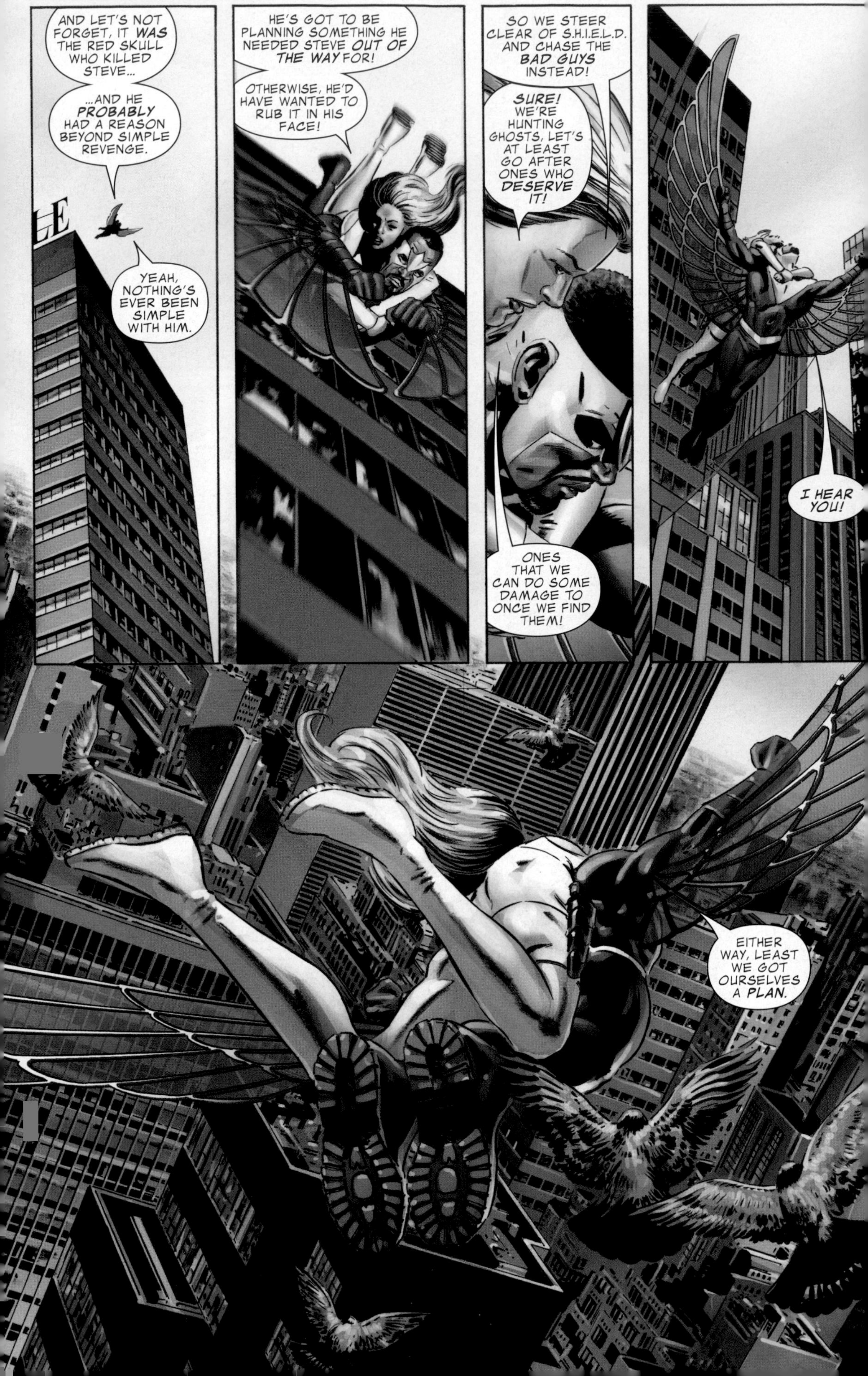
AND LET'S NOT FORGET, IT WAS THE RED SKULL WHO KILLED STEVE...
...AND HE PROBABLY HAD A REASON BEYOND SIMPLE REVENGE.
YEAH, NOTHING'S EVER BEEN SIMPLE WITH HIM.
HE'S GOT TO BE PLANNING SOMETHING HE NEEDED STEVE OUT OF THE WAY FOR!
OTHERWISE, HE'D HAVE WANTED TO RUB IT IN HIS FACE!
SO WE STEER CLEAR OF S.H.I.E.L.D. AND CHASE THE BAD GUYS INSTEAD!
SURE! WE'RE HUNTING GHOSTS, LET'S AT LEAST GO AFTER ONES WHO DESERVE IT!
ONES THAT WE CAN DO SOME DAMAGE TO ONCE WE FIND THEM!
I HEAR YOU!
EITHER WAY, LEAST WE GOT OURSELVES A PLAN.

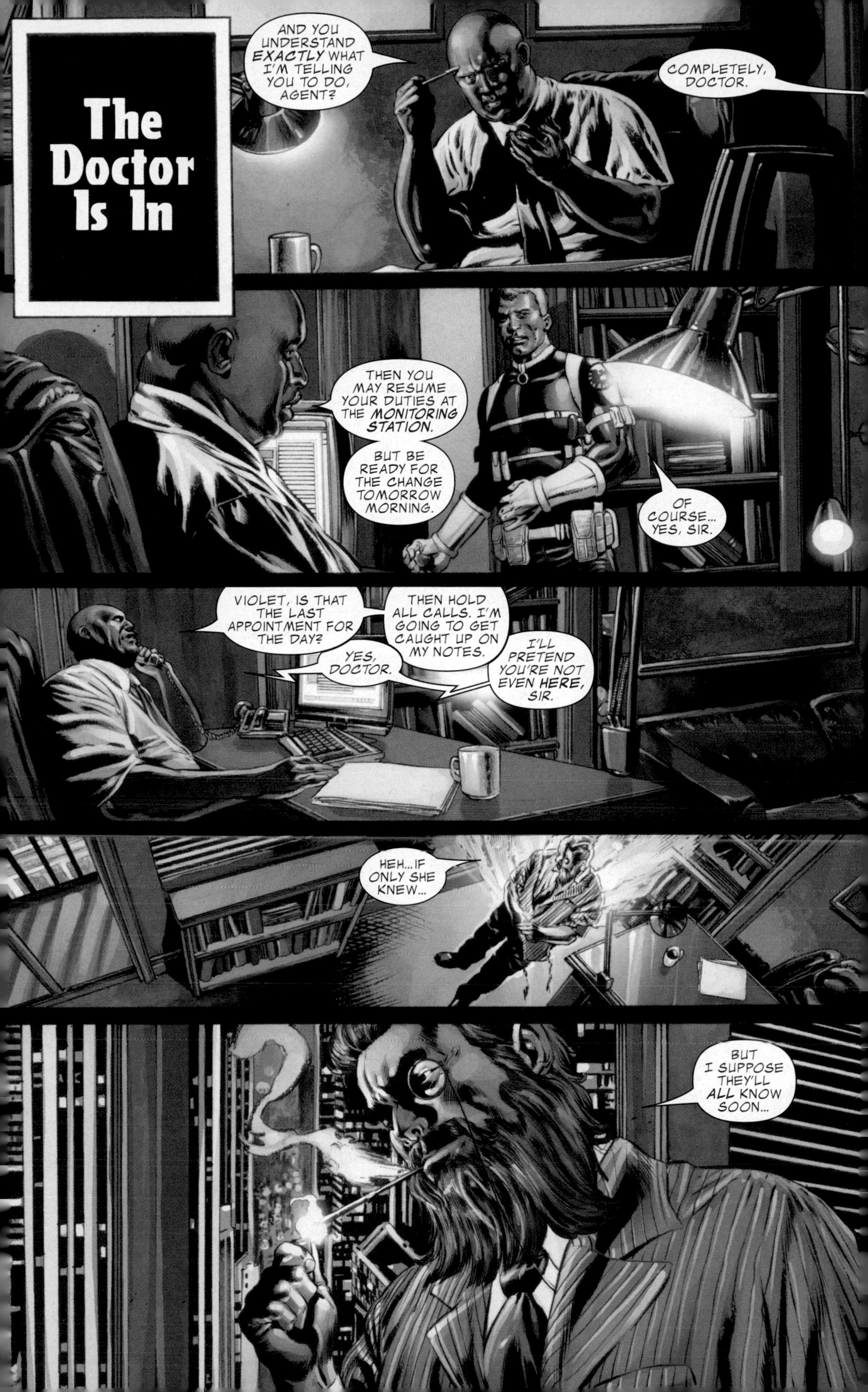

The Doctor Is In
AND YOU UNDERSTAND EXACTLY WHAT I'M TELLING YOU TO DO, AGENT?
COMPLETELY, DOCTOR.
THEN YOU MAY RESUME YOUR DUTIES AT THE MONITORING STATION.
BUT BE READY FOR THE CHANGE TOMORROW MORNING.
OF COURSE... YES, SIR.
VIOLET, IS THAT THE LAST APPOINTMENT FOR THE DAY?
YES, DOCTOR.
THEN HOLD ALL CALLS. I'M GOING TO GET CAUGHT UP ON MY NOTES.
I'LL PRETEND YOU'RE NOT EVEN HERE, SIR.
HEH...IF ONLY SHE KNEW...
BUT I SUPPOSE THEY'LL ALL KNOW SOON...

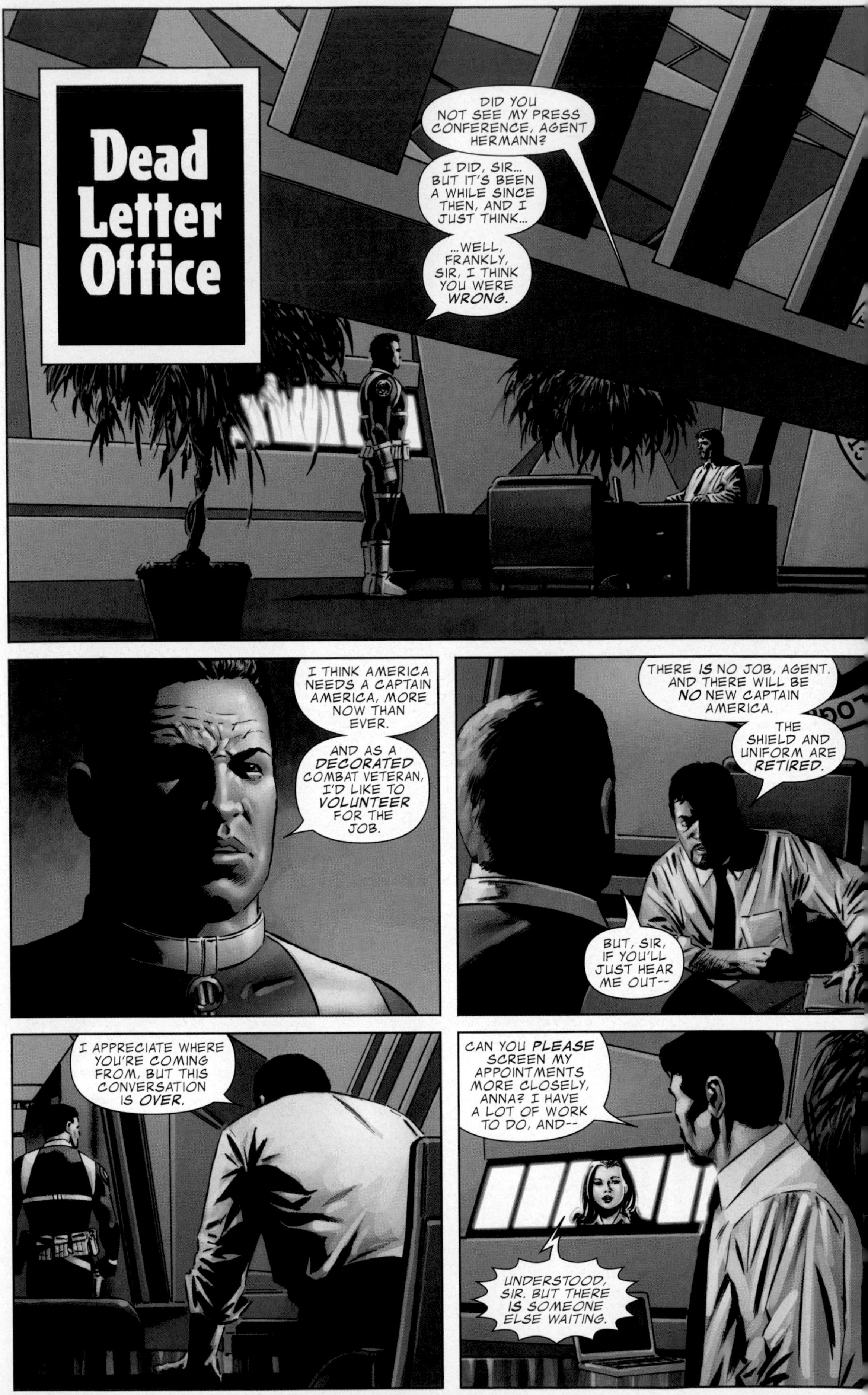
Dead Letter Office
DID YOU NOT SEE MY PRESS CONFERENCE, AGENT HERMANN?
I DID, SIR... BUT IT'S BEEN A WHILE SINCE THEN, AND I JUST THINK...
...WELL, FRANKLY, SIR, I THINK YOU WERE WRONG.
I THINK AMERICA NEEDS A CAPTAIN AMERICA, MORE NOW THAN EVER.
AND AS A DECORATED COMBAT VETERAN, I'D LIKE TO VOLUNTEER FOR THE JOB.
THERE IS NO JOB, AGENT. AND THERE WILL BE NO NEW CAPTAIN AMERICA.
THE SHIELD AND UNIFORM ARE RETIRED.
BUT, SIR, IF YOU'LL JUST HEAR ME OUT--
I APPRECIATE WHERE YOU'RE COMING FROM, BUT THIS CONVERSATION IS OVER.
CAN YOU PLEASE SCREEN MY APPOINTMENTS MORE CLOSELY, ANNA? I HAVE A LOT OF WORK TO DO, AND--
UNDERSTOOD, SIR. BUT THERE IS SOMEONE ELSE WAITING.

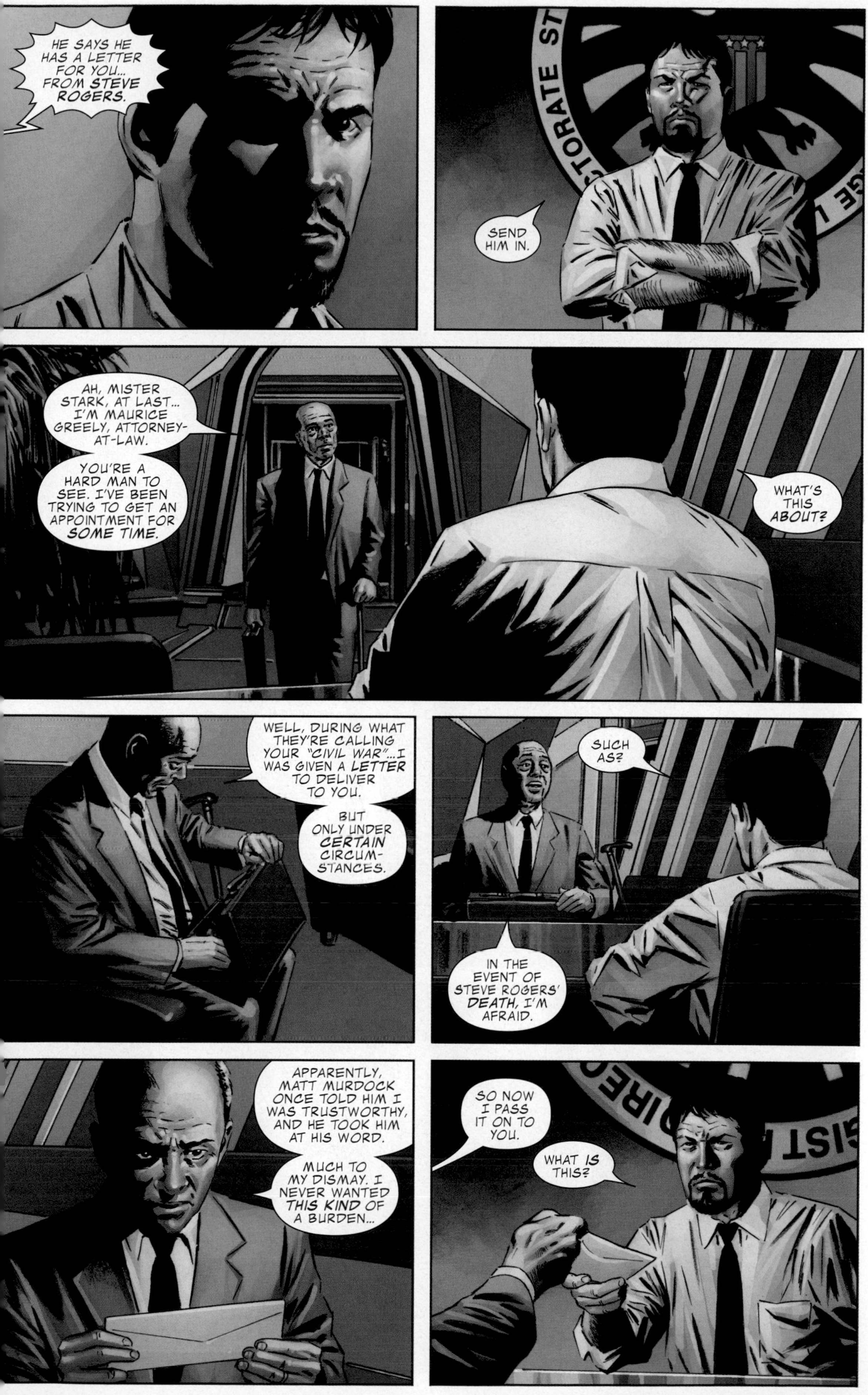
HE SAYS HE HAS A LETTER FOR YOU... FROM STEVE ROGERS.
SEND HIM IN.
AH, MISTER STARK, AT LAST... I'M MAURICE GREELY, ATTORNEY-AT-LAW.
YOU'RE A HARD MAN TO SEE. I'VE BEEN TRYING TO GET AN APPOINTMENT FOR SOME TIME.
WHAT'S THIS ABOUT?
WELL, DURING WHAT THEY'RE CALLING YOUR "CIVIL WAR"...I WAS GIVEN A LETTER TO DELIVER TO YOU.
BUT ONLY UNDER CERTAIN CIRCUM-STANCES.
SUCH AS?
IN THE EVENT OF STEVE ROGERS' DEATH, I'M AFRAID.
APPARENTLY, MATT MURDOCK ONCE TOLD HIM I WAS TRUSTWORTHY, AND HE TOOK HIM AT HIS WORD.
MUCH TO MY DISMAY. I NEVER WANTED THIS KIND OF A BURDEN...
SO NOW I PASS IT ON TO YOU.
WHAT IS THIS?

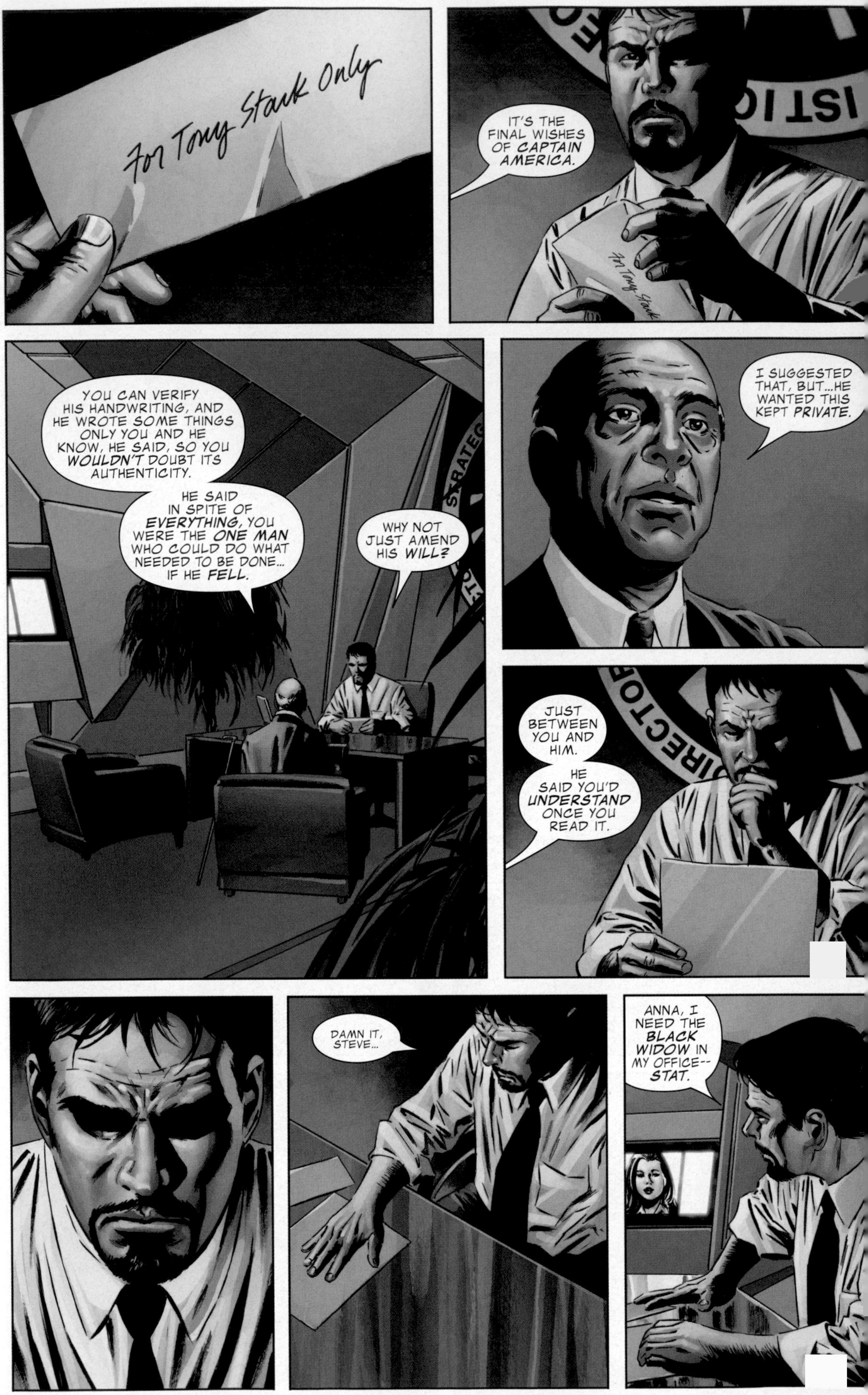
For Tony Stark Only
IT'S THE FINAL WISHES OF CAPTAIN AMERICA.
YOU CAN VERIFY HIS HANDWRITING, AND HE WROTE SOME THINGS ONLY YOU AND HE KNOW, HE SAID, SO YOU WOULDN'T DOUBT ITS AUTHENTICITY.
HE SAID IN SPITE OF EVERYTHING, YOU WERE THE ONE MAN WHO COULD DO WHAT NEEDED TO BE DONE... IF HE FELL.
WHY NOT JUST AMEND HIS WILL?
I SUGGESTED THAT, BUT...HE WANTED THIS KEPT PRIVATE.
JUST BETWEEN YOU AND HIM.
HE SAID YOU'D UNDERSTAND ONCE YOU READ IT.
DAMN IT, STEVE...
ANNA, I NEED THE BLACK WIDOW IN MY OFFICE-- STAT.

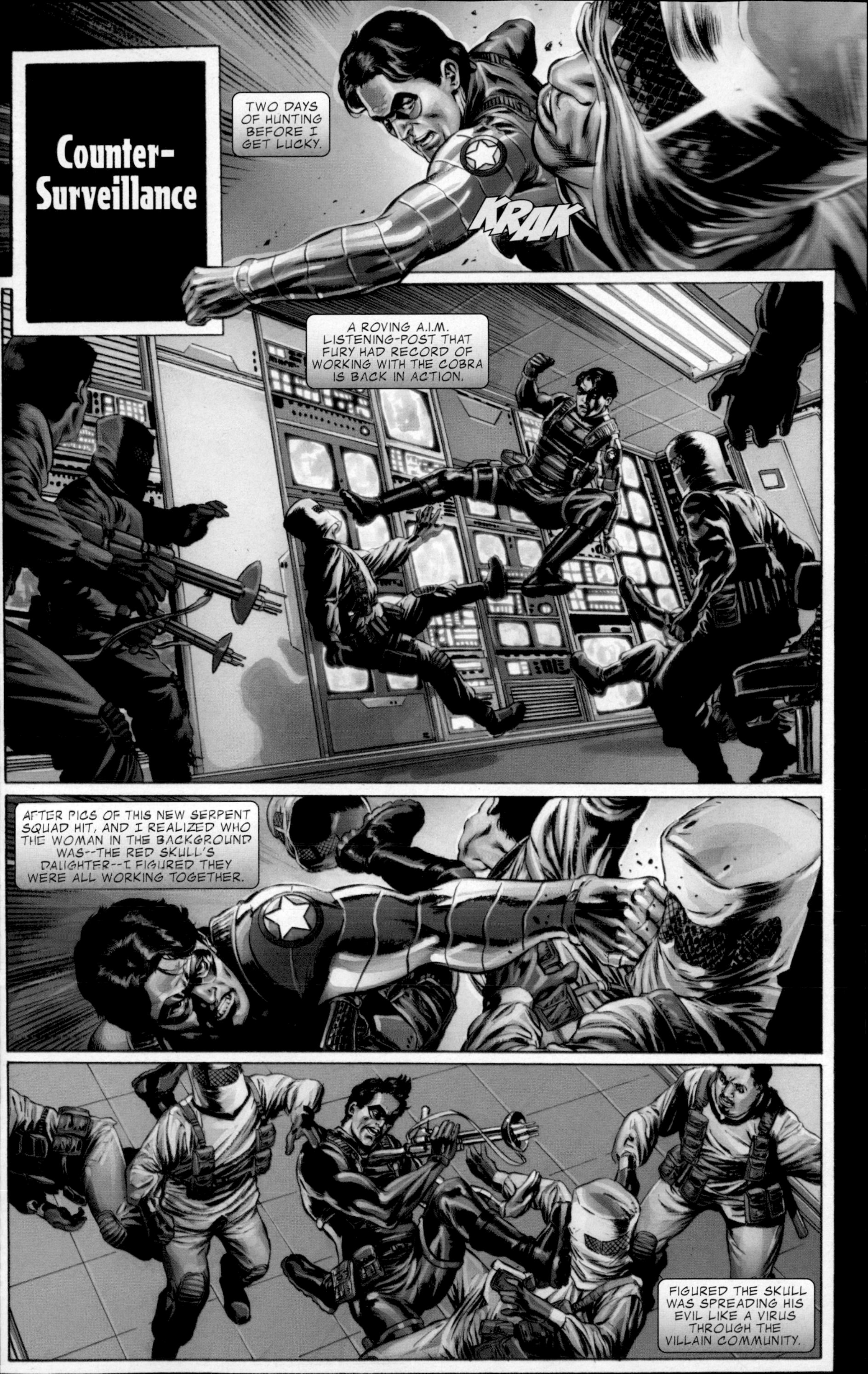
Counter-Surveillance
TWO DAYS OF HUNTING BEFORE I GET LUCKY.
KRAK
A ROVING A.I.M. LISTENING-POST THAT FURY HAD RECORD OF WORKING WITH THE COBRA IS BACK IN ACTION.
AFTER PICS OF THIS NEW SERPENT SQUAD HIT, AND I REALIZED WHO THE WOMAN IN THE BACKGROUND WAS--THE RED SKULL'S DAUGHTER--I FIGURED THEY WERE ALL WORKING TOGETHER.
FIGURED THE SKULL WAS SPREADING HIS EVIL LIKE A VIRUS THROUGH THE VILLAIN COMMUNITY.

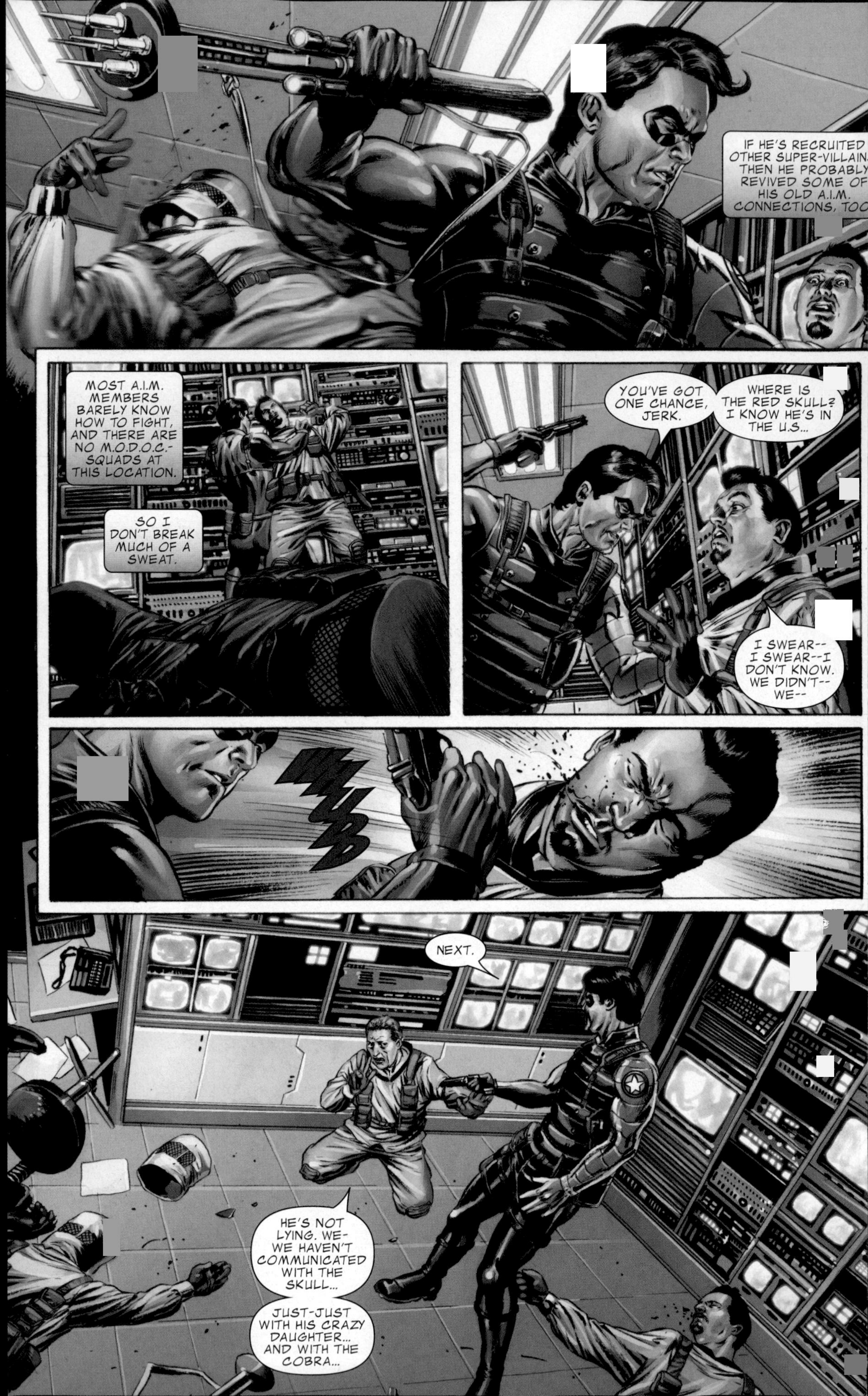
IF HE'S RECRUITED OTHER SUPER-VILLAINS, THEN HE PROBABLY REVIVED SOME OF HIS OLD A.I.M. CONNECTIONS, TOO.
MOST A.I.M. MEMBERS BARELY KNOW HOW TO FIGHT, AND THERE ARE NO M.O.D.O.C.-SQUADS AT THIS LOCATION.
SO I DON'T BREAK MUCH OF A SWEAT.
YOU'VE GOT ONE CHANCE, JERK.
WHERE IS THE RED SKULL? I KNOW HE'S IN THE U.S...
I SWEAR-- I SWEAR--I DON'T KNOW. WE DIDN'T-- WE--
NEXT.
HE'S NOT LYING. WE-WE HAVEN'T COMMUNICATED WITH THE SKULL...
JUST-JUST WITH HIS CRAZY DAUGHTER... AND WITH THE COBRA...

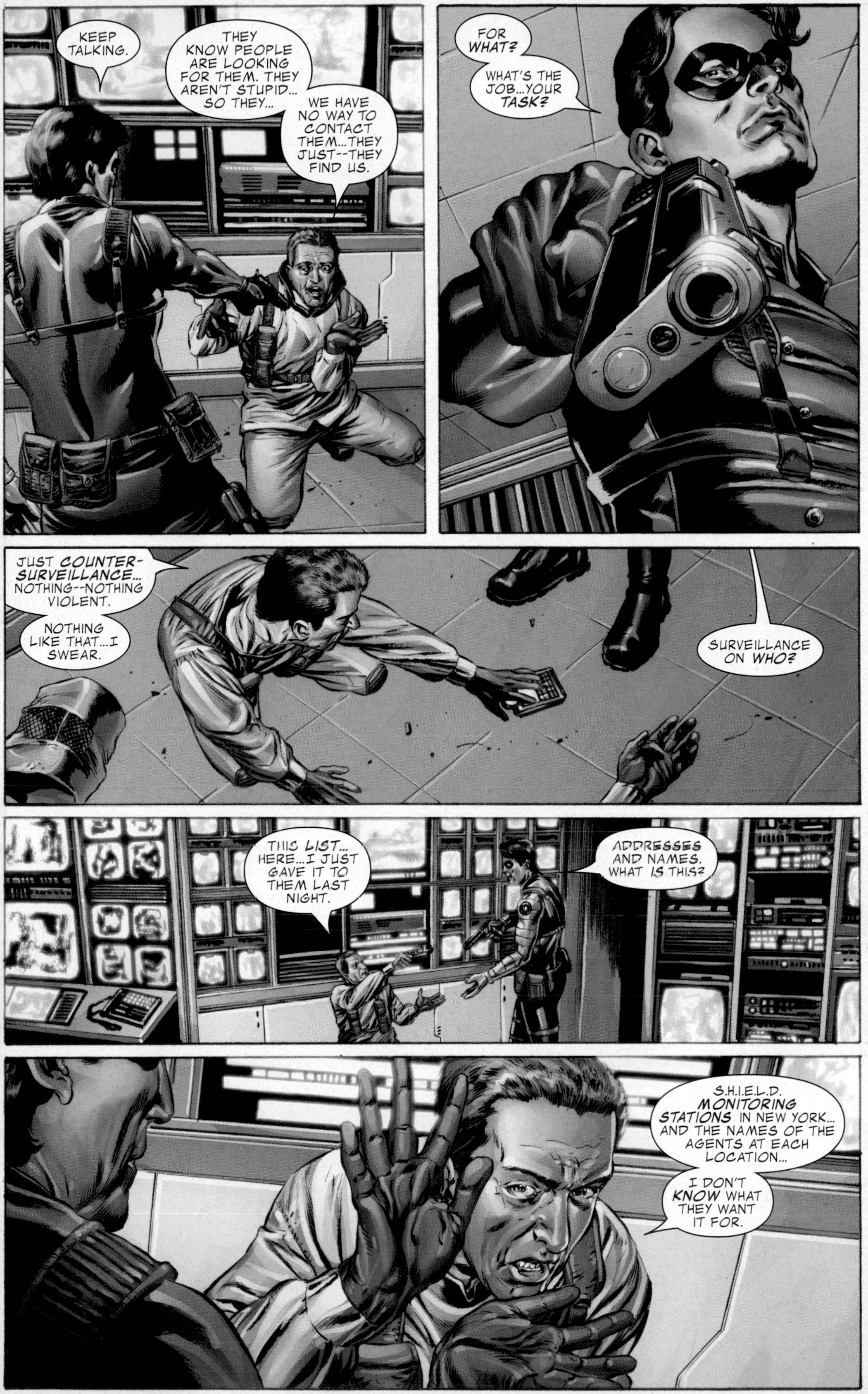
KEEP TALKING.
THEY KNOW PEOPLE ARE LOOKING FOR THEM. THEY AREN'T STUPID... SO THEY...
WE HAVE NO WAY TO CONTACT THEM...THEY JUST--THEY FIND US.
FOR WHAT?
WHAT'S THE JOB...YOUR TASK?
JUST COUNTER-SURVEILLANCE... NOTHING--NOTHING VIOLENT.
NOTHING LIKE THAT...I SWEAR.
SURVEILLANCE ON WHO?
THIS LIST... HERE...I JUST GAVE IT TO THEM LAST NIGHT.
ADDRESSES AND NAMES. WHAT IS THIS?
S.H.I.E.L.D. MONITORING STATIONS IN NEW YORK... AND THE NAMES OF THE AGENTS AT EACH LOCATION...
I DON'T KNOW WHAT THEY WANT IT FOR.

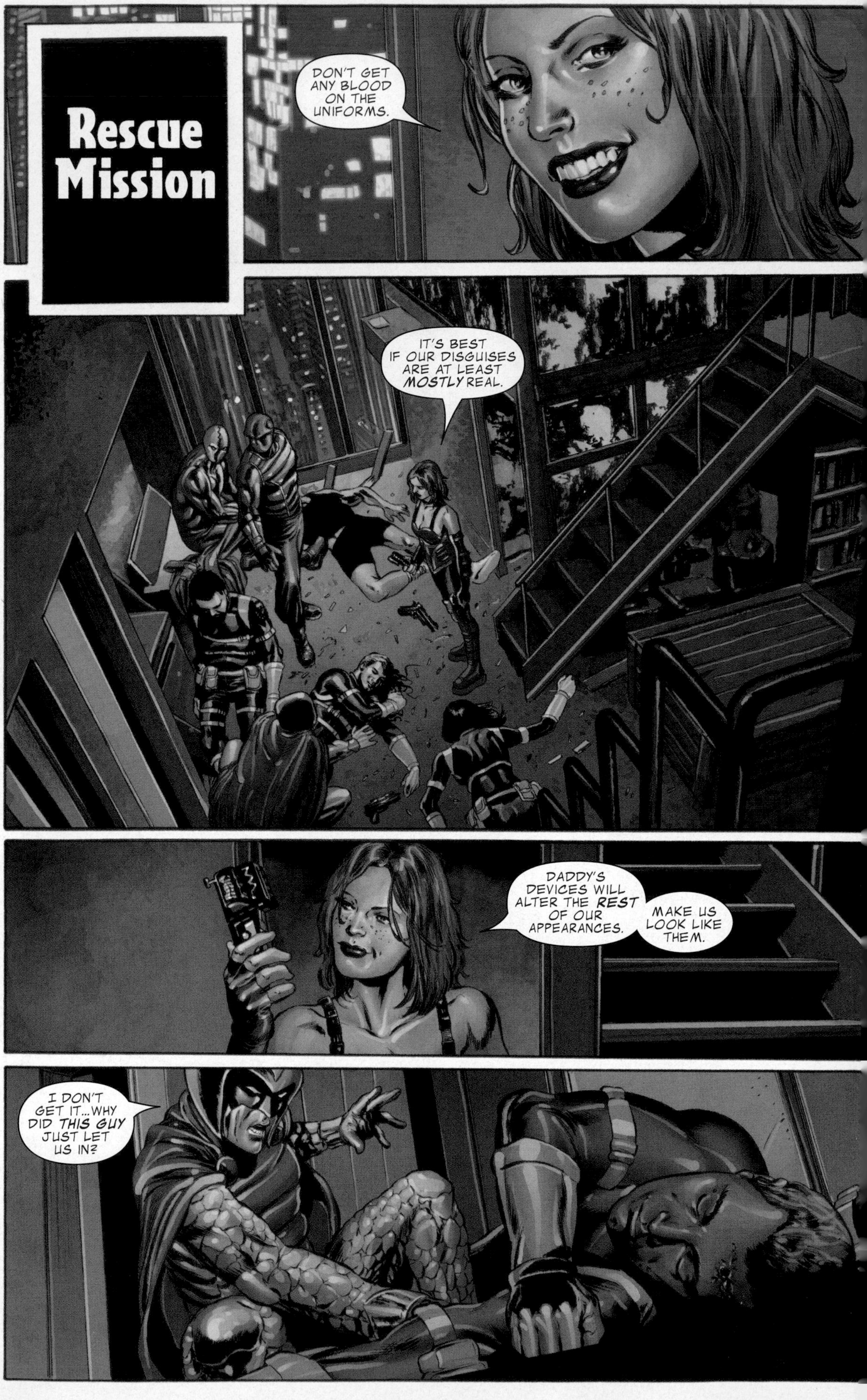

Rescue Mission
DON'T GET ANY BLOOD ON THE UNIFORMS.
IT'S BEST IF OUR DISGUISES ARE AT LEAST MOSTLY REAL.
DADDY'S DEVICES WILL ALTER THE REST OF OUR APPEARANCES.
MAKE US LOOK LIKE THEM.
I DON'T GET IT...WHY DID THIS GUY JUST LET US IN?

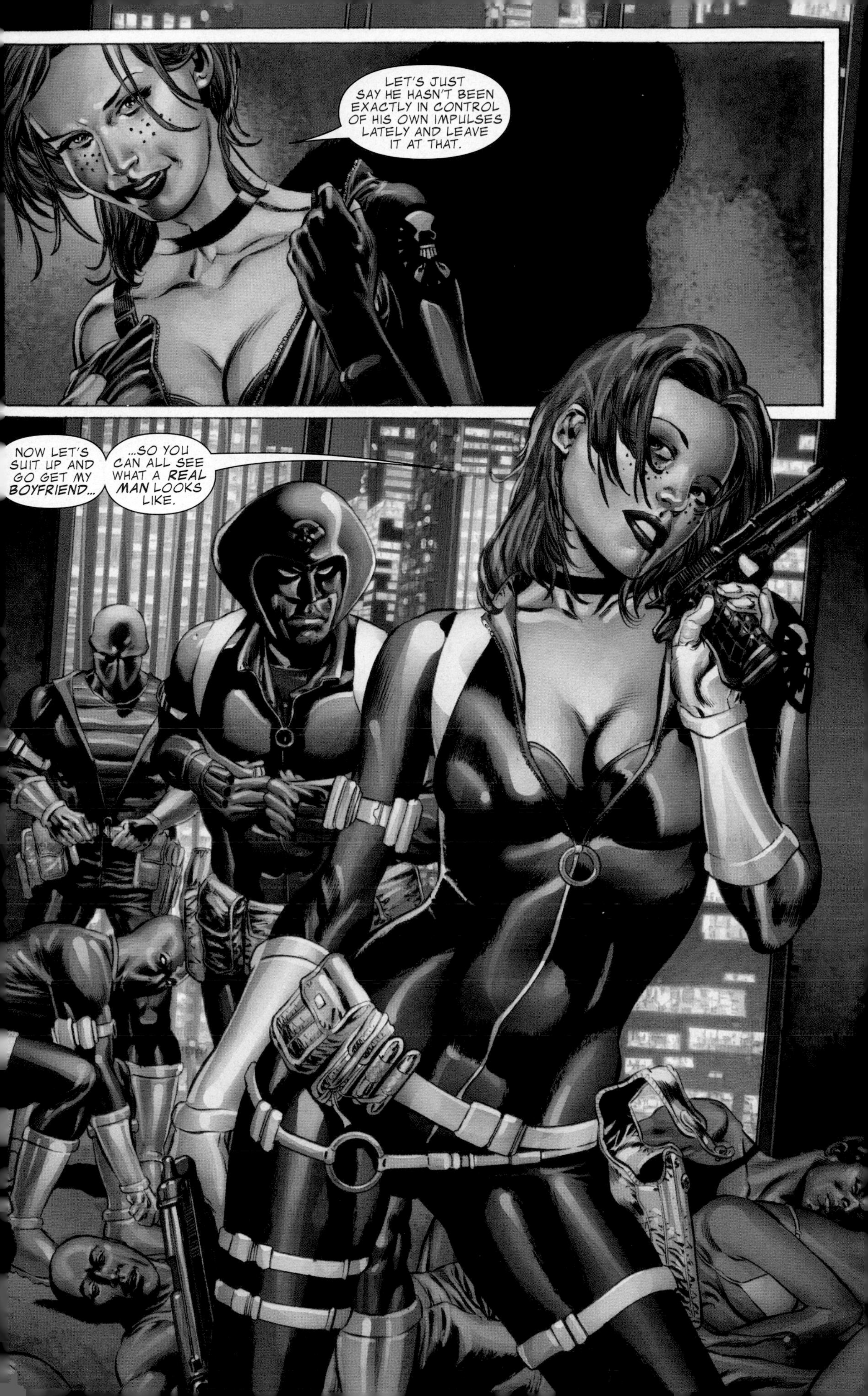
LET'S JUST SAY HE HASN'T BEEN EXACTLY IN CONTROL OF HIS OWN IMPULSES LATELY AND LEAVE IT AT THAT.
NOW LET'S SUIT UP AND GO GET MY **BOYFRIEND**...
...SO YOU CAN ALL SEE WHAT A **REAL MAN** LOOKS LIKE.

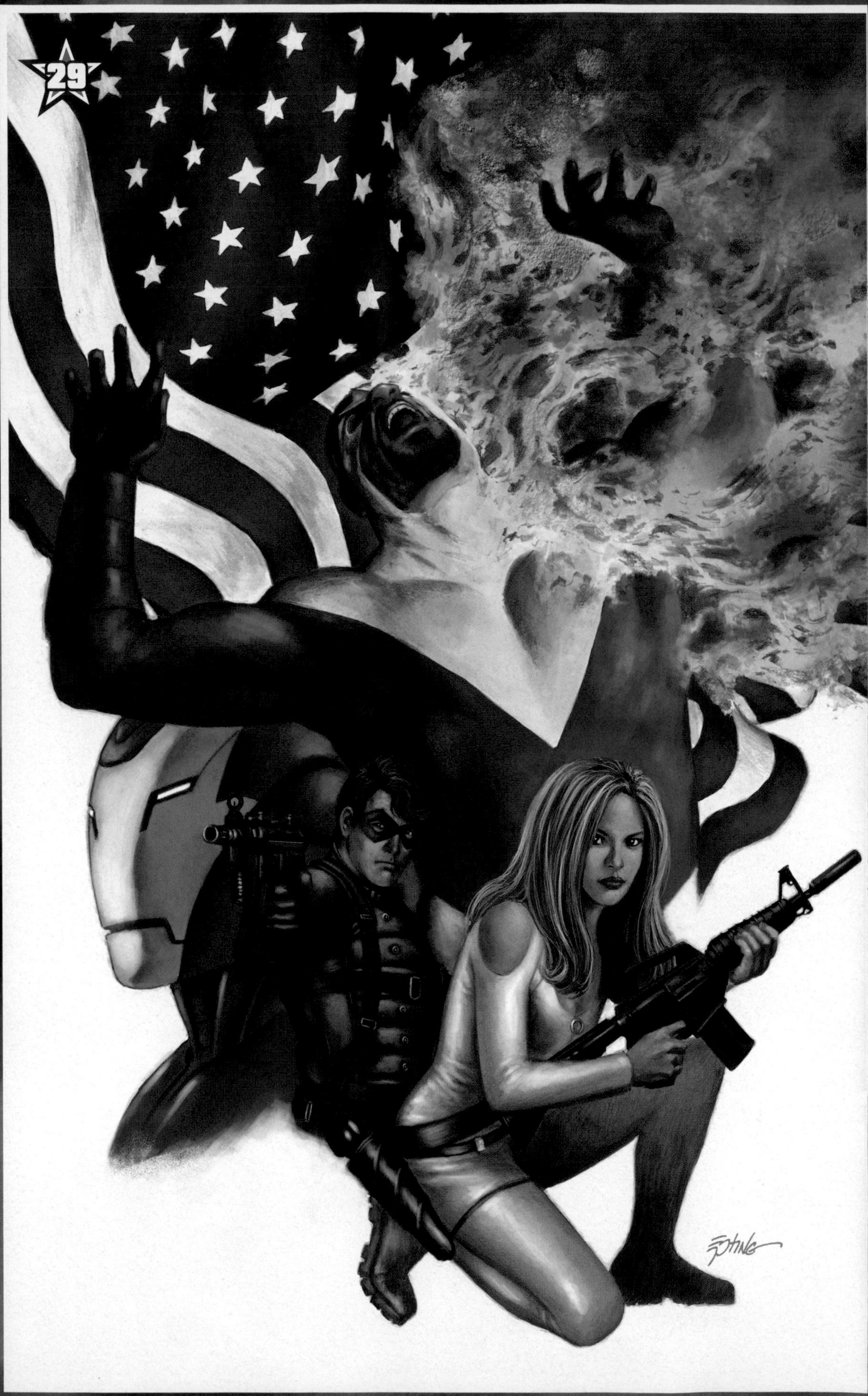
29

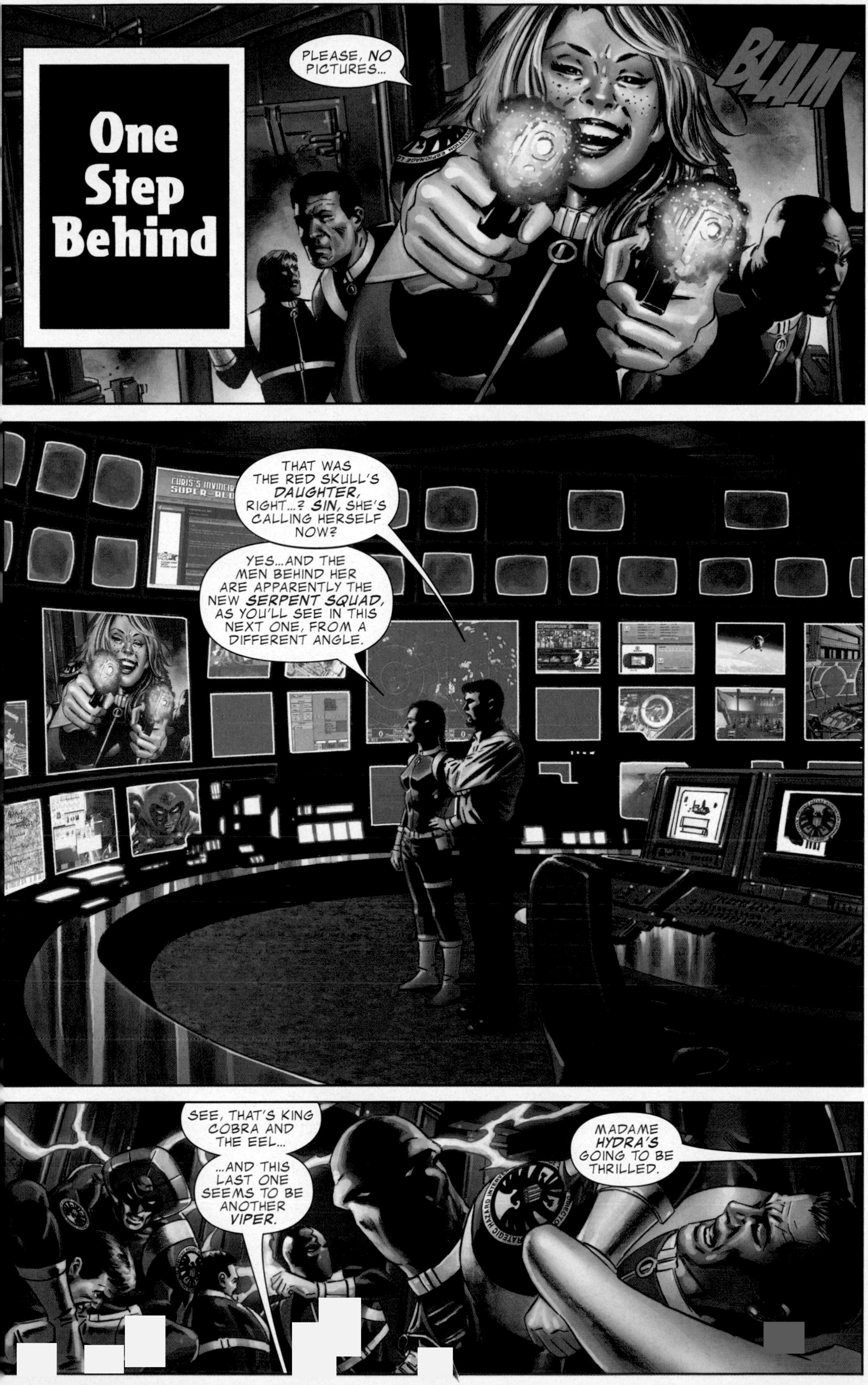
One Step Behind
PLEASE, NO PICTURES...
BLAM
THAT WAS THE RED SKULL'S DAUGHTER, RIGHT...? SIN, SHE'S CALLING HERSELF NOW?
YES...AND THE MEN BEHIND HER ARE APPARENTLY THE NEW SERPENT SQUAD, AS YOU'LL SEE IN THIS NEXT ONE, FROM A DIFFERENT ANGLE.
SEE, THAT'S KING COBRA AND THE EEL...
...AND THIS LAST ONE SEEMS TO BE ANOTHER VIPER.
MADAME HYDRA'S GOING TO BE THRILLED.

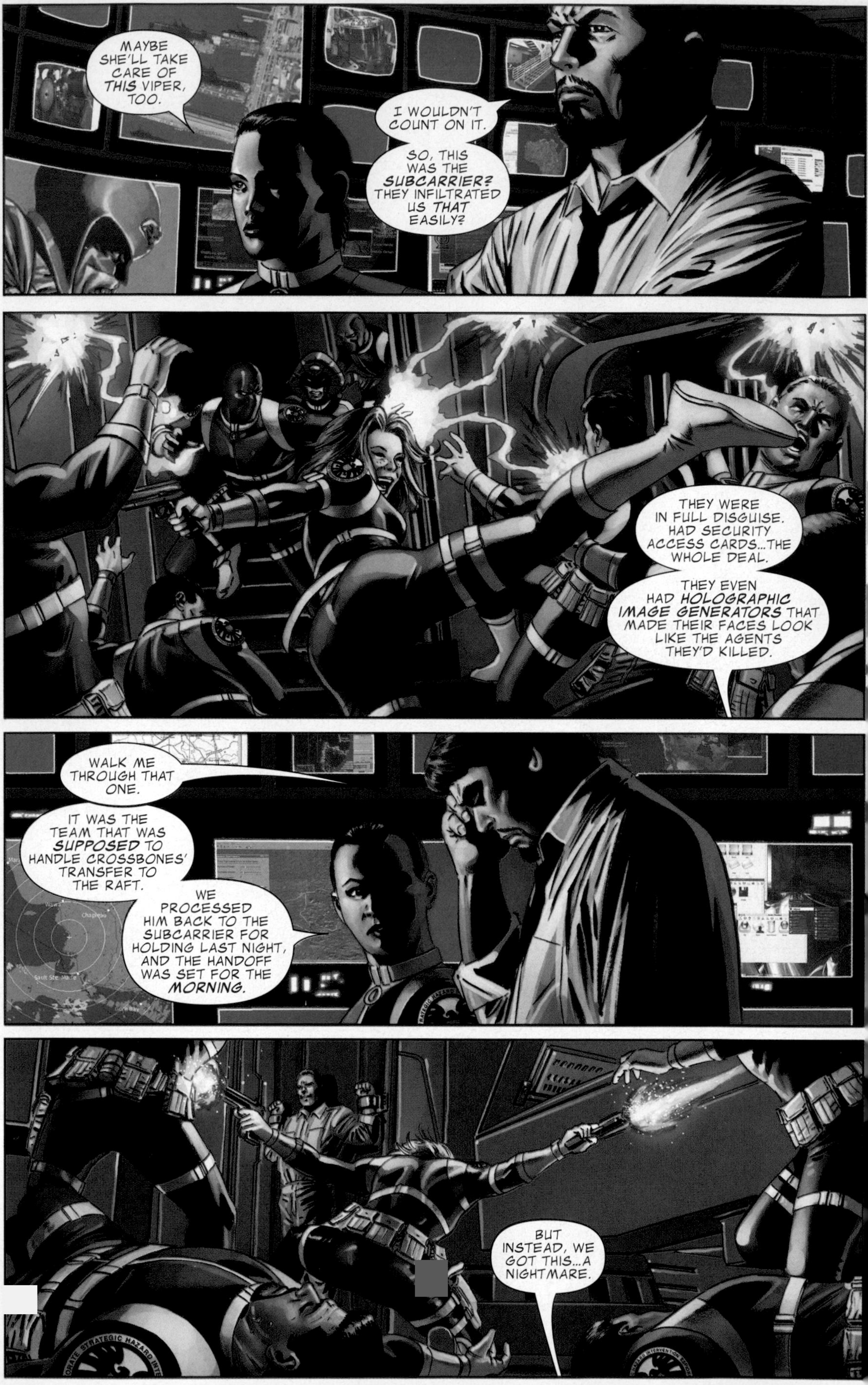
MAYBE SHE'LL TAKE CARE OF THIS VIPER, TOO.
I WOULDN'T COUNT ON IT.
SO, THIS WAS THE SUBCARRIER? THEY INFILTRATED US THAT EASILY?
THEY WERE IN FULL DISGUISE. HAD SECURITY ACCESS CARDS...THE WHOLE DEAL.
THEY EVEN HAD HOLOGRAPHIC IMAGE GENERATORS THAT MADE THEIR FACES LOOK LIKE THE AGENTS THEY'D KILLED.
WALK ME THROUGH THAT ONE.
IT WAS THE TEAM THAT WAS SUPPOSED TO HANDLE CROSSBONES' TRANSFER TO THE RAFT.
WE PROCESSED HIM BACK TO THE SUBCARRIER FOR HOLDING LAST NIGHT, AND THE HANDOFF WAS SET FOR THE MORNING.
BUT INSTEAD, WE GOT THIS...A NIGHTMARE.

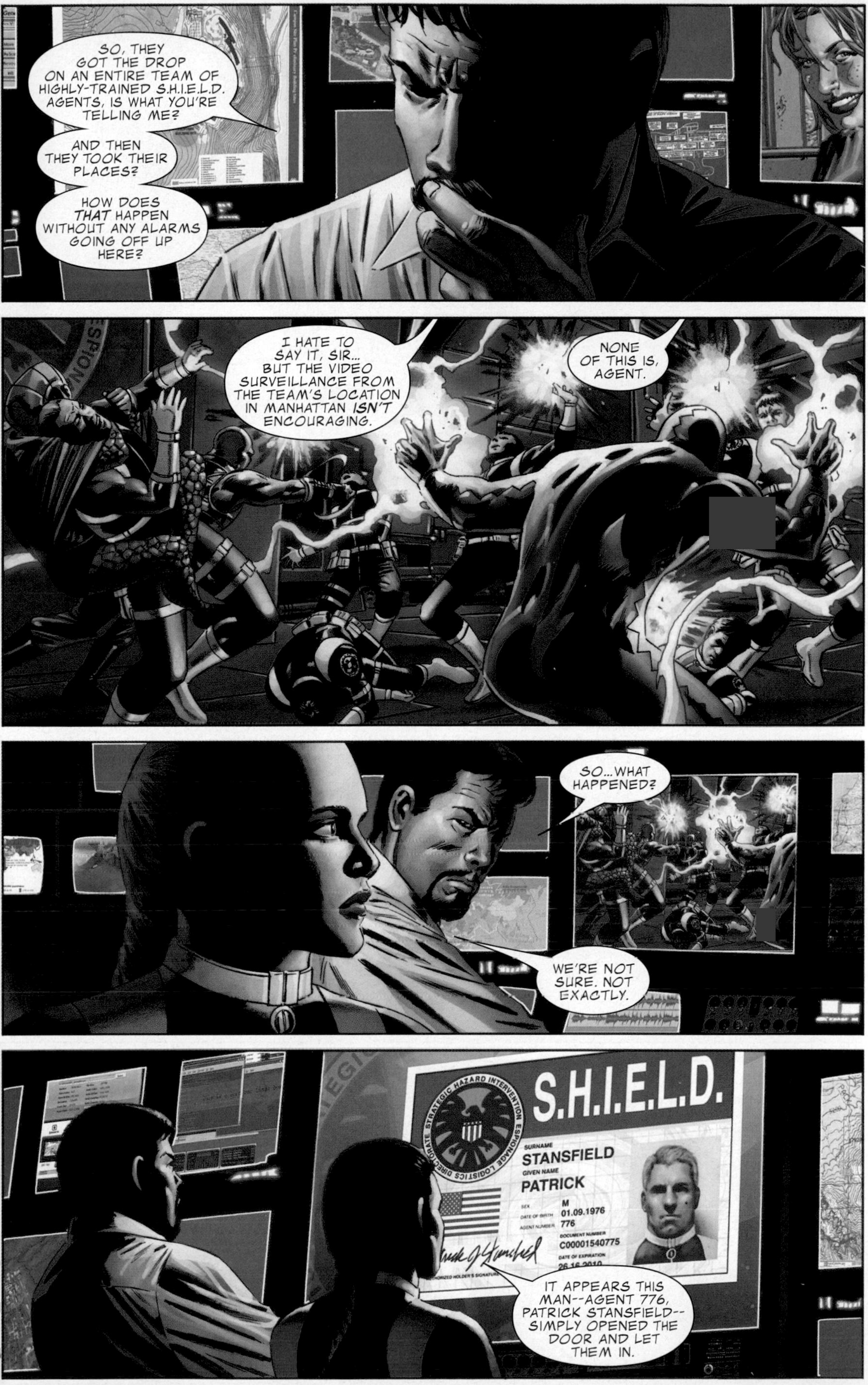
SO, THEY GOT THE DROP ON AN ENTIRE TEAM OF HIGHLY-TRAINED S.H.I.E.L.D. AGENTS, IS WHAT YOU'RE TELLING ME?
AND THEN THEY TOOK THEIR PLACES?
HOW DOES *THAT* HAPPEN WITHOUT ANY ALARMS GOING OFF UP HERE?
I HATE TO SAY IT, SIR... BUT THE VIDEO SURVEILLANCE FROM THE TEAM'S LOCATION IN MANHATTAN *ISN'T* ENCOURAGING.
NONE OF THIS IS, AGENT.
SO...WHAT HAPPENED?
WE'RE NOT SURE. NOT EXACTLY.
S.H.I.E.L.D.
STRATEGIC HAZARD INTERVENTION ESPIONAGE LOGISTICS DIRECTORATE
SURNAME
STANSFIELD
GIVEN NAME
PATRICK
SEX
M
DATE OF BIRTH
01.09.1976
AGENT NUMBER
776
DOCUMENT NUMBER
C00001540775
DATE OF EXPIRATION
IT APPEARS THIS MAN--AGENT 776, PATRICK STANSFIELD--SIMPLY OPENED THE DOOR AND LET THEM IN.

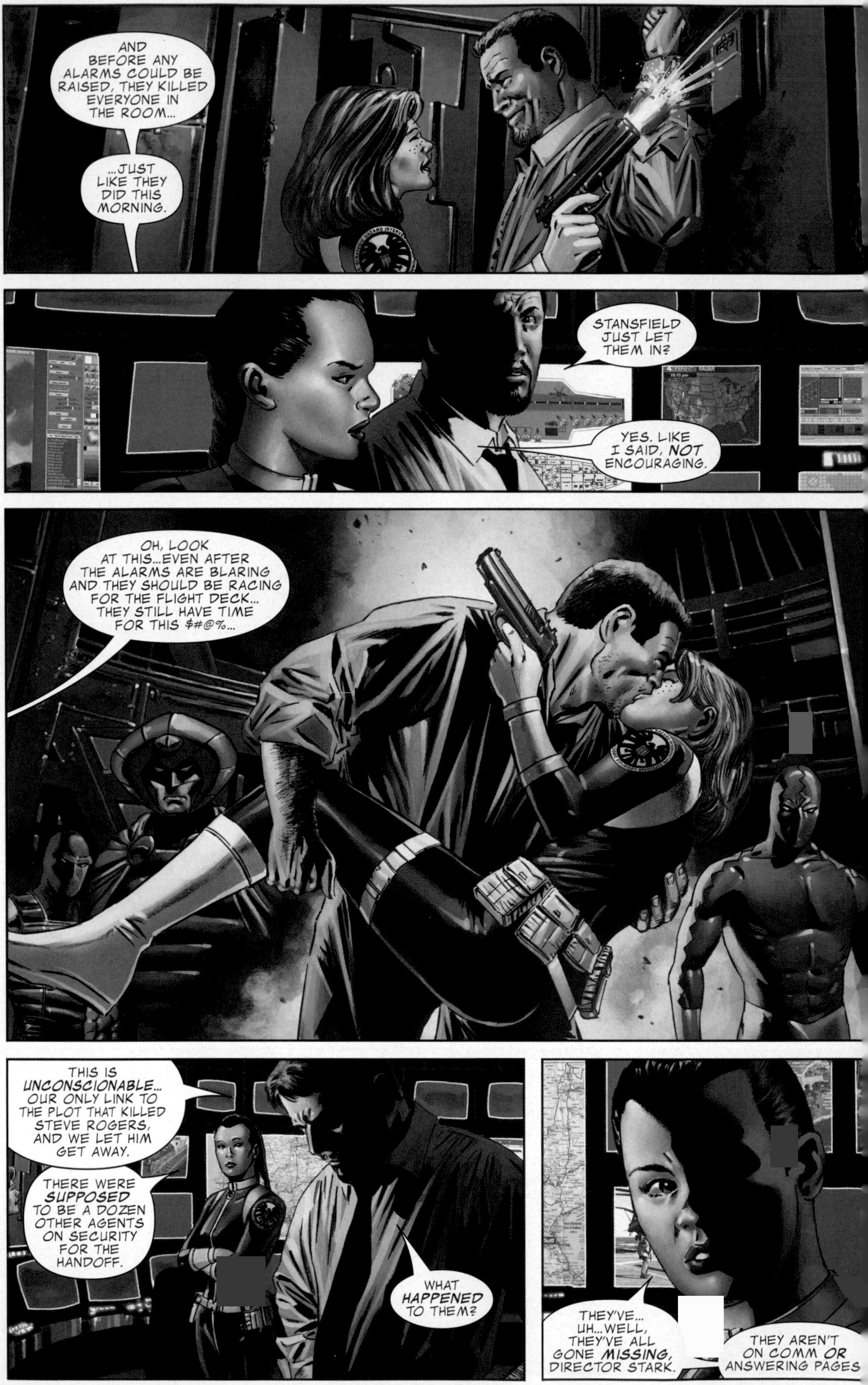
AND BEFORE ANY ALARMS COULD BE RAISED, THEY KILLED EVERYONE IN THE ROOM...
...JUST LIKE THEY DID THIS MORNING.
STANSFIELD JUST LET THEM IN?
YES. LIKE I SAID, NOT ENCOURAGING.
OH, LOOK AT THIS...EVEN AFTER THE ALARMS ARE BLARING AND THEY SHOULD BE RACING FOR THE FLIGHT DECK... THEY STILL HAVE TIME FOR THIS $#@%...
THIS IS UNCONSCIONABLE... OUR ONLY LINK TO THE PLOT THAT KILLED STEVE ROGERS, AND WE LET HIM GET AWAY.
THERE WERE SUPPOSED TO BE A DOZEN OTHER AGENTS ON SECURITY FOR THE HANDOFF.
WHAT HAPPENED TO THEM?
THEY'VE... UH...WELL, THEY'VE ALL GONE MISSING, DIRECTOR STARK.
THEY AREN'T ON COMM OR ANSWERING PAGES

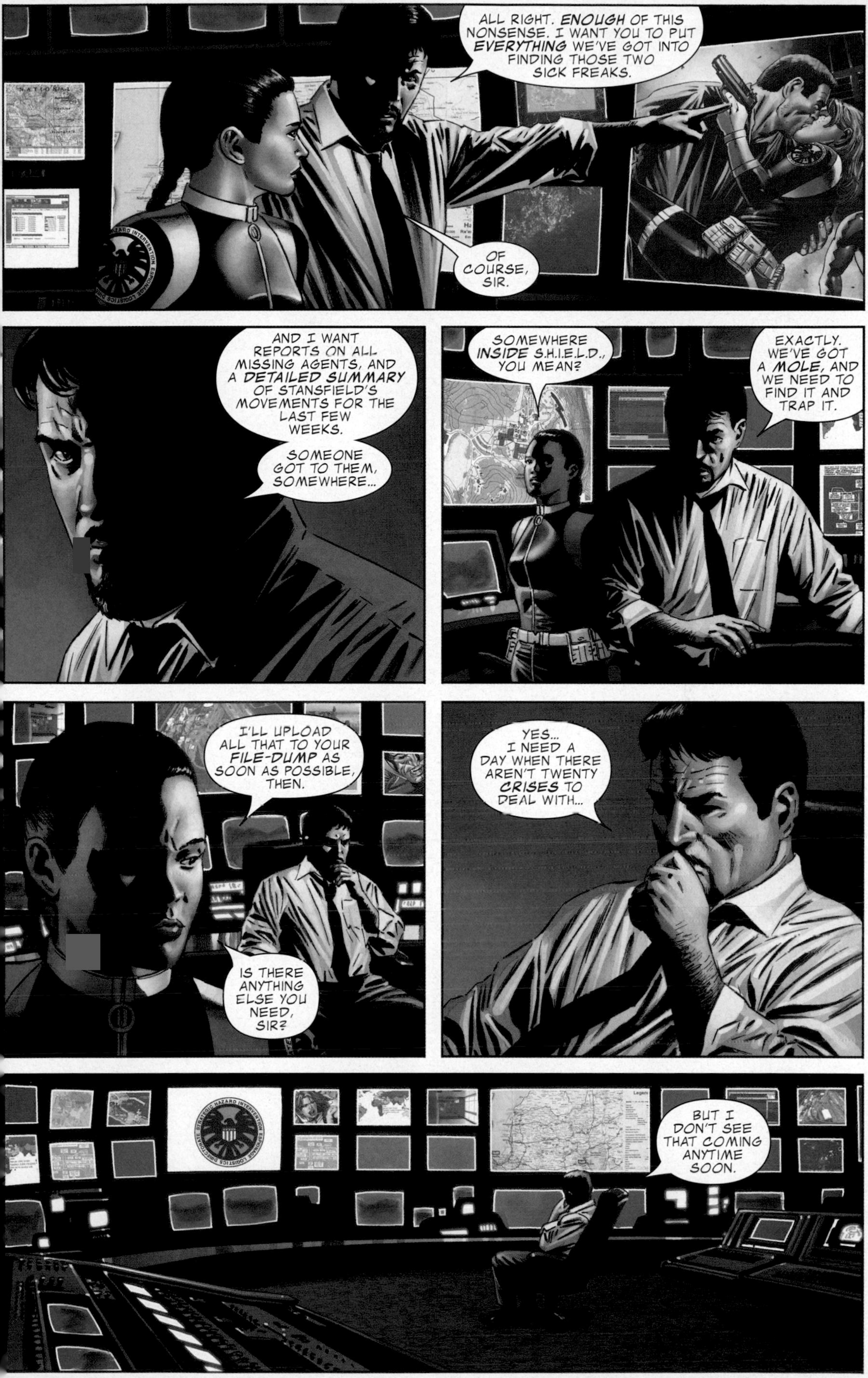
ALL RIGHT. ENOUGH OF THIS NONSENSE. I WANT YOU TO PUT EVERYTHING WE'VE GOT INTO FINDING THOSE TWO SICK FREAKS.
OF COURSE, SIR.
AND I WANT REPORTS ON ALL MISSING AGENTS, AND A DETAILED SUMMARY OF STANSFIELD'S MOVEMENTS FOR THE LAST FEW WEEKS.
SOMEONE GOT TO THEM, SOMEWHERE...
SOMEWHERE INSIDE S.H.I.E.L.D., YOU MEAN?
EXACTLY. WE'VE GOT A MOLE, AND WE NEED TO FIND IT AND TRAP IT.
I'LL UPLOAD ALL THAT TO YOUR FILE-DUMP AS SOON AS POSSIBLE, THEN.
IS THERE ANYTHING ELSE YOU NEED, SIR?
YES... I NEED A DAY WHEN THERE AREN'T TWENTY CRISES TO DEAL WITH...
BUT I DON'T SEE THAT COMING ANYTIME SOON.

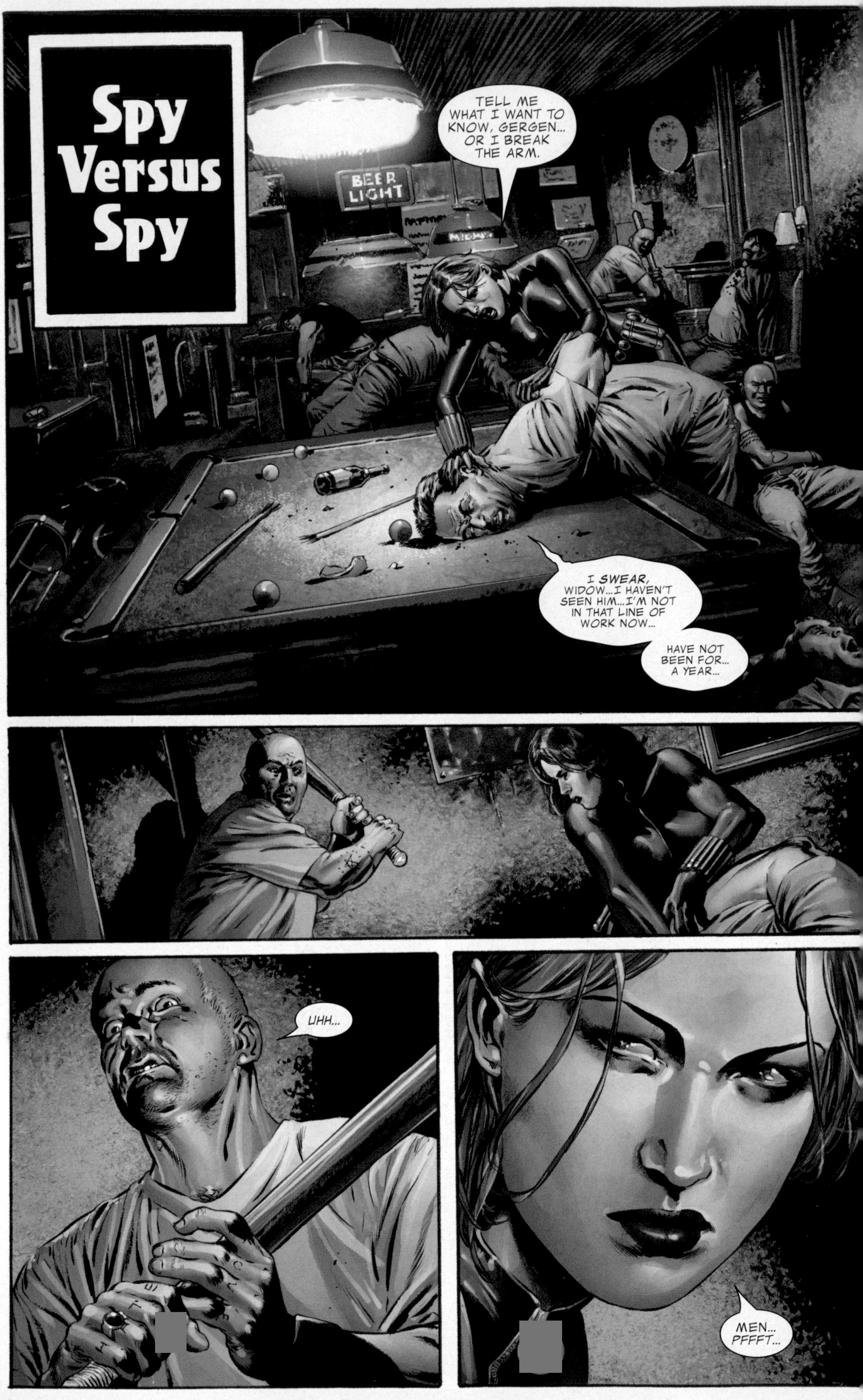
Spy Versus Spy
TELL ME WHAT I WANT TO KNOW, GERGEN... OR I BREAK THE ARM.
BEER LIGHT
I SWEAR, WIDOW...I HAVEN'T SEEN HIM...I'M NOT IN THAT LINE OF WORK NOW...
HAVE NOT BEEN FOR... A YEAR...
UHH...
MEN... PFFFT...

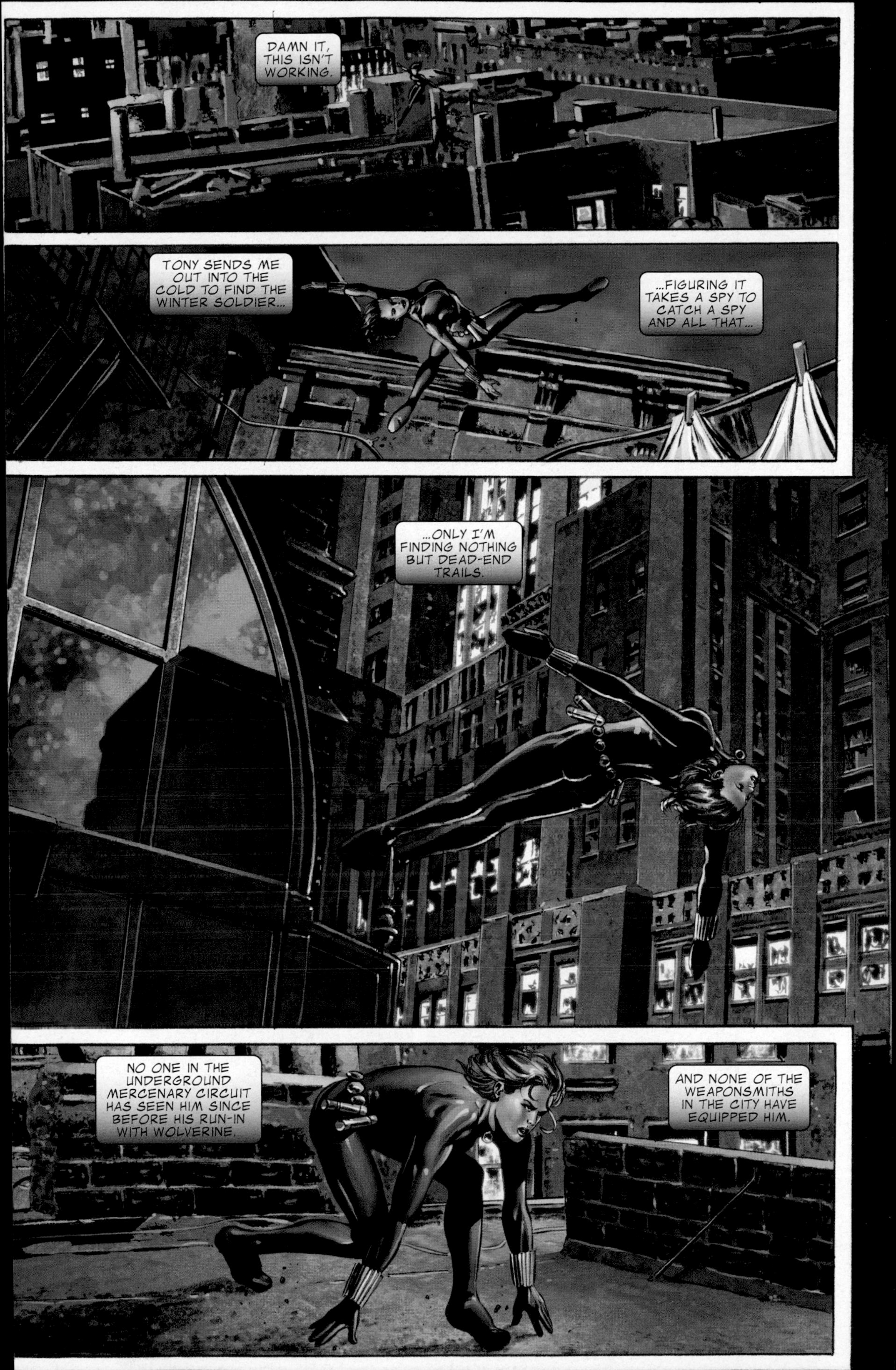
DAMN IT, THIS ISN'T WORKING.
TONY SENDS ME OUT INTO THE COLD TO FIND THE WINTER SOLDIER...
...FIGURING IT TAKES A SPY TO CATCH A SPY AND ALL THAT...
...ONLY I'M FINDING NOTHING BUT DEAD-END TRAILS.
NO ONE IN THE UNDERGROUND MERCENARY CIRCUIT HAS SEEN HIM SINCE BEFORE HIS RUN-IN WITH WOLVERINE.
AND NONE OF THE WEAPONSMITHS IN THE CITY HAVE EQUIPPED HIM.

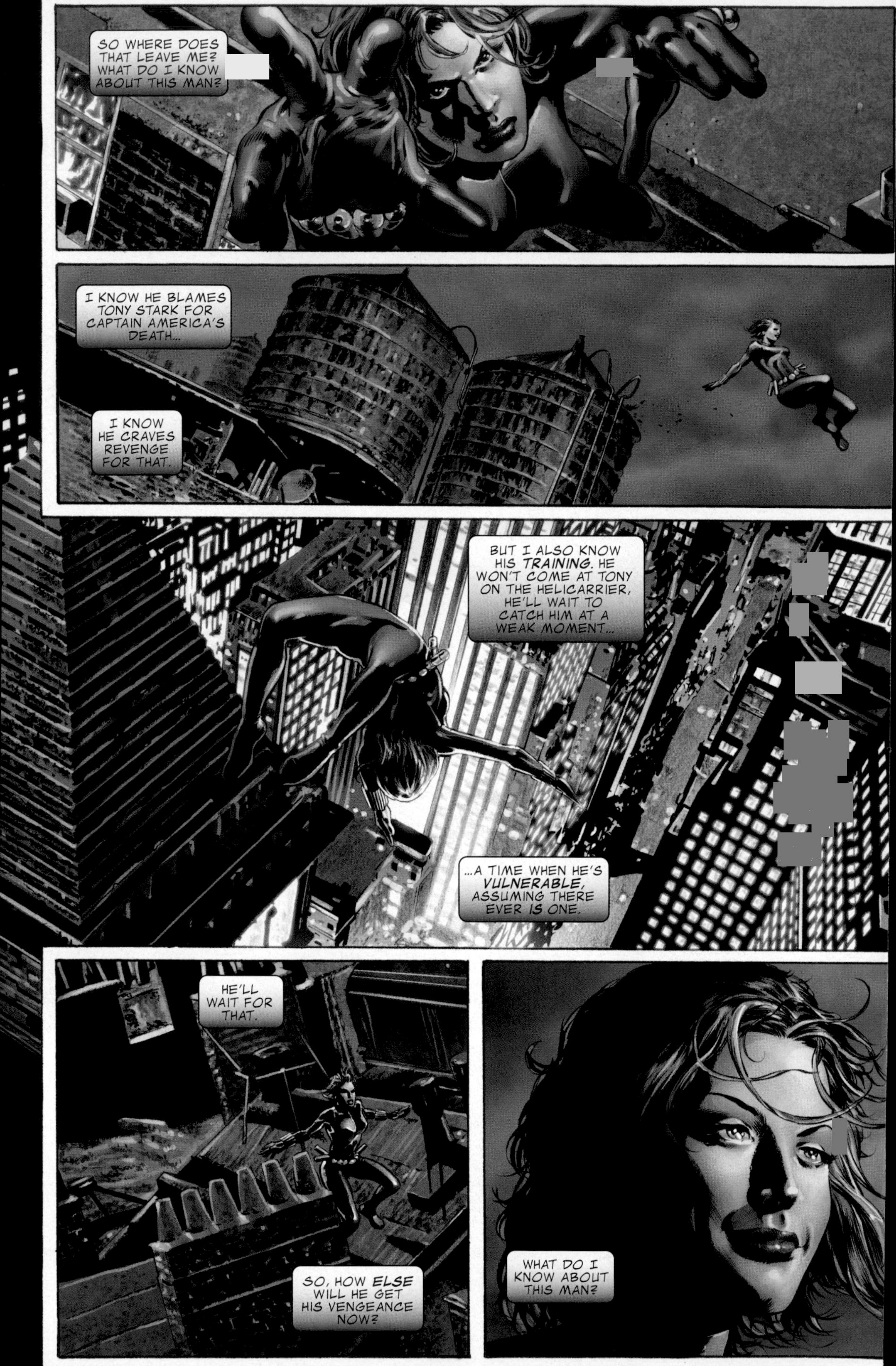
SO WHERE DOES THAT LEAVE ME? WHAT DO I KNOW ABOUT THIS MAN?
I KNOW HE BLAMES TONY STARK FOR CAPTAIN AMERICA'S DEATH...
I KNOW HE CRAVES REVENGE FOR THAT.
BUT I ALSO KNOW HIS *TRAINING*. HE WON'T COME AT TONY ON THE HELICARRIER, HE'LL WAIT TO CATCH HIM AT A WEAK MOMENT...
...A TIME WHEN HE'S *VULNERABLE*, ASSUMING THERE EVER *IS* ONE.
HE'LL WAIT FOR THAT.
SO, HOW *ELSE* WILL HE GET HIS VENGEANCE NOW?
WHAT DO I KNOW ABOUT THIS MAN?

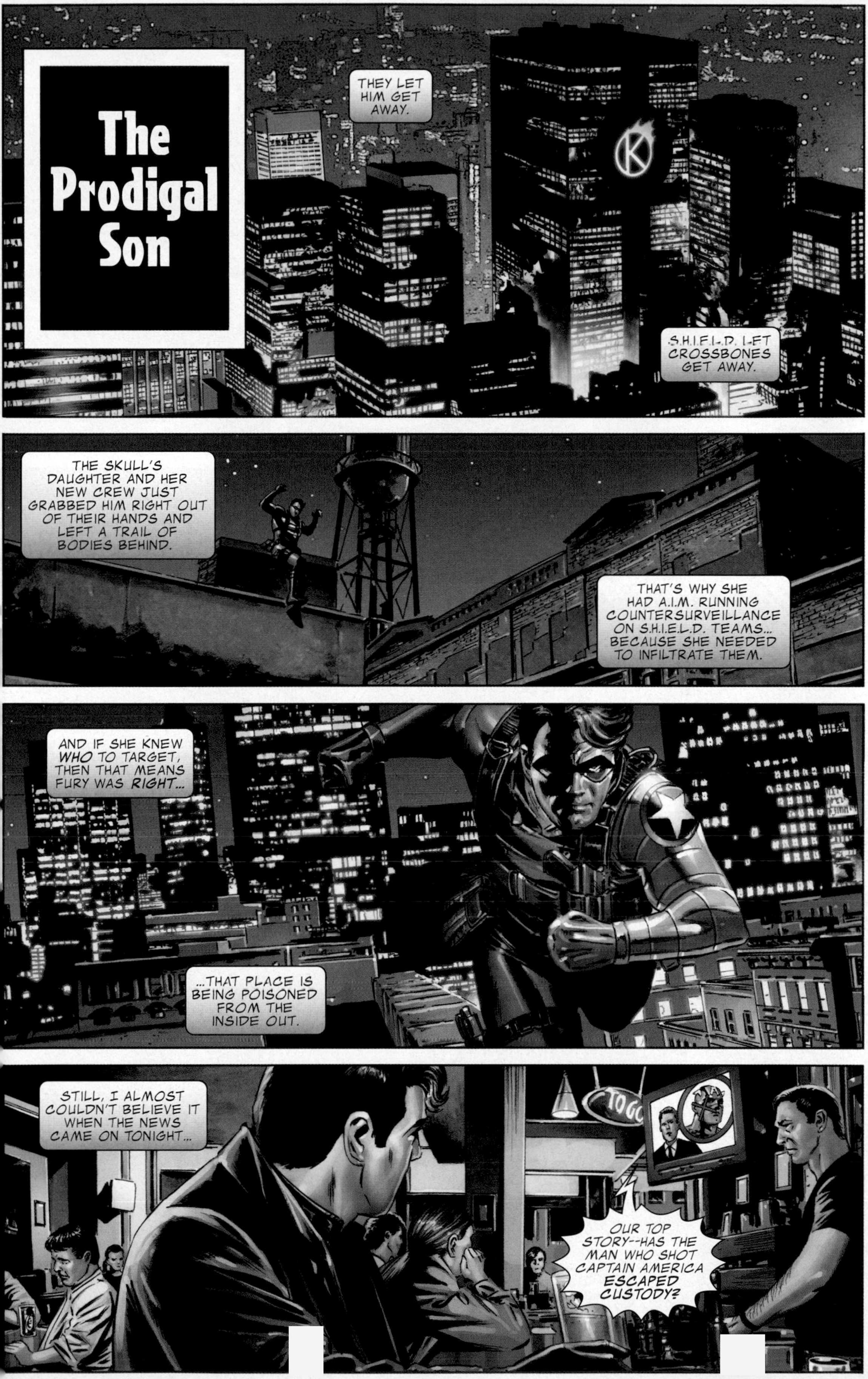
The Prodigal Son
THEY LET HIM GET AWAY.
S.H.I.E.L.D. LET CROSSBONES GET AWAY.
THE SKULL'S DAUGHTER AND HER NEW CREW JUST GRABBED HIM RIGHT OUT OF THEIR HANDS AND LEFT A TRAIL OF BODIES BEHIND.
THAT'S WHY SHE HAD A.I.M. RUNNING COUNTERSURVEILLANCE ON S.H.I.E.L.D. TEAMS... BECAUSE SHE NEEDED TO INFILTRATE THEM.
AND IF SHE KNEW WHO TO TARGET, THEN THAT MEANS FURY WAS RIGHT...
...THAT PLACE IS BEING POISONED FROM THE INSIDE OUT.
STILL, I ALMOST COULDN'T BELIEVE IT WHEN THE NEWS CAME ON TONIGHT...
OUR TOP STORY--HAS THE MAN WHO SHOT CAPTAIN AMERICA ESCAPED CUSTODY?

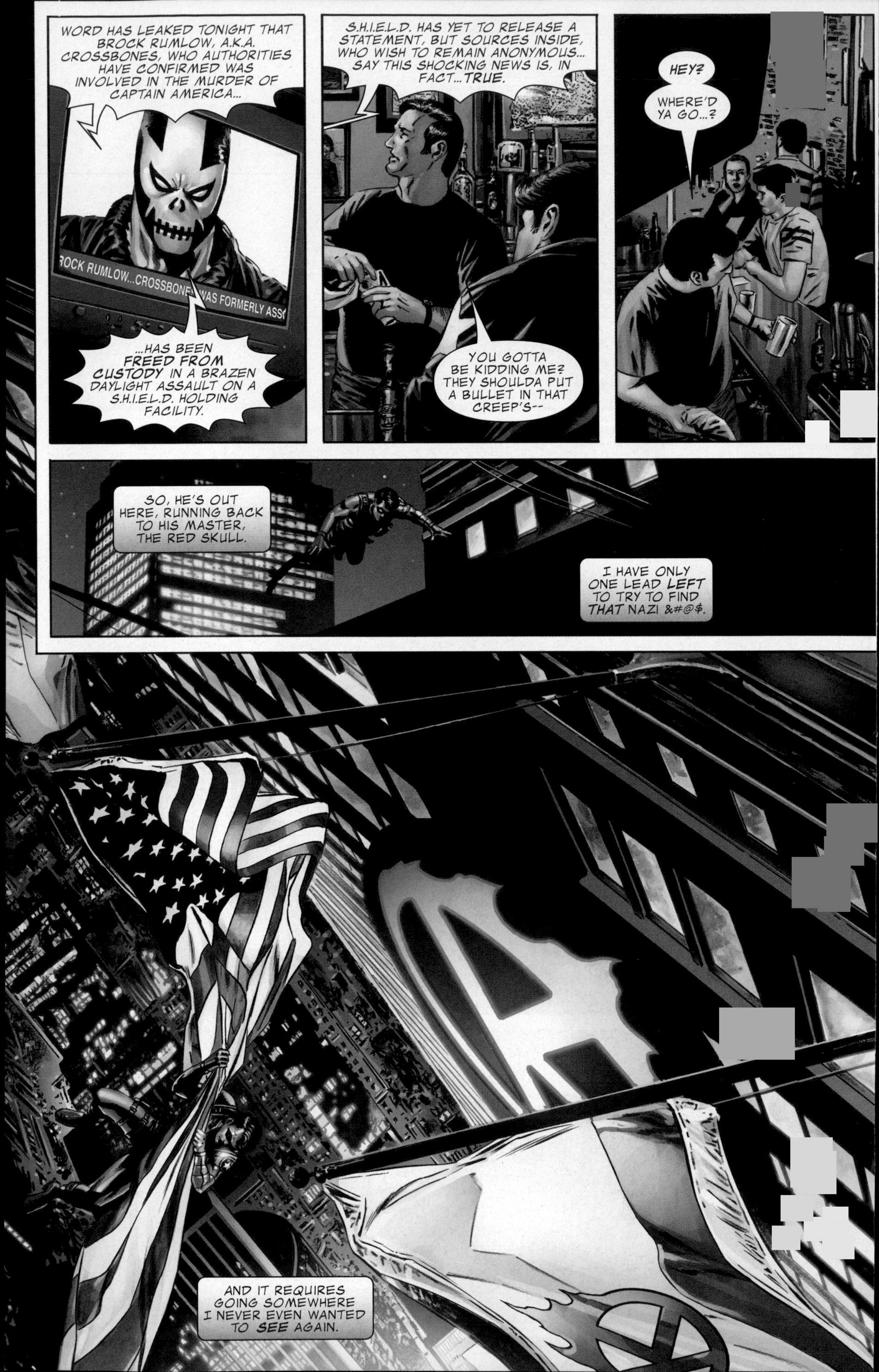
WORD HAS LEAKED TONIGHT THAT BROCK RUMLOW, A.K.A. CROSSBONES, WHO AUTHORITIES HAVE CONFIRMED WAS INVOLVED IN THE MURDER OF CAPTAIN AMERICA...
ROCK RUMLOW...CROSSBONES WAS FORMERLY ASS
...HAS BEEN FREED FROM CUSTODY IN A BRAZEN DAYLIGHT ASSAULT ON A S.H.I.E.L.D. HOLDING FACILITY.
S.H.I.E.L.D. HAS YET TO RELEASE A STATEMENT, BUT SOURCES INSIDE, WHO WISH TO REMAIN ANONYMOUS... SAY THIS SHOCKING NEWS IS, IN FACT...TRUE.
YOU GOTTA BE KIDDING ME? THEY SHOULDA PUT A BULLET IN THAT CREEP'S--
HEY?
WHERE'D YA GO...?
SO, HE'S OUT HERE, RUNNING BACK TO HIS MASTER, THE RED SKULL.
I HAVE ONLY ONE LEAD LEFT TO TRY TO FIND THAT NAZI &#@$.
AND IT REQUIRES GOING SOMEWHERE I NEVER EVEN WANTED TO SEE AGAIN.

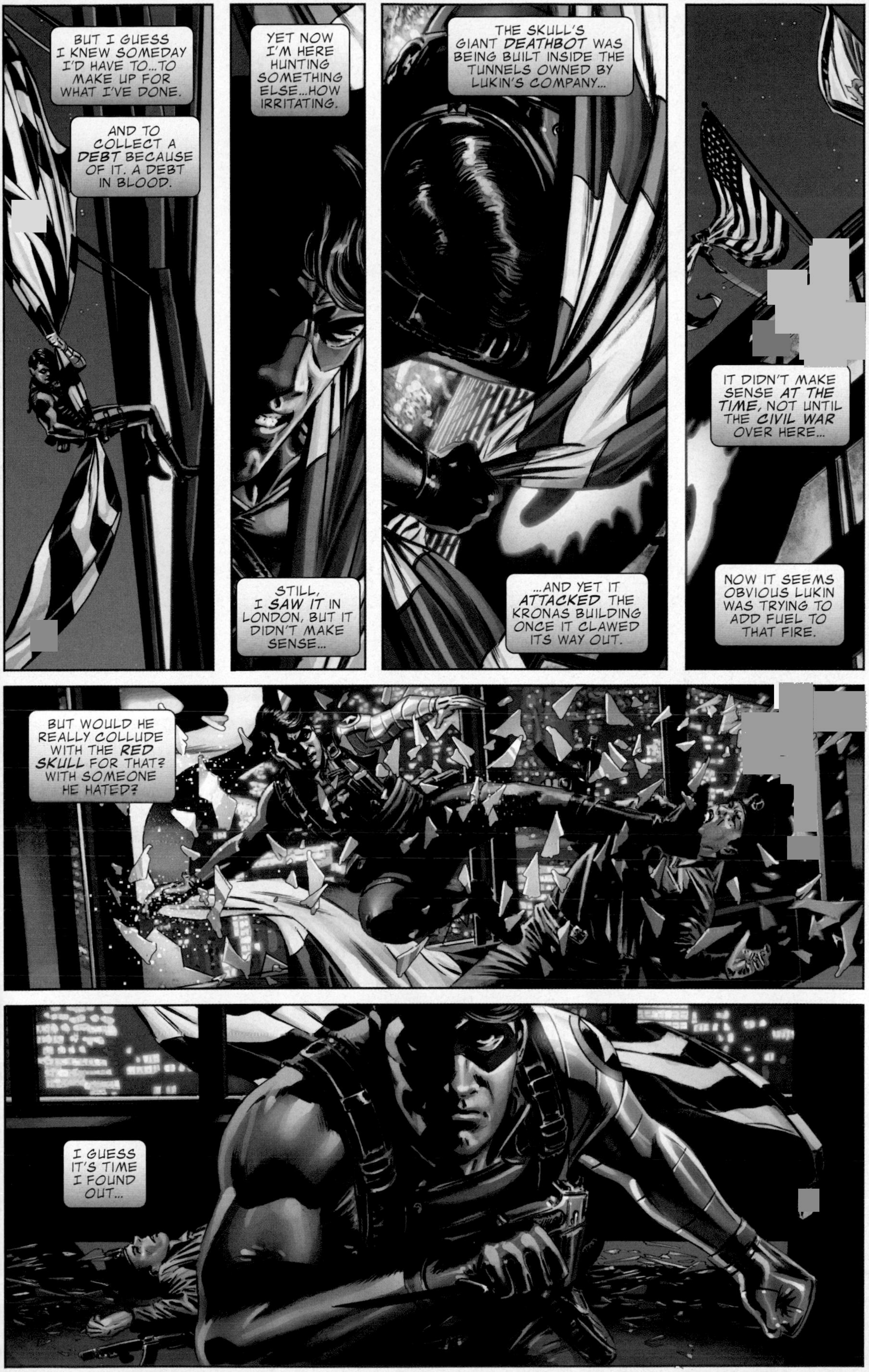

BUT I GUESS I KNEW SOMEDAY I'D HAVE TO...TO MAKE UP FOR WHAT I'VE DONE.
AND TO COLLECT A DEBT BECAUSE OF IT. A DEBT IN BLOOD.
YET NOW I'M HERE HUNTING SOMETHING ELSE...HOW IRRITATING.
STILL, I SAW IT IN LONDON, BUT IT DIDN'T MAKE SENSE...
THE SKULL'S GIANT DEATHBOT WAS BEING BUILT INSIDE THE TUNNELS OWNED BY LUKIN'S COMPANY...
...AND YET IT ATTACKED THE KRONAS BUILDING ONCE IT CLAWED ITS WAY OUT.
IT DIDN'T MAKE SENSE AT THE TIME, NOT UNTIL THE CIVIL WAR OVER HERE...
NOW IT SEEMS OBVIOUS LUKIN WAS TRYING TO ADD FUEL TO THAT FIRE.
BUT WOULD HE REALLY COLLUDE WITH THE RED SKULL FOR THAT? WITH SOMEONE HE HATED?
I GUESS IT'S TIME I FOUND OUT...

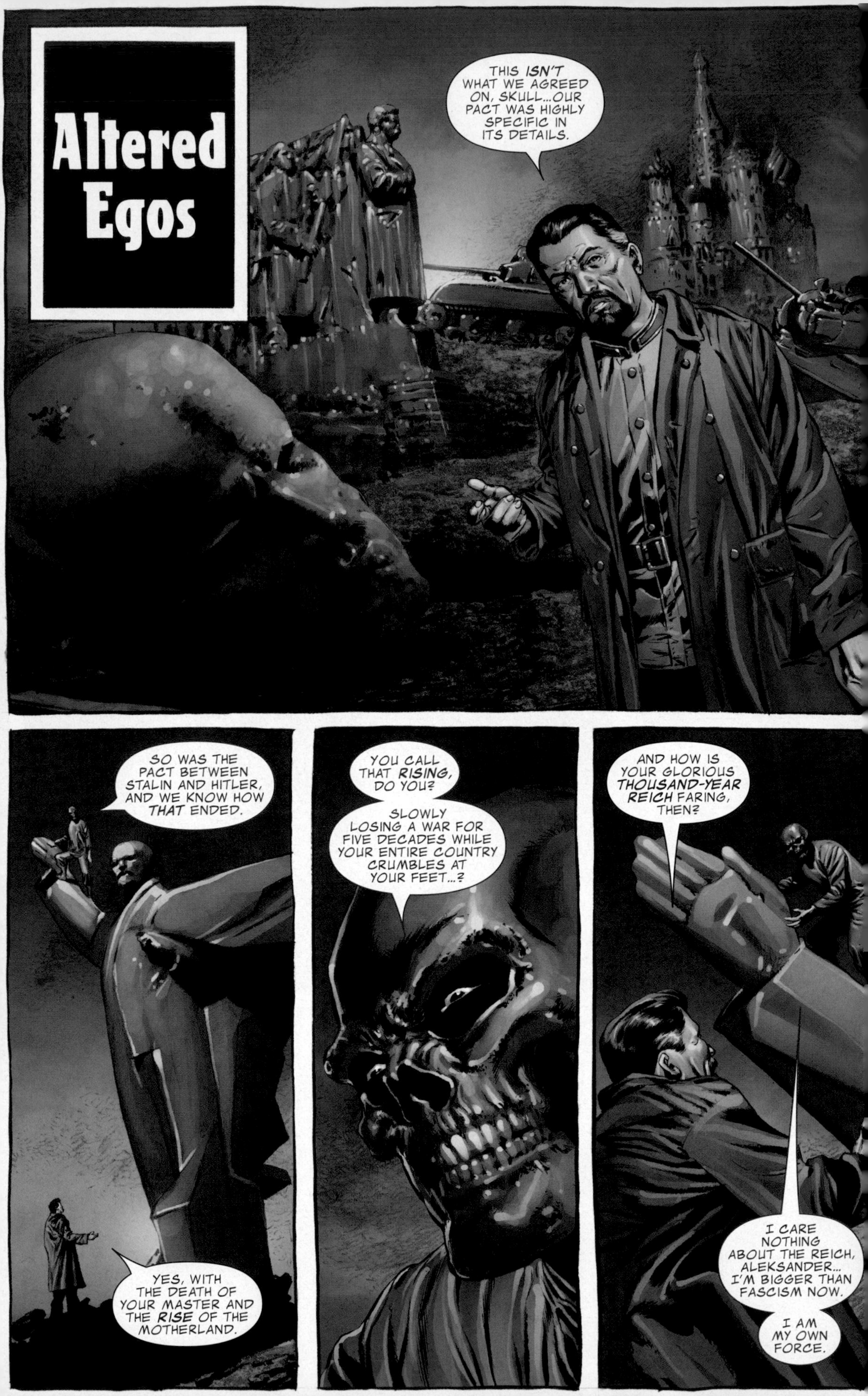
Altered Egos
THIS ISN'T WHAT WE AGREED ON, SKULL...OUR PACT WAS HIGHLY SPECIFIC IN ITS DETAILS.
SO WAS THE PACT BETWEEN STALIN AND HITLER, AND WE KNOW HOW THAT ENDED.
YES, WITH THE DEATH OF YOUR MASTER AND THE RISE OF THE MOTHERLAND.
YOU CALL THAT RISING, DO YOU?
SLOWLY LOSING A WAR FOR FIVE DECADES WHILE YOUR ENTIRE COUNTRY CRUMBLES AT YOUR FEET...?
AND HOW IS YOUR GLORIOUS THOUSAND-YEAR REICH FARING, THEN?
I CARE NOTHING ABOUT THE REICH, ALEKSANDER... I'M BIGGER THAN FASCISM NOW.
I AM MY OWN FORCE.

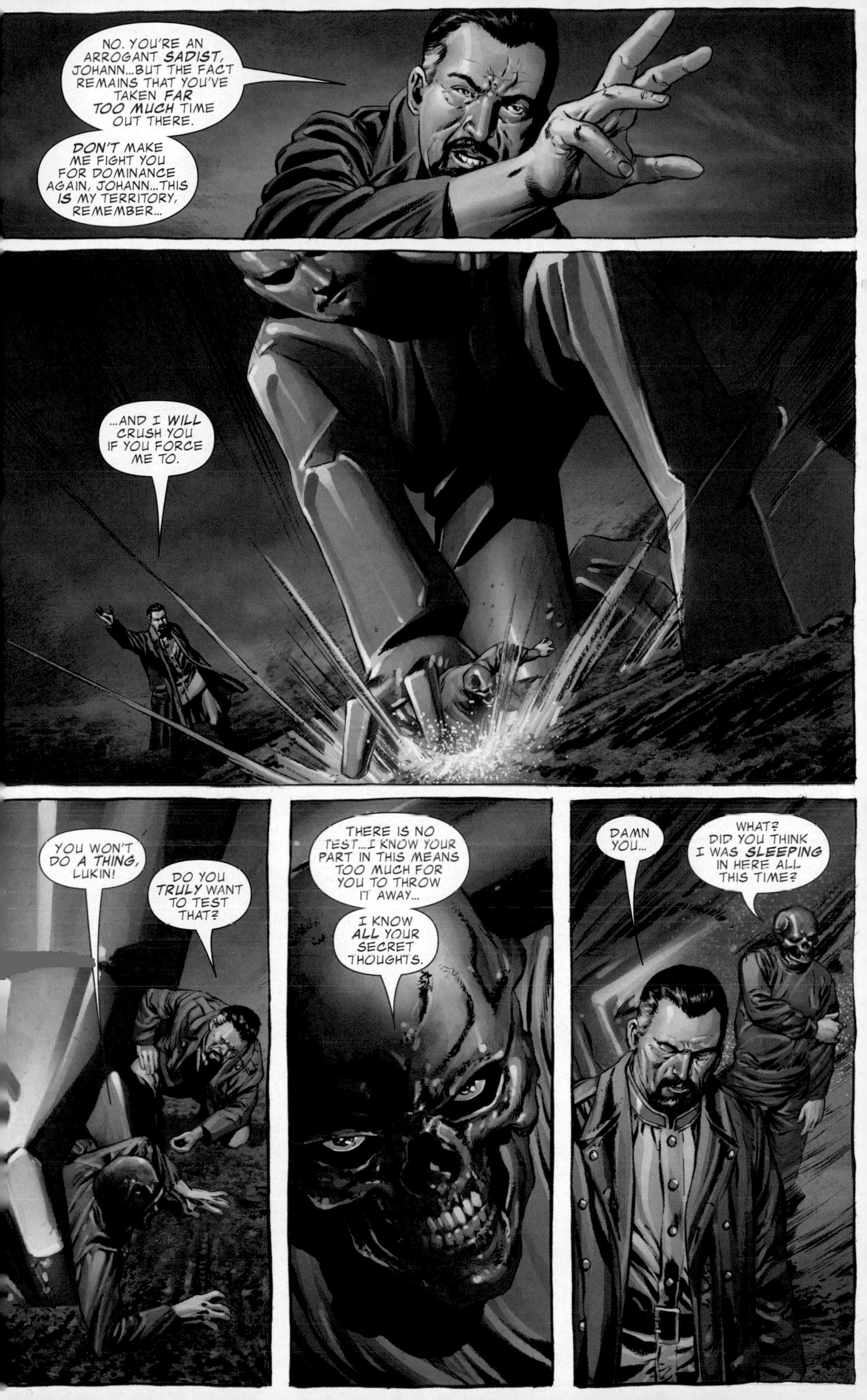
NO. YOU'RE AN ARROGANT SADIST, JOHANN...BUT THE FACT REMAINS THAT YOU'VE TAKEN FAR TOO MUCH TIME OUT THERE.
DON'T MAKE ME FIGHT YOU FOR DOMINANCE AGAIN, JOHANN...THIS IS MY TERRITORY, REMEMBER...
...AND I WILL CRUSH YOU IF YOU FORCE ME TO.
YOU WON'T DO A THING, LUKIN!
DO YOU TRULY WANT TO TEST THAT?
THERE IS NO TEST...I KNOW YOUR PART IN THIS MEANS TOO MUCH FOR YOU TO THROW IT AWAY...
I KNOW ALL YOUR SECRET THOUGHTS.
DAMN YOU...
WHAT? DID YOU THINK I WAS SLEEPING IN HERE ALL THIS TIME?

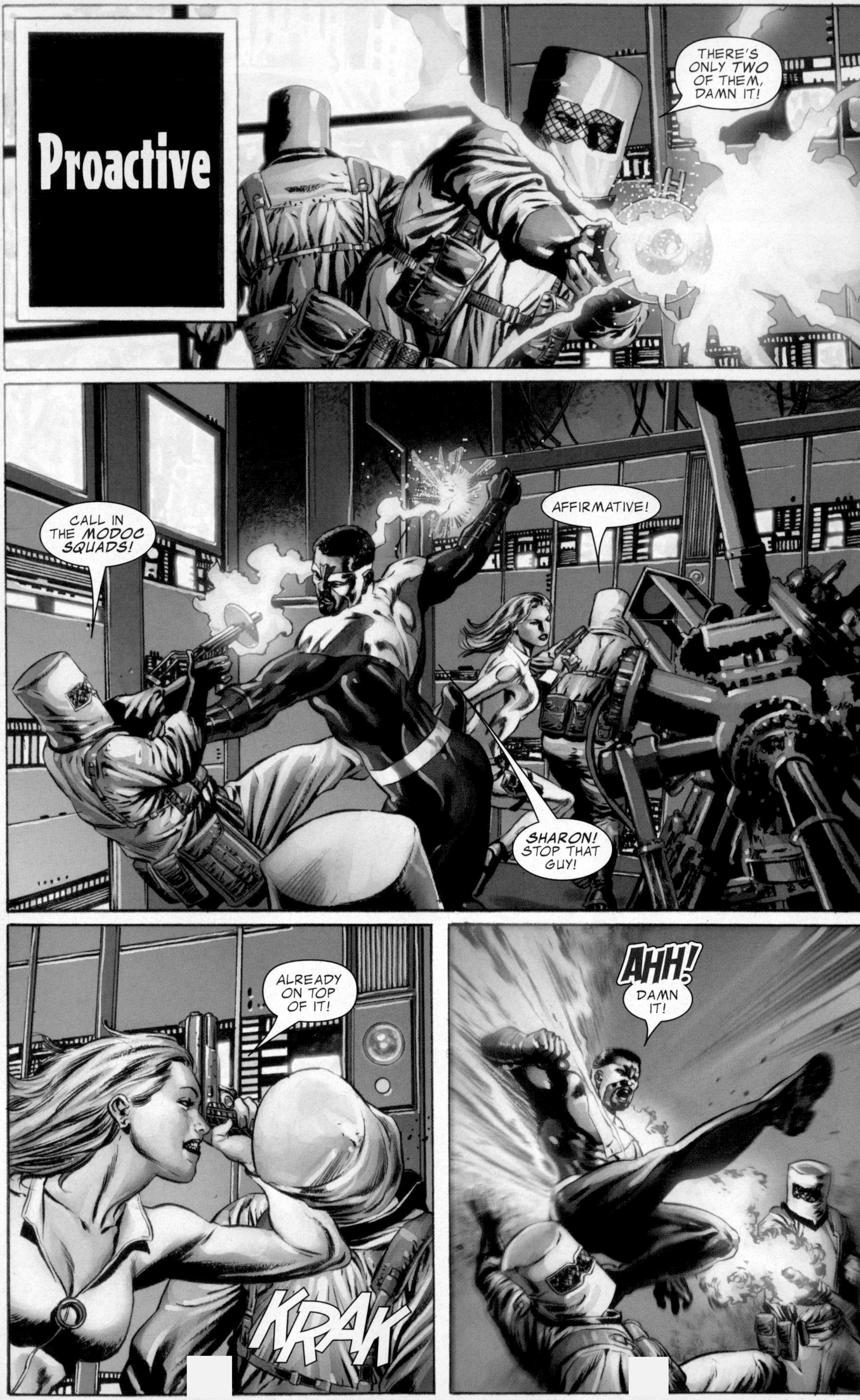
Proactive
THERE'S ONLY TWO OF THEM, DAMN IT!
CALL IN THE MODOC SQUADS!
AFFIRMATIVE!
SHARON! STOP THAT GUY!
ALREADY ON TOP OF IT!
KRAK
AHH! DAMN IT!

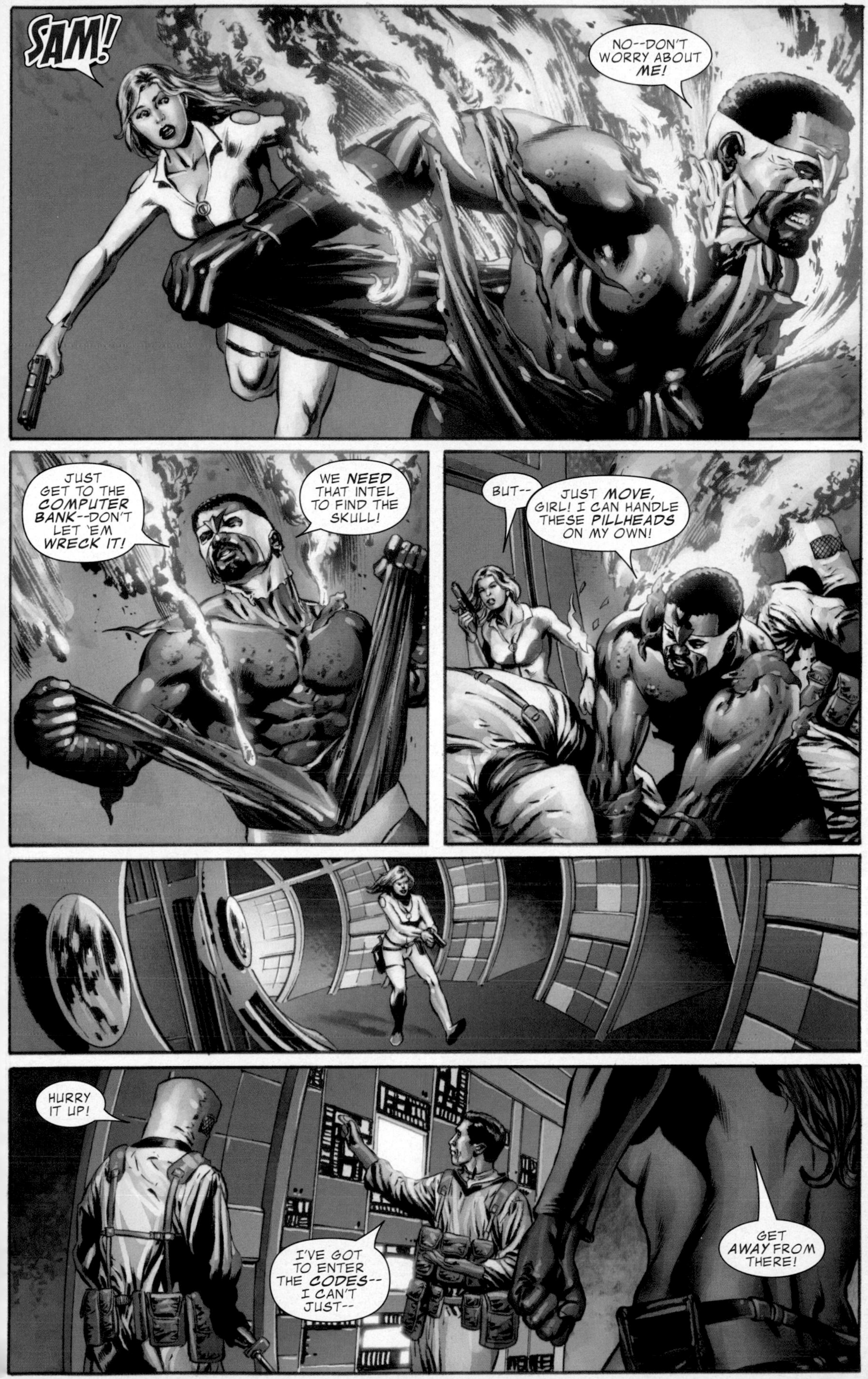
SAM!
NO--DON'T WORRY ABOUT ME!
JUST GET TO THE COMPUTER BANK--DON'T LET 'EM WRECK IT!
WE NEED THAT INTEL TO FIND THE SKULL!
BUT--
JUST MOVE, GIRL! I CAN HANDLE THESE PILLHEADS ON MY OWN!
HURRY IT UP!
I'VE GOT TO ENTER THE CODES-- I CAN'T JUST--
GET AWAY FROM THERE!

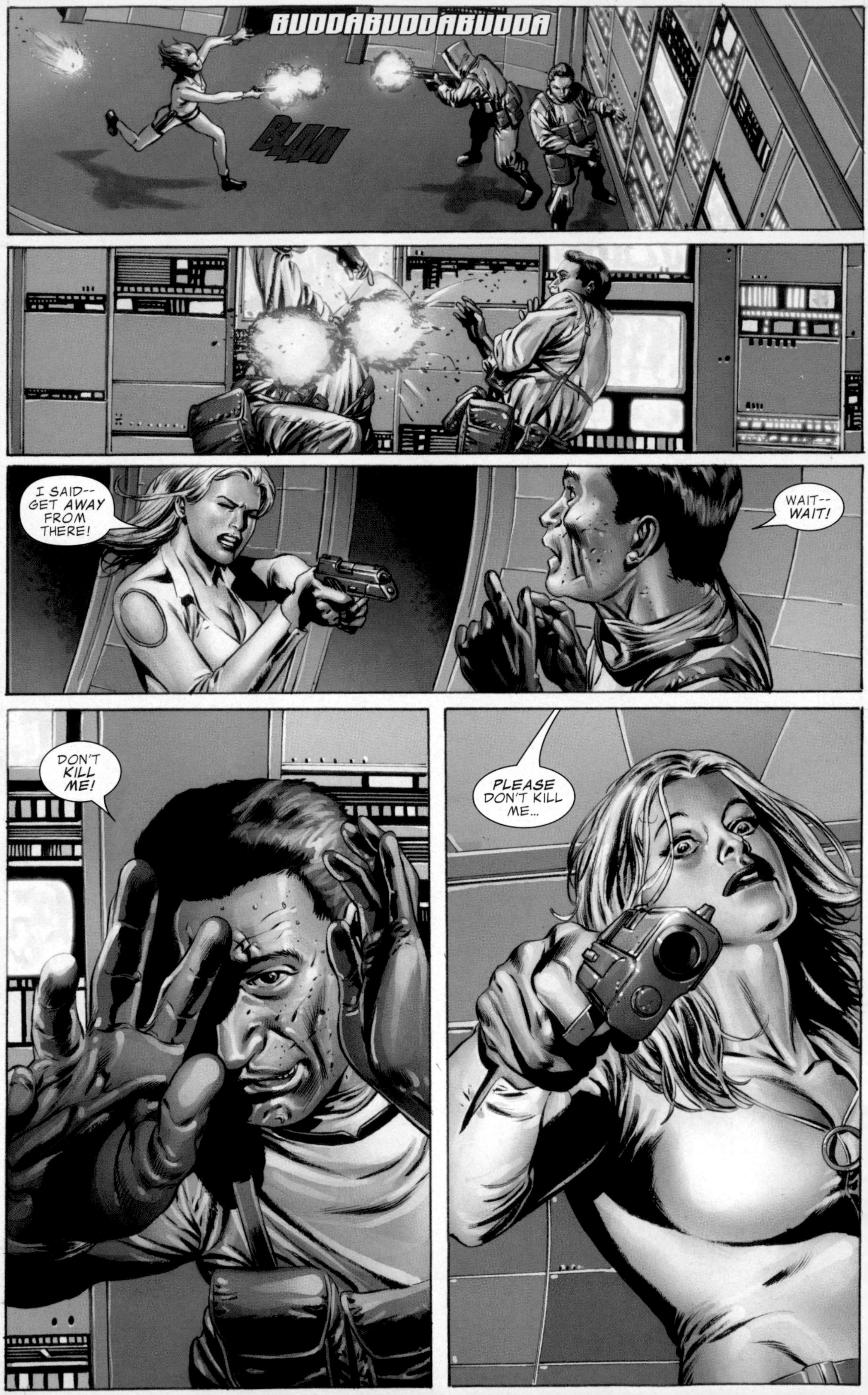
BUDDABUDDABUDDA
BLAM
I SAID-- GET AWAY FROM THERE!
WAIT-- WAIT!
DON'T KILL ME!
PLEASE DON'T KILL ME...

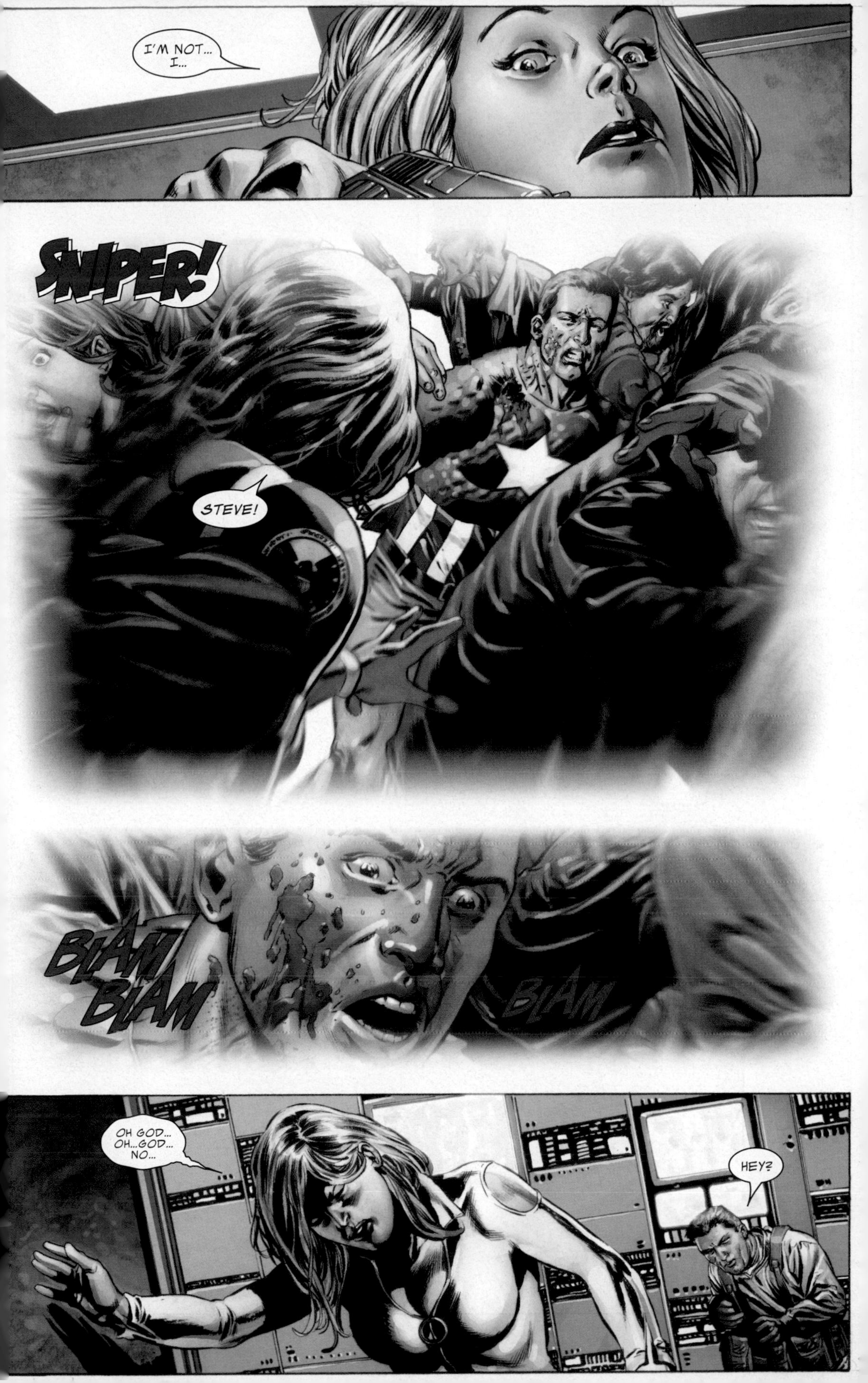
I'M NOT...
I...
SNIPER!
STEVE!
BLAM
BLAM
BLAM
OH GOD...
OH...GOD...
NO...
HEY?

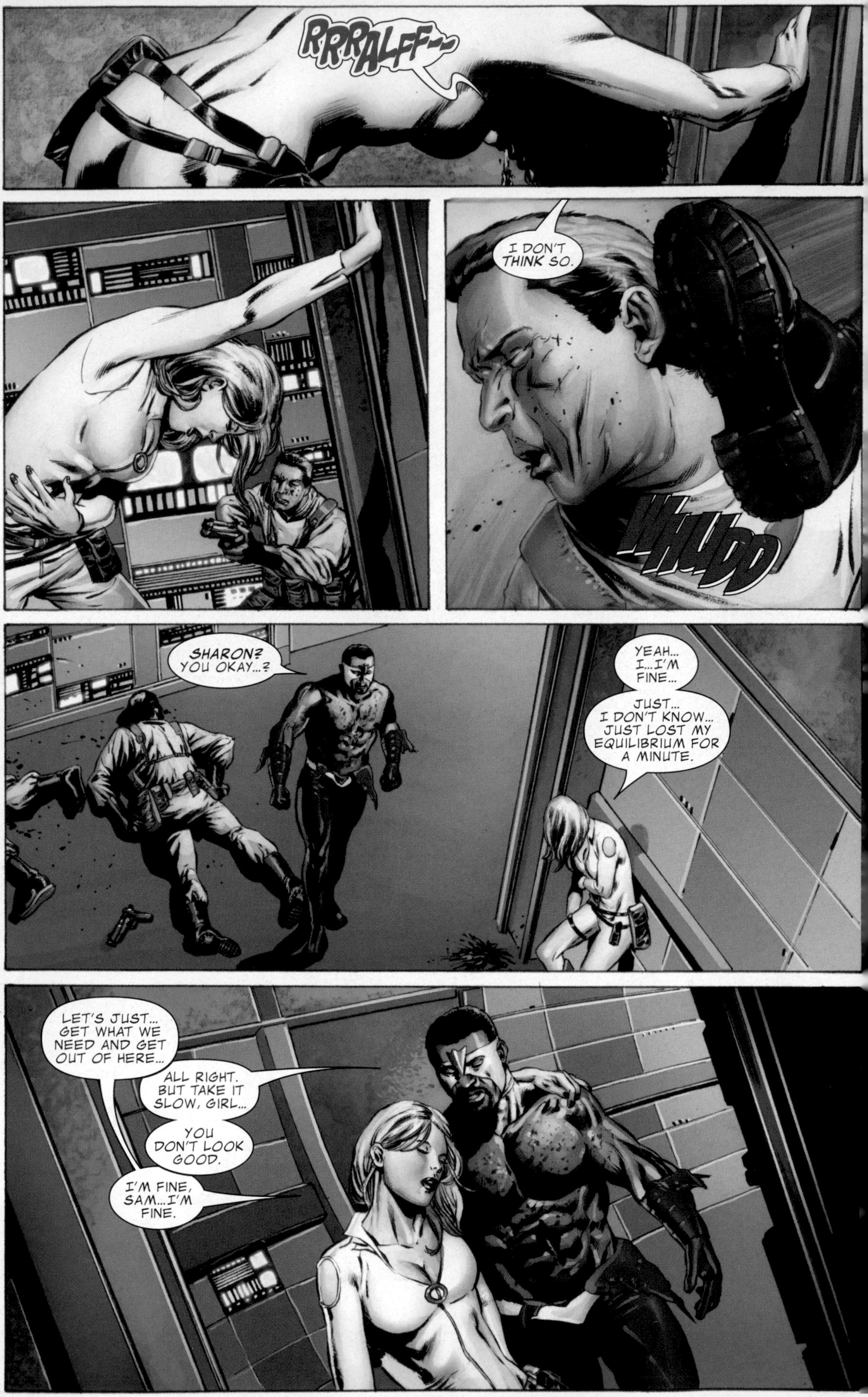

RRRALFF--
I DON'T THINK SO.
WHUDD
SHARON? YOU OKAY...?
YEAH... I...I'M FINE...
JUST... I DON'T KNOW... JUST LOST MY EQUILIBRIUM FOR A MINUTE.
LET'S JUST... GET WHAT WE NEED AND GET OUT OF HERE...
ALL RIGHT. BUT TAKE IT SLOW, GIRL...
YOU DON'T LOOK GOOD.
I'M FINE, SAM...I'M FINE.

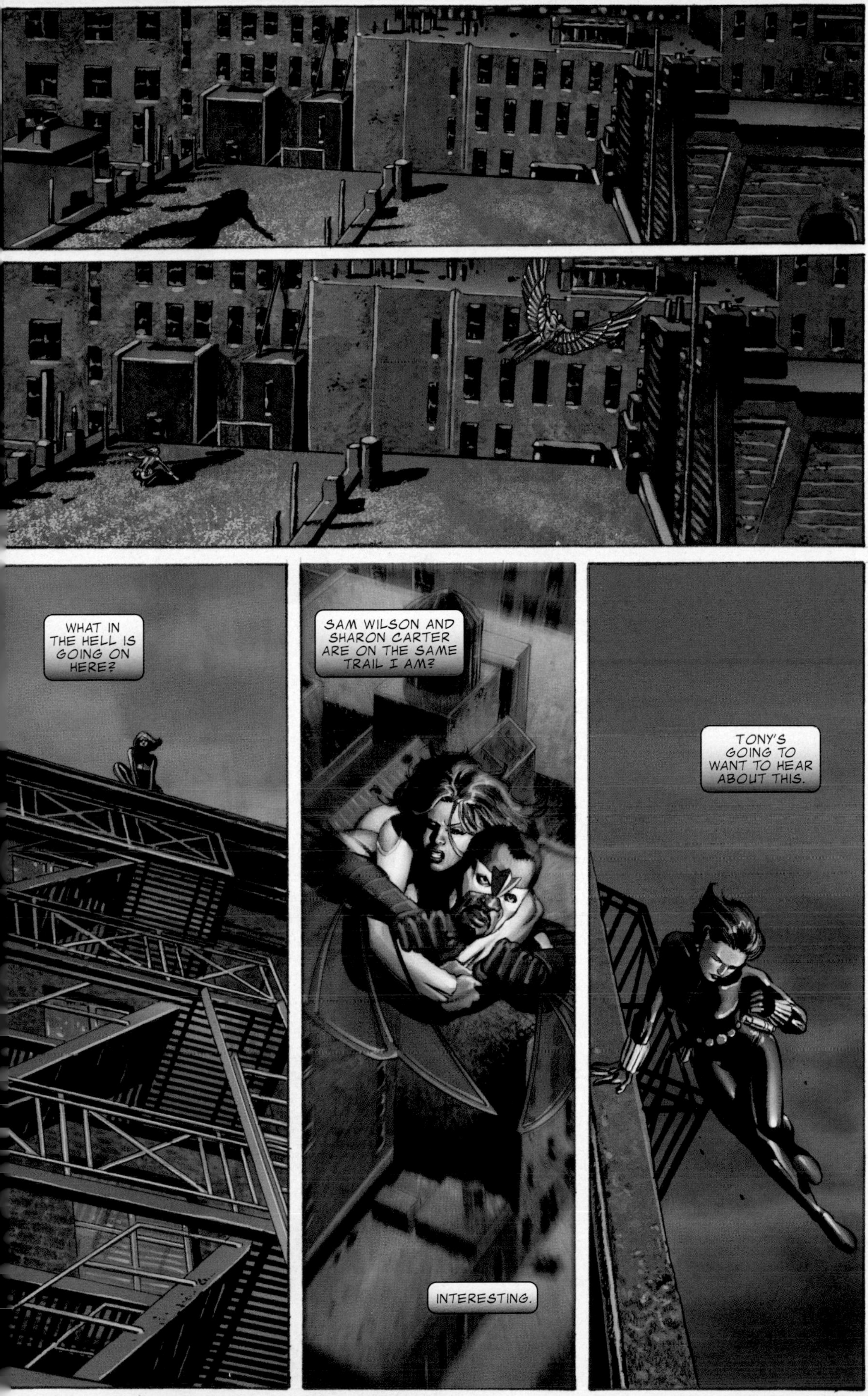
WHAT IN THE HELL IS GOING ON HERE?
SAM WILSON AND SHARON CARTER ARE ON THE SAME TRAIL I AM?
INTERESTING.
TONY'S GOING TO WANT TO HEAR ABOUT THIS.

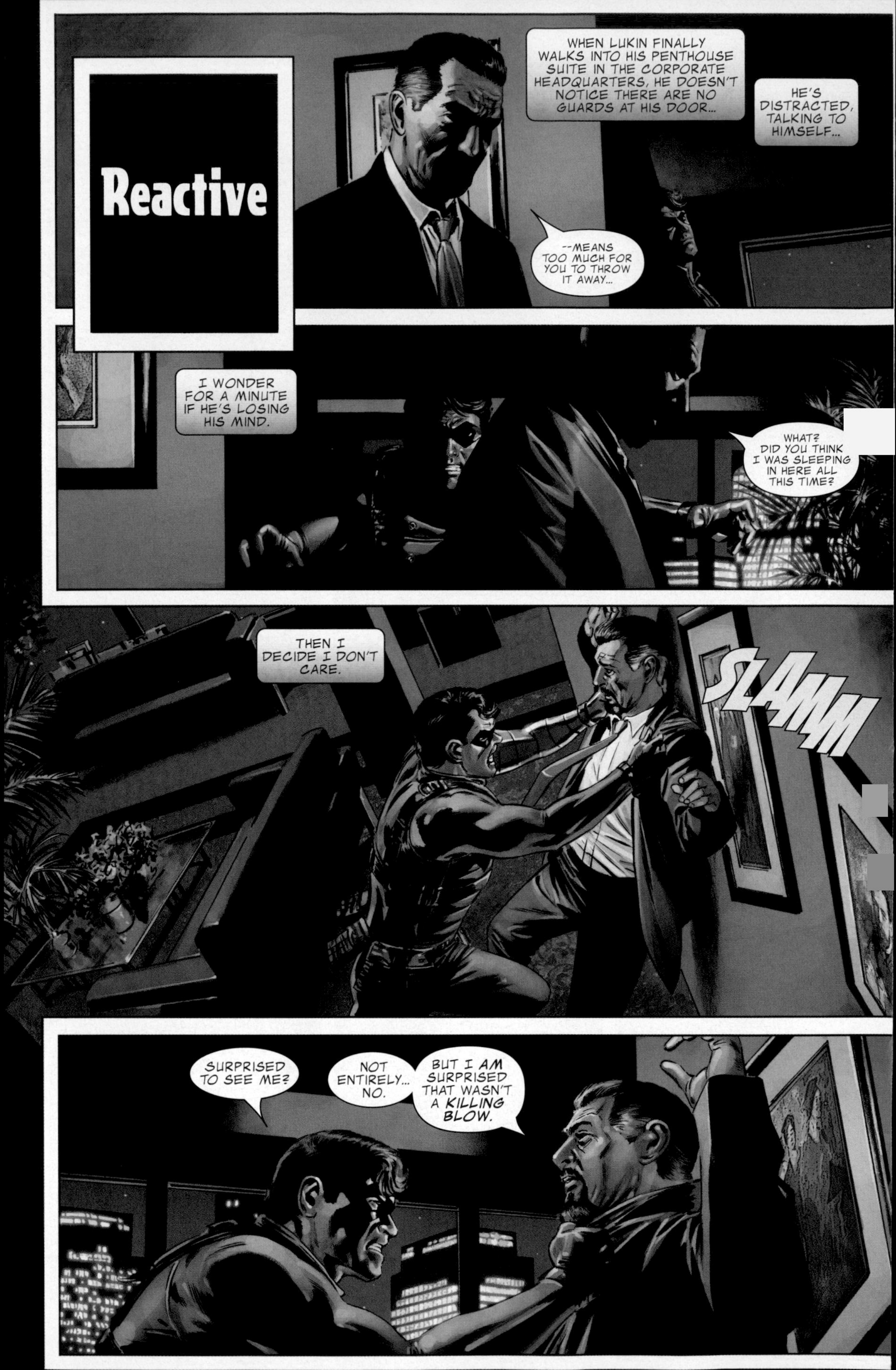
Reactive
WHEN LUKIN FINALLY WALKS INTO HIS PENTHOUSE SUITE IN THE CORPORATE HEADQUARTERS, HE DOESN'T NOTICE THERE ARE NO GUARDS AT HIS DOOR...
HE'S DISTRACTED, TALKING TO HIMSELF...
--MEANS TOO MUCH FOR YOU TO THROW IT AWAY...
I WONDER FOR A MINUTE IF HE'S LOSING HIS MIND.
WHAT? DID YOU THINK I WAS SLEEPING IN HERE ALL THIS TIME?
THEN I DECIDE I DON'T CARE.
SLAMM
SURPRISED TO SEE ME?
NOT ENTIRELY... NO.
BUT I *AM* SURPRISED THAT WASN'T A *KILLING BLOW.*

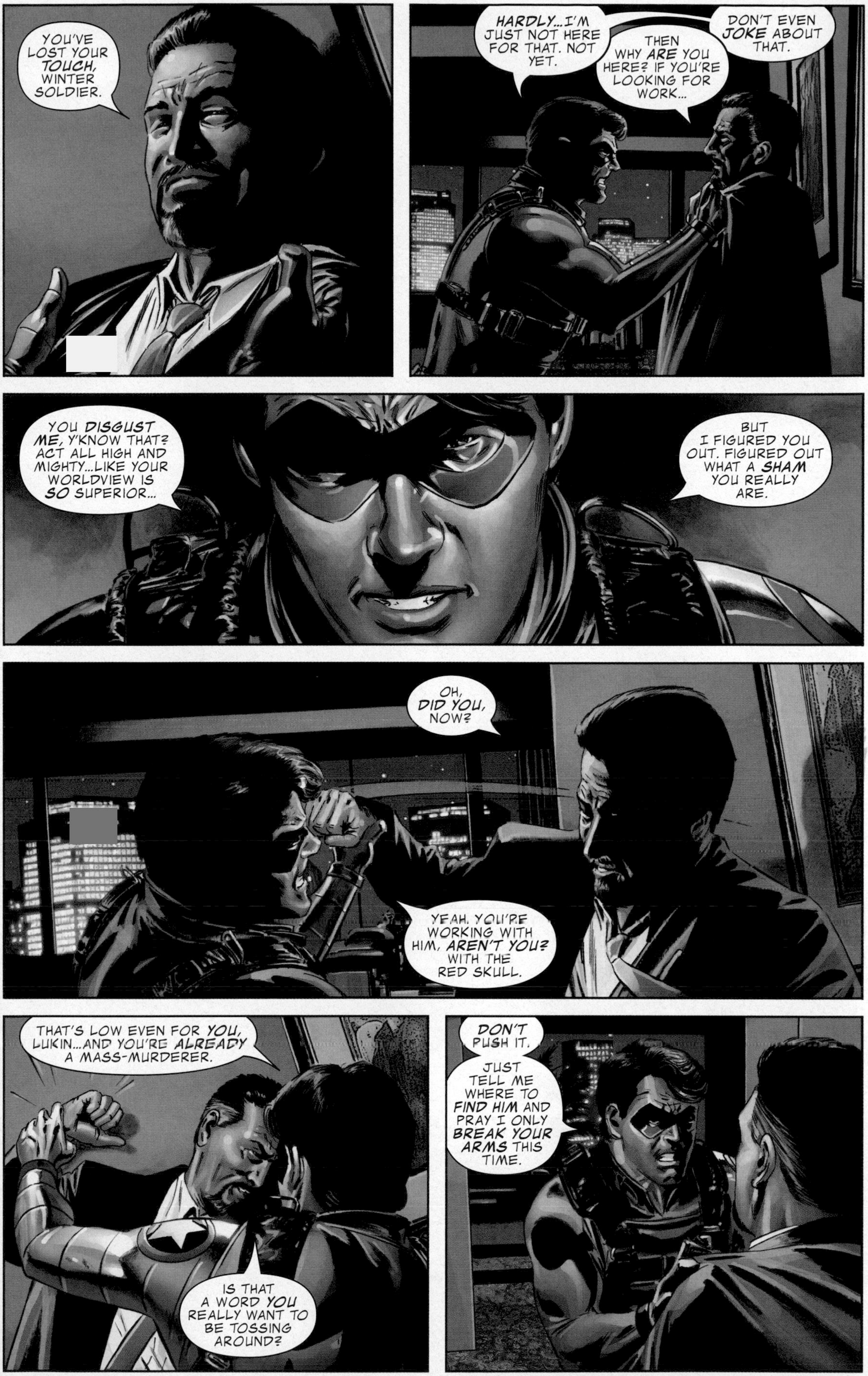
YOU'VE LOST YOUR TOUCH, WINTER SOLDIER.
HARDLY...I'M JUST NOT HERE FOR THAT. NOT YET.
THEN WHY ARE YOU HERE? IF YOU'RE LOOKING FOR WORK...
DON'T EVEN JOKE ABOUT THAT.
YOU DISGUST ME, Y'KNOW THAT? ACT ALL HIGH AND MIGHTY...LIKE YOUR WORLDVIEW IS SO SUPERIOR...
BUT I FIGURED YOU OUT. FIGURED OUT WHAT A SHAM YOU REALLY ARE.
OH, DID YOU, NOW?
YEAH. YOU'RE WORKING WITH HIM, AREN'T YOU? WITH THE RED SKULL.
THAT'S LOW EVEN FOR YOU, LUKIN...AND YOU'RE ALREADY A MASS-MURDERER.
IS THAT A WORD YOU REALLY WANT TO BE TOSSING AROUND?
DON'T PUSH IT.
JUST TELL ME WHERE TO FIND HIM AND PRAY I ONLY BREAK YOUR ARMS THIS TIME.

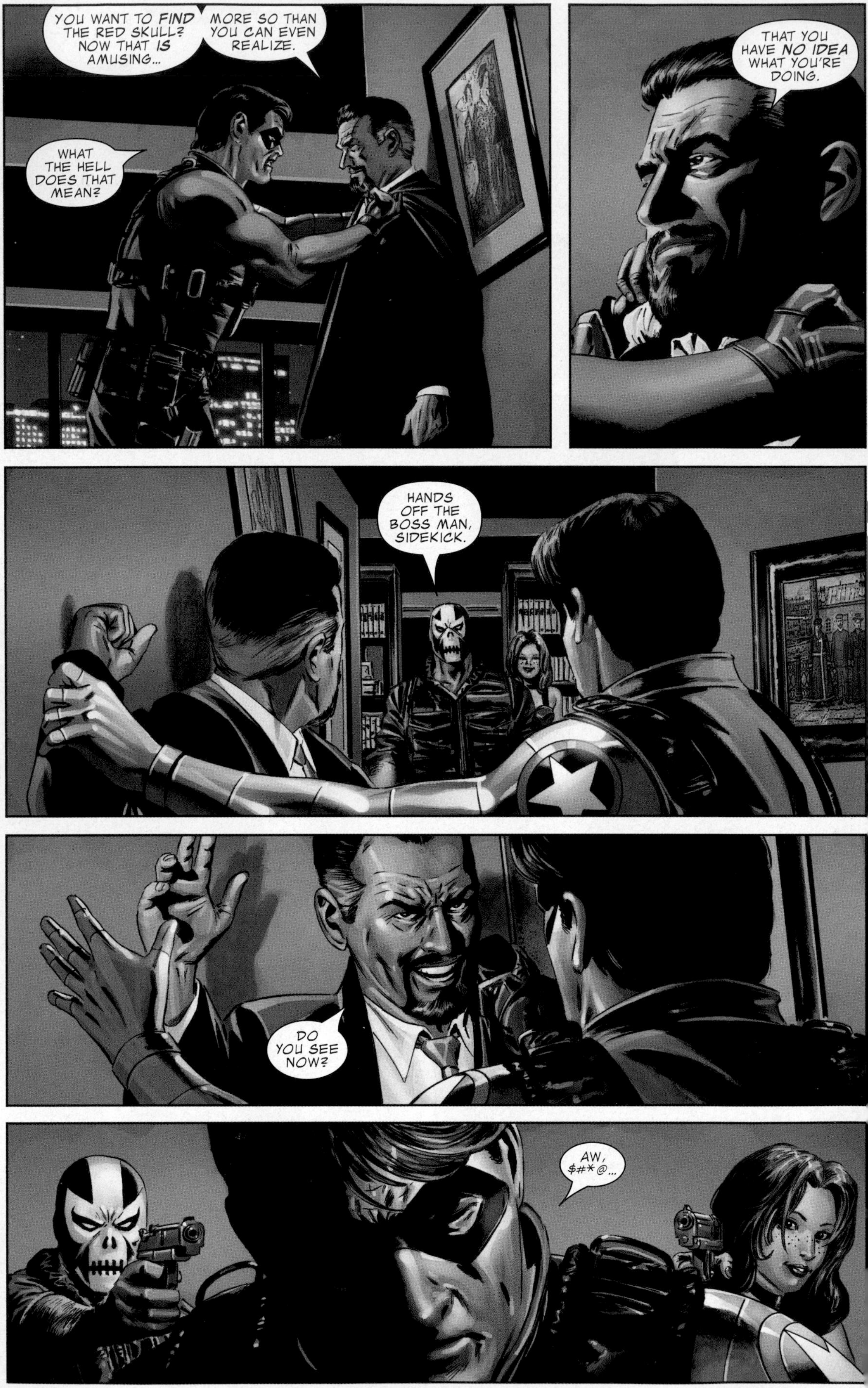
YOU WANT TO FIND THE RED SKULL? NOW THAT IS AMUSING...
MORE SO THAN YOU CAN EVEN REALIZE.
WHAT THE HELL DOES THAT MEAN?
THAT YOU HAVE NO IDEA WHAT YOU'RE DOING.
HANDS OFF THE BOSS MAN, SIDEKICK.
DO YOU SEE NOW?
AW, $#*@...

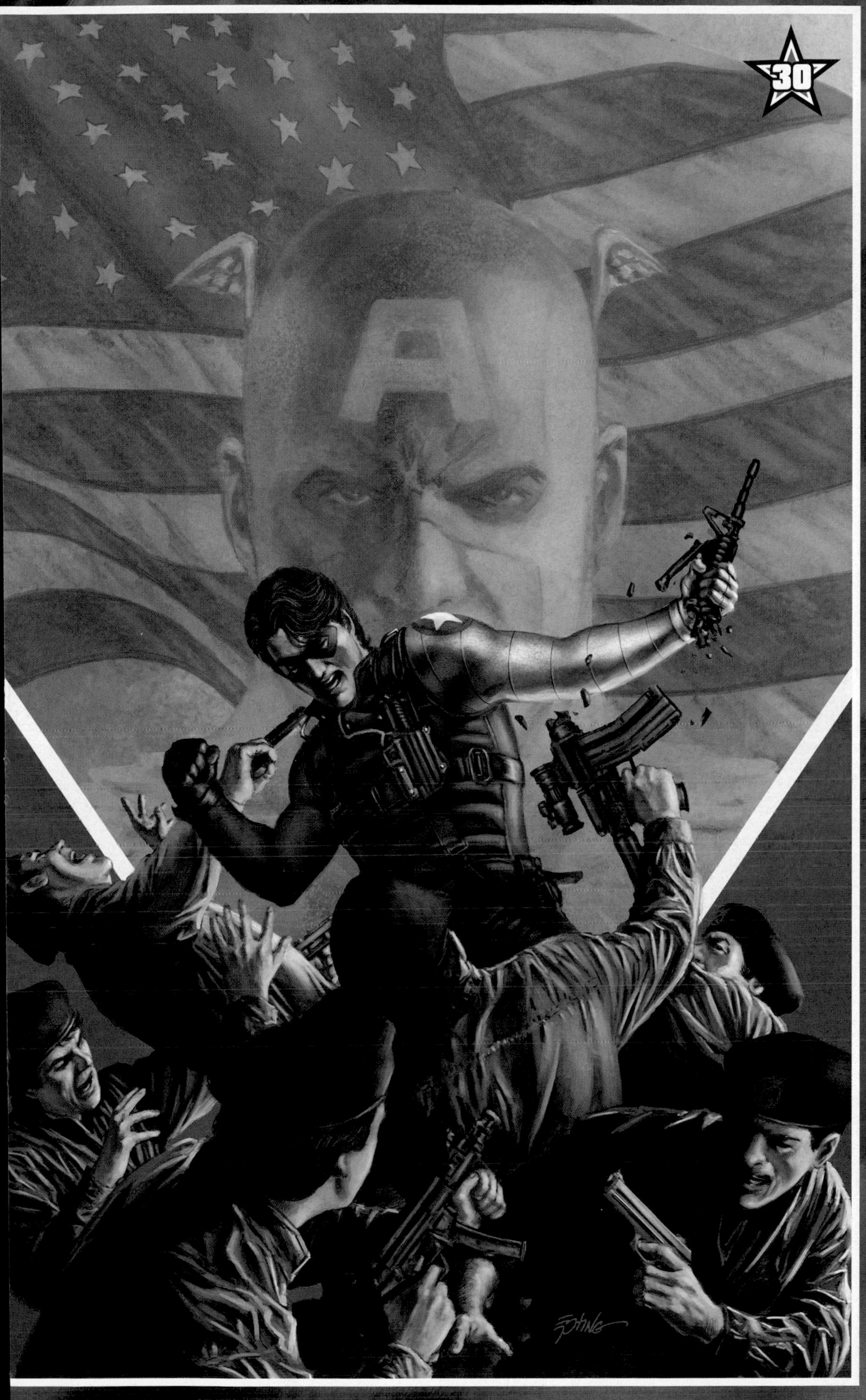
30

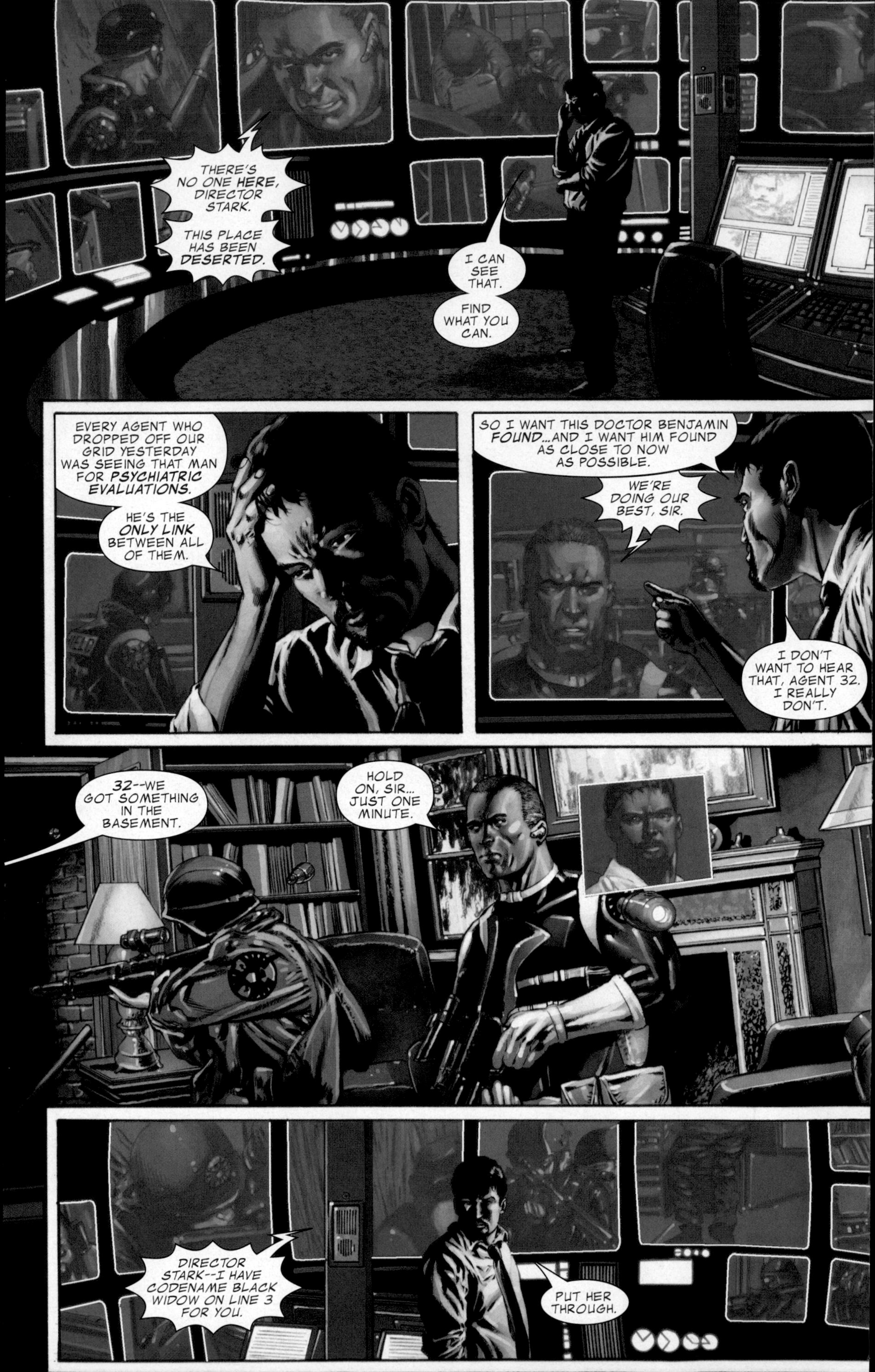
THERE'S NO ONE HERE, DIRECTOR STARK.
THIS PLACE HAS BEEN DESERTED.
I CAN SEE THAT.
FIND WHAT YOU CAN.
EVERY AGENT WHO DROPPED OFF OUR GRID YESTERDAY WAS SEEING THAT MAN FOR PSYCHIATRIC EVALUATIONS.
HE'S THE ONLY LINK BETWEEN ALL OF THEM.
SO I WANT THIS DOCTOR BENJAMIN FOUND...AND I WANT HIM FOUND AS CLOSE TO NOW AS POSSIBLE.
WE'RE DOING OUR BEST, SIR.
I DON'T WANT TO HEAR THAT, AGENT 32. I REALLY DON'T.
32--WE GOT SOMETHING IN THE BASEMENT.
HOLD ON, SIR... JUST ONE MINUTE.
DIRECTOR STARK--I HAVE CODENAME BLACK WIDOW ON LINE 3 FOR YOU.
PUT HER THROUGH.

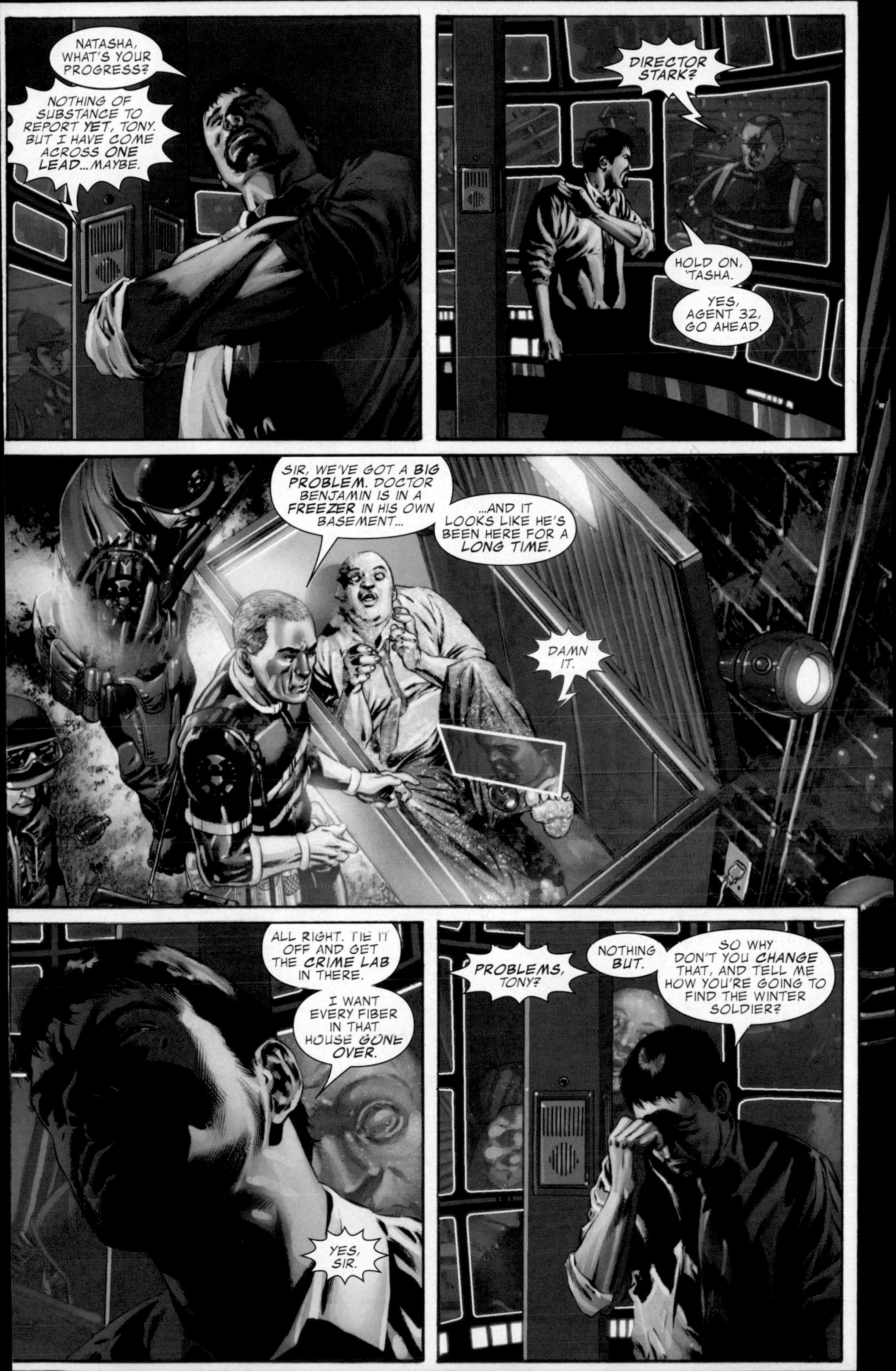
NATASHA, WHAT'S YOUR PROGRESS?
NOTHING OF SUBSTANCE TO REPORT YET, TONY. BUT I HAVE COME ACROSS ONE LEAD...MAYBE.
DIRECTOR STARK?
HOLD ON, 'TASHA.
YES, AGENT 32, GO AHEAD.
SIR, WE'VE GOT A BIG PROBLEM. DOCTOR BENJAMIN IS IN A FREEZER IN HIS OWN BASEMENT...
...AND IT LOOKS LIKE HE'S BEEN HERE FOR A LONG TIME.
DAMN IT.
ALL RIGHT. TIE IT OFF AND GET THE CRIME LAB IN THERE.
I WANT EVERY FIBER IN THAT HOUSE GONE OVER.
YES, SIR.
PROBLEMS, TONY?
NOTHING BUT.
SO WHY DON'T YOU CHANGE THAT, AND TELL ME HOW YOU'RE GOING TO FIND THE WINTER SOLDIER?

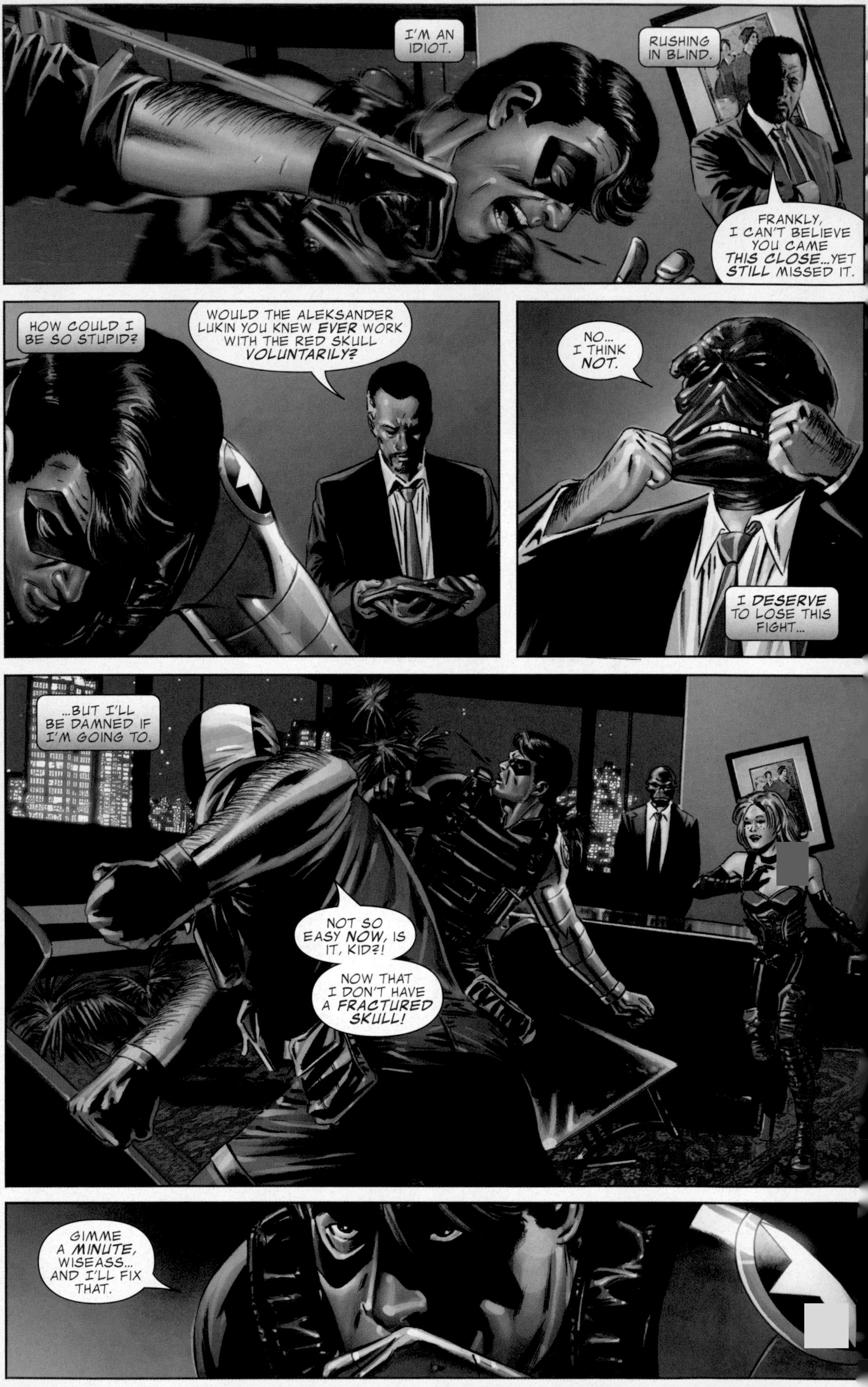
I'M AN IDIOT.
RUSHING IN BLIND.
FRANKLY, I CAN'T BELIEVE YOU CAME THIS CLOSE...YET STILL MISSED IT.
HOW COULD I BE SO STUPID?
WOULD THE ALEKSANDER LUKIN YOU KNEW EVER WORK WITH THE RED SKULL VOLUNTARILY?
NO... I THINK NOT.
I DESERVE TO LOSE THIS FIGHT...
...BUT I'LL BE DAMNED IF I'M GOING TO.
NOT SO EASY NOW, IS IT, KID?!
NOW THAT I DON'T HAVE A FRACTURED SKULL!
GIMME A MINUTE, WISEASS... AND I'LL FIX THAT.

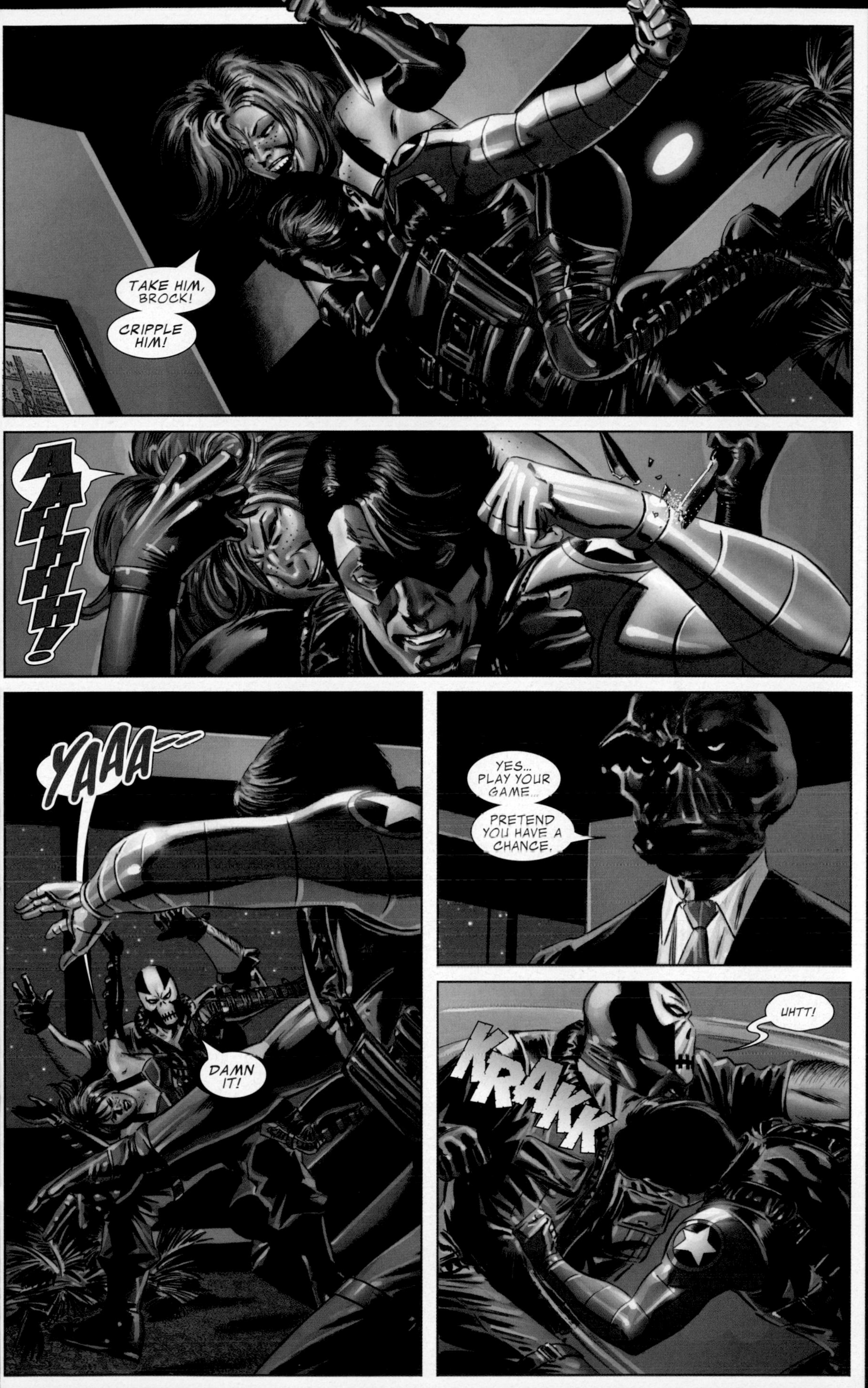
TAKE HIM, BROCK!
CRIPPLE HIM!
AAHHHH!
YAAA--
DAMN IT!
YES... PLAY YOUR GAME...
PRETEND YOU HAVE A CHANCE.
KRAKK
UHTT!

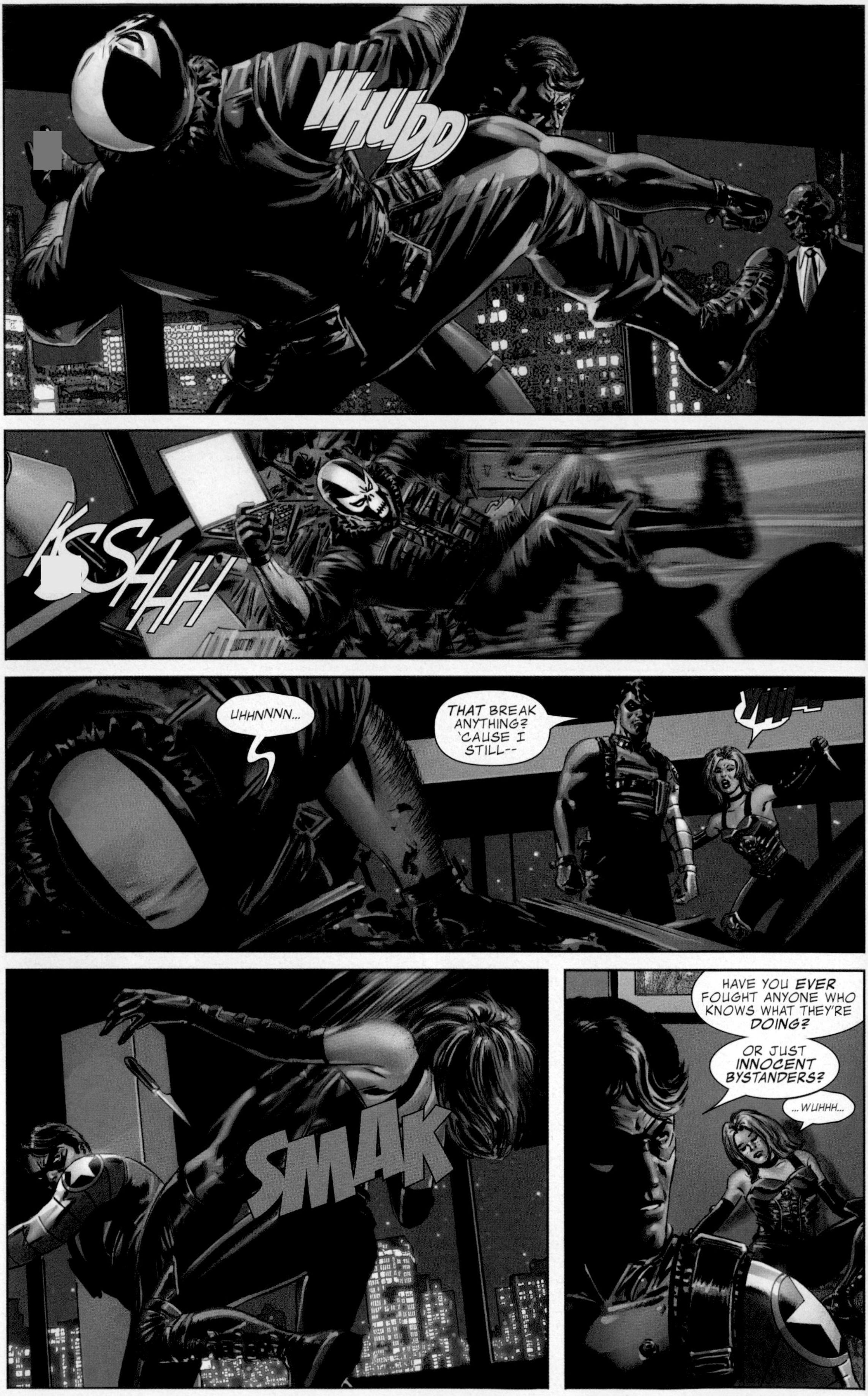
WHUDD
KSHHH
UHHNNNN...
THAT BREAK ANYTHING? 'CAUSE I STILL--
SMAK
HAVE YOU EVER FOUGHT ANYONE WHO KNOWS WHAT THEY'RE DOING?
OR JUST INNOCENT BYSTANDERS?
...WUHHH...

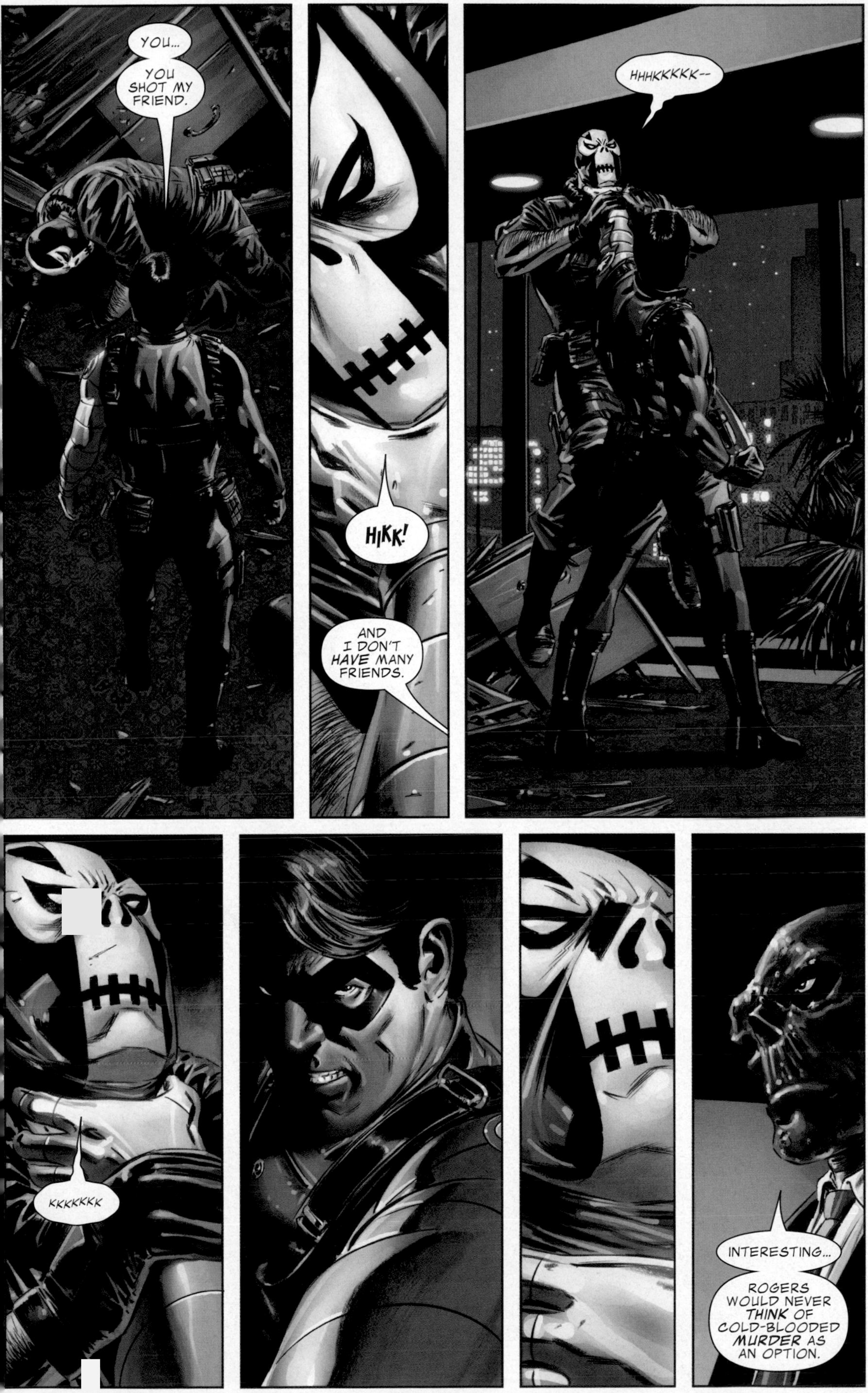
YOU...
YOU SHOT MY FRIEND.
HIKK!
AND I DON'T HAVE MANY FRIENDS.
HHHKKKKK--
KKKKKKK
INTERESTING...
ROGERS WOULD NEVER THINK OF COLD-BLOODED MURDER AS AN OPTION.

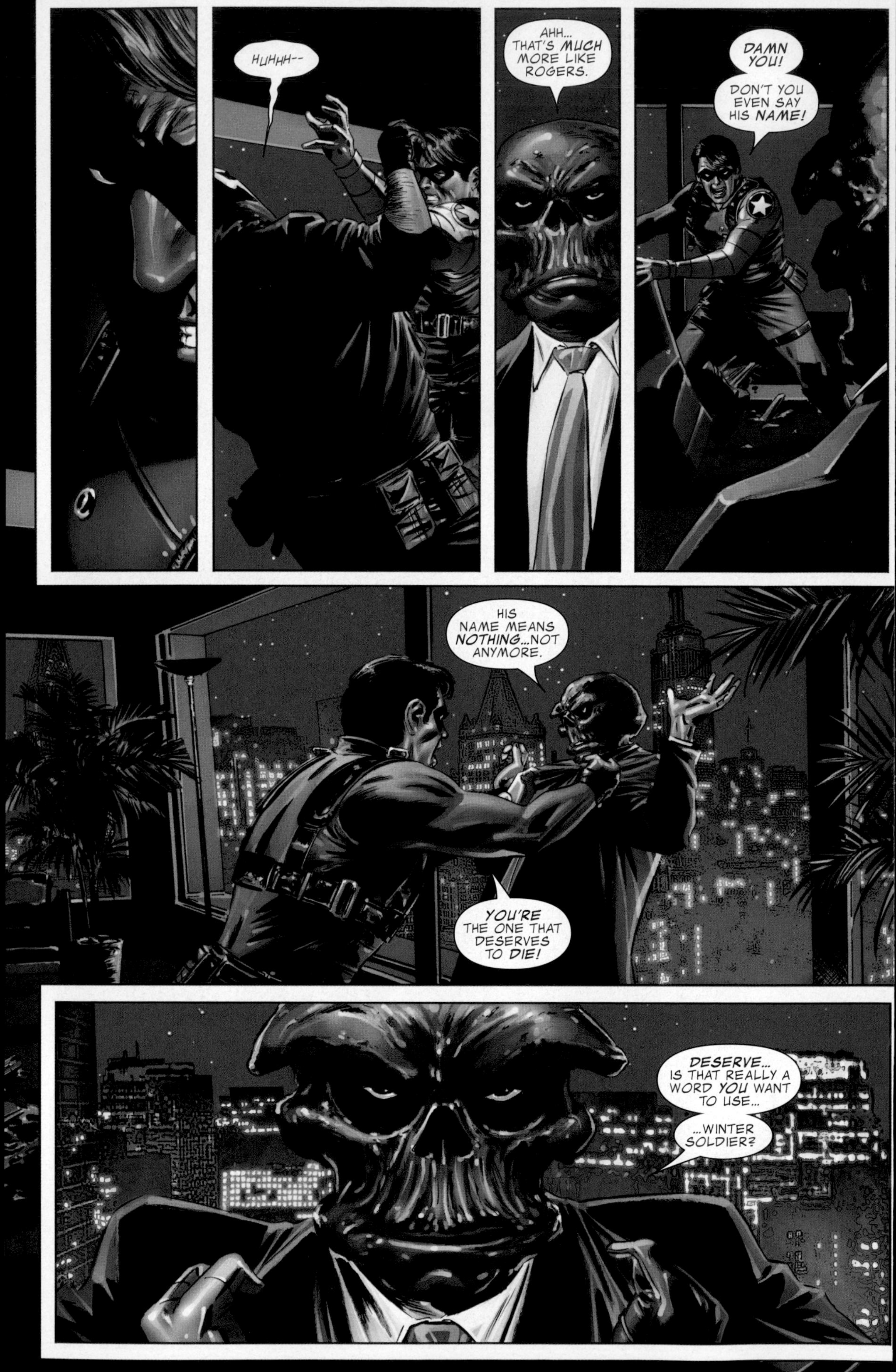
HUHHH--
AHH... THAT'S MUCH MORE LIKE ROGERS.
DAMN YOU!
DON'T YOU EVEN SAY HIS NAME!
HIS NAME MEANS NOTHING...NOT ANYMORE.
YOU'RE THE ONE THAT DESERVES TO DIE!
DESERVE... IS THAT REALLY A WORD YOU WANT TO USE...
...WINTER SOLDIER?

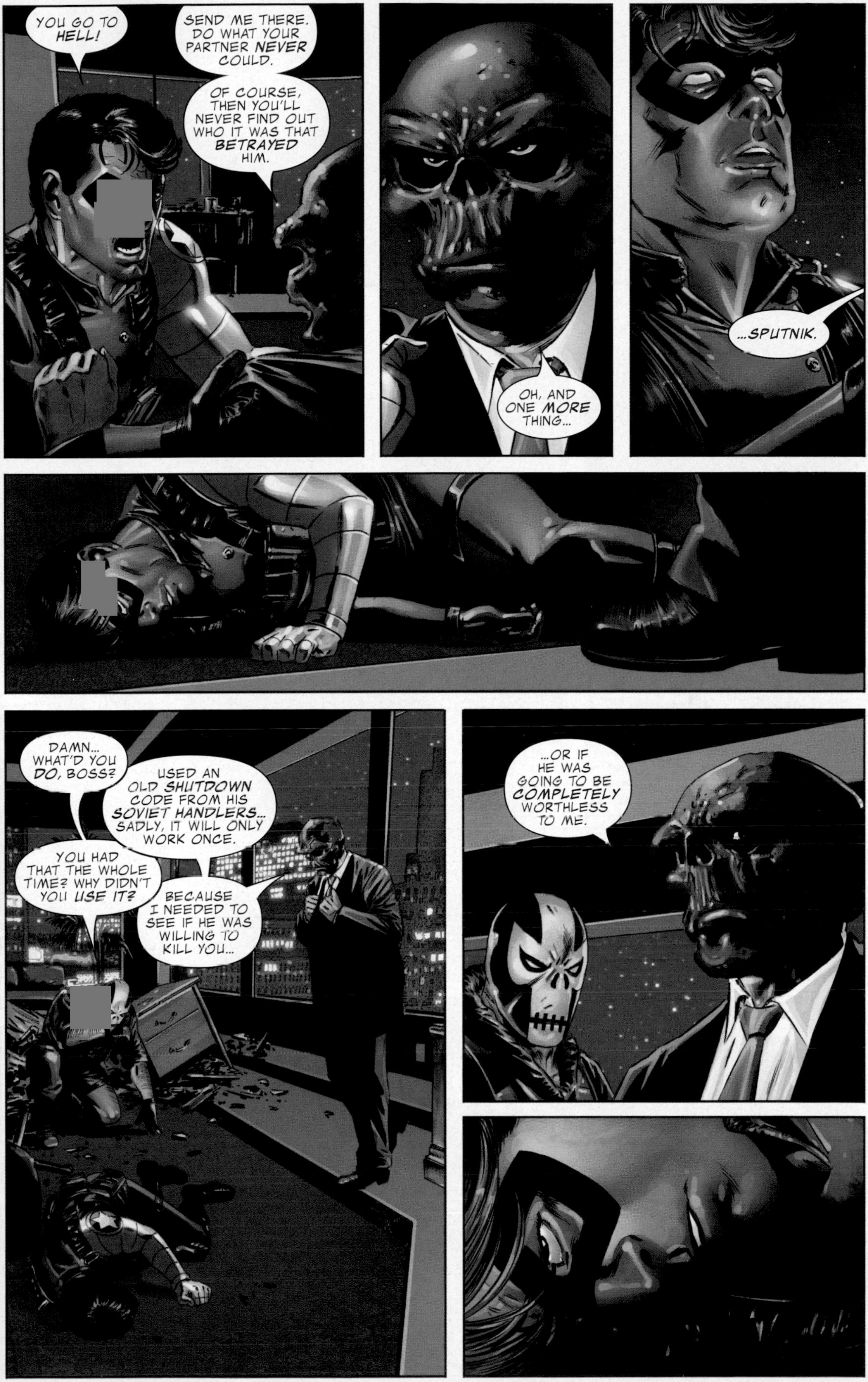
YOU GO TO HELL!
SEND ME THERE. DO WHAT YOUR PARTNER NEVER COULD.
OF COURSE, THEN YOU'LL NEVER FIND OUT WHO IT WAS THAT BETRAYED HIM.
OH, AND ONE MORE THING...
...SPUTNIK.
DAMN... WHAT'D YOU DO, BOSS?
USED AN OLD SHUTDOWN CODE FROM HIS SOVIET HANDLERS... SADLY, IT WILL ONLY WORK ONCE.
YOU HAD THAT THE WHOLE TIME? WHY DIDN'T YOU USE IT?
BECAUSE I NEEDED TO SEE IF HE WAS WILLING TO KILL YOU...
...OR IF HE WAS GOING TO BE COMPLETELY WORTHLESS TO ME.

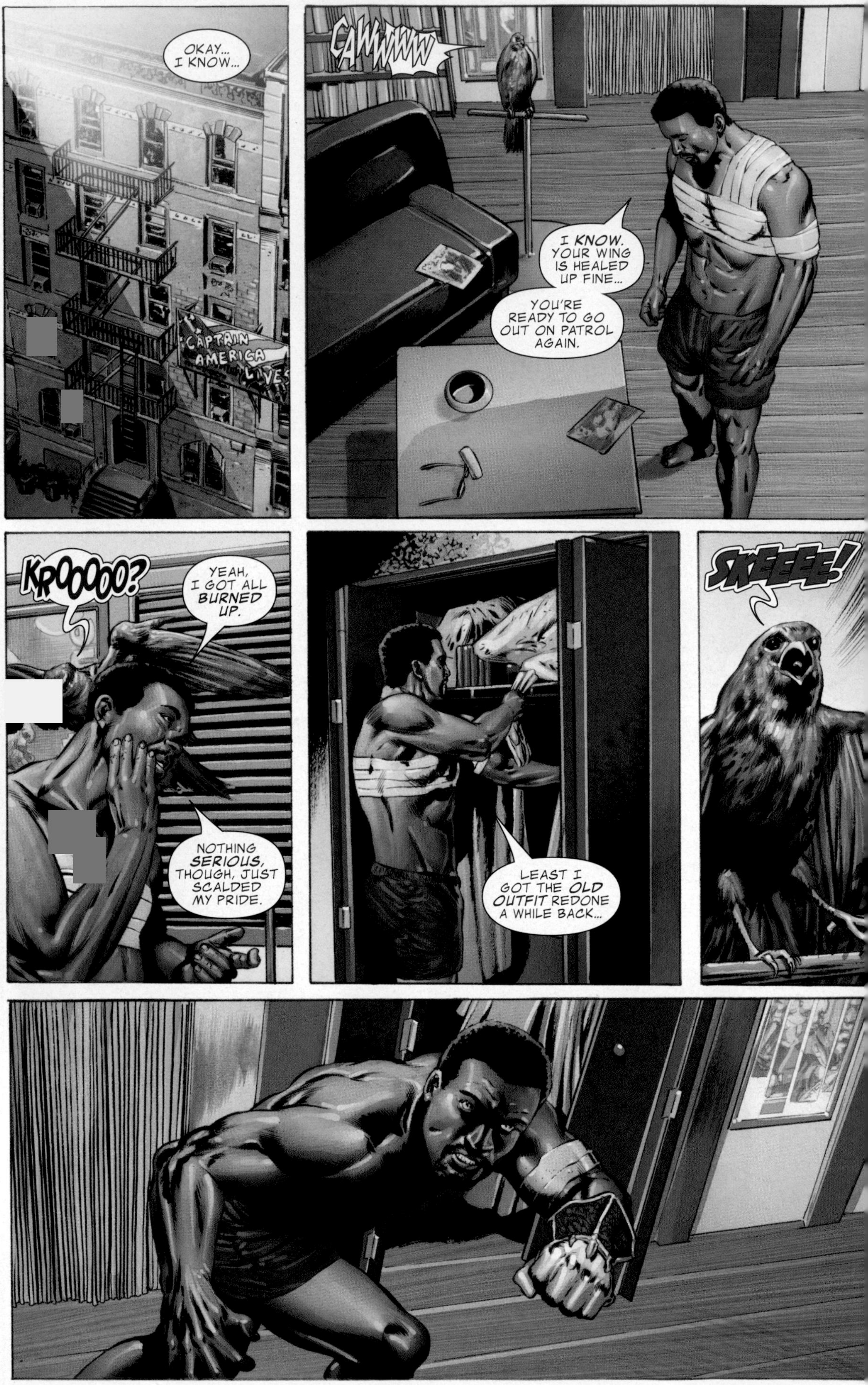
OKAY... I KNOW...
CAPTAIN AMERICA LIVES
CAWWWW
I KNOW. YOUR WING IS HEALED UP FINE...
YOU'RE READY TO GO OUT ON PATROL AGAIN.
KROOOOO?
YEAH, I GOT ALL BURNED UP.
NOTHING SERIOUS, THOUGH, JUST SCALDED MY PRIDE.
LEAST I GOT THE OLD OUTFIT REDONE A WHILE BACK...
SKEEEE!

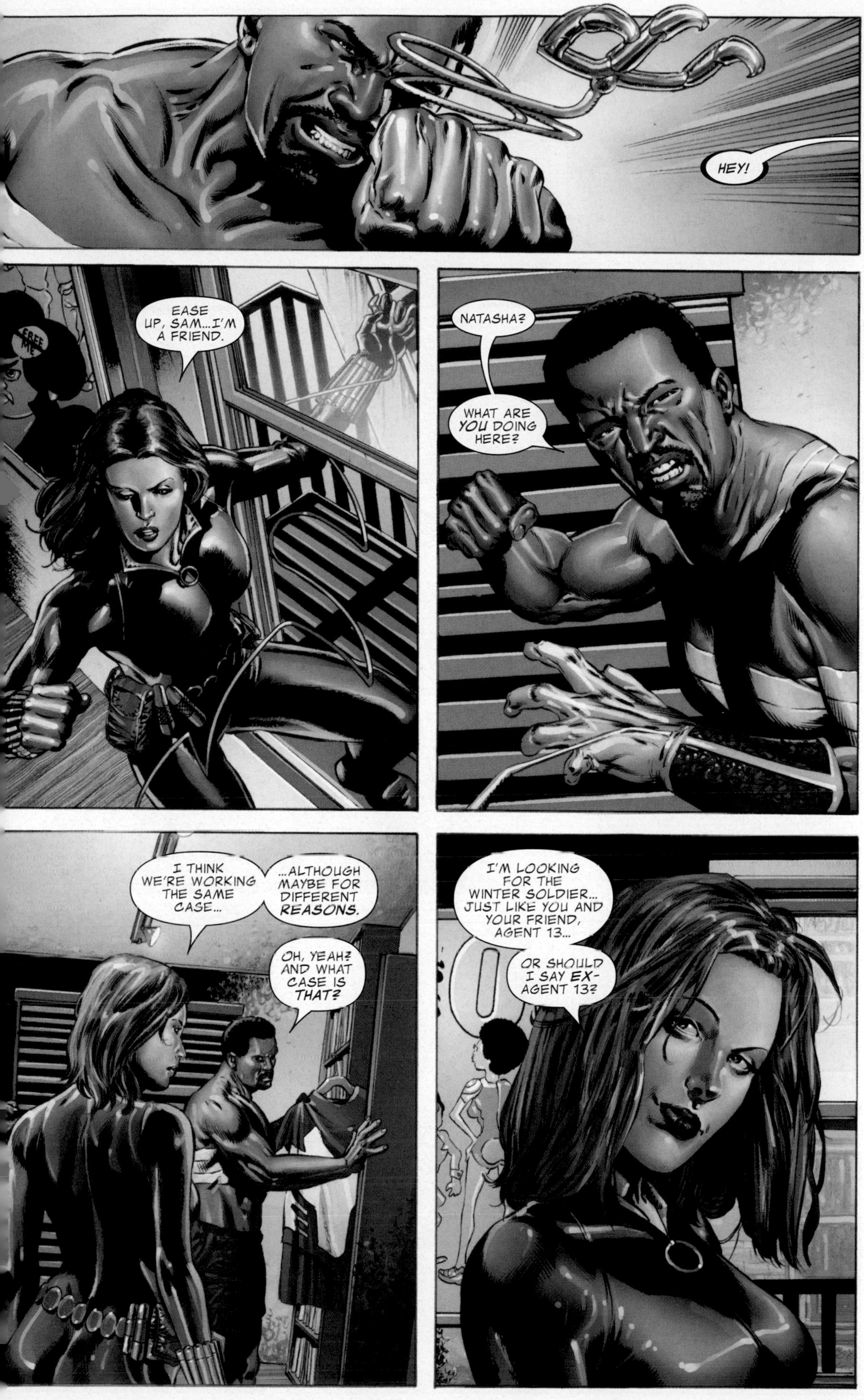
HEY!
EASE UP, SAM...I'M A FRIEND.
FREE ME
NATASHA?
WHAT ARE YOU DOING HERE?
I THINK WE'RE WORKING THE SAME CASE...
...ALTHOUGH MAYBE FOR DIFFERENT REASONS.
OH, YEAH? AND WHAT CASE IS THAT?
I'M LOOKING FOR THE WINTER SOLDIER... JUST LIKE YOU AND YOUR FRIEND, AGENT 13...
OR SHOULD I SAY EX-AGENT 13?

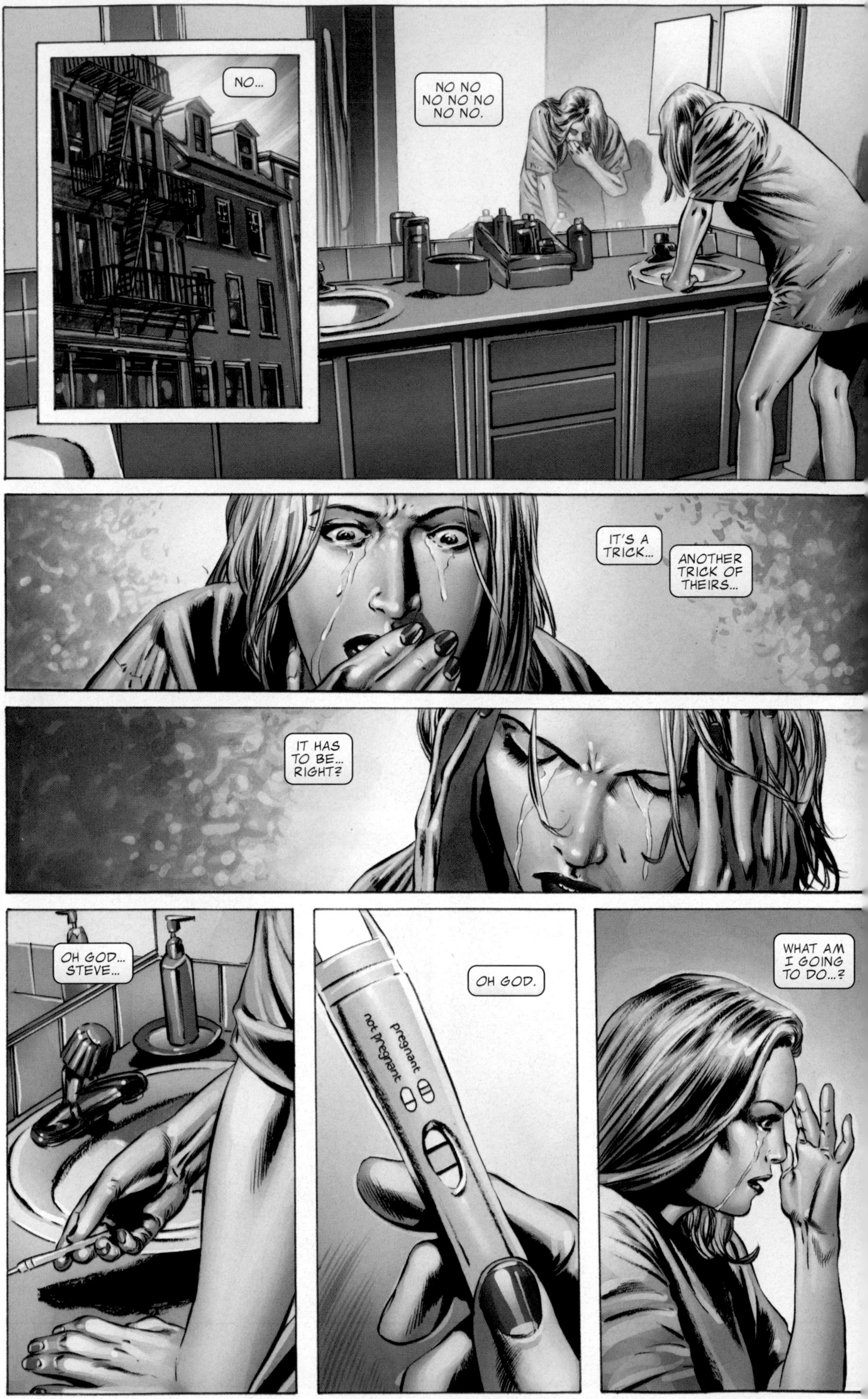
NO...
NO NO NO NO NO NO NO NO.
IT'S A TRICK...
ANOTHER TRICK OF THEIRS...
IT HAS TO BE... RIGHT?
OH GOD... STEVE...
OH GOD.
pregnant
not pregnant
WHAT AM I GOING TO DO...?

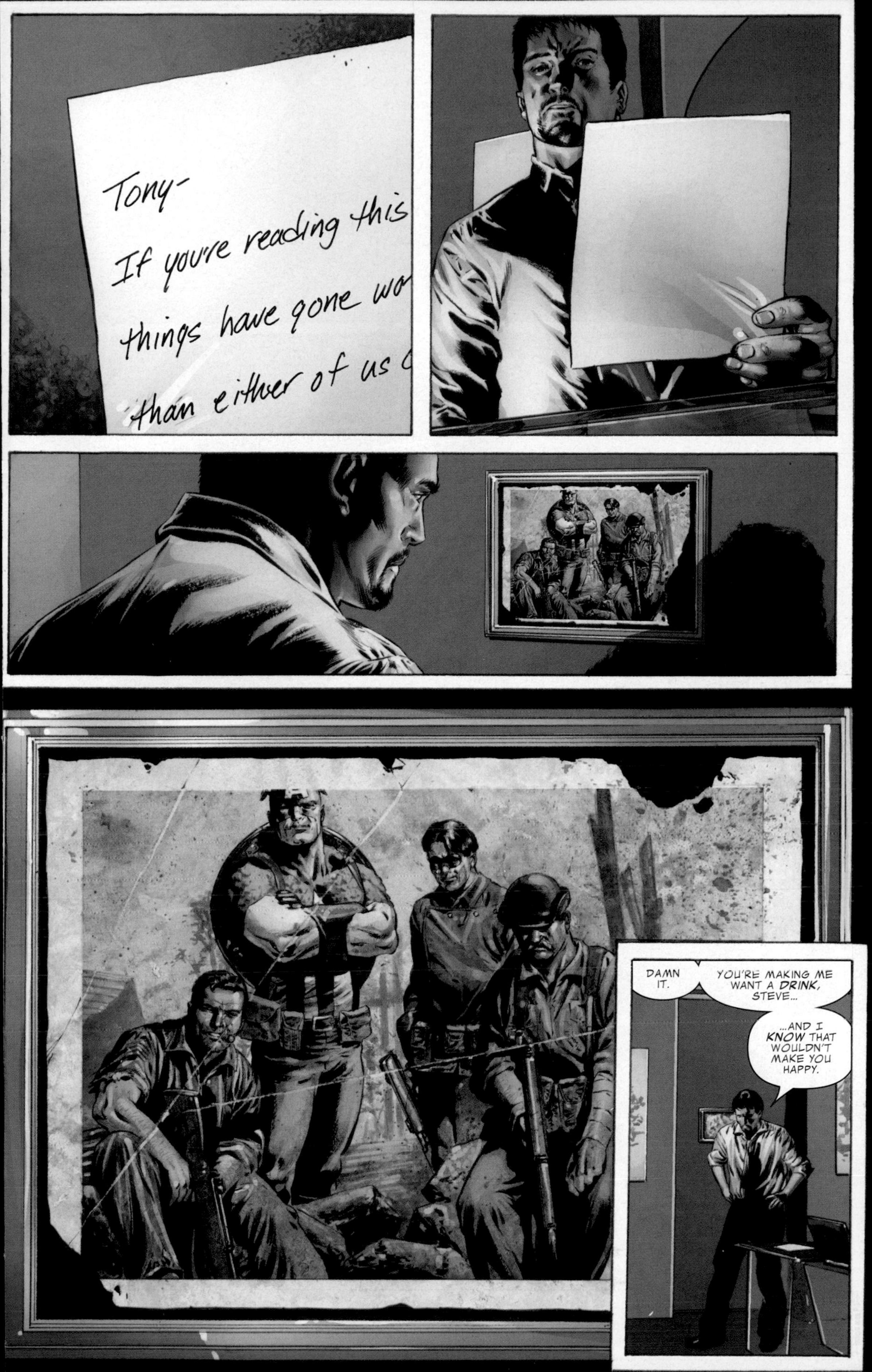
Tony-
If you're reading this
things have gone wo
than either of us c
DAMN IT.
YOU'RE MAKING ME WANT A DRINK, STEVE...
...AND I KNOW THAT WOULDN'T MAKE YOU HAPPY.

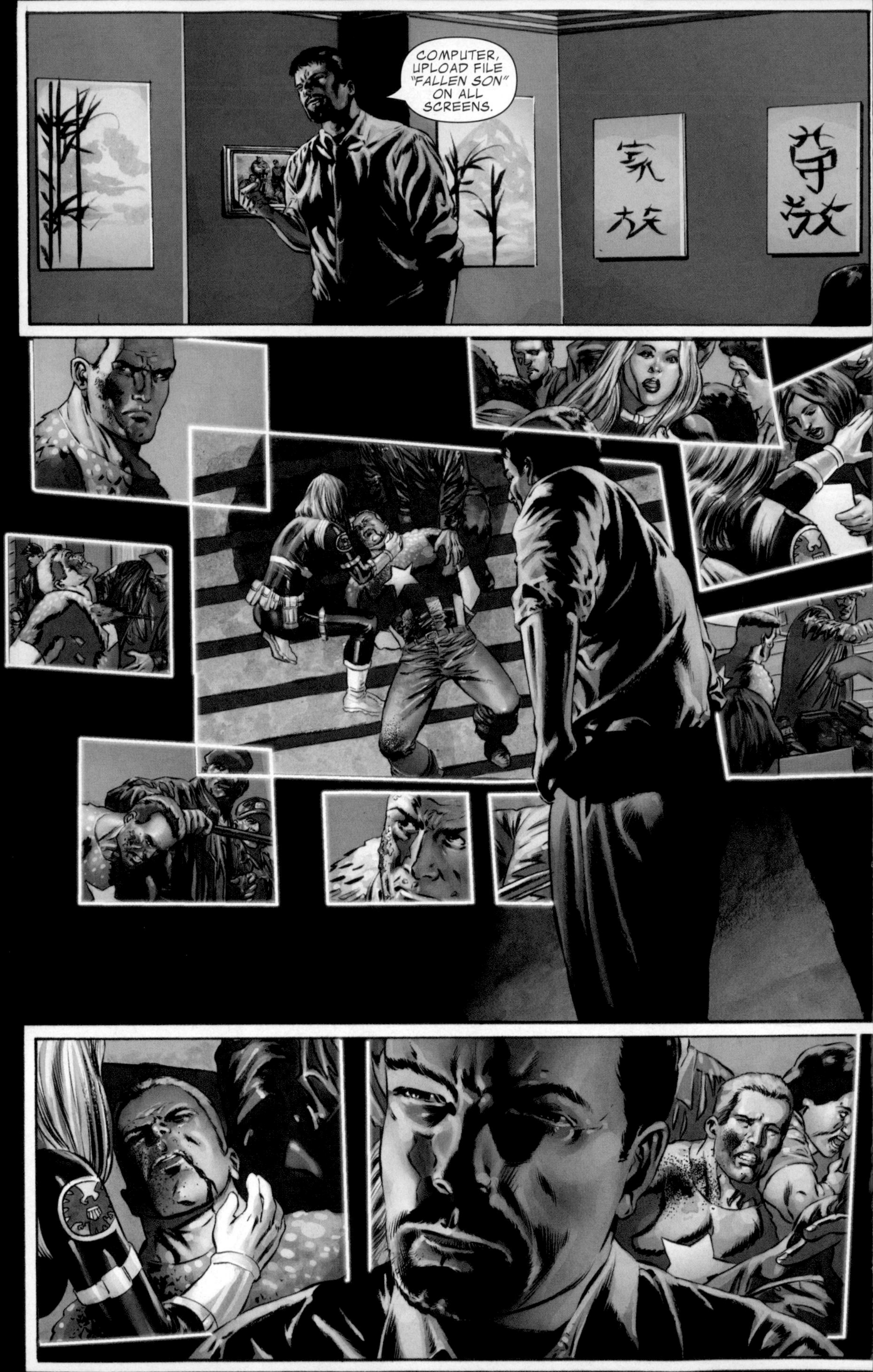
COMPUTER, UPLOAD FILE "FALLEN SON" ON ALL SCREENS.

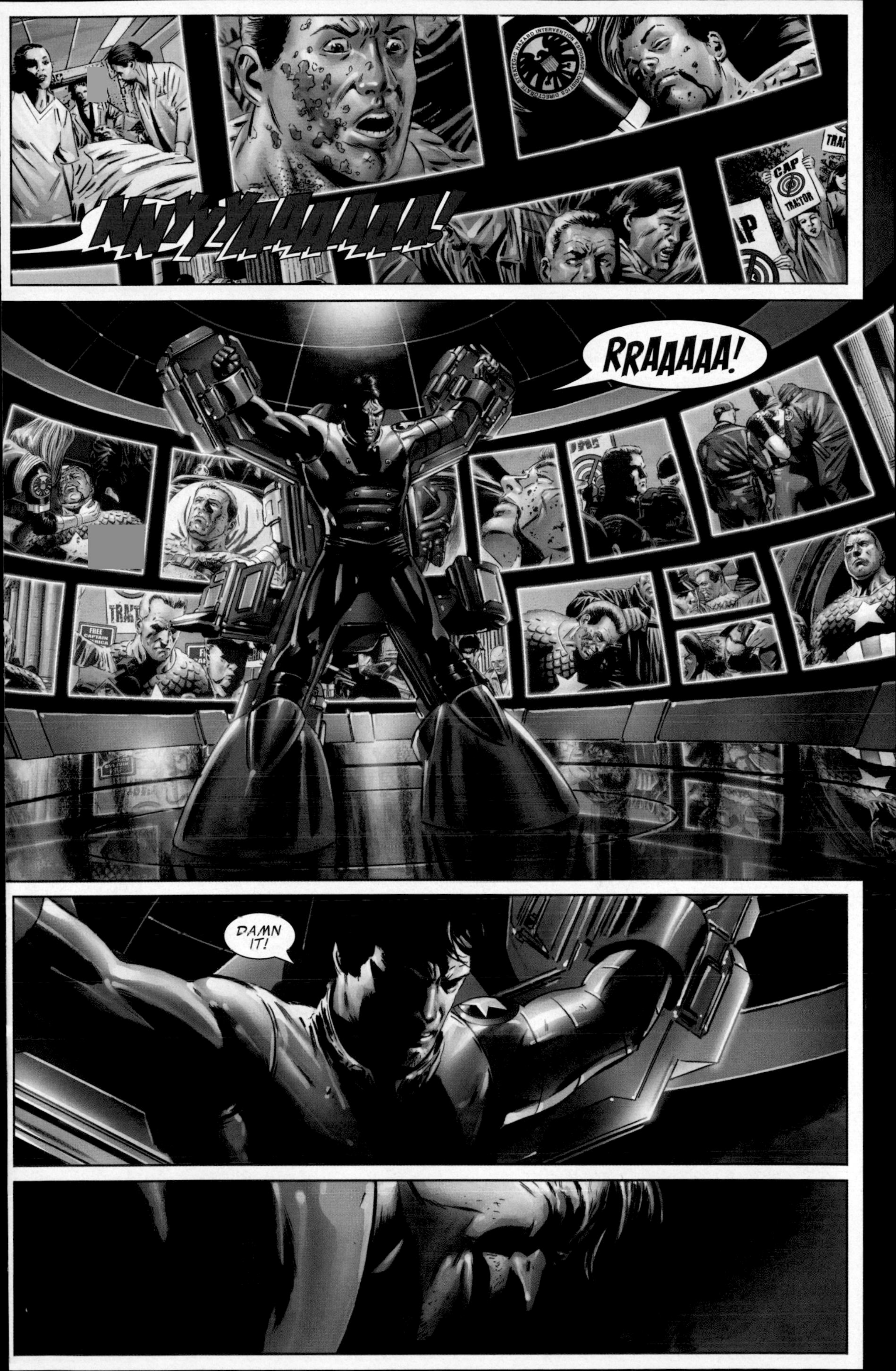
STRATEGIC HAZARD INTERVENTION ESPIONAGE LOGISTICS DIRECTORATE
CAP TRAITOR
NNYYAAAAAA!
RRAAAAA!
FREE CAPTAIN AMERICA
DAMN IT!

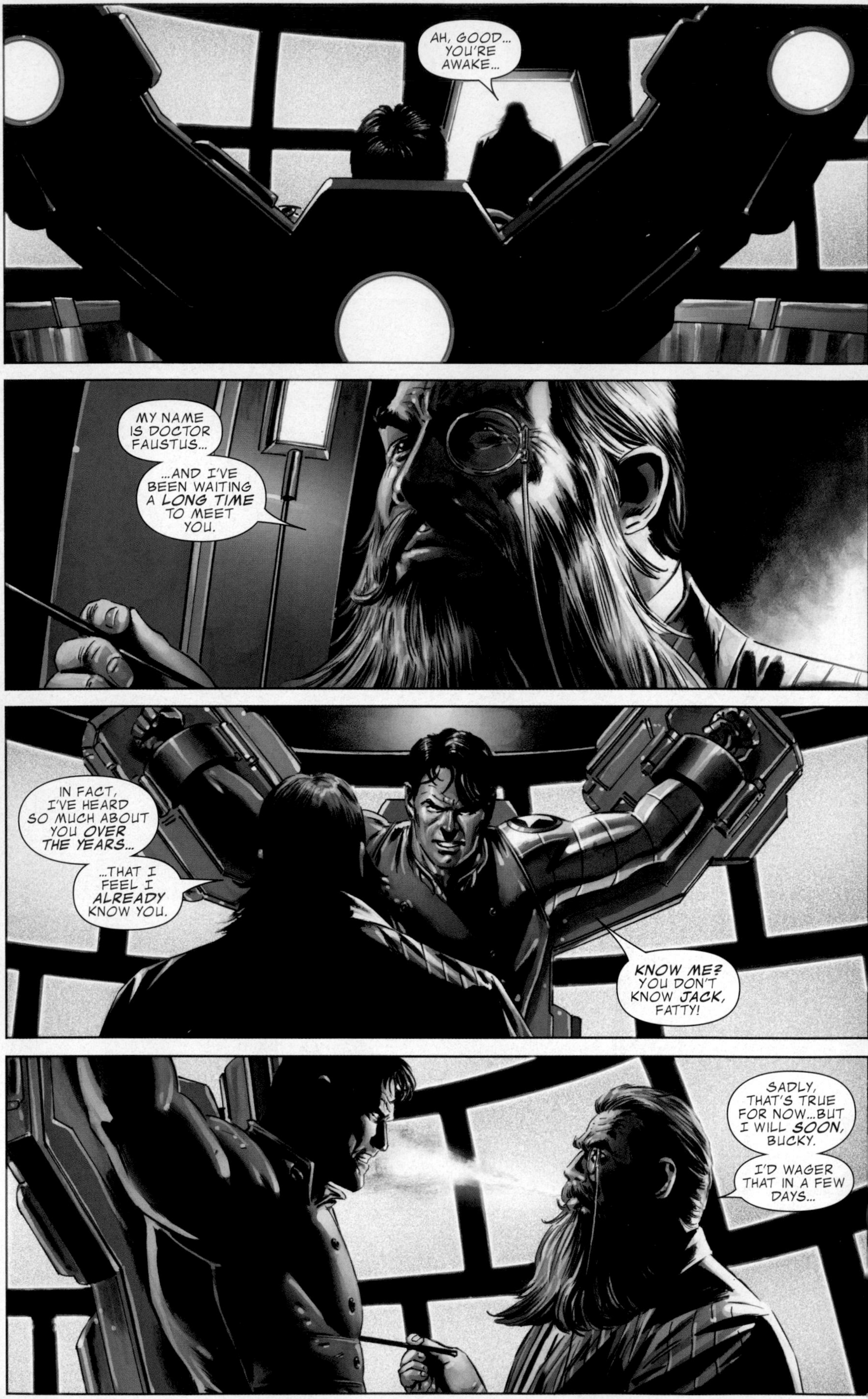
AH, GOOD... YOU'RE AWAKE...
MY NAME IS DOCTOR FAUSTUS...
...AND I'VE BEEN WAITING A LONG TIME TO MEET YOU.
IN FACT, I'VE HEARD SO MUCH ABOUT YOU OVER THE YEARS...
...THAT I FEEL I ALREADY KNOW YOU.
KNOW ME? YOU DON'T KNOW JACK, FATTY!
SADLY, THAT'S TRUE FOR NOW...BUT I WILL SOON, BUCKY.
I'D WAGER THAT IN A FEW DAYS...

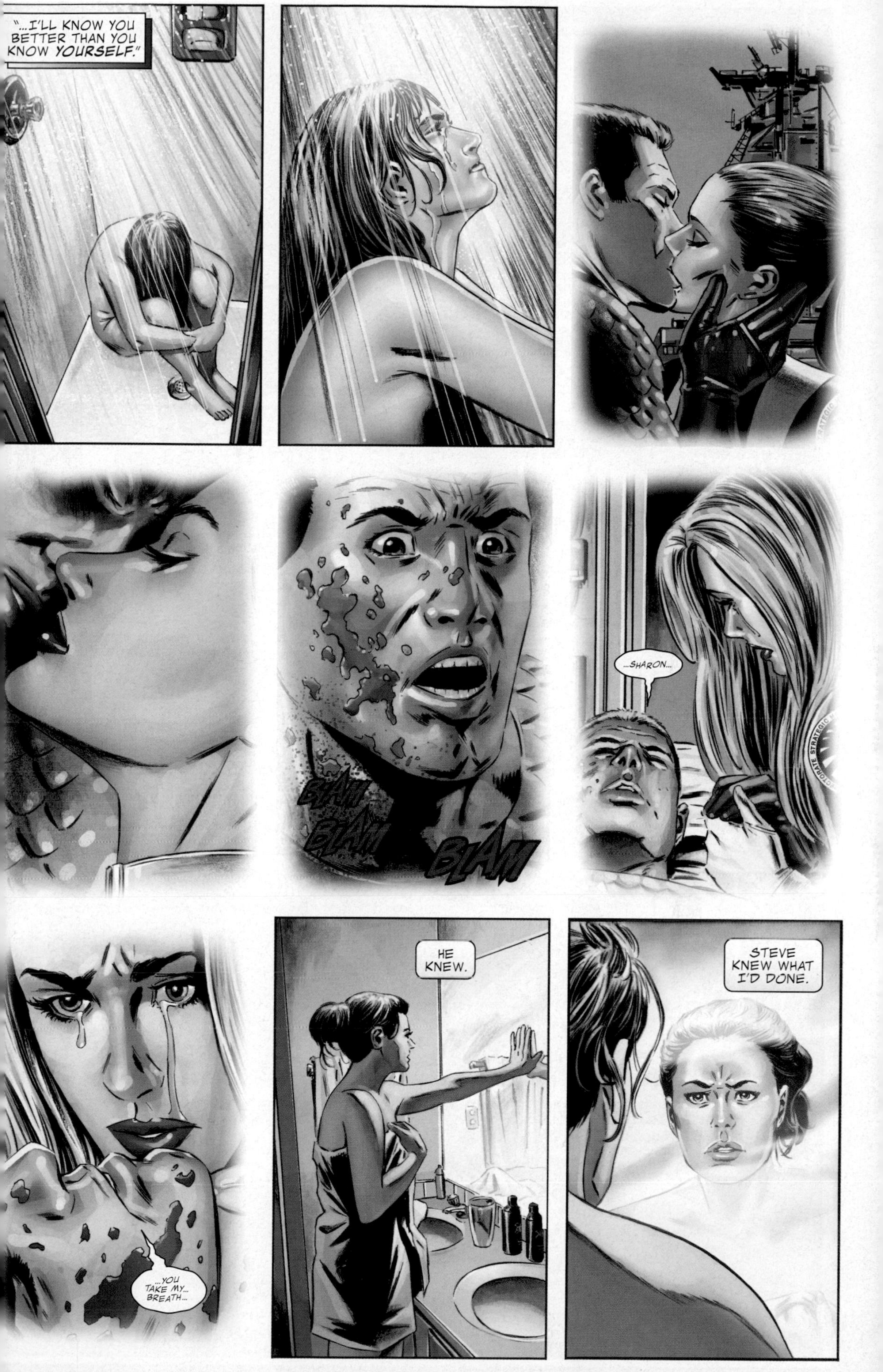
"...I'LL KNOW YOU BETTER THAN YOU KNOW YOURSELF."
BLAM
BLAM
BLAM
...SHARON...
...YOU TAKE MY... BREATH...
HE KNEW.
STEVE KNEW WHAT I'D DONE.

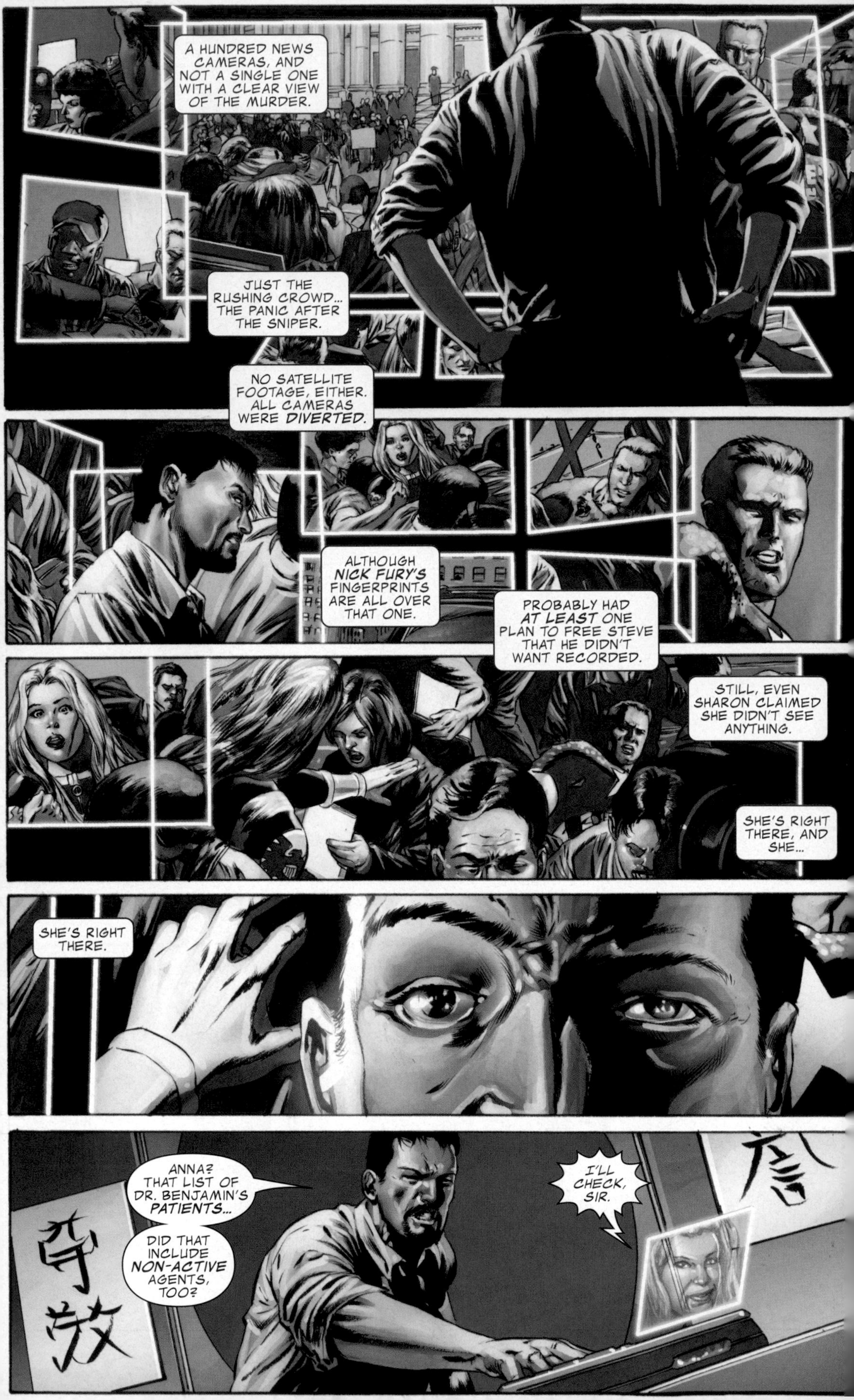
A HUNDRED NEWS CAMERAS, AND NOT A SINGLE ONE WITH A CLEAR VIEW OF THE MURDER.
JUST THE RUSHING CROWD... THE PANIC AFTER THE SNIPER.
NO SATELLITE FOOTAGE, EITHER. ALL CAMERAS WERE *DIVERTED*.
ALTHOUGH *NICK FURY'S* FINGERPRINTS ARE ALL OVER THAT ONE.
PROBABLY HAD *AT LEAST* ONE PLAN TO FREE STEVE THAT HE DIDN'T WANT RECORDED.
STILL, EVEN SHARON CLAIMED SHE DIDN'T SEE ANYTHING.
SHE'S RIGHT THERE, AND SHE...
SHE'S RIGHT THERE.
ANNA? THAT LIST OF DR. BENJAMIN'S *PATIENTS*...
DID THAT INCLUDE *NON-ACTIVE* AGENTS, TOO?
I'LL CHECK, SIR.

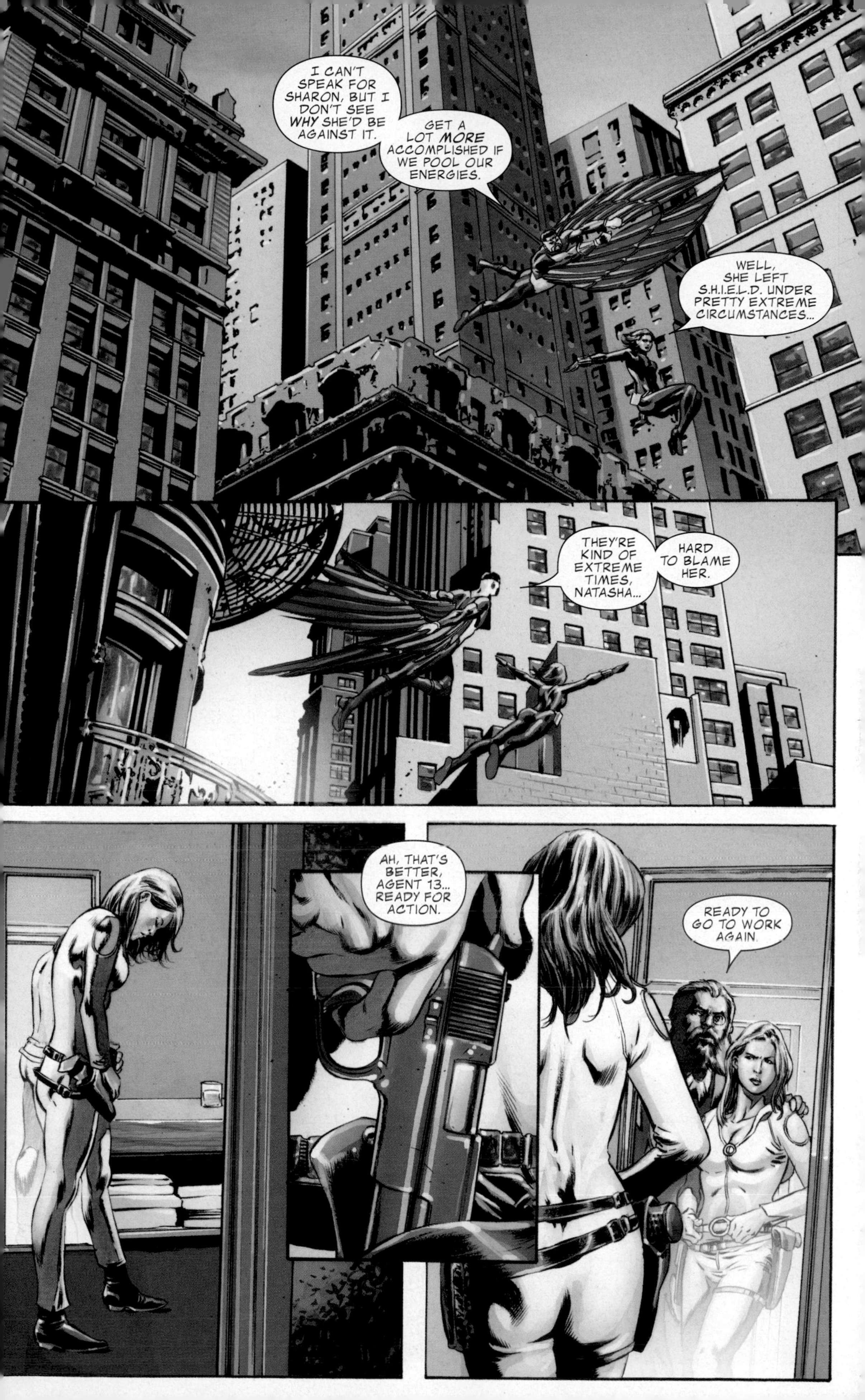
I CAN'T SPEAK FOR SHARON, BUT I DON'T SEE WHY SHE'D BE AGAINST IT.
GET A LOT MORE ACCOMPLISHED IF WE POOL OUR ENERGIES.
WELL, SHE LEFT S.H.I.E.L.D. UNDER PRETTY EXTREME CIRCUMSTANCES...
THEY'RE KIND OF EXTREME TIMES, NATASHA...
HARD TO BLAME HER.
AH, THAT'S BETTER, AGENT 13... READY FOR ACTION.
READY TO GO TO WORK AGAIN.

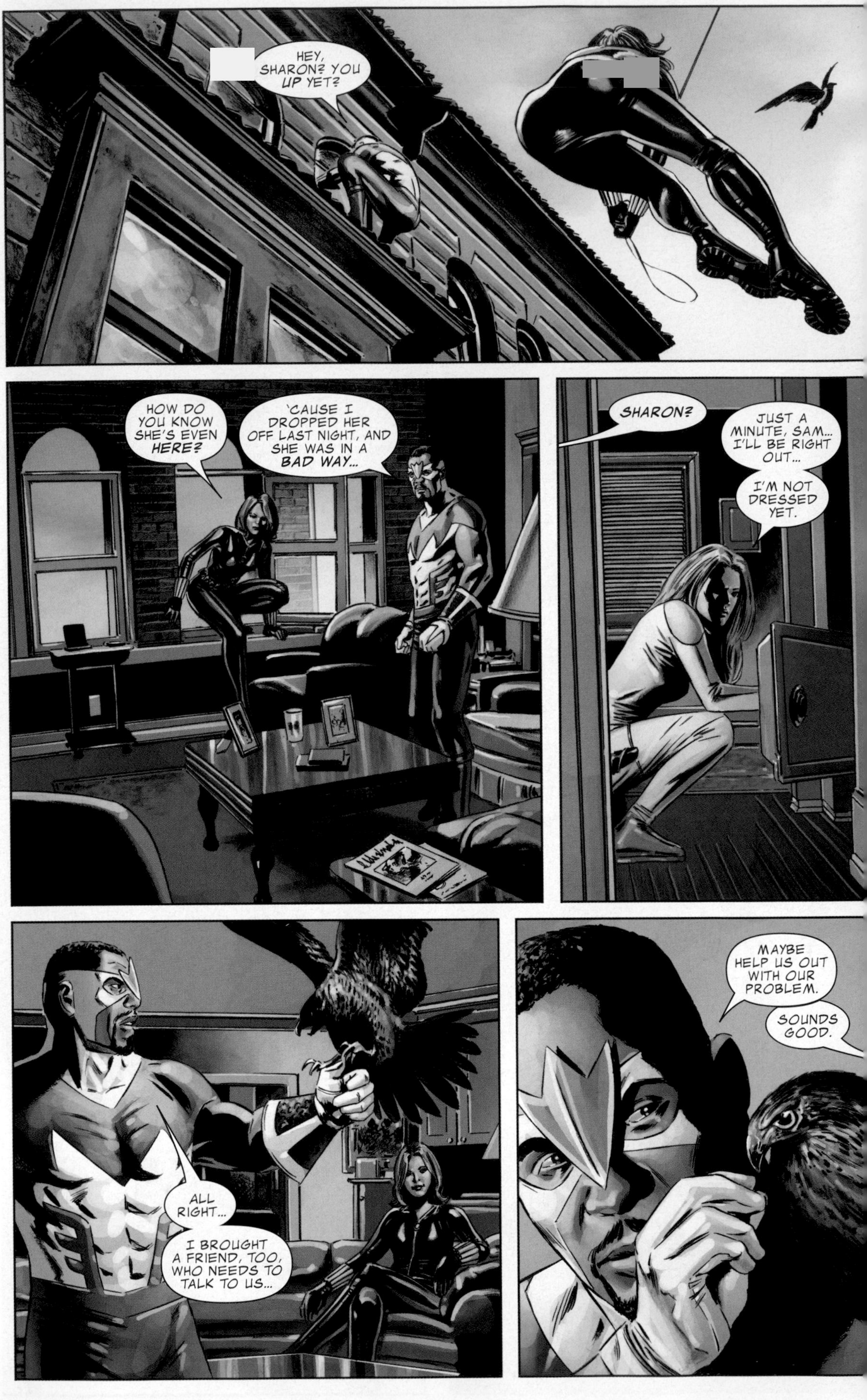
HEY, SHARON? YOU UP YET?
HOW DO YOU KNOW SHE'S EVEN HERE?
'CAUSE I DROPPED HER OFF LAST NIGHT, AND SHE WAS IN A BAD WAY...
SHARON?
JUST A MINUTE, SAM... I'LL BE RIGHT OUT...
I'M NOT DRESSED YET.
ALL RIGHT...
I BROUGHT A FRIEND, TOO, WHO NEEDS TO TALK TO US...
MAYBE HELP US OUT WITH OUR PROBLEM.
SOUNDS GOOD.

DAMN IT.

SMART ENOUGH TO SEE THE FUTURE...

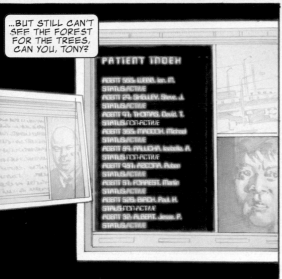

...BUT STILL CAN'T SEE THE FOREST FOR THE TREES, CAN YOU, TONY?

PATIENT INDEX

AGENT 565: WEBB, Ian. M.
STATUS: ACTIVE
AGENT 29: SHELLEY, Steve. J.
STATUS: ACTIVE
AGENT 47: THOMAS, David. T.
STATUS: NON-ACTIVE
AGENT 365: MADOCK, Michael
STATUS: ACTIVE
AGENT 89: PALUCHA, Isabelle. A.
STATUS: NON-ACTIVE
AGENT 481: ACOTA, Ruben
STATUS: ACTIVE
AGENT 51: FORREST, Merle
STATUS: ACTIVE
AGENT 526: BIRCH, Paul. K.
STATUS: NON-ACTIVE
AGENT 32: ALBERT, Jesse. P.
STATUS: ACTIVE

STATUS: NON-ACTIVE
AGENT 982: EDMUNDS, Gary. M.
STATUS: ACTIVE
AGENT 56: GEORGE, David. P.
STATUS: ACTIVE
AGENT 13: CARTER, Sharon
STATUS: NON-ACTIVE
AGENT 77: BISHOP, David
STATUS: ACTIVE
AGENT 572: GONZALEZ, Alberto
STATUS: NON-ACTIVE

THERE WAS NO REASON TO SUSPECT HER...AND NO EVIDENCE...

I STILL SHOULD'VE SEEN IT.

NATASHA, COME IN.

WE HAVE A BIG PROBLEM.

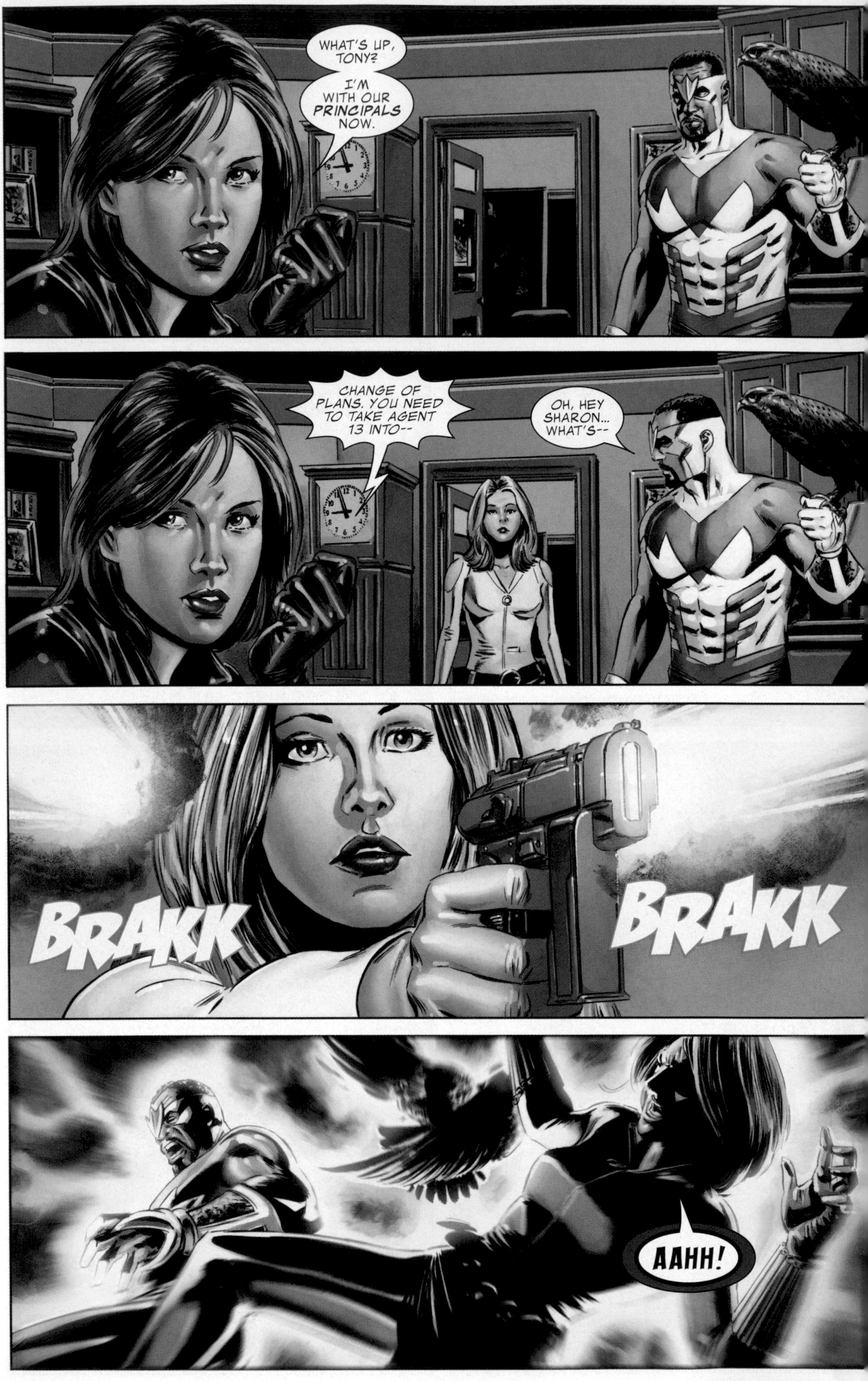
WHAT'S UP, TONY?
I'M WITH OUR PRINCIPALS NOW.
CHANGE OF PLANS. YOU NEED TO TAKE AGENT 13 INTO--
OH, HEY SHARON... WHAT'S--
BRAKK
BRAKK
AAHH!

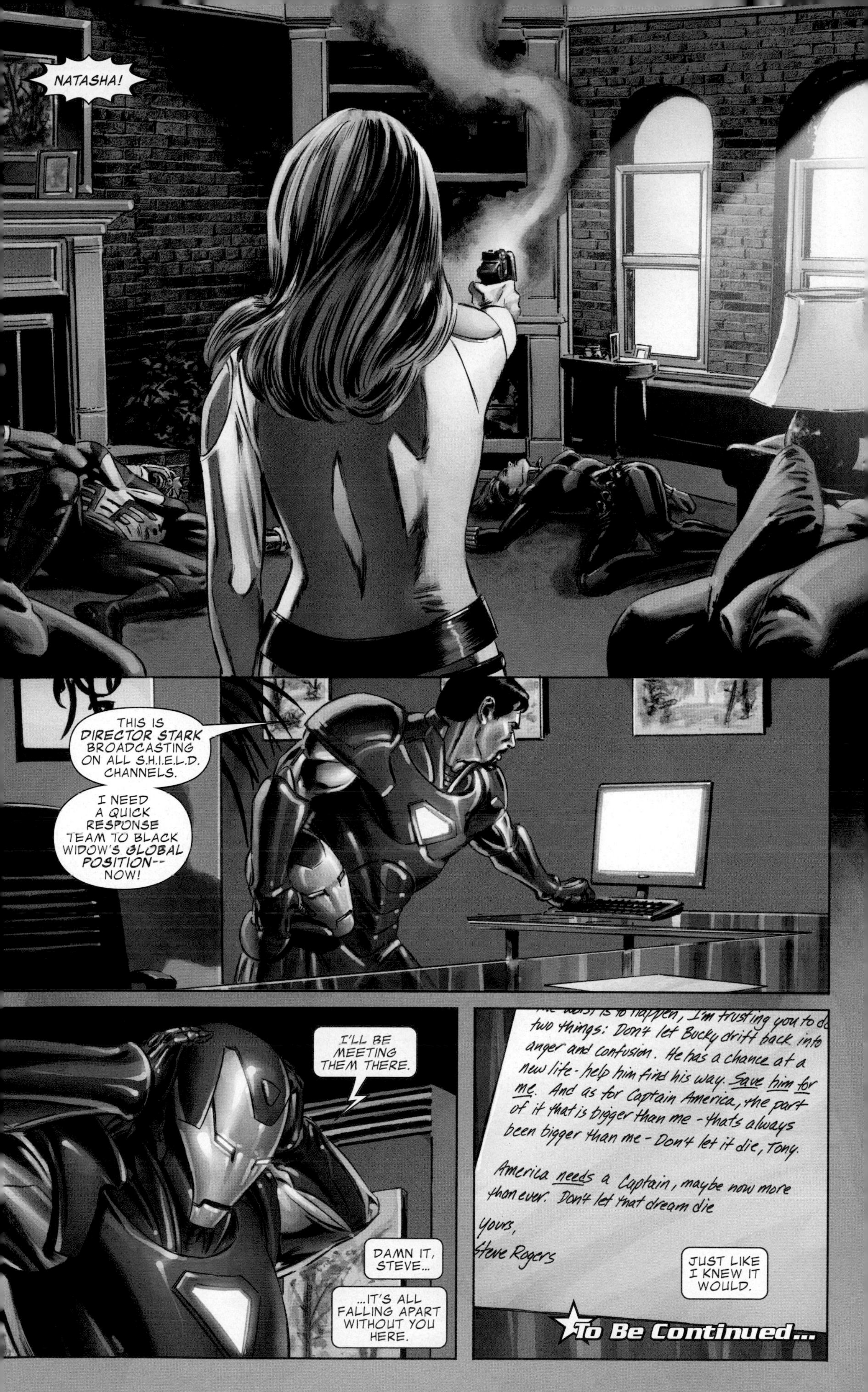
NATASHA!
THIS IS DIRECTOR STARK BROADCASTING ON ALL S.H.I.E.L.D. CHANNELS.
I NEED A QUICK RESPONSE TEAM TO BLACK WIDOW'S GLOBAL POSITION-- NOW!
I'LL BE MEETING THEM THERE.
DAMN IT, STEVE...
...IT'S ALL FALLING APART WITHOUT YOU HERE.
is to happen, I'm trusting you to
two things: Don't let Bucky drift back into
anger and confusion. He has a chance at a
new life - help him find his way. Save him for
me. And as for Captain America, the part
of it that is bigger than me - thats always
been bigger than me - Don't let it die, Tony.
America needs a Captain, maybe now more
than ever. Don't let that dream die
Yours,
Steve Rogers
JUST LIKE I KNEW IT WOULD.
To Be Continued...

VARIANT COVER TO *CAPTAIN AMERICA* #25 BY ED MCGUINNESS

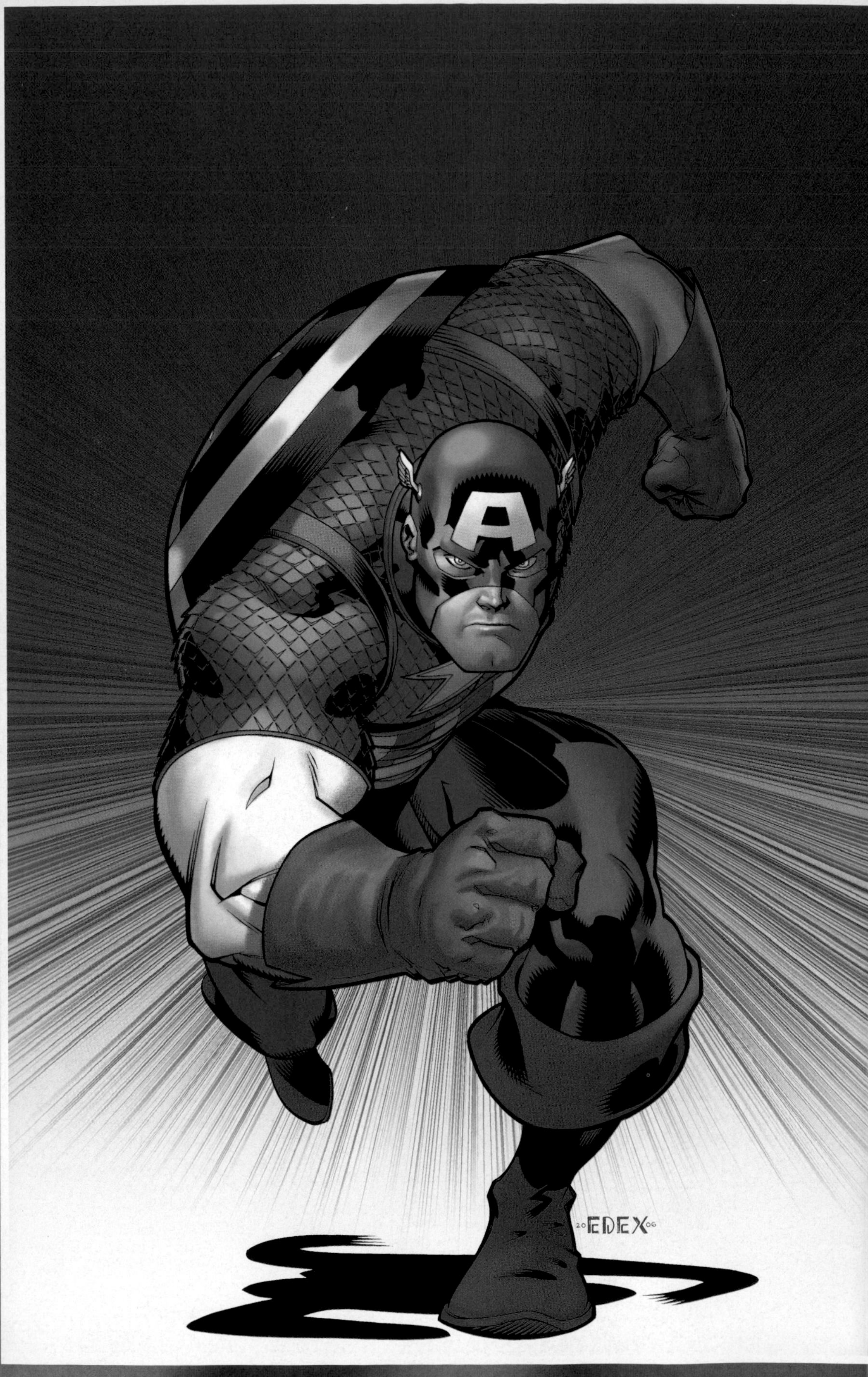
20 EDEX 06

WIZARD WORLD LOS ANGELES VARIANT COVER TO *CAPTAIN AMERICA* #25 BY JOHN CASSADAY

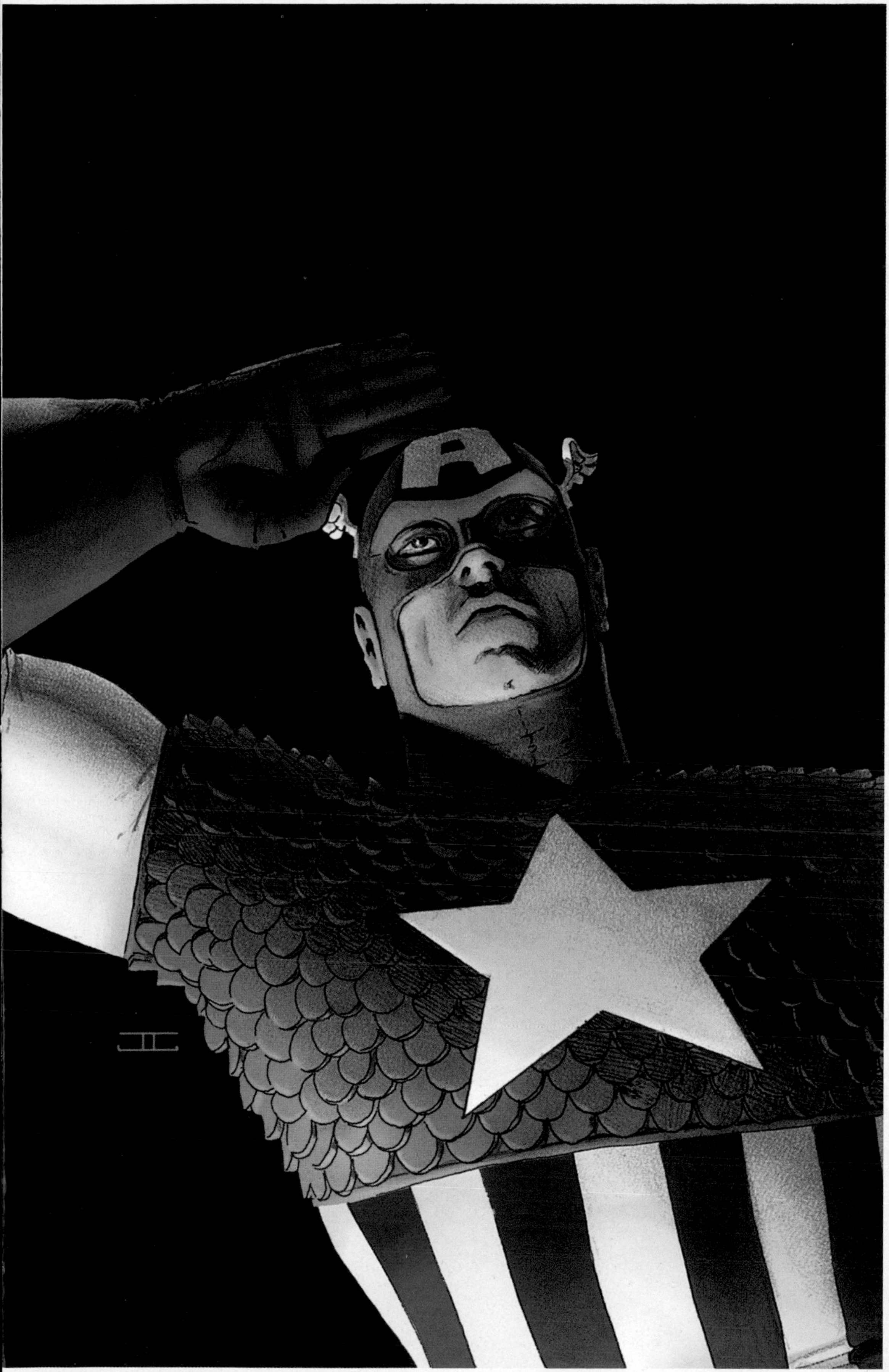

UNUSED COVER TO *CAPTAIN AMERICA* #25 BY STEVE EPTING

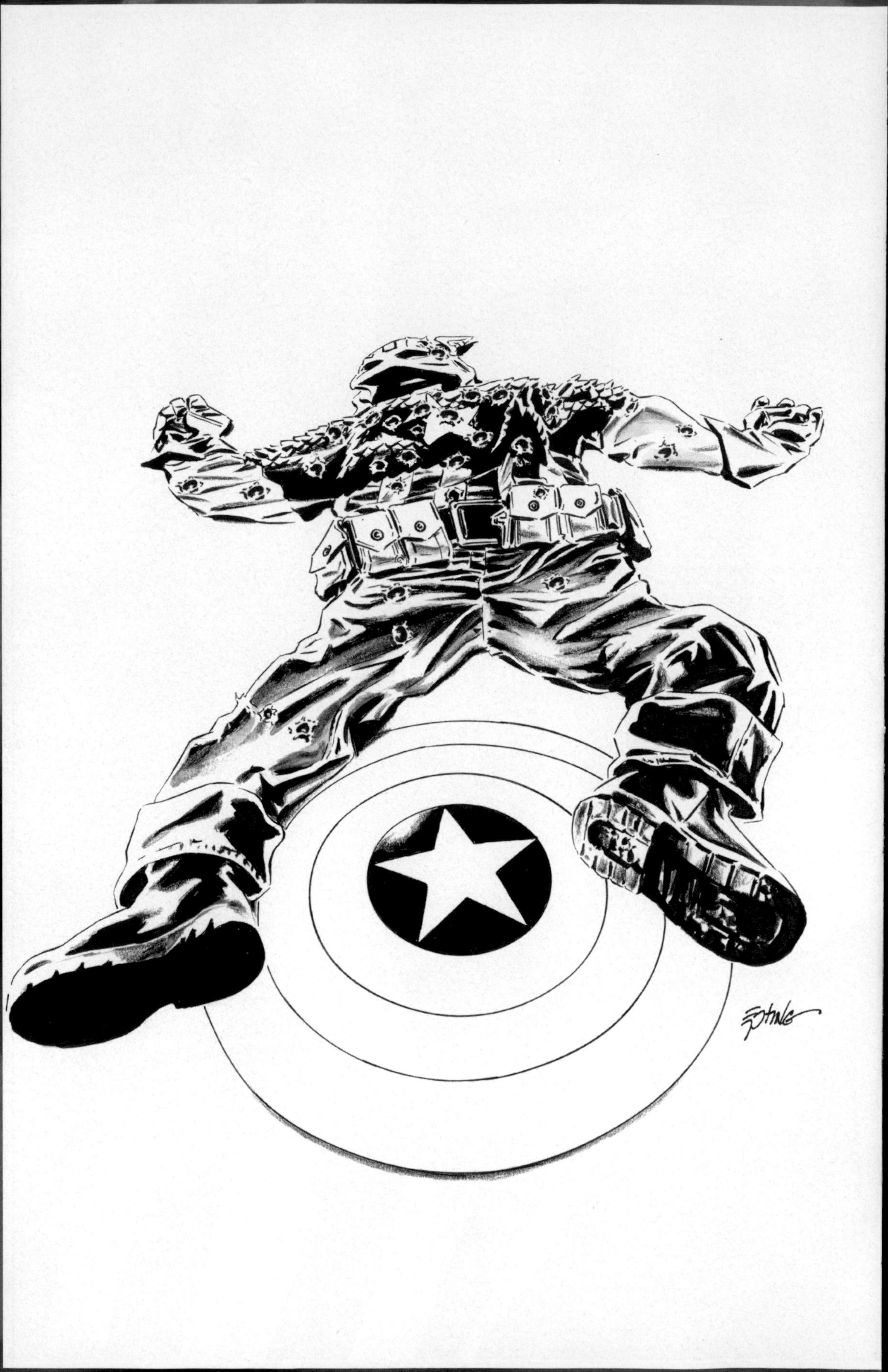

COVER TO *CAPTAIN AMERICA #25 DIRECTOR'S CUT* BY STEVE EPTING

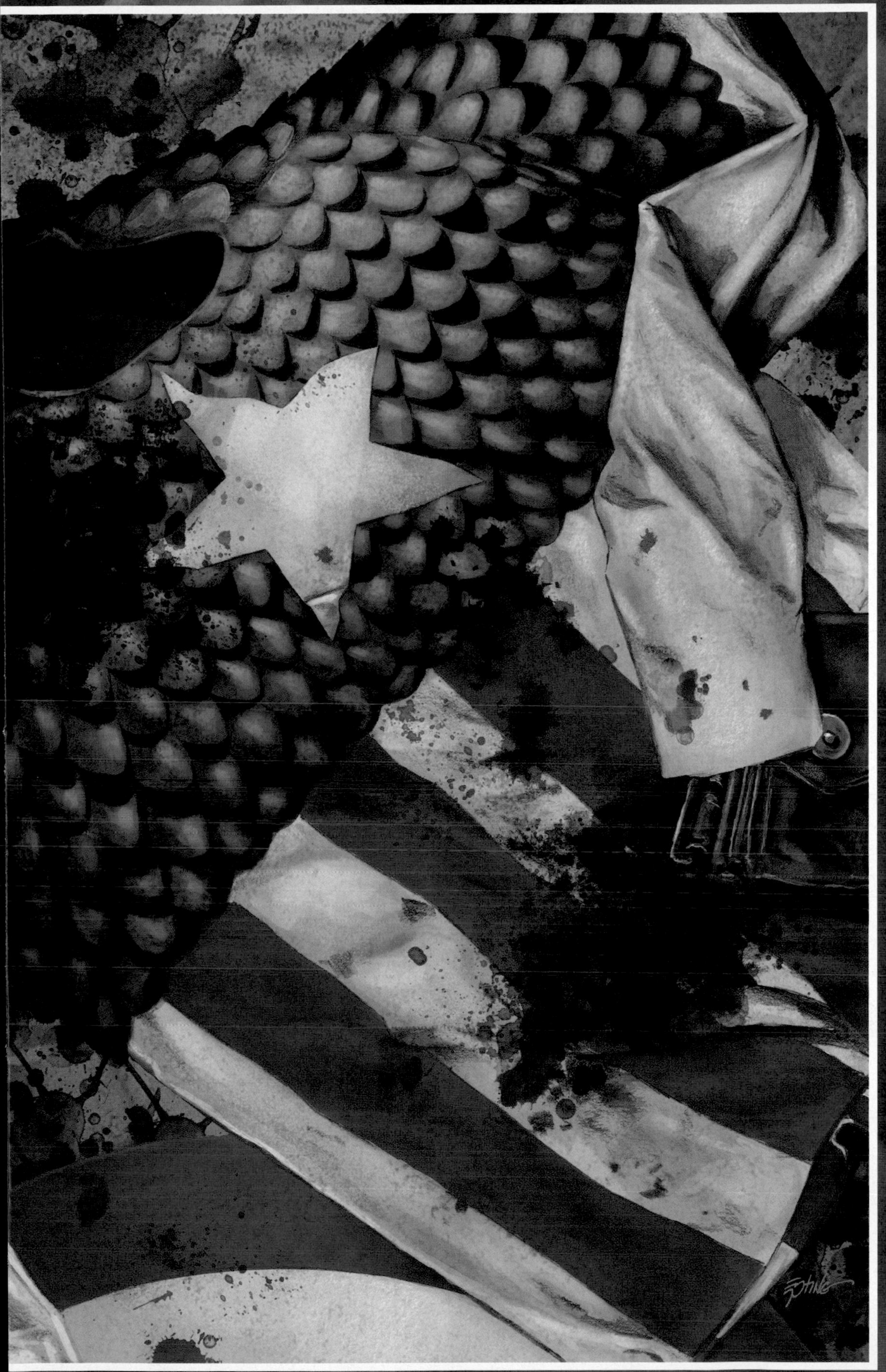

IN THE TRENCHES

Keep it secret, keep it safe. That was the directive given by the highest authority. No, not Gandalf talking about the One Ring; I mean the death... THE death. The death that would cap off Civil War. The death that sent shock waves through the comic community. The death that rocked the news world. No one could know about the **DEATH OF CAPTAIN AMERICA**.

Of course, that wasn't entirely true. After the unprecedented media attention **Civil War** had garnered, major media outlets were continually coming to us for more news on the event. When it came time to place the story of the death of one of comic's most beloved icons, we called up comic fan and journalist extraordinaire Ethan Sacks of the *Daily News* here in New York. Ethan was brought in at the last second so as to preserve this secret but still within enough time to pitch and write up his story and ensure it good coverage for the day ***Captain America #25*** hit stands. And then we all went radio silent and crossed our fingers that no word would leak out.

Finally, March 7th came and we had succeeded in taking the world by surprise! I hadn't even left the house for work that morning when my father called and I knew that this was going to be far bigger than any of us had originally thought. When dealing with mainstream stories, I never tell my dad what we are doing. If a mortgage banker in Nashville, TN, hears about something related to Marvel comics, then I know we've tapped the mainstream. He called, groggy from just waking up, and said "I can't believe you did it. How could you kill Captain America?" Apparently he was in a hotel in lower Alabama on a business trip and had turned on a cable news channel where they were debating if this was the right time to kill off the Sentinel of Liberty with America in the war on terror. It wasn't even 7:30 a.m. and not a single comic store had opened yet.

MEDIA SPOTLIGHT

DAILY NEWS
DEATH OF A LEGEND

Writer Ed Brubaker proudly displays his story making the front page.

Milestones

RETROSPECTIVE

He fought Nazis, cold war baddies, even his own oppressive government. In his latest comic, Marvel superhero **Captain America** was assassinated on the way to court, where he hoped to talk up civil liberties. Will he, like the once deceased Superman, be back? Says publisher Dan Buckley: "He's very dead right now."

From the *Los Angeles Times*, March 8, 2007

Interview
WITH STAN LEE

NEWSWEEK: What was your reaction to the sudden death of Captain America?

"I was a little bit shocked. America could use a man like that right now—the ultimate patriot."

—Captain America's former writer and superhero to comics fans

From *Newsweek*, March 19, 2007

hed the office, the phone and email y. Et[illegible]s story had hit the wire at ready over 200 print and 400 online ‹ed it up, not to mention the countless stations bombarding us with interview N already had an amazing piece edited t stoked the fires even more. Everyone piece of Cap's death. Along with our ?.R. firm, I was in charge of coordinating a ıslaught the comic world hadn't seen in over ıde. And I loved every minute of it. Marvel blisher Dan Buckley stationed himself at his iome office and handled all telephone interviews. Ed Brubaker (on Pacific time) was roused to do ocal media and radio call-in shows. We hired a car ervice to drive Joe Quesada to various TV stations ıround the city, but when that proved to be too slow o meet the demanding pace of the news crews, we brought him back here (in full television make-up) ınd had the crews conduct interviews in the Marvel bullpen. There were news stories about the number of news stories this event was getting. By the end of he day, we'd had dozens of TV appearances, and he story had driven people to comic shops like no other in recent memory.

The dust didn't settle for a few weeks. By the time all was sai[illegible] done, every major network, radio program, newspaper, and internet site had all covered the life and death of Marvel's Fallen Son. The passing of Steve Rogers had brought comics back into the mind of the general public and retailers were still receiving calls from people they had never seen in their stores before, everyone asking for a copy of ***Captain America #25***. But the crowning moment had to be on the March 12th edition of the **COLBERT REPORT**, when Stephen Colbert, a long-time fan and friend to Marvel, was presented Cap's shield per Captain America's "final wishes." Colbert humbly accepted the shield and awarded it a permanent place of honor on the set of the **COLBERT REPORT**.

Cap's been dead now for a few months, and it doesn't look like he's giving into the naysayers who thought this was a fake-out or short-term stunt. As hard as it is to believe, Steve Rodgers is gone from comics. I'd like to think, after over a half-century of battles, we gave Captain America a proper send off.

Jim McCann
Marvel Sales & Marketing

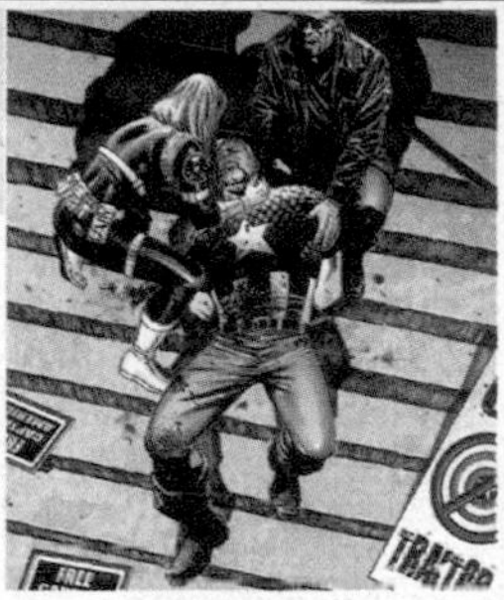

NEW YORK. The epic run of comic book icon Captain America closes as his creators decide it's time to kill him off.

A Telling End for a Superhero

The quintessential American superhero is dead. Captain America fell to a sniper's bullets in last week's edition of the comic. The news seemed laden with ill portent as the republic grapples with an unstable stock market and an unpopular war. "We really need him now," lamented retired cocreator Joe Simon, 93.

Developed in 1941, Captain America gained his world class strength after being injected with "super-soldier serum" to fight the Nazis. Captain America took on a number of real-world enemies, including Communists. The tale stayed timely to the end. He was killed after leading other superheroes in refusing to register with the government as "a weapon of mass destruction," arguing it was a violation of civil rights. Marvel execs in **New York** said the end was a long time coming and made for a "compelling story." But in comics, not even death is final. A Captain America movie is a possibility. ●

With Will Sullivan, Anna Mulrine, Bret Schulte, and the Associated Press

From *U.S. News & World Report*, March 19, 2007

QUICK TAKES

Superhero shot, and it's for real

Captain America is dead. But will he stay that way?

In the latest issue of his comic book, Steve Rogers, the star-spangled hero with the gleaming shield and World War II roots, is shot to death — and his publisher, Marvel Comics, pledges that it is neither a dream, a hoax nor a short-term stunt.

The issue hit stands on Wednesday and shows the iconic hero gunned down on the steps of a federal courthouse; he was arriving there as a fugitive, a resistance leader to a federal Superhero Registration Act that has been a key Marvel story line for the last year.

The role of homeland rebel is a far cry from the hero's early days. He first appeared in March 1941 and became the most popular of the purely patriotic comic characters drawn up for wartime duty and by far the most enduring of them.

Marvel has plans for a "Captain America" movie in the next few years, so there is cause to wonder whether the character (or at least the costume) will make a return of some sort.

— Geoff Boucher

From *Time Magazine*, March 26, 2007

As a Superhero, the Captain Changed Along With America

By Jonathan V. Last

Last Wednesday morning, while most people kibitzed about Scooter Libby over their morning coffee, Captain America was murdered on the steps of the federal courthouse in New York. Captain America (real-life identity: Steve Rogers) is survived by his crime-fighting partner, Bucky, and his girlfriend, Sharon Carter, who may have fired the fatal shots while under the control of the evil Dr. Faustus. Such are the perils of romance.

The death of Captain America became, quite improbably, a minor cultural event. According to Joe Quesada, the editor in chief of Marvel Comics, Marvel made the decision to kill Cap 18 months ago, while it was plotting the direction of its seven-issue limited series "Civil War," which details the rift between heroes following a law that required superheroes to register with the government.

Marvel kept the decision to kill Cap secret. The final issue of "Civil War" was released in February, and last week issue 25 of "Captain America" arrived on the doorsteps of the nation's 2,000 comic-book shops.

Owners unpacking the boxes of new inventory were shocked to find Cap lying dead in a hospital on the final page. There was a flurry of chatter on the Internet. Within hours, the wire services picked up the story, and people crowded into neighborhood comic-book shops. By noon, the issue was sold out and fetching hefty sums on eBay.

* * *

There is an old joke about death in the comic-book world: No one stays dead except Bucky, Jason Todd and Uncle Ben. Over the years Superman, Phoenix, Green Arrow and a legion of other heroes have perished, only to be resurrected by their publishers [illegible]. Even this Bucky Clause of hero death has begun unraveling as both Bucky and Jason Todd (who replaced Dick Grayson as Robin) were recently brought back to life. This was, in fact, the second time Captain America journeyed to the undiscovered country.

Cap was born in March 1941, when a scrawny Steve Rogers tried to enlist in the Army. Rejected because of his feeble physique, Rogers volunteered for a secret government program attempting to create a super soldier through genetic enhancement. Alas, just as all robots eventually rebel and kill their masters, all government attempts at genetic manipulation are doomed to go awry.

The scientist heading the super-soldier program ended up dead, but Steve Rogers became a specimen of physical perfection, with heightened reflexes and enhanced strength. The Army sent him into battle with a red, white and blue shield and the moniker Captain America.

The cover of the first issue of Captain America showed Cap socking Hitler with a right cross nearly a year before America declared war on Germany. A champion of American freedom, Cap's popularity soared during World War II as he battled Nazis and the Japanese with Bucky at his side.

After the war, sales of Captain America dwindled; the title was canceled in 1950. As Bradford Wright details in "Comic Book Nation," Marvel brought Cap back several years later as a

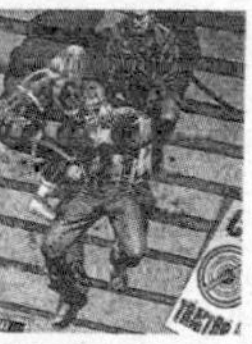

Cold Warrior: "Captain America ... Commie Smasher." This time, he and Bucky fought communist agents "who hid behind the privileges of a free society in order to subvert American institutions." The series sold poorly and was dropped after a few issues.

Captain America changed with the times. He returned in 1964 and found renewed fame, but not as the same rock-jawed, stalwart soldier. In 1969 he was paired with the first African-American superhero, the Falcon. In one small sign of how comics were evolving, the Falcon's alter ego, Sam Wilson, was a Harlem social worker.

As Vietnam raged, Captain America stayed home. In 1971 Marvel's Stan Lee wrote that Cap "simply doesn't lend himself to the John Wayne type character he once was" and that he "could not see any of [Marvel's] characters taking on the role of super-patriotism in the world as it is today." Instead, Cap became a Great Society superhero, battling, as Mr. Wright puts it, "poverty, racism, pollution, and political corruption."

Consider this monologue from a '70s issue in which Cap muses: "I'm like a dinosaur—in the cro-magnon age! An anachronism—who's out-lived his time! This is the day of the anti-hero—the age of the rebel—and the dissenter! It isn't hip—to defend the establishment!—only to tear it down! And, in a world rife with injustice, greed, and endless war—who's to say the rebels are wrong? . . . I've spent a lifetime defending the flag—and the law! Perhaps I should have battled less—and questioned more!"

While he avoided Vietnam, Captain America dove head-on into Watergate. He took up arms against a thinly veiled version of the Nixon White House, which was linked to a McCarthyite conservative political group called the Committee to Regain America's Principles, or "CRAP." But this CREEP knock-off wasn't merely attempting to re-elect the president using dirty tricks. Instead, CRAP was a front for a cabal of actual fascists who were plotting to take over the country. The leader of the conspiracy was, naturally, the president.

After being duped by the president, Cap dropped his hero name and became, briefly, "Nomad, the man without a country."

Given his political progress it is not surprising that by the time "Civil War" began, Cap was quoting Thomas Paine and couching his opposition to the superhero registration act in terms of civil liberties. Marvel now seems poised to use his death as the focus of a large-scale debate on the balancing of freedom and security.

* * *

"Captain America" will probably return. Ed Brubaker, the current writer of the series, won't divulge details, but comments in an interview with the Web site Comic Book Resources, "I've got the next two years of Cap plotted, if that says anything." Fans have already concocted several plausible resurrection scenarios.

But before looking toward his next incarnation, it's worth pausing to appreciate that even at this late date, Captain America's death still meant something. Partially, this was due to the simple fact that Marvel was able to keep his murder a surprise—something of a wonder in an age when every other happening comes prehyped and presold. (Mr. Quesada reveals that the editors went to great lengths to keep the secret, engaging in a quiet campaign of disinformation and even going so far as to leak fake covers to throw fans off the scent.)

Ultimately, it is wonder that we need most from comic books. The wonder that a man can fly or that a skinny American kid with a stout heart can pick up a shield and deck the Führer. With his death last week, Captain America gave us that sense of wonder once more.

Mr. Last is online editor of The Weekly Standard.

From the *Wall Street Journal*, March 13, 2007

CAPTAIN AMERICA #25 ART BY STEVE EPTING

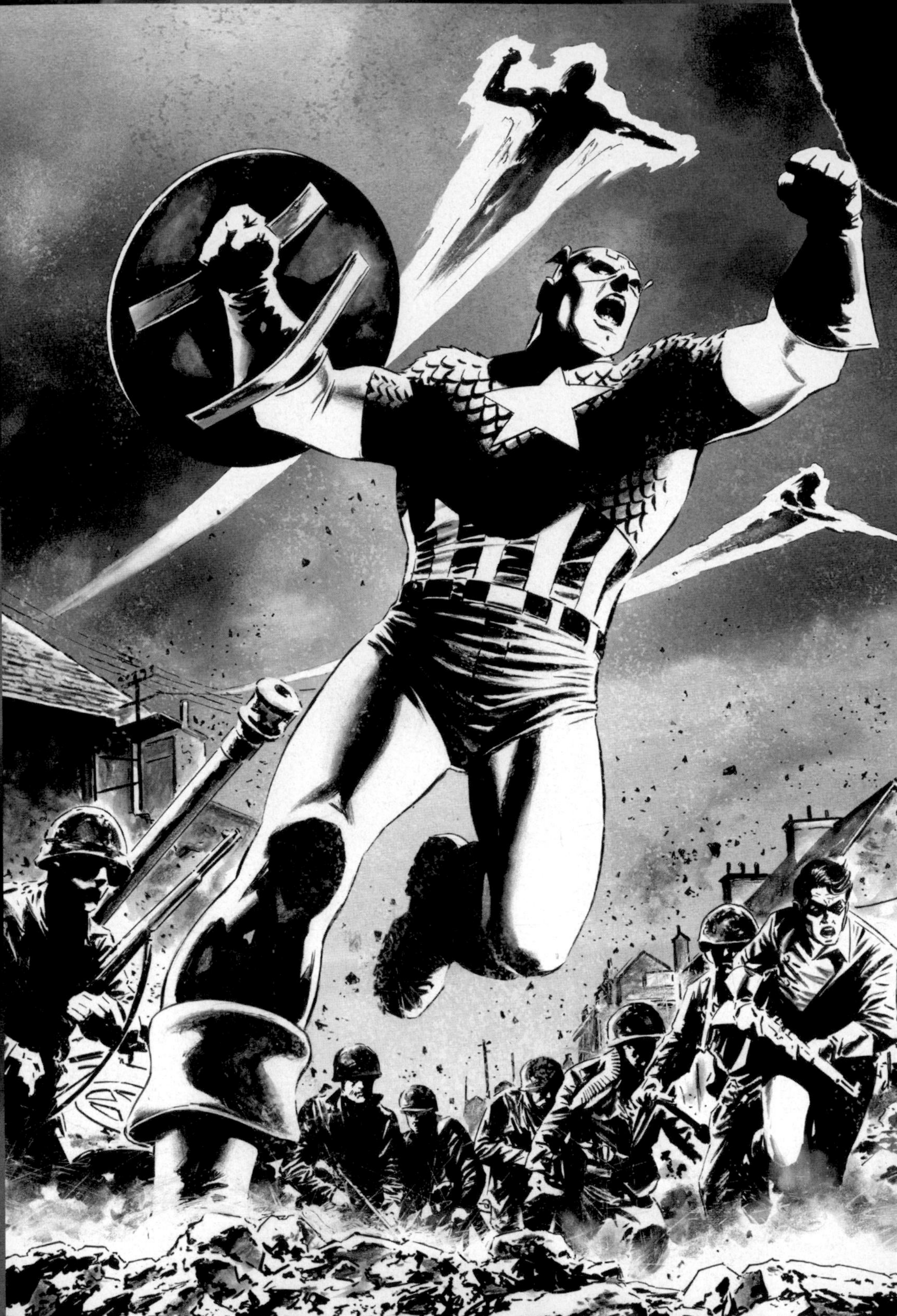

PAGE 3

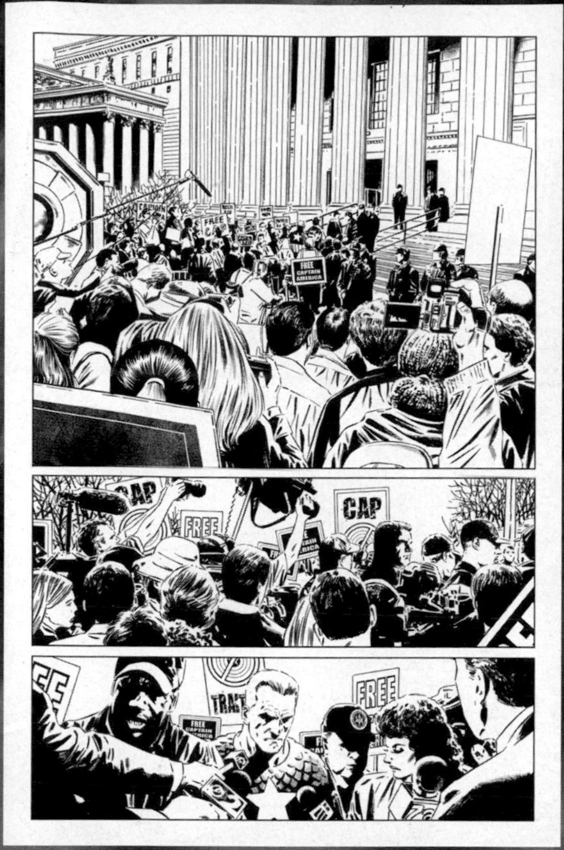
FREE CAPTAIN AMERICA
CAP
FREE
CAP
FREE

PAGE 12

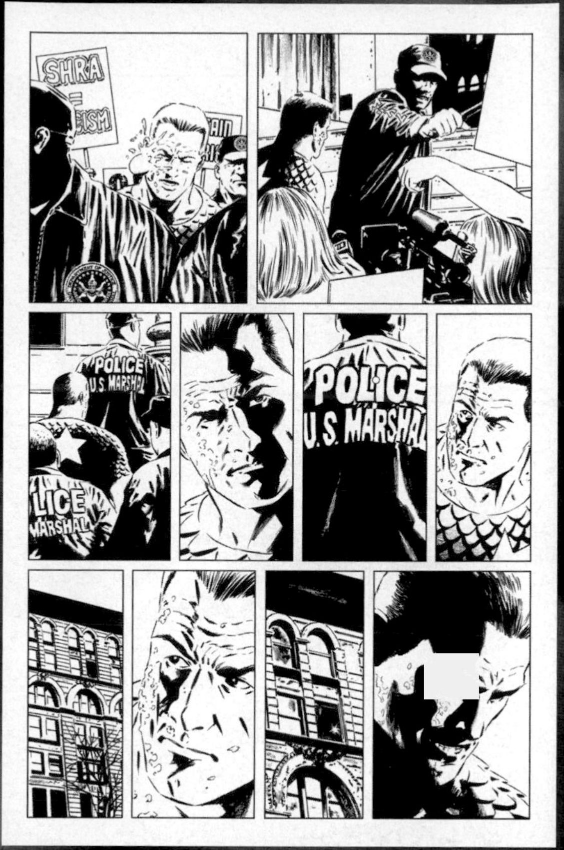
SHRA
POLICE U.S. MARSHAL
POLICE U.S. MARSHAL

PAGE 13

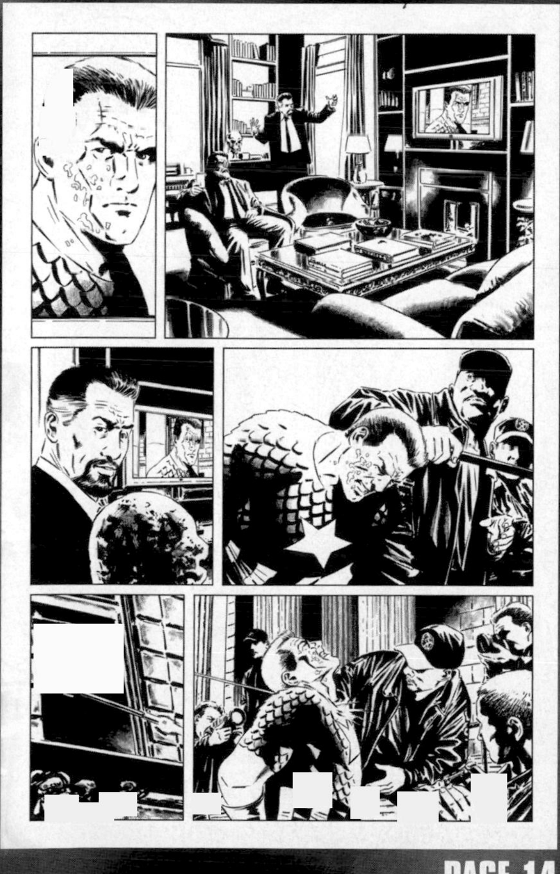

PAGE 14

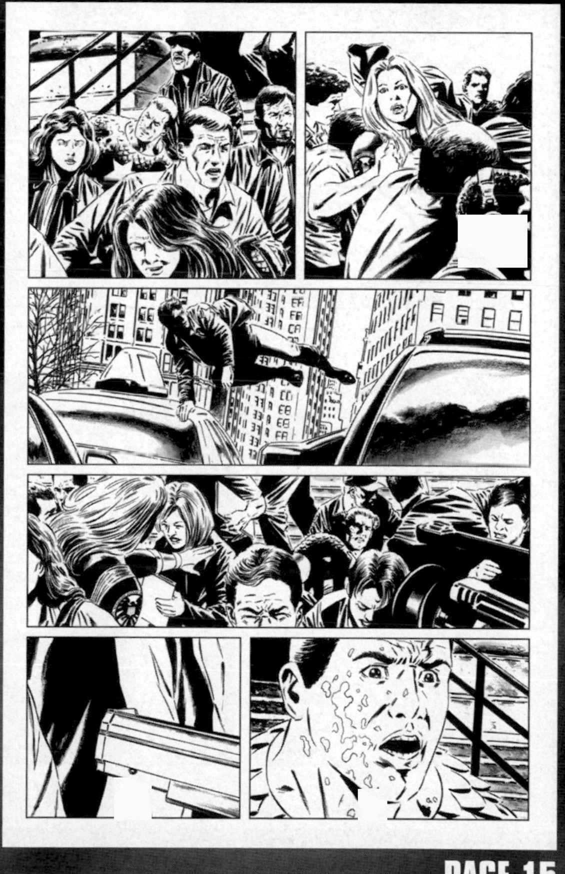

PAGE 15

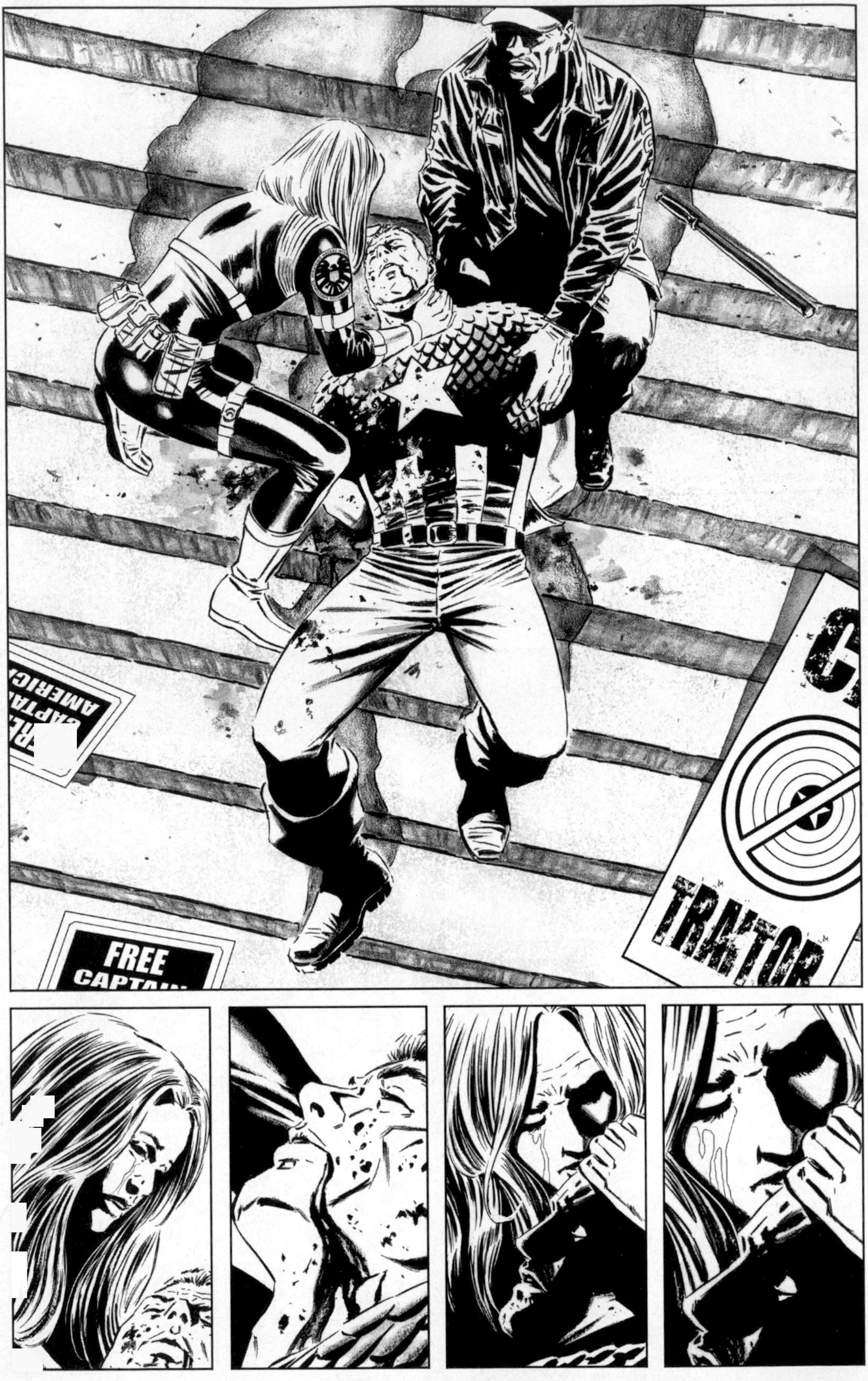
CAPTAIN AMERICA
FREE CAPTAIN
TRAITOR